The Moral Self

Studies in Contemporary German Social Thought (partial list)
Thomas McCarthy, General Editor

The Moral Self

edited by Gil G. Noam and Thomas E. Wren

in cooperation with Gertrud Nunner-Winkler
and Wolfgang Edelstein

The MIT Press, Cambridge, Massachusetts, and London, England

This book was set in New Baskerville at The MIT Press and was printed and bound in the United States of America.

Library of Congress Cataloging-in-Publication Data

The Moral self / edited by Gil G. Noam and Thomas E. Wren in cooperation with Gertrud Nunner-Winkler and Wolfgang Edelstein.
      p.   cm. — (Studies in contemporary German social thought)
   Includes bibliographical references and index.
   ISBN 0-262-14052-7
   1. Ethics—Psychological aspects. 2. Moral development.
3. Ethics I. Noam, Gil G. II. Series.
BJ45.M67   1992
170—dc20   92-21501
                                                      CIP

Contents

Introduction: Building a Better Paradigm

Thomas E. Wren and Gil G. Noam

Over the past decade an increasing number of psychologists and philosophers have invoked the concept of a moral self to account for the grip that moral demands, values, and ideals have on people's lives. Weaving together various strands from philosophical and psychological theories of personality, cognitive development, ethics, and metaethics, these theorists and empirical researchers have tried to show that morality is at once a cultural field within which we live our lives and an interior psychological space at the center of our personal being. That there is more than one way to chart this space is indicated by the variety of approaches taken by the contributors to this volume. They all, however, begin with the conviction that if we are to fully understand either the moral domain or the domain of the self, we must consider these domains in relation to each other, both as cognitive systems and as spheres of personal existence. The latter (e.g., emotion, motivation, personality, and biography) were kept out of sight as long as moral development was studied within a purely cognitive, decontextualized paradigm that focused on universal structures of moral judgment. But the restrictiveness of that paradigm is now increasingly obvious, even to those (including some of the authors in this volume) who have contributed most to it.

The discussion in these pages continues the dialogue between philosophy and psychology begun in *The moral domain: Essays in the ongoing discussion between philosophy and the social sciences.*[1] Like that volume, this one has its roots in a working conference convened at Ringberg Castle in Germany by the Max Planck Institute for

Human Development and Education (Berlin) and the Max Planck Institute for Psychological Research (Munich) and organized by Wolfgang Edelstein, Gil G. Noam, and Gertrud Nunner-Winkler. The conference participants, selected either because of their writings on morality and moral development or because of their work on the structure and development of the self, were asked to address the question of how these two domains relate to each other. Their shared inquiry during and after Ringberg has produced the following essays, all of which were written specifically for this volume. In spite of their diverse theoretical traditions and methodologies, the authors agree on the need to build a better paradigm, either by significantly revising the cognitive-developmental model of moral judgment or perhaps by replacing it altogether with a less judgment-centered model capable of incorporating the valuable insights provided by cognitive-developmental theory.

The book opens with a set of essays focused on the conceptual foundations that must underlie any paradigm of moral selfhood (part I) and then features essays proposing models that can be thought of as prototypes of the paradigm in question (part II). These models are put into play in the last set of essays (part III), which are empirical studies embodying and extending many of the principal ideas of the previous sections.

Although this volume is based on the conviction that the two domains of morality and self are linked, it is not altogether clear whether this linkage is conceptual or psychological or both. In fact, it is a matter of some debate whether the concepts of morality and moral judgment are analytically tied to certain dimensions of the personal domain or only empirically correlated with them. Just a few years ago the relationship between the moral and personal domains was not considered especially problematic, and hence was not part of psychology's basic research agenda. This was largely due to the influential work of Lawrence Kohlberg, who carried to its logical conclusions the Piagetian notion of thought as interiorized action. Kohlberg believed that moral judgment and moral behavior are conceptually as well as causally reciprocal, two moments of a single personal unity, and that moral development is the cognitive career of an individual self in the social world.

Subsequent research by cognitive developmentalists and others has led moral psychology beyond this rather cozy picture of the way in which moral thought and action are related to each other (see Wren, 1991; Noam, 1993). The aftermath of this research—which has covered such varied topics as the role of emotion and motivation in moral experience, the evolution of personality and personal identity, and the methodological issues involved in tapping moral and personal experience—is that moral psychology finds itself "between paradigms." It is now clear that we must anchor morality—lived morality, which is cognized, felt, *and* acted on—in our concept of a developing and experiencing person. Without yielding to the temptation to return to the easier days of pre-Kohlbergian theory, in which thought was incidental to moral action, we must move beyond the standard cognitive-developmental paradigm to create more adequate ways of understanding what it means to be a moral self.

Accordingly, the essays in this volume address the following overlapping sets of concerns:

The diversity of moral outlooks: questions about the one or many definitions of morality, the possibility of universal moral principles, the culture-specificity of virtues and other moral values, the distinction between structures and contents of moral reasoning, the three-way relationship between moral philosophy and empirically based theory and moral practice, etc.

The dynamics of the constitution of the moral self: questions about the power of psychoanalytic models of the growth of self and identity, the role of biography and autobiography in self-understanding and moral conduct, the function of distortions and defenses, the role of will and ego strength in personal development, etc.

Cognitive and noncognitive prerequisites of psychological development in moral competence: questions about reflexive consciousness and one's self-concept, second-order desires and beliefs, objective and subjective points of view, social constructions of self, etc.

Motivation and moral personality: questions about the role of morality in a person's identity, the role of intersubjective motives in family and friendship relationships, personal identity, and the passage from moral judgment to action, etc.

Although not all the authors in this volume work within the cognitive-developmental paradigm, they all take it into account in order to go beyond it or transform it. For instance, they each recognize that individuals find moral judgments motivating, though they have different explanations for why this is the case and correspondingly different conceptions of human motivation and moral cognition. Each believes that moral maturity involves increased autonomy, self-esteem, and other sorts of ego strengths. And finally, each addresses, directly or indirectly, the question posed by Thrasymachus to Socrates and passed on down the ages: Why (and how) do people follow their considered moral judgments even when doing so is not to their own personal advantage? Taken together, these essays do not constitute a grand synthesis or a single integrated statement, nor do they say the final word on how our theories of morality and the self should be transformed. Instead, they provide a window onto the process of theory building and empirical investigation in an extremely important area of philosophical and social science inquiry.

Heartfelt thanks are due to those who have made it possible to complete this volume: to the Spencer Foundation, which funded Thomas Wren's work on this book; to the Institute for Advanced Study (Berlin), the John Alden Trust, and the Hall-Mercer Foundation, which supported Gil Noam's work on this and other projects; to Larry Cohen and Alan Thwaits of The MIT Press for their support, advice, hard work, and patience; to Stuart Krahn for the preparation of the index; to Barbara Panza and Mark Johnson for editorial assistance; and to Donna McLaughlin-Travis of the Loyola University Center for Instructional Design for helping to format the book. Finally, loving thanks are due to families and friends who put up with so much for so long while this book was being produced, especially our wives, Carol Wren and Maryanne Wolf.

Note

1. Most of the essays in *The moral domain* (edited by T. E. Wren in cooperation with W. Edelstein and G. Nunner-Winkler, 1990) appeared in somewhat different versions in the German volume, *Die Bestimmung der Moral* (edited by Edelstein and Nunner-Winkler, 1989). In a similar arrangement, the present volume has a German counterpart, *Moral und Person* (edited by W. Edelstein, G. Nunner-Winkler, and G. Noam, 1993), published concurrently although with some differences in format and content.

xi

References

Edelstein, W., and Nunner-Winkler, G., Eds. (1989). *Die Bestimmung der Moral.* Frankfurt: Suhrkamp.

Edelstein, W., Nunner-Winkler, G., and Noam, G., Eds. (1993). *Moral und Person.* Frankfurt: Suhrkamp.

Noam, G. (1993). Ego development: True or false? *Psychological Inquiry* 4:43–49.

Wren, T. E., Ed. (1990). *The moral domain: Essays in the ongoing discussion between philosophy and the social sciences.* Cambridge: MIT Press.

Wren, T. E. (1991). *Caring about morality: Philosophical perspectives in moral psychology.* Cambridge: MIT Press, and London: Routledge.

I

Conceptual Foundations

The Role of Identity in the Constitution of Morality

Ernst Tugendhat

The two main questions of moral philosophy are, first, what is a moral rule (or judgment or system) and what does it mean to justify it? And second, what are the moral rules that can be justified today? My speaking of the "constitution of morality" (in the title of this paper) can be understood in the sense of either one of these questions. I shall contend in this paper that neither the formal sense of morality (in the sense of a moral system) nor what we call "our morality" can be understood without recurring to a concept of personal-social identity.

What Is a Moral Rule?

By the question "What is a moral rule?" I mean to raise the issue of the significance of the modal expressions contained in moral judgments ("ought," "must," "may not," and "cannot").[1] There are notoriously many kinds of "ought." The moral "ought" differs from most others in that it connotes obligation. Therefore, the question concerning the significance of the modal words in the moral context is identical with the question of what we are to understand under moral obligation. It is also identical to what we normally mean when we use the words "moral" and "immoral," not because "morality" encompasses all the moral rules but because we happen to use these words as substitutes for the moral modal words ("It is immoral to crucify the cat" = "You mustn't crucify the cat").

How can we clarify any of these modal usages (moral or nonmoral) in the first place? We should ask, I think, what happens (what is the case) if the subject does not act as he should (ought, must).

Let me begin with some preparatory steps. To understand what we mean when we make a moral judgment of "ought," we have to explore the connections with other judgments and also certain feelings which, because of their analytical connections with the "ought" judgments, can lead us to understand the conceptual environment within which they are made. These other judgments are judgments of praise and blame. And the feelings I have in mind are the feelings of indignation, resentment, and shame (also guilt). These feelings are the feelings we have (in third, second, and first person correspondingly) when we feel that something that happened is morally bad. These feelings are thus analytically connected with (they actually imply) judgments of blame. Do the judgments of blame or praise contain anything special that permits one to say something of interest about "ought" judgments? Yes. When you praise or blame a person, you say that she is good or bad, or has done something good or bad. This use of "good" and "bad" is unique. This is the only context in which these words are used as simple predicates. To connect this point up with "ought" judgments: the use of the moral modal words is analytically connected with an evaluation of persons (and actions) not in some respect (good for, good as), but *as such.*

The understanding of morality thus boils down to the question of how we are to understand this evaluation of persons as such. Here it appears sensible to connect this type of evaluation with the entire scope of evaluations of activities of persons. There are many dimensions in which we do things more or less well. As children we are socialized partly by acquiring all kinds of skills, and throughout life this remains a dominant source of our self-value. By doing socially esteemed things, we acquire a sense of self-esteem if things go well. If they don't, we feel shame.

In all these cases the attribution of value is relative. I am being esteemed or depreciated in my capacity as cook, as violinist, as father. It seems to me plausible to understand the special place of moral evaluation in connection with these valuations of persons relative to specific skills. This means that we should also understand moral evaluative statements whose surface use is predicative as attributive in their deep-structure: "She is bad" = "She is a bad person." (The only alternative would be to take the predicative use as ultimate, and in my opinion, this leads nowhere: the words "good" and "bad," so understood, have no clear meaning, and in the hands of a philosopher, this would lead to all sorts of inventions.) Whereas all other appraisals of human acting contain a specific perspective, a perspective of a specific skill (cooking, violin playing, etc.), either the moral appraisal contains no perspective (this would be the case if we should have to take the predicative use as ultimate) or (if the predicative use is implicitly attributive) the perspective is general: one is good not as a cook or violin player but as a person or member of the community or member of society.

We can now say that at the same time that children are being socialized into all sorts of special skills, they are also being socialized into one fundamental skill, which is the skill of behaving as a member of the community or, more generally, as a member of society. This skill, like all skills, contains a scale that runs from very bad to very good, a scale from depreciation to esteem, and it consists precisely in performing well according to the moral rules (of that society). This means in turn that the moral rules are the rules of this fundamental skill (of being a person, a member of the community, a member of society).

The relationship between doing well (badly) in this fundamental skill and in other skills can be well grasped in the way in which it is mirrored in the different forms of *shame*. Shame is, in general, the feeling of (real or imagined) loss of value in the eyes (or possible eyes) of others. Now this loss (or lack) of value can relate to anything I consider mine, such as bodily features, my outward circumstances, or what other people with whom I identify do (my relatives, my compatriots). But within this large sphere there is an inner region of shame that refers to things I myself do, and to this region belong all my incompetencies in the different skills, and they are felt the more poignantly the more important they are to my role in society. And then there is within this inner region an innermost core, and this is moral shame. If my exposition is correct, then moral shame must consist in a sense of devaluation in the eyes (or possible eyes) of others that concerns the core of my social being: myself, not as a cook, etc., but as a person, a member of society. That this central shame is distinguished from the other forms of shame is documented, e.g., by the fact that Aristotle, in his analysis of shame, considers moral shame only. More significant is that in all the languages of our culture as far back as Ancient Greek, not having the capacity for shame, shamelessness, refers only to this central shame (Ger., "schamlos"; Sp., "sinvergüenza"; Lat., "impudens"; Gr., "anaischyntos"). Notice also that what one is ashamed of can be called a *disgrace (Schande)* only in the moral sense.

How can the difference be grasped conceptually? In the first place, by recurring once again to the activities of praise and blame, and in the second, by attending to the connection in which these activities and moral shame stand to the other moral feelings (indignation, etc.). The words "praise" and "blame" ("Lob" and "Tadel") do not seem to apply to the same domain of discourse. Praise can be of anything one is good at. Blame, on the other hand, seems restricted to the moral case. In the case of particular skills, we criticize but do not blame. Criticism is the more general concept. To criticize is to point out a deficiency in relation to a given standard of excellence. To blame, on the other hand, means to point out a deficiency that is not thus relative: the action is bad, simpliciter; it is a deficiency of the person. We criticize actions but blame persons.

We can see the decisive connections if we include moral feelings, in particular, indignation. Blame normally includes indignation. It would be rather superficial to think that because indignation is defined as the feeling that includes a judgment of blame, it cannot in its turn help in understanding blame. In addition to the pure judgment, indignation includes emotional upset vis-à-vis the immoral action. The reason for this emotional reaction is that the immoral action jeopardized the common ground, the very foundations of the community, with which the indignant person identifies. Whereas moral judgment is normally accompanied by indignation, an ordinary value judgment (criticism) cannot be accompanied by indignation. Indignation (or possible indignation) is what distinguishes blame from personal value judgments in general. The possibility of indignation is not to be interpreted as a simple emotional addition. The possibility of indignation is a matter of content; it is essential for enabling the judgment to refer not to a standard of a specific skill but to the common social ground. It is important to see clearly the line of thought here: at first I could only point out that this value judgment does not concern a specific skill and that it somehow refers to the person as such. But so far this is an empty claim. It is only indignation that gives us the clue as to what is in question in moral judgments.

Only now can we understand what is the distinguishing mark of moral shame within shame in general. Shame in general is the (supposed) loss of value in the eyes of others. But these eyes are normally cool; there is no emotional counterpart to shame in those who put me to shame except in the extreme case of ridicule. In the case of moral shame, however, the faces of others are indignant. If somebody performs badly in some skill or other, others neither are indignant nor hold any other analogous emotion. The reason is clear: in other skills the performer's only problem is that he is doing badly (we can be sorry for him or laugh at him; these are other-regarding emotions, they do not stand for an emotional shock of the person himself). But when he is doing badly morally, this is not just his own business, it is as if he were breaking a contract. We stand aghast. Thus indignation is the exact mirror image of moral shame: shame is fear of others' indignation, since indignation is part of the intentional content of shame. This is why the most terrible thing for the morally evaluating person is that his opposite may not have the capacity for shame, that he is "shameless" (psychologists call it lack of moral sense) and hence capable of doing anything. And this, of course, is why in all languages this word is also used as a strong word of abuse.

Let us quickly take stock before taking the last step. Normative moral judgments ("One can't do that") led us to corresponding personal evaluations ("You are bad"), and these in turn can only be explained by reference to shame and indignation. The cognitivist will tend to understand this line of thought as if the moral rule were the self-subsistent star and the rest the tail attached to it, but the priorities are the other way around: it is only from indignation that the evaluation of a person as person ("bad" *sans phrase*) gets its sense, and it is only from this vantage point that the modal words in moral judgments are to be understood. This line of thought cannot be turned around, because the moral modal words ("ought," etc.) have no independent meaning. I can now apply the criterion for understanding the moral "ought" that I laid claim to at the beginning: What happens if somebody does not do what he "ought" to in this sense? He will face indignation, or alternatively, be put to shame. This is the specific inner social sanction that gives the moral "ought" *its sense*. (That we "ought" to act so does not mean that it is rational, that if you don't, you will not get what you aim at, or that it is part of the game, that if you don't you do not play this game. Rather, it means that if you don't, you incur a sanction, although one of a very special type. Anybody who thinks that this sanction is only something secondary must volunteer to say what he thinks is primary.)

The last step is to make clear in what sense indignation and shame are connected with a specific social identity. In the case of shame, it is obvious that there is such an identity: in moral shame we experience a lack of value of the self, not in respect to specific qualities of the person but of the person as person. To be sure, this still sounds very abstract, but since moral shame and indignation belong together, we can see that the personal identity here in question is the social identity that is the common ground for the person potentially put to shame and those persons potentially in indignation, understanding of course that all members of society function always in both possible roles. What is the common ground? Obviously it is not to be understood in analogy to a carpet on which we find ourselves standing but rather as intersubjectively constituted. The clue lies again in indignation and hence in praise and blame. Both imply a demand to behave in specific ways (the moral rules). This demand is, within a community, universal and reciprocal. At the same time one can see that the indignant person not only demands that she and everybody else behave in this way but also positively identifies with these norms and assumes that everybody else (even the person who arouses her indignation) does too. This double aspect has been beautifully brought out by Freud, even though only for the individual case. Freud speaks of the superego in the first case and the ego ideal in the second. The positive identification with the ego ideal (one wishes to be such and such) is a condition for internalizing the sanctioning and punishing superego. This complicated structure, namely, that everybody *wishes* to be so and at the same time *demands* of himself and all others to be so, constitutes the moral system of a society. The society (in *this* sense of "society") is not first there and then develops such a system. Rather, the society is constituted by this system.

Can we now say what it means to justify a moral norm? I think I can say it at least in relation to traditionalist moralities, by which I mean moralities founded on religion and myth and primarily restricted to a particular community. I shall come to the issue of justifying modern morality in the next section. In a traditional morality, justification consists in showing that the norm to be justified is a consequence of the religious foundations. Like any justification, this one, of course, enters into the normative beliefs themselves. To trespass a norm incurs indignation because the norm belongs to the religious belief system that is the common ground.

To clarify some doubtful points of what I have said, let me answer a few questions. First, what kind of an identity is moral identity? Surely it is not the identity of an individual as such. Indeed not, it is a qualitative identity ("I understand myself as a such and such"). Furthermore, it is an identity that is essentially intersubjective. But is this moral identity *the* primary intersubjective identity, basic to all other intersubjective identities and basic also to one's personal self-understanding? I think it is, but it is not necessary to make any such strong claims. The hierarchy of values by which a person understands herself can, in principle, be left open. Moral identity is simply the identity that has been described.

Second, how are conventional social norms and moral norms to be distinguished? I think by two interconnected criteria: conventional norms do not contain a claim to justify, and a person who breaks them is not considered to be bad. It does, I have to admit, seem possible to feel indignation at somebody who breaks a conventional norm, and in that case "indignation" would have to be admitted to be a wider concept than moral indignation. This cannot create any trouble, however, because we get the indignation that we need for morality by taking the indignation that corresponds to unqualified personal value judgments.

Third, in earlier attempts I have been criticized for restricting morality by definition to social morality. But notice that social morality as here conceived does not restrict morality to social contents. It leaves open the possibility of moral obligations to oneself or to animals, but moral sanction, the meaning of obligation, is socially defined. I follow G. H. Mead in saying that of course an individual can differ from society in his moral views. But then he must expect society to accept his views. This is implied in his saying that X is wrong, etc.

Fourth, when I spoke of the "common ground," I used two alternative formulations: the foundations of the community or those simply of society. I used to think that the first corresponds to a traditional morality, the second to a modern morality. But a traditionalist morality seems to be more complicated. There certainly is a community of those who believe. But are their obligations restricted to themselves, to the members of their particular community, or are they universal or in part universal? In a morality like that of Christianity the latter is clearly the case, but probably something of the sort is even true of primitive moral systems. This seems to me to be a matter of empirical research. The conception here presented can leave the question open.

Moral Justification in Modernity

What I have shown is a general structure of identity that appears to be the necessary basis of any set of moral norms. Of course, any society with a specific morality would thus far have this general structure with a differently specified identity. The question now to be considered is, What is the specific identity of that morality which remains when there are no nonempirical beliefs to sustain it?

We have to face a preliminary question first: can a morality without religious or metaphysical assumptions be justified? Several contemporary philosophers, Rawls and Habermas for example, maintain that in content this morality must be understood along Kantian lines ("Consider all people as equal objects of respect"), and I agree. But concerning the possible justification of this morality, Rawls and Habermas have taken opposite views. Rawls believes that such a morality cannot be justified at all; one can only hope that most people agree. Habermas believes that he is able to justify morality in one stroke, on the basis of the conditions of discourse. I think that his attempts are circular, and more generally I think that no wholesale justification of morality is possible at all. For what would a justification look like? Empirical it cannot be. Analytical it also cannot be, since a substantial moral view cannot be thought to follow from meanings (or conditions of discourse) alone. On the other hand, it is irksome to think that moral views are arbitrary. In fact, if we had to give up our objective moral judgments, which presuppose justifiability, we would have to give up our entire moral way of speaking and furthermore have to change a lot of our intersubjective behavior (reproaching, resentment, indignation). What we must expect, therefore, is some sort of partial justification. In the last resort, we can only show a way of life and must leave it up to individuals whether they want it (this way of life being analogous to the religious systems that in the case of traditional moralities are the points of reference for justification).[2]

In contrast to the cognitivist and the empirical researcher, the philosopher (not as theorist but as reflecting person) faces the question not of what are people's actual moral views but of what results do we come to if we reflect on the problems of morality without religious or other transcendent premises. Morality is something made (although not arbitrarily), not something found (Mackie, 1977). By saying "without transcendent premises," I mean it is made by paying due regard to all pertinent natural factors.

There seems to me to be two such factors: first, our natural propensity to compassion and sympathy, and second, the interest in having tacit agreements with the others to observe a system of rules if the others observe them too. The first of these factors is the starting point of Schopenhauer but also of utilitarianism. By itself, it certainly cannot achieve what it is supposed to. For compassion and sympathy are limited in scope, vary from person to person, and are counteracted by the contrary feelings of sadism and spiteful glee. Most important, there is no obligation in any of these feelings: they carry with them no moral "ought." The contractarian argument, on the other hand, lies at the foundation of Kant's view and other Golden Rule conceptions. Here we undoubtedly have an incipient morality with a specific set of moral rules, a concept of obligation, and a clear sense in which such a system is justified. It is justified in the sense that it is rational to submit to this system. The moral rules generated by contractarian deliberation are in large part the rules that the cognitivist imagines he finds on his Mount Sinai tablets (they are generated, not found). This set of moral rules is indeed so natural that it is a kernel within all moral systems.

But the shortcomings of this contractarian morality are equally obvious and have always been insisted upon: (1) The obligation within this system is by definition maintained merely by external sanctions. Accordingly, it is not based on evaluation (we cannot use the words "good" and "bad"), and there is no space for indignation (or shame). (2) Besides, contractarian morality does not by itself have universal scope (J. L. Mackie, the strongest contemporary advocate of this morality, points out that it can be the morality within a group of thieves; see Mackie, 1977), nor is it necessarily egalitarian.

I think we should accept the fact that we might be stuck with this truncated form of morality. Its limitations should not blind us to the fact that it is our surest natural possession. I doubt that there is another independent point of departure if we renounce such transcendent premises as Kant's Practical Reason. So we must see how these deficiencies can be mended.

Our first step must be to see whether the contractarian outlook allows for a genuine morality (a genuine morality being of the structure described in the first part of this paper). Can we say that it is in the interest of everyone to wish that everyone has a conscience (feelings of shame and indignation) in relation to those norms that the contractarian point of view is able to generate? Yes we can, but it is hopeless to try to base this full-fledged morality on contractarian considerations. Conscience cannot be instrumentalized; this is semantically not possible. If I say that my reasons for making certain moral claims (that such and such is bad or good) are that making such claims is in my interest (bad or good for me), I have therewith canceled those claims. It certainly remains possible that a contractarian justification of this full-fledged morality has a collateral, strengthening function, but a justification of this morality cannot be given on these lines.

At this point I must come back to what I said in the first part of the paper about moral identity. Now that we are no longer dealing with a particular society, the identity in question can only consist in understanding oneself as a member of *society*. This means as somebody on whom others can count, but "count" in what sense, and "member of society" in what sense? I submit that these senses are spelled out by the moral rules generated in the contractarian position. From the point of view of understanding oneself as a member of society, these moral rules are maintained not because it is profitable to me but because it is demanded from the point of view of this identity, from the point of view of what is often aptly called "the moral community," and this means that not acting accordingly leads to shame and indignation. (The extreme case of indignation is expulsion from the moral community, which shows that all indignation has an inclination in this direction. For a person who is amoral, who does not consider himself a member of the moral community, indignation has no sting, and this shows that moral sanction is truly internal.)

What is the exact import of this justification by reference to understanding oneself as a member of society? We must contrast it both with justification by reference to traditional moral identities and with contractarian justification. Contractarian justification connects the norms with normal, empirical interests. Traditionalist justification connects them with an identity that is in turn supported by religious and other transcendent beliefs. The justification that we are now faced with refers not to such interests as everybody can be presumed to have but to a conception of oneself and others, an "identity," yet not one that is supported by something. This justification thus appears to be tenuous indeed. Every one of us has to ask (and implicitly has always asked and answered) the question of whether he *wants* to consider himself a member of the moral community. The possibility of justifying moral norms and even the very possibility of being able to speak of a moral "ought" depend on this wanting. Does this sound unsatisfactory? Why should we want to do any better? (Or would not better be worse?) We cannot connect the moral norms with anything in the *heavens*. And is not the connection between wanting and obligation correct? It is artificial to think that morality is something out there independent of all of us and our wanting to stand in the moral dimension. As a matter of fact, it seems that the great majority of people want to be members of the moral community (it would be interesting to investigate why this is so). Of course, we have to distinguish between wanting to be members of the moral community (wanting to be able to reproach, to be indignant, etc.) and wanting to be moral. The latter is, of course, something quite different, though many philosophers, beginning with Plato, have not seen this important distinction.

Saying that morality depends on us seems to be opening the doors for relativism. But this is not the case. The identity of being a member of society is a conception of this world (without transcendent beliefs), and it is entirely general ("of society"). It therefore contains only what has been generated empirically on a contractarian basis and nothing else.

From this prohibition of any normative concepts over and above those that constitute a moral community, it also seems to follow that this morality is necessarily universal and egalitarian. The contractarian was free to decide with whom he was going to make his contract. But with the conception of behaving as a member of society, any restriction of scope needs additional reasons and justification. It is restriction, not nonrestriction, that needs additional justification. Similarly, any distinction in value between different classes or groups or races would need additional reasons.

I must admit that there are some norms that may claim admittance to morality but are not generated on the contractarian basis, such as considerateness toward animals and small children, but this issue concerns only the question of even further widening the scope of the same norms beyond what could be contractarian partners. Especially in the case of animals, the other source of a natural morality, compassion, here voices its claims. The question of whether and how to work this other source of morality into the fabric of obligation is difficult, and this is not the place to enter upon this thorny question.

Notes

1. My paper (Tugendhat, 1990) of the first Ringberg conference was already dedicated to this question, but it must have appeared excessively abstract and "philosophical" (to judge from the introduction by the editors of the German edition; see Edelstein and Nunner-Winkler, 1990). The Kohlbergian prejudices of the Ringberg community in favor of a "cognitive" conception of moral judgments were not auspicious for an attempt to identify the meaning of the moral "ought" with a motivational factor. Indeed, if my analysis of the moral "ought" is correct, the cognitive stance is not only wrong but devoid of sense. The attempt to furnish all of us with more or less innate little Mount Sinai tablets, slowly forming, to be sure, can only be understood as a hasty reaction to modern relativism. The trouble is that these tablets, when conceived cognitively without any motivational weight, are only ghostly replicas. They do not really deserve the name "morality," and this is precisely what makes it so important to insist once again on the question of what morality is.

2. To anticipate the cognitivist who stops me again at this point and claims that valid moral rules are just right, correct, or something of the sort and don't even need justification, I ask him what he has to say about obligation toward animals. This obligation does not appear in his Mount Sinai tablets (see n. 1) with either a plus or a minus sign. Why consider only the easy cases?

References

Edelstein, W., and Nunner-Winkler, G. (1990). From the introduction to the German edition. In T. E. Wren (Ed.), *The moral domain: Essays in the ongoing discussion between philosophy and the social sciences.* Cambridge: MIT Press.

Mackie, J. L. (1977). *Ethics: Inventing right and wrong.* London/Harmondsworth: Penguin.

Tugendhat, E. (1990). The necessity for cooperation between philosophical and empirical research in the clarification of the meaning of the moral "ought." In T. E. Wren (Ed.), *The moral domain: Essays in the ongoing discussion between philosophy and the social sciences.* Cambridge: MIT Press.

On the Necessity of Ideals

Harry Frankfurt

Freedom, Individuality, and Necessity

Our culture places a very high value on a certain ideal of freedom, according to which a person is to have varied alternatives available in the design and conduct of his life.[1] For a long time we have been fundamentally committed to encouraging a steady expansion of the range of options from which people can select. This commitment has been rather lavishly provided with technological, institutional, and ideological support. Moreover, it has become morally entrenched: we admire individuals and societies that promote freedom, and we deplore practices or circumstances that impair it. The more a society leaves it up to its members to determine individually the direction of their energies and the specification of their goals, and the more reasonable possibilities it offers them, the more enlightened and humane we consider it.

Our conception of ideal freedom is limited, to be sure, by considerations of legitimacy. Even those most enthusiastically devoted to freedom acknowledge that some courses of action are morally or in other ways unacceptable. As time has gone on, however, these constraints have been progressively relaxed. Corresponding to the proliferation of possibilities engendered by increasing technological and managerial sophistication, there has been a steady and notable weakening of the ethical and social constraints on legitimate choices and courses of action. Thus the expansion of freedom has affected not only what can be done but what is permissible as well. This combination of endlessly more masterful technical control and increasingly uncritical permissiveness has generated a tendency whose limit would be a culture in which everything is possible and anything goes.

Another ideal also enjoys considerable vitality, though devotion to it is perhaps not quite so pervasive or so orthodox as the commitment to freedom. This is the ideal of individuality, construed in terms of the development of a distinctive and robust sense of personal identity. To the extent that people find this ideal compelling, they endeavor to cultivate their own personal characters and styles and to decide autonomously how to live and what to do. Insofar as men and women have attained genuine individuality, they know their own minds. Furthermore, they have formed their minds not by merely imitating others but through a more personalized and creative process in which each has discovered and determined independently what he himself is.

Enlarging the range of available and permitted alternatives entails, of course, diminishing the scope of necessity in human life. It narrows the extent to which people find that circumstances allow them no choice but to follow a particular course of action. But as the ideal of freedom is more closely approached, the progressive reduction of necessity tends to undermine that ideal; and it also tends to undermine the ideal of individuality. For it is true both of freedom and of individuality that they *require* necessity.

Freedom and Autonomy in Conflict

We very commonly assume that whenever our freedom is expanded, our lives are thereby enriched. But this is true only up to a point. Reducing the grip of necessity may not in fact enhance our enjoyment of freedom. For if the restrictions on the choices that a person is in a position to make are relaxed too far, he may become, to a greater or lesser degree, disoriented with respect to where his interests and preferences lie. Instead of finding that the scope and vigor of his autonomy are augmented as the range of choices open to him broadens, he may become volitionally debilitated by an increasing uncertainty both concerning how to make decisions and concerning what to choose.

That is, extensive growth in the variety of a person's options may weaken his sense of his identity. The task of evaluating and ranking a considerably enlarged number of alternatives may be too much for him; it may overload his capacity to make decisions firmly grounded in a steady appreciation of what he really values and desires. Though he may have been able to find his way easily among a relatively small number of options, when he confronts a substantially wider array of possibilities, his understanding of his own interests and priorities will likely become less decisive. He may well discover, then, that his confidence in his preferences and predilections—a confidence established when the alternatives he needed to consider were fewer and more familiar—is drastically undermined. He may experience an unsettling diminution in the clarity with which he comprehends who he is. His grasp of his own identity may thus be radically disturbed.

Now suppose that someone is in a position to select from a field of alternatives that has not merely been extended but has no boundaries at all. Suppose, in other words, that every conceivable course of action is both available and eligible for choice. If the limits of choice have genuinely been wiped out, some possible courses of action will affect the person's desires and preferences themselves and hence bring about profound changes in his volitional character. It will be possible, then, for him to change those aspects of his nature that determine what choices he makes. He will be in a position to redesign his own will.

In that case, however, he will have to face his alternatives without a definitive set of goals, preferences, or other principles of choice. If his will becomes whatever he chooses to make it, no will can be unequivocally his until he has decided what will to choose. Any volitional characteristics that he may have prior to making that choice will be merely adventitious and provisional, for he has not committed himself to them and can alter them as he wants. Accordingly, no choice to which these characteristics lead will be fully or wholeheartedly his own. He is not volitionally equipped to make truly autonomous choices until he chooses how his choices are to be made.

But how is it possible for him to make that choice? What is to guide him in choosing, when the volitional characteristics by which his choices are to be guided are among the very things that he must choose? Under these conditions there is in him no fixed point from which a self-directed volitional process can begin. Erasing the boundaries within which his freedom was confined leaves him with too little volitional substance. No choice that he makes can be regarded as having originated in what we could meaningfully identify as his own will.

Unless a person makes choices within restrictions from which he cannot escape by merely choosing to do so, the notion of self-direction, of autonomy, cannot find a grip. Someone free of all such restrictions is so vacant of identifiable and stable volitional tendencies and constraints that he cannot deliberate or make decisions in any conscientious way. If he nonetheless does remain in some way capable of choice, the decisions and choices he makes will be altogether arbitrary. They cannot possess authentically personal significance or authority, for his will has no determinate character.

There is, then, a reciprocal conflict or strain between freedom and individuality. The latter requires limits that the former tends to erase. With total freedom, there can be no individual identity. This is because an excess of choice impairs the will. Without individuality, on the other hand, freedom loses much of its point. The availability of alternatives counts, after all, only for someone who has a will of his own. It should come as no surprise that when there is a steady inclination *both* to urge a general expansion of freedom *and* to encourage the development of autonomy, things begin to go wrong.

Limits of the Will

What limits does an autonomous will require? What are the volitional necessities whose elimination or attenuation threatens individuality and freedom? The most fundamental, I believe, pertain to what a person cares about, what he considers important to him. This is not primarily either a cognitive or an affective matter. Cognitive and affective considerations are its sources and grounds. But while it is based on what a person believes and feels, caring is not the same as believing or feeling. Caring is essentially volitional; that is, it concerns one's will. The fact that a person cares about something or considers it important to himself does not consist in his holding certain opinions about it; nor does it consist in his having certain feelings or desires. His caring about it consists, rather, in the fact that he *guides* himself by reference to it. This entails that he purposefully direct his attention, attitudes, and behavior in response to circumstances germane to the fortunes of the object about which he cares. A person who cares about something is, as it were, invested in it. By caring about it, he makes himself susceptible to benefits and vulnerable to losses depending upon whether what he cares about flourishes or is diminished. We may say that in this sense he *identifies* himself with what he cares about.

About certain things that are important to him, a person may care so much, or in such a way, that he is subject to a kind of necessity. Because of this necessity, various courses of action that he would otherwise be able to pursue are effectively unavailable to him. It is impossible for him to pursue them. He may well possess the knowledge and skill required for performing the actions in question; nonetheless, he is unable to perform them. The reason is that he cannot bring himself to do so. It is not that he cannot muster the necessary *power*. What he cannot muster is the *will*. He is held in the grip of a volitional necessity that renders certain actions impossible for him—not by depriving him of the capacity to perform them but by making it impossible for him to use that capacity.

Consider a mother who reaches the conclusion, after conscientious deliberation, that it would be best for her to give up her child for adoption, and suppose that she decides to do so. When the moment arrives for actually giving up the child, however, she may find that she cannot go through with it—not because she has reconsidered the matter and changed her mind but because she simply cannot bring herself to give her child away. Similarly, there are reports that military officers refused to carry out orders to begin launching nuclear weapons, when they believed that the orders were not part of a test but were intended actually to bring about a nuclear strike. Since these officers had volunteered for their assignments, they were presumably unaware of the limits within which their wills were bound. When the chips were down, however, they discovered that in fact they could not bring themselves to do what they had believed they would be willing to do.

When a person is subject to this sort of volitional necessity, it renders certain actions *unthinkable* for him. These actions are not genuinely among his options. He cannot perform any of them, because he is prevented by a volitional constraint: that is, he cannot *will* to perform them. Even though he may think it would be best for him to perform one of the actions, he *cannot bring himself* to perform it. He cannot volitionally organize himself in the necessary way. If he attempts to do so, he runs up against the *limits of his will*. This is shown by the fact that he is unable to perform the action even when all the nonvolitional conditions for his performing it (e.g., opportunity, knowledge, and power) are satisfied.

A person who cannot bring himself to perform a certain action has a powerful aversion, which effectively limits his conduct. But finding it unthinkable to perform an action is not the same as being irresistibly averse to performing it. In cases of volitional necessity, the aversion is not only irresistible; it is also in some way endorsed by the person. Furthermore, endorsing the aversion is something that he cares about. Indeed, his conduct is constrained so effectively precisely because of the fact that, whether consciously or not, he endorses the aversion and cares about maintaining it. Thus, he resists making any efforts to do what he remains deeply averse to doing.

This distinguishes situations in which one finds an action *unthinkable* from those in which one's inability to choose effectively is due to addiction, terror, or some other variety of overwhelming compulsion or inhibition. In situations of the former kind, but not in those of the latter, the effectiveness of the person's incapacity derives from the fact that the person considers that incapacity to be important to him. This also accounts for the rather notable peculiarity that when a person discovers that it is unthinkable for him to perform a certain action, or to refrain from performing it, he does not ordinarily experience the constraint as moving or obstructing him against his will. Although he may not know it, the fact is that the constraint is itself imposed by his will. For this reason he experiences his submission to it less as a defeat than as a liberation.

The necessities of the will are, of course, subject to change. What is unthinkable for a person at one time may not be unthinkable for him at another, as a consequence of alterations in the contingent circumstances from which volitional necessities derive. A person may even find it possible deliberately to alter the necessities that bind his will. Needless to say, however, he cannot alter them by a sheer act of will. A person cannot redesign his own volitional nature simply by making up his mind that what has been unthinkable for him is no longer so. Ordinary inhibitions and aversions may sometimes be overcome by strenuous efforts of will. But a genuine necessity of the will could hardly be susceptible to alteration in that way.

A person for whom an action is unthinkable may be in a position to alter his will by means less immediate and direct than the exercise of willpower alone. However, undertaking to make the unthinkable thinkable might itself be something that the person cannot bring himself to do. Then it is not only unthinkable for him to perform the action in question; it is also unthinkable for him to form an effective intention to become willing to perform it. His will is constrained by an aversion to the very idea of making that change in himself. He cannot bring himself to endorse that idea. To be sure, changes in circumstances might bring about a change in his will. But he cannot change his will by any deliberate effort of his own. He is subject to a necessity that, in this sense, defines an absolute limit. And this necessity is unequivocally constitutive of his nature or essence as a volitional being.

Volitional Necessity and Identity

In every triangle, the sum of the interior angles is equal to 180 degrees. The triangle may be scalene, isosceles, or equilateral, but in no triangle does the sum of the interior angles equal either more or less than 180 degrees. This is a necessary condition for being a triangle; it constitutes part of the essence of triangularity. Triangles have, as it were, no choice. They cannot help satisfying the condition in question; doing so defines the generic identity of a triangle as the type of thing it is. The idea that the identity of a thing is to be understood in terms of conditions essential for its existence is one of the oldest and most compelling of the philosophical principles that guide our efforts to clarify our thought. To grasp what a thing is, we must grasp its essence, namely those characteristics without which it cannot be what it is. Thus the notions of necessity and identity are intimately related.

Of course, the necessity that binds a triangle to its essential nature is only a conceptual or logical necessity. This type of necessity has to do with the organization of our ideas and our language. It governs how things are described and classified. But it does not govern, nor is it even pertinent to, the careers of the things themselves. It is not a real force, and it has no effect on what actually happens in the world. The fact that a figure cannot be a triangle unless it possesses the characteristics essential to triangularity has no influence on whether or not a certain triangular figure retains these characteristics or is altered in such a way as to lose them.

It seems to me that when we talk about the essential nature of a person, the issue is analogous. It is likewise a matter of the person's necessary characteristics. In this case, however, the necessity is not merely conceptual. Here the necessity does not pertain only to how the person is to be classified or described. The constraints imposed by volitional necessity are not constraints merely upon thought and language. Volitional necessity constrains the person himself, by limiting the choices he can make.

The essential nature of a person is constituted by his necessary *personal* characteristics. These characteristics have to do particularly with his nature as a person, rather than with his nature as a human being or as a biological organism of a certain type. They are especially characteristics of his will. In speaking of the personal characteristics of someone's will, I do not mean to refer simply to the desires or impulses that move him. We attribute impulses, desires, and motives even to infants and animals, creatures that cannot properly be said either to be persons or to possess wills. The personal characteristics of someone's will are reflexive, or higher-order, volitional features. They pertain to a person's efforts to negotiate his own way among the various impulses and desires by which he is moved, as he undertakes to identify himself more intimately with some of his own psychic characteristics and to distance himself from others.

To be a *person* entails having evaluative attitudes (not necessarily based on moral considerations) toward oneself.[2] A person is a creature prepared to endorse or repudiate the motives from which he acts and to organize the preferences and priorities by which his choices are ordered. He is disposed to consider whether what attracts him is actually important to him. Instead of responding unreflectively to whatever he happens to feel most strongly, he undertakes to guide his conduct in accordance with what he really cares about.

To the extent that a person is constrained by volitional necessities, there are certain things that he cannot help willing or that he cannot bring himself to do. These necessities substantially affect the actual course and character of his life. But they affect not only what he does: they limit the possibilities that are open to his will, that is, they determine what he cannot will and what he cannot help willing. Now the character of a person's will constitutes what he most centrally is. Accordingly, the volitional necessities that bind a person identify what he cannot help being. They are in this respect analogues of the logical or conceptual necessities that define the essential nature of a triangle. Just as the essence of a triangle consists in what it must be, so the essential nature of a person consists in what he must will. The boundaries of his will define his shape as a person.

Ideals

Without attempting to analyze the nature or basis of volitional necessity, I suggest that its force is in certain respects similar to the force of love. This force is somewhat paradoxical. Love *captivates* us, but even while we are its captive we find that it is in some way liberating. Love is *selfless*, but it also enables us in some way to feel most truly ourselves. Moreover, it seems that love would not be so liberating or so enhancing if its grip on us were not so overpowering and so far outside our immediate voluntary control.

Only by virtue of the necessity that it imposes upon us does love intensify our sense of identity and of freedom. We cannot help loving what we love, nor can we make ourselves love by a mere act of will. The value of loving for us derives precisely, at least in part, from the very fact that whether we love is not up to us. The importance of loving to us would be lost if we could love something or cease to love it merely by deciding to do so. The self-fulfillment and freedom that love provides depend upon the very necessity that love entails.

If someone loves nothing, it follows that he has no ideals. Now an ideal is a limit. A person's ideals are concerns that he cannot bring himself to betray. They entail constraints that, for him, it is unthinkable to violate. Suppose that someone has no ideals at all. In that case, nothing is unthinkable for him; there are no limits to what he might be willing to do. He can make whatever decisions he likes and shape his will just as he pleases. This does not mean that his will is free. It means only that his will is anarchic, moved by mere impulse and inclination. For a person without ideals, there are no volitional laws that he has bound himself to respect and to which he unconditionally submits. He has no inviolable boundaries. Thus he is amorphous, with no fixed identity or shape.

If someone has no ideals, there is nothing that he cannot bring himself to do. Moreover, since nothing is necessary to him, there is nothing that he can be said essentially to be. To be sure, he may have a number of persistent psychological dispositions or traits; he may exhibit various consistent patterns of inclination and choice. But any stable volitional characteristics he may have are products of impersonal causal influences. They are not consequences of his wanting to be a person of a certain sort or to devote himself to a certain kind of life; they are not fixed by his will itself but by contingencies external to it. In other words, his will is governed entirely by circumstances rather than by any essential nature of its own. None of his volitional characteristics is necessary to him, since none derives from his own nature.

This means that he lacks a personal essence, which would comprise the necessary conditions of his identity. For this reason, there is no such thing for him as genuine integrity. After all, he has no personal boundaries whose inviolability he might set himself to protect. There is nothing that he is essentially. What he is at any given time is no more than what he happens then to be, which is merely accidental.

The ideals that define the essential nature of a person need not be moral ideals, in the sense in which morality is especially a matter of how a person relates himself to the interests of others. The most decisive boundaries of a person's life may derive from imperatives of tradition, of style, of intellect, or of some other mode of ambition. This leaves open what characteristics an ideal must possess to serve its function of limiting a person and specifying his identity. To a surprising extent, philosophers have neglected this important question, and I will not pursue it here.[3] Another important question, which has also been neglected and which I shall also not undertake to discuss, concerns the basis on which a person can reasonably make a choice from among various worthy ideals.[4]

It may seem inappropriate to suggest that problems of choice and justification can arise with respect to what I have characterized as necessities. What cannot be helped, it would appear, does not depend upon being chosen, nor, accordingly, does it require justification. But while it is true that a person can no more choose or decide on the limits of his will than he can simply choose or decide on what he will love, we must not conclude from this that he has nothing whatever to say about the matter. From the fact that what binds us to our ideals is love, it does not follow that our relationship to them is wholly noncognitive. There is considerable room for reason and argument in the clarification of ideals and in the evaluation of their worthiness. Even in romantic love, after all, there is generally more to the story than being swept blindly off one's feet.

Reason and Love

It is widely supposed that the two most precious capacities of our species, which make human life distinctively valuable and interesting, are that we can reason and that we can love. Each of these capacities is fully realized only when a person finds himself constrained by a kind of necessity. In the former case, it is the cognitive necessity of logic; in the latter, it is the volitional necessity of love. Reason is universal, in the sense that its dictates are equally binding on everyone. On the other hand, love is particular: the fact that I am devoted to certain ideals, or the fact that I love someone, does not lead me to think that anyone who does not do the same is making a mistake. The question of whom one is to love cannot be settled by developing a rigorous proof, nor can one rigorously demonstrate which ideals are properly to define the boundaries of one's will. This should not be taken to entail, however, that our volitional necessities must merely be acknowledged as givens—that is, accepted passively as brute facts with respect to which deliberation and rational critique have no place. The relationship between love and reason is an ancient philosophical theme, which it would be well for us to explore anew.[5]

Notes

1. Throughout this essay personal pronouns are used in the generic rather than in any gendered sense.

2. See Tugendhat's discussion (1990 and in this volume) of the connections between personal identity, evaluative judgments, and moral emotions.

3. But see the chapters in this volume by Blasi, Rorty, Tugendhat, and Wren.

4. Parts of this question are addressed by Haste (in this volume) and Nunner-Winkler (1990 and in this volume).

5. For further discussion of some of the themes elaborated in this essay, see Frankfurt (1988).

References

Frankfurt, H. (1988). *The importance of what we care about.* New York: Cambridge University Press.

Nunner-Winkler, G. (1990). Moral relativism and strict universalism. In T. E. Wren (Ed.), *The moral domain: Essays in the ongoing discussion between philosophy and the social sciences.* Cambridge: MIT Press.

Tugendhat, E. (1990). The necessity for cooperation between philosophical and empirical research in the clarification of the meaning of the moral "ought." In T. E. Wren (Ed.), *The moral domain: Essays in the ongoing discussion between philosophy and the social sciences.* Cambridge: MIT Press.

What It Takes to Be Good

Amélie Oksenberg Rorty

Moral Systems as Practical Directives for Character Formation

"Without dramatis personae, moral philosophy is poetry."

It takes a great deal of ability and skill to lead a morally significant life, and to carry ideals or principles to their effective realization. If the point of being moral were to pass the judgments of a court of morality, having good will might be sufficient. Even if the point of morality were solely to avoid doing wrong—no mean feat, to be sure—moral systems might not have to investigate the dispositions and habits that are exercised in a constructively moral life. If the primary concern of morality were to articulate a morality of prohibition, and if there were a sharp and workable distinction between the morality of omission and that of commission, moral philosophy might well proceed without a detailed characterization of the traits necessary for realizing moral ideals and principles in action. On the (questionable) assumption that the capacities required to refrain from doing wrong are available to Everyman, moral philosophy might in principle be independent of moral psychology and moral education.

But most traditional moral philosophy is not limited to an analysis of minimal negative morality, the morality of prohibition. Most moral philosophers also go beyond minimal positive morality, an account of the basic principles that ground universal obligations. Even philosophers who, like Kant, are primarily known for their analyses of the preconditions for the *possibility* of morality were also concerned to describe the character of an active moral agent. Traditional moral philosophers considered their tasks incomplete until they specified the mentality and motivational structure of reliable moral agents who could be counted on to affect the world in a certain way.

Of course, philosophical systems of morality are complex enterprises, conjoining a number of quite different tasks. Different philosophers have focused on distinctive aspects of the multifaceted directions of morality. Some have concentrated on specifying the presuppositions of (what they take to be) the common moral understanding and moral practice. Others have attempted to formulate the ideals toward which we should strive. Still others seek to articulate the principles that should regulate just and right conduct. Although these various investigations are in a way independent of one another, although a philosopher can concentrate on one approach to morality without engaging herself in all the others, a complete moral system analyzes the interrelations among these various issues. All of them involve a theory about what is best and worst in human nature, an account of how to bypass or transform the worst so as to allow the best to flourish. The point of understanding morality is, after all, to affect moral practice. But since moral practice is fundamentally affected by the character of agents, by their habits and motives, and since the structures of social and political institutions centrally form a people's habits and motives, moral philosophy is incomplete unless it carries its analyses of moral principles, ideals, or the presuppositions of morality to an account of the character of the moral agent and how best to form it.

There are several reasons for any moral philosophy—whatever the directions of its ideals or principles—to attend to the details of the development of moral character. Enlarging minimal negative morality to minimal positive morality and again to substantive positive morality requires progressively greater attention to moral psychology. Any norm, ideal, or obligation that can legitimately make claims on us must be capable of being realized by us. If *ought* implies *can*, normative morality bears a burden of psychological proof: it must determine the basic traits of the agents presumptively subject to the claims of any particular moral directive. Even though we need to develop and teach the capacities and traits that make active substantive morality possible, we still need to determine what is possible in order to specify what is obligatory or ideal. A responsible moral theorist cannot rest content with specifying the moral capacities and traits whose development is only conceptually possible. She must also specify the conditions that transform moral capacities into active dispositions and habits. For those concerned to live in a just society, the point of understanding principles of justice is not solely to characterize general principles that might hold for angels, Martians, or demons. Political philosophers are presumably also committed to specifying the conditions of justice as they can be applied to their own society. Principles of justice remain empty until they are contextually specified as realizable in a specific historical and political situation. By no means the least of the conditions that constrain and direct theories of justice are psychological conditions: the mentality, primary motives, and habits on which social institutions rely and which they are obliged to foster. To be sure, the perspective of abstract justice provides a critique for the psychology fostered by specific social arrangements; yet a formal theory of justice suited to a species psychologically constructed quite differently from us can have no claims on our ideals, let alone on the directions of our practices.

Furthermore, realizing the point of ethics—the application of ethical commitment and ethical understanding to practice—requires more than a relatively unconflicted good will capable of being guided by practical reason; it also requires many specific active skills and dispositions. The kind of psychological analysis required by a substantive morality moves from the psychology of capacity to the psychology of performance, from the psychology of understanding, will, and commitment to the psychology of action.

We become moral agents through a process of transformation that affects virtually every aspect of our character. Though the capacities for rational agency, for emotion and steadfast commitment, may well be necessary for morality, they are obviously not sufficient to transform a wanton into a moral person, even for the narrow morality of the will or for the discursive morality that is primarily expressed in public discussion. There is no single pivotal point or fulcrum that can transform a wanton into a genuinely respectful, cooperative citizen and friend. In any case, rationality, *caritas*, a good will, and the habit of acting from moral principle are not single, unitary active powers. These terms are placeholders, covering a vast array of psychological and characterological capacities, abilities, and skills that vary independently of one another and need to be developed and sustained.

Not only a person's self-conception as expressed in her principles and ideals but also her binding commitments and motives, not only her capacity to take an impartial or altruistic standpoint but also patterns of salience in perception and imagination, specific categorial frames for organizing experience, posture and tone of voice, a sense of timing and tact—all these and more—are engaged in and presupposed by active morality. How we act—our manner and tone in what we do—is an essential part of *what* we do. Of course, the surface description of what we do (march or refuse to march, vote the accused guilty or innocent) is morally significant. But our rationale for what we do, blending, as it does, the reasons and causes that individuate our actions, is also morally significant. It is manifest in the *ways* we act: harshly or hesitantly, abruptly or sorrowfully. The substantive description of our actions (voting the accused guilty in a sorrowful and compassionate way that conveys our recognition that we too might be standing in the dock if circumstances had been only slightly different) tells the fuller moral story of our action. Indeed, even in such large political matters as international negotiations, what matters is often the manner in which participants accord the kind of respect that can be recognized cross-culturally. Sadly for us, we may lack the abilities and skills to adjust the tone and manner of our actions even when we possess the best rational reflection supported by the most resolute rational will, accompanied by the noblest of self-ideals and emotional commitments. Only when rational reflection and the best of ideals succeed in forming our *petites perceptions*, our spontaneous reactions, our faces and our gestures, do we come within hailing distance of morality. Only then are our principles, ideals, and commitments substantively realized, and only then do they become more than wishes and words whose directions are more frequently expressed in shame or regret than in action.

In principle, we possess as standard issue equipment the capacities required for the minimal negative morality that articulates universal prohibitions and the minimal positive morality that enjoins general universal commands. Normally, minimal morality does not require abilities that can only be acquired in just social conditions. But minimal morality by no means exhausts our moral repertoire or our moral obligations. These progressively extend to the basic decent "good enough" morality of neighborliness and good citizenship, to reliably playing a social role. While minimal morality normally involves all-or-none performances, the morality of decency can vary both in region and in degrees. A person can be a morally constructive colleague but a deplorable husband, a good neighbor but a corrupt politician. Universal capacities for minimal morality do not assure the morality of decency. Though the morality of decency is not self-sacrificing or self-denying, it does require a certain level of education and training. It is vulnerable to erosion by harsh circumstances and is, under normal circumstances, best sustained by a relatively sound social system. Within the morality of decency, we can distinguish the morality of a righteous will, which involves the general commitment to do what is right for the right reason, from significant morality, which involves active dispositions to generate morally appropriate intentions and to fulfil those intentions in well-formed action. This distinction can be refined still further. Saintliness involves acting well for the appropriate reasons and from the best motives. It is usually unselfconscious and never self-congratulatory. But because of the way that our vulnerabilities generate narrowly self-protective motives, and the way that our exuberance can generate sheerly playful motives, saintliness is, and perhaps should be, out of our reach. To be righteous, a person's motives (whatever they may be) must either coincide with, or be capable of being overruled by, the requirements of morality (whatever they may be). But if the morality of saintliness is too demanding, the morality of righteousness is incomplete. By itself, it does not generate or assure the richness or detail of a morally significant life. Significant morality requires a rich and appropriate array of specific intentions and motives as well as a robust array of abilities to execute these effectively. It leaves the world a better place for our activity, beyond the contribution that might be made by the sheer existence of yet one more merely righteous will.

The point of moral life moves beyond the will successfully passing the judgment of a court of righteousness, toward acting well to fulfill the principles of morality (or as it may be, the will of Allah). After all, a cheap and easy way of passing the court of righteousness is to remain minimalist about having intentions. A robust significant morality goes beyond intending little so that one can intend clean. A person with a pure will and an exquisitely precise moral sensibility, who understands and is committed to morally sound procedural principles for communicative discourse, but lacks the ability to follow his judgments and directions in action may be charming, perhaps tragic, but after a time his pretensions to morality sound hollow. Even if he is committed to a set of ideals that he takes as necessary for his identity, even if he suffers moral shame—internalized communal indignation—when he violates his moral principles, his pretensions to morality are a mockery unless he generally succeeds in acting from his commitments and principles. To characterize someone as moral on the grounds that he has certain general *capacities* is to praise with faint damns; and to hold such a person morally responsible in social and political situations where nothing is done to develop those capacities—to place them in active, working order—is to displace the real locus of moral responsibility.[1]

This is a conceptual as well as a moral issue. The goodness of a person's will is determined by the propriety of her intentions, however these may be measured in any particular moral system. A generalized good will, a generalized intention to act in accordance with duty, is a second-order intention. By itself, it does not command a particular policy, a principle, a course of action, or even, for that matter, a particular intention. Intentions are individuated and defined by their rationales and by their typical action directions.[2]

But it requires considerable astuteness to understand what is at the heart of each duty, to know what is commanded in each situation. The generalized commitment to do the right thing, even the generalized commitment to do the right thing for the right reason, does not necessarily by itself assure the abilities required to carry out that commitment. As Kant himself realized, executive morality—carrying the good will to its fulfillment in particular intentions and action—requires the practical virtues: the range of skills and attitudes generally required and exercised in acting effectively and well. When morality is executive as well as legislative, when it is robust as well as righteous, it requires the capacities and abilities necessary to realize moral principles, to actualize their purport in the right way on the right objects at the right time. (Consider the parallel: in principle, the general capacity for critical rationality might be equally distributed. But the abilities required to construct the relevant productive lines of thought that are the point of being rational do not appear to be equally distributed. It is unjust to hold individuals responsible for being rational when it takes educative training to develop the generalized *capacity* for rationality into the many detailed *habits* of thought required for its active exercise.)

Without treating any of these traits, habits, and abilities as exhaustive or mutually exclusive, we can sketch a list of intellectual and character traits, abilities, and skills that a robust significant morality requires and that normally are also personally as well as socially beneficial.[3]

1. Cognitive and intellectual abilities

•the ability to perceive preventable harms, satisfiable needs, and realizable benefits

•foresight and lateral sight, an active disposition to think comparatively and systematically, forming all-things-considered judgments of reflective equilibrium

•imagination and resourcefulness, inventiveness, ingenuity

•a detailed and contextualized sense of proportion and priorities

•openness to novelty and to correction that is nevertheless resolute against the lure of distraction by remote or notional possibilities

2. Character and executive traits

•an informed empathic and generous understanding

•a nondefensive objectivity, a recognition of one's limitations

•a sense of humor, wild and free

•energy, persistence, and a capacity to deal with conflict and frustration constructively

•an active ability to act in accordance with one's judgment of what is best

•a sense of empowerment to make one's causes visible and audible, the ability to elicit and give cooperation, an active recognition of the background mutual aid needed for the success of most projects[4]

•a sense of (culturally and contextually variable) timing, tact, and expressiveness, knowing when to press and when to pause, when to sympathize closely and when to withdraw, when to listen and when to advise, when and how to praise and blame

3. Skills

•a set of skills that enable the appropriate performance of well-formed intentions. Many of these are acquired, and most vary with social needs and with a person's situation.

To be sure, a person doesn't have to have all of these to be within hailing distance of robust significant morality. Moral luck reigns in this domain. Morally significant traits, abilities, and skills are not equally distributed, and they require benign circumstances for their best development and exercise. Moreover, these traits do not themselves assure their appropriate use. Many can be used well or ill, beneficently or harmfully. Still for all of that, we need a healthy number and a tasteful and well-balanced array to realize the best of general intentions.[5] Fortunately, some abilities and skills are not necessary. Moral competence does not require any particular moral theory, or indeed any particular kind of moral theory, nor need moral agents take on morality as a project for themselves, exhorting themselves to excellence and evaluating their motives and actions. Indeed, too acute and persistent attention to their own motives and directions might well distract agents from their primary focus on the tasks at hand. And while moral agents must respect and respond to questions and criticisms from their fellows, active and reliable habits neither require nor presuppose explicit justification. Although morality involves acting in accord with the best or most justified course, a highly competent moral agent need not articulate or defend the principles of her action.

The same is true for the centrally important civic discussions about what principles and virtues should regulate and direct institutions. A community's deliberations about just political procedures presupposes the same heterogeneous range of perceptual, emotional, cognitive, motivational, and behavioral dispositions exercised in substantive morality. Just as there is no fulcrum, no pivotal point that adjusts the wide range of traits required for morality, so none assures the impartial and mutually respecting rationality of public deliberation. It is not enough for participants in the discussions of public life to understand and follow the general rules of good-willed rationality. They must also be morally sensitive to the needs and nuances, the hesitations and insecurities, of their fellows. Respect goes beyond acknowledging the rational will of others; it goes beyond acknowledging the need to justify the principles of one's actions to one's fellows in terms they can understand.[6] It moves toward highly complex psychological attitudes of tact, timing, and empathy; it requires a detailed understanding of the effects of being disempowered as well as the skills that would empower the dispossessed to participate in public life. Without civic virtue, there is no true rationality; and without a benign social system and sound institutions of moral education, there is no civic virtue. In the domain of practice, there is no royal road, no purely formal characterization of a robust substantive rationality capable of constructive as well as consistent or universalized practical intelligence. Indeed, except at the level of purely formal validity, determining whether a procedural rule is substantively rational and fair already presupposes substantive value judgments against which consistency or equity is measured. But even more significantly, it requires that these value judgments become realized in the details of practice. It is character—the vast range of perceptual, categorial, behavioral habits—that carries principled value judgments to their realization in practice.

The full realization of morality requires not only a sound set of principles but also a robustly formed character, that is, a configuration of the minute dispositions that affect the ways in which a person acts. Morality is in the details; it not only affects what a person chooses to do but also how she acts. A person expresses a sound character not only in a steadfast commitment to principles but also in the modality and manner of her thoughts and behavior.[7] Morality goes far beyond a capacity for self-control, for being directed by justice and duty rather than by inclination or desire. As readers of novels know, it includes the active dispositions to be helpful and emotionally empathic as well as prudent and principled.

Though they understand the role of character in action, recent virtue theorists are still working within a frame of a morality of righteousness. And though post-Kantian theorists of virtue from Matthew Arnold to Philippa Foot understand the need to develop a wide range of morally relevant dispositions, they attempt to find a single capacity that determines the morality of a person's character. But locating moral virtue in one capacity loses all the advantages of virtue theory: no single trait or principle differentiates the moral virtues from the vast range of dispositions, abilities, skills, and habits required to act well.[8] Moral systems designed to produce *correct moral judgment, correct moral decision,* or *correct moral feeling* assume that agents are strongly unified, have hierarchical structures, and have a central homuncular capacity that elicits and directs the vast array of abilities and habits that form action.

There are roughly three versions of such systems: intellectualist theories focus on rationality as the pivot of morality, voluntarist theories focus on the correctness of the will as fundamental, and *caritas* theories focus on a central emotional capacity like love or benevolence.[9] All three assume that a person's traits are, or can be, centrally unified: they attempt to locate a panoptical point that not only scans the vast array of dispositions and habits that affect action but also commands and regulates their exercise. All three tend to ignore the social and political conditions required for developing and exercising the central capacities of morality. The responsibility for developing (what is, after all, merely) a capacity is left to the individual, as if she could bootstrap herself to ramify that capacity throughout her psychology so as to affect her habits and actions.

If there were such a pivotal point for morality—as *caritas* or a good will or the range of intellectual virtues (say cleverness, ingenuity, the ability rapidly and accurately to make complex inferences, even the capacity to form impartial judgments)—it would be insufficient for civic virtue. Of course, no one, certainly not Kant himself, thought that such traits could assure virtue by themselves. The claim was rather that *caritas,* good will, rationality, or a commitment to just procedural principles is a necessary precondition for the very possibility of morality. But if there is a distinctive and specific moral domain, it has many presuppositions and preconditions: an empathic imagination, a well-formed character that doesn't suffer from the disorders that disconnect thought from action, a civic polity that actively promotes moral development. The intellectual virtues that are ingredient in civic virtue—a sound and clear sense of priorities, an imaginative and vivid understanding of what is relevant to public welfare, gifts of eloquent persuasion—are also character virtues. Because their exercise is highly sensitive to situation and context, they are not readily formulated in principles or rules. In any case, the principles that articulate them are so general that applying these virtues requires the very character virtues that they are meant to guide. In principle, one can recognize, understand, and develop rules and principles relatively late in life by a purely intellectual process (if there is such a thing). Perhaps one can acquire the capacities for internalized indignation by developing a vivid empathic imagination, by carefully reading novels and newspapers. But for an individual to qualify as a moral person, rather than as a potentially moral person, that capacity must be finely developed and exercised.

The virtues required to use and apply those principles (or to form that conception of the self) are, like other habits and dispositions, acquired and developed by practice and imitation. We do not develop them by understanding them or even by considering ourselves committed to them as an essential part of our identities. We cannot acquire substantive morality solely by acquiring the right cognitive or psychological attitudes. Moreover, those attitudes are necessary for morality only if they actively embed the minutiae of perception, emotion, and habits that form morally significant action. The common parental command, "Do as I say, not as I do" expresses the unrealistic dream that words and thoughts can substitute for models, that an evocative description can replace the minutiae of imitation.

The role of developing the imagination—particularly through reading literature and drama—is, as many have recently argued, central to developing moral sensibilities, particularly to refining moral perception. But while such sensibility may be necessary for morality, it is not sufficient. It is as difficult to carry imagination to practice as it is to act from rules and principles. Imitation and practice are necessary for both. Unless they are expressed in the smallest nuances of practice, the principles of justice—however clearly and intelligently understood—can at best introduce the beneficial complexity of internal psychological conflict. We imitate and reproduce the characterological morality of models—the morality of their bones and sinews, of their gestures and tones of voice—far more surely than whatever rules or principles articulate their ideals or commitments. In the hands and on the faces of the vicious, the best of noble or rational principles become deadly weapons. Just as good-willed rationality, regarded as a purely intellectual faculty, cannot assure virtue, so too rationality and rational good-willed respect cannot assure just conditions for debate about the forms of public life.

For similar reasons, philosophical theory—regarded as a purely analytic and speculative activity—cannot even begin to construct the conditions for fair and rational deliberation. Of course that's not news: no one ever for a moment thought that philosophy could replace politics, or that philosophy is immune to the diseases of demagogic politics, or that rationality (whatever it may be) is sufficient for the fullness of life. The thought was rather: erst kommt die philosophie, dann kommt die morale; und *dann* kommt . . . well, whatever it might be: forming just public institutions, developing an appropriate educational system, and so on. The contribution of philosophy to morality is thought to be propaedeutic: to analyze the principles of civic virtue and its most general preconditions. But since the preconditions for civic virtue are practical as well as theoretical, since just institutions and a sound system of moral education are among the central preconditions for the possibility of civic virtue, a moral philosophy that modestly limits itself to describing the conditions for just deliberation, to articulating the rules and principles that govern fair-mindedness, is radically and dangerously incomplete.

Nor can the affective conditions of morality be assured by a sound philosophical analysis of the logical and psychological relations between a person's identity as a social being and some particular moral affect. Of course, no sensible philosopher ever believed that an analysis of the preconditions of the possibility of morality can by itself even begin to move toward the realization of those conditions. To be useful, such an analysis must also move to practical matters: to describing the childhood and the sociopolitical institutions— particularly the wide range of educative institutions including not only schools but museums and the mass media—that (whether we like it or not) effectively form civic character, whether it is just or unjust. Taking our substantive convictions to heart and hands, we should move from Kant, Rawls, and Habermas to Montesquieu, Rousseau, and Jefferson, from analyzing the preconditions for the possibility of . . . to drawing up curriculum for . . . , turning our attention to those institutions which, in our time and in our place, form our habits of mind and action. The appropriate fusion of an ideal of rational good will with the minutiae of our way of acting and interacting is formed in childhood, in the politics of the playground and the fantasies of bedtime stories. A range of educative institutions, bridging the private and the public spheres, the economic and the cultural domains, are centrally and ultimately responsible for the morality of a polity's citizens. They are responsible for developing our moral capacities into active working habits. Only after such habits are appropriately formed and developed, appropriately supported and sustained, can responsibility for morality be placed on individuals.

A number of philosophers have argued for the fusion of empirical moral psychology with ethics.[10] Moral philosophy is also, in the nature of the case, normative and practical, that is, political. Because it programmatically requires restructuring educational institutions, the philosophical task becomes describing the institutional and social processes that form the moral citizen. You might think it sufficient to describe the end product, the mentality and modus operandi of the moral citizen. But an ideal cannot be described without specifying *for whom* it is an ideal, under what conditions. The empirical studies that support philosophical ethics are local and historical: not only psychology generally, but also the psychology of a specific people, at a specific time and place, economically and politically situated as they are; not just education pure and simple but also education for *these* people with this history, these neighbors, and these problems.

We might well be concerned that bringing philosophers into the political arena endangers both philosophy and politics. On the one hand, nature's politicians can probably lead nature's philosophers like lambs to the slaughter, and on the other hand, self-consciously politicized philosophers may fear that their reforming zeal endangers their self-critical impartiality. In any case, merging politics and moral philosophy opens the door to the political control of truth. But nothing—not even philosophy and genuinely rational deliberation about the highest and best things—can keep us out of the territory of power politics. Certainly the point of articulating conditions for rationality—the point of stressing rationality and impartiality—is to keep us out of the hands of the charismatic bullies, power mongers of all kinds, intellectual and rhetorical as well as political demagogues. But nothing less than everything—the minutiae of Socratic shrewdness, the endless (and empowered) persistent examination of civic life and its institutions—can keep us out of the hands of bullies, rhetorical or political. Our question really is, What does it take to develop a Socratic questioner with practical wisdom? For it is people, not ideas or positions, who bully or are bullied. And the only way of "arming and strengthening" ourselves against power mongers is to focus on moral education, on the formation and direction of certain kinds of people.

The Desirability of Moral Diversity

"There is no action without interaction."

Because establishing the conditions for morality is a task that must engage rulers, civic virtue is a precondition for moral virtue. But civic virtue requires a wide range of character traits. It requires a Socratic questioner with constructive practical wisdom. Constructing sound political arrangements requires persuasion as well as impartial self-criticism, shrewd economic planning as well as a steadfast commitment to principles of justice. But these and other character configurations are relatively specialized. Plato, for one, thought that we enter into communities precisely because there is a division of labor among relatively specialized psychological types. The varieties of mentality are quite different from one another: they have distinctive perceptual, categorial, and value orientations. The type of childhood and the kind of education that can promote the best development of each variety might differ markedly. A sound political system requires a range of distinctive types of agents, each with distinctive talents and abilities suited to different types of occupations. But different mentalities are best developed by different types of early education: they require different sorts of models to imitate, distinctive sorts of playground games and storybooks. Different mentalities bring distinctive preoccupations, different perspectives on common, social life, different sets of priorities and values, and they often move individuals in different directions in moral and political life. We can distinguish the varieties of psychological types required by a society in a number of different ways: by their temperaments, by their practical orientation toward what is salient for them, by their cognitive styles, by the directions of their distinctive self-defining ideals, by their motivational structures. Plato's account of the connections between the natural division of psychological talent and the political division of labor gives us a start in characterizing the varieties of psychological and moral temperaments. Every polity needs citizens engaged in the economy of production and exchange. It needs citizens who are primarily focused on the care and welfare of their fellows, nurturers of various sorts. Their skills may vary considerably: some, like physicians, are attentive to bodily needs; others have intellectual and practical skills that suit them to become policy makers; still others are inclined to become educators of young children. A polity needs intellectuals and artists, citizens attempting to understand the world around them, engaged in envisioning and evaluating unrealized possibilities. It needs those skilled in persuading their fellows. It also needs vigilant protectors of various kinds, protectors against both internal and external aggression.

We can divide, group, and articulate these social functions and psychological types in different ways. And indeed, different polities, each with distinctive geopolitical needs, benefit by grouping and articulating social functions in distinctive ways, each developing and clustering the capabilities and skills of their citizens in ways that best suit their specific situations and needs. Nevertheless, however they are divided or grouped, each of these social functions requires and produces a specific orientation and mentality, a set of perceptual and categorial saliences. Each orientation has a distinctive type of action-guiding values, priorities, and satisfactions; each has a distinctive sense of what is important, a sense that forms the most general directions of one's motivational structure. At their best, in the best kind of polity, these various functions are harmonious and mutually supportive, or at the very least they acknowledge and respect one another's contributions. In any case, none of these functions and psychological types ever appear in pure form; any viable psychology is to some extent hybridized. Those engaged in production and exchange also standardly have a competitive if not downright combative streak; artists often also develop a mercantile mentality; at least some intellectuals are also nurturers and educators. Nevertheless, an individual's configuration of traits reveals a pattern of dominance and specialization.

Although in principle different types of moral agents can share general values, their occupations and preoccupations give them distinctive action-guiding orientations. Though in the best of circumstances they can agree on general principles, their immediate and short-range priorities differ. In a sense, they differ ethically (that is, characterologically) and morally (that is, in their specific social interactions). To put it dramatically, there are distinctive types of persons, and distinctive ways of being a person, with distinctive modes of realizing and organizing whatever general capacities individuals think are necessary for substantive morality, each providing an individual with a distinctive phenomenological sense of her own moral identity.

Under the best of circumstances, individuals with various moral mentalities acknowledge the advantages of moral pluralism; they recognize that they benefit from their differences. We can think of modern society as a palimpsest, composed of a number of distinct types of pluralism superimposed upon one another.[11] A polity is best served by keeping demographic, cultural, political, interest, class, moral pluralism independent of one another, so that individuals and groups are cross-classified and the interests of each group remains distinct, without reductively collapsing into those of the others. The psychological pluralism required by a complex society does not, of course, coincide with cultural, demographic, or political pluralism, nor is it fully expressed in the varieties of traditional moral systems. Nevertheless, a sound political system is well served when its citizens represent the mentality and psychology of a wide and apparently competing range of distinctive moral systems.

Practical political life requires considerable diversity of moral as well as psychological orientations. It requires an Aristotelian striver after excellence who disdains counting costs or benefits in matters of honor and esteem, a *phronimos* who takes honorable, sound ends for granted in solving the endless particular crises of practical life, and an ironic Socratic questioner who puts these basic values under continuous, grueling cross-examination. But we also need an upright Kantian, a universalizer impartially oriented to justice and committed to egalitarian principles and public justification of policy, a person of rectitude focused not on excellence or honor but on truthfulness, reliability, and steadfastness independently of social utility. Yet we could not do without eudaimonically oriented social planners who insist that policies and principles be justified by their service to welfare. We would also be morally impoverished without Hume's citizens of civil sensibility, capable of precise and well-developed empathic imaginations. Complex social life requires tactful delicacy of manners, an ability to adjust the tone of actions appropriately to their contexts, finely graded deftness of speech and demeanor, gifted in the insufficiently celebrated nurturing partiality of kinship and friendship.

But every Hume requires a Rousseau to unmask social corruption and to insist on the need and primacy of autonomy. We need exuberant, disrespectful firebrands who emphasize individual liberty and individual rights and who unmask the hidden interests of traditional, convention-ridden morality. But we also need those who expose the Romantic cult of autonomy and question the metaphysical foundations of individualism, who press the importance of consequentialist, welfare-oriented social policies.

The morally relevant skills and abilities central to these various moral values are relatively specialized. The ideal agents projected by different moral systems not only have distinctive priorities and values; they also differ in their characteristic skills and modes of organizing experience, their ways of structuring decisions. Humean tact is not always accompanied by the ingenuity of the Aristotelian *phronimos*; the just Kantian might make a very cool friend. Some stress traits that shine in war; others those that preserve peace. Some focus on the skills required by a growing industrial society; others promote the traits of a theocratic society. Even in the same culture, different moral systems favor different context-dependent abilities: some focus on abilities required in law courts, while others concentrate on those required for sound parenting. Except at the most general, and nearly banal, level of abstraction, these ideal agents would not make the same policy recommendations for roles for the arts and public institutions in moral development, nor would they stress the development of the same character traits. Even when major traditional theories attempt to accommodate the insights of their rivals (as, for instance, when Kant acknowledges the need to develop a range of compassionate civic virtues or when neo-utilitarians argue for the need to develop virtues independent of the calculation of utilities), there remains some tension and even mutual suspicion about where the primary focus of morality and moral education should be.

In truth, unless the focus is placed in a system of checks and balances, each of these moral emphases, if left to rule the moral field on its own, fails to address some of our basic moral needs. Indeed, unless an emphasis is pressed by some opposition, it runs the danger of going amok, transforming virtue into a classically tragic flaw, sometimes a vice. Whether or not we acknowledge it, we depend on moral pluralism, on a variety of well-developed distinctive yet complementary moral mentalities. Morality is not the enterprise of a person who, as it happens, necessarily depends on others. Rather, it is the enterprise of a community that, as it happens, necessarily forms agents who can and should act independently of one another. To keep itself alert and honest, improvisatory and just, a community requires some members who are rigid hawks of justice, some who are focused on indignation, and some who calculate future benefits, looking inward or backward only when it serves the future. To be sure, we might well fear that practical polyphony can turn into chaotic cacophony. Which among the various types should be stressed varies with time and circumstance. It cannot be determined by rules or principles; it is under constant negotiation.

None of this entails any of the objectionable forms of arbitrariness or relativism. Once historical circumstances are specified, there is a nonrelative diagnosis of the dominant social and political problems. Moral diversity is compatible with strong moral realism. It allows that distinctive problems arising in specific situations command distinctive solutions. The solutions are distinct; the command is objectively grounded. Though it often differs contextually, there is an appropriate balance and distribution of power among the various moral mentalities. But there is no single nostrum, no single set of institutions or rules, that prevents chaos. The therapies against the disorders of radical pluralism are always local and particular, and like other modes of therapies, they do not always succeed.

A Rough Sketch of Types of Moral Education

"The child is the parent of the citizen."

Each of the ideal models projected by the major traditional moral systems is developed in a different way, in a different kind of social setting. These systems presuppose a general theory of the structure of premoral agency, a theory about the relation between rationality and desire, about standard basic motives and aspirations, about the role of the imagination in choice. Indeed, one fruitful way of characterizing the differences among the major traditional theories is by distinguishing their views on the raw materials with which morality begins, the transforming processes of moral thought and moral development, and the desired outcome, a particular kind of moral mentality or moral agency.

Unfortunately, most contemporary moral theorists concentrate on describing the ideal end product of the transforming processes of morality. With some exceptions, they neglected the processes and institutions of moral education. Their own orientations lead them to ignore the political and educative dimensions that were an essential part, and indeed the primary focus, of traditional moral systems. Presumably, this neglect is explained by the liberal decision to leave substantive moral education to the private sphere. In any case, theorists give little attention to the development of a soundly functioning psychological and moral pluralism and to the kinds of social and political, formal and informal, institutions engaged in educative processes. What is central to the life of a polity, the structuring of the character of its citizens, is left to chance of culture, religion, domesticity, or the self-forming and self-reforming struggles of individuals.

We can project the "before" and "after" of traditional moral theories. Aristotle presents a relatively detailed profile of the psychological and intellectual structure of the person of practical wisdom. It would be illuminating to project the profiles of Humean, Kantian, utilitarian moral agents, and even of the Nietzschean creative free spirit, the "antimoralist." In what terms do they perceive and categorize their experience? What are their characteristic preoccupations and activities? How do they regulate their actions? What are their relations to their spouses, friends, fellow citizens, parents, and children? What, according to each theory, are the premoral materials from which we build moral character? Does the moral person act against or with the grain of the original material? How does the moral agent deal with apparent moral conflicts? Is there a moral dimension to responses to works of art and to the natural environment? We need a phenomenological description of a day in the moral life of an Aristotelian *phronimos*, a Humean civil citizen, a Kantian person of good will, a utilitarian, a Nietzschean free spirit.

Once we understand the structure and dynamics of the moral personality projected by each of these traditional theories, we need to understand the processes of their development as moral agents. How are the raw materials, the endowments of "natural psychology" transformed through the processes of moral education? What is the primary focus of that education: how is the appropriate balance among (various conceptions of) rationality, the imagination, and the emotions conceived, and how is that balance developed? Do the very processes of moral education leave their traces on the adult moral agent? (An authoritarian method of moral development leaves its mark; the modes of admiration and imitation leave theirs; and a method that stresses the processes of group consensus also affects the tenor and direction of action.) Who are the primary agents in moral development: parents, peers, poets, political structures? What role do the arts play in moral development? What kind of praise, blame, and responsibility conduce to moral development?

Aristotelians see moral development as involving the development of minute action-forming habits, guided and directed by practical reason. Because living things naturally attempt to fulfill their best potentialities, moral development does not require acquiring a special set of capacities or motives. Nevertheless, exercising the virtues requires skill, and most skills are acquired by imitation and practice. Practical rationality is a central human capacity, to be developed for its own sake, but it is also an essential key to the development and exercise of other constituents of a flourishing life. Aristotle is, of course, no egalitarian: the person of practical wisdom is just but not impartial; he places civic loyalty and civic dignity above (what we have come to think of as) general human compassion. His characteristic virtues are practical astuteness, a range of debating and rhetorical skills, measured boldness. Like Odysseus, he has no particular compunction about lying, and he measures justice proportionally to nobility rather than by a principle of universalizability. Though a political system structured by an Aristotelian person of practical wisdom seems to offend our egalitarian moral sensibilities, still any polity without a solid number of *phronimoi* is in practical difficulty.

Stoics and neo-Stoics like Kant see the task of ethics to bring a person to his true identity as a rational being. Like Aristotle, they hold that morality involves rational control or direction of thought and action. But they have a very different conception the way in which human fulfillment involves rationality. Aristotelian ethics is oriented to *eudaimonia*; it is situated in the polis. Greek Stoic morality achieves practice through *theoria*. Individuals reach their true selves when they identify themselves with Mind as the cosmic order. This may involve recognizing the citizen as an integral part of the cosmic order, Mind as locally realized in a particular body in a particular situation. But the Stoic citizen identifies with his capacities for *recognition* and *reflection* rather than with the contingent content of his capacities and talents or with the structure and situation of his polis. Praxis becomes intellectualized: what really matters in what a person does is his understanding of his action and practice. The Stoic conception of the transforming processes of moral education and development differs from Aristotle's conceptions in two ways: For Aristotle, the essence of moral development is the development of habits of all kinds: habits of perception and speech, habits of reflective thought and of action. For Stoics, including neo-Kantians as well as classical Stoics, the essence of moral education lies in developing the capacity for detached, rational reflection. But despite surface similarities, the details and emphases of the two views are dramatically different as they affect the development and tenor of the morality of *la vie quotidiènne*.

Hume sees morality as involving the development and refinement of social sentiments, particularly the sense of justice. These sentiments arise from the practices of cooperation as naturally enlarged by the mechanism of sympathy. They are developed by the imagination, by its natural tendency to vivify the needs and conditions of our fellows. At best, the associations and enlivening powers of the imagination and sympathy are checked and balanced by critical historical reflection on experience in "an attempt to introduce the method of experimental reasoning into the moral sciences." The motivating sentiments, enriched by an empathic imagination, function best to promote the activities of the civilized citizen when they are combined with "reflection from a distant view." Since morality involves exercising appropriate patterns of imaginative empathy and a critically reflective sense of justice, the moral educator focuses on developing patterns of imaginative association that are accurate and reflective rather than fanciful and idiosyncratic. The study of history, as a reflective and analytic chronicle of political experience and experiments—should supplement the study of literature, as it enlarges the sentiments.

Mill sees morality as involving reconciliation of eudaimonistic self-interest and social meliorism. Moral development involves transforming crude egoistic hedonism into a capacity for the "higher" civilized pleasures, whose appropriate configuration and balance constitute happiness, developing capacities for rational calculation, developing the habits and capacities for acting in accord with the utilitarian calculus of promoting the general welfare.

Besides characterizing types of moral development historically projected by various traditional moral theories, we can also distinguish strategies of moral development, each with distinct moral advantages and disadvantages:

1. Close imitative modeling along with the formation of political and social institutions (Plato and Aristotle)

2a. Legendary hagiography of idealized models (lives of the saints)

2b. Hagiography with sensory and image training (Loyola)

3. Characteristic play, focused on cooperative problem solving, leader-follower adventures, reproducing stereotypic roles, or team versus individual competition (Montessori, Dewey)

4. Situational, experiential learning (Rousseau, Dewey)

5. Principled forming of the will (Kant, Arnold)

6. Forming of sentiments (Hume, Tolstoi)

Moral Systems versus Moral Theories

"Practice makes perfect."

Construing moral system as practical and political directives permits a much more generous interpretation of moral agreement and disagreement than is possible when moral systems are construed as competing theories about the good or about justice. To be sure, it is possible to formulate and articulate a moral system as a theory about (as it may be) human thriving or the conditions for justice. But because moral systems are directed to the realization of values through action and activity, translating the practical orientation of moral pluralism into competing theories runs the danger of missing their point. It transforms the aims of action into the aims of inquiry.

Although they centrally include both analytic and empirical investigations, moral systems are not appropriately construed on the model of competing scientific theories, to be demonstrated or falsified. They should rather be understood on the model of shared practice-oriented deliberations in which the participants begin with a range of vague and ambiguous mutually constraining aims and principles, whose priorities typically vary in different contexts. The precise action-guiding claims of the diverse aims cannot be fully specified in advance of the dialogic deliberative process.[12] The minutiae of continuous practice-oriented, contingency-sensitive interactive deliberation presses toward gradual closure: it moves from general to more determinate programs, sometimes by opposition, sometimes by elaboration or improvisation. When deliberation goes well, what emerges is a further determination, a further specification, of our several aims and intentions. When things go well, we emerge with a program that suits us all, but only temporarily. A slightly less happy resolution produces a set of grudgingly accepted compromises. The worst outcome declares a winner, with the loser retreating to gather forces for another attack, often a sneak surprise.

Fundamentally, the attempt to characterize what it takes to be good is directed to answering the question, "What should we do?" When we treat this as a practical question calling for a proposal of the form "Let's now . . . ," what matters is satisfactory convergence in practice, rather than agreement about theory. Although we are practically and morally bound to justify our decisions, and to convince our fellows, by advancing all manner of arguments and theories, coming to a sound convergence about what to do does not require that we all have the same (good) reasons for doing so. The conditions for convergence in practice are different from those for agreement about the truth of a theory.

The distinction between the two modes of agreement is not that between practical activity on the one hand and science on the other. Practical arrangements involve all manner of straightforwardly verifiable claims and predictions, and scientific investigations involve all manner of shared practices. The distinction between theory and practice is a distinction between activities directed to discovering truth (as it might be expressed in unambiguous propositions) and activities directed at achieving some other good. To be sure, agreement in practice presupposes a minimal pidgin mutual understanding. But this kind of basic agreement does not depend on the participants sharing, or even understanding, one another's interpretations of their activities, the rules or principles that govern their activities, or their respective reasons for accepting them. What matters in practical cooperation is that the same state of affairs will satisfy all parties over a reasonable period of time.

Rawls's method of reflective equilibrium presents one of the most estimable models for constructing a moral system.[13] Instead of selecting a single primary normative stance and attempting to do justice to competing principles by setting them up as side constraints, the method of reflective equilibrium involves a mutual adjustment of the most abstract principles or aims with a range of considered convictions about just and fair outcomes. This method has the advantage of attempting to balance competing claims in a way that allows for their mutual criticism and correction. It acknowledges the provisional and relatively arbitrary character of initial commitments and provides a way in which we can refine, revise, and specify them.

But the method of reflective equilibrium can itself be interpreted in several ways. Construed in one way, it is a method to guide the construction of a demonstrable *theory*, one which is Janus-faced with the rejection of alternative theories. Ideally, we should disambiguate the principles of a theory, and ideally, we should develop well-defined procedures for determining what they entail. Our desire to articulate and demonstrate a rational reconstruction of our fundamental beliefs is powerful and admirable. It is powerful because relinquishing it seems to threaten rationality itself and because we think that rational principles are our only defense against the ravages of power politics. And it is admirable because it presses us to explain and to justify ourselves to our fellows. But even the most powerful and legitimate of desires cannot always be satisfied. Construed as a theory, a moral system is too general to provide practical guidance, or it has a host of competitors with equally serious claims to our allegiance.

But construed as a method for producing a *system of practice* rather than a theory, the method of reflective equilibrium is a method of constructing a dynamic system of mutual checks and balances among the diverse aims and interests of different moral systems. So construed, it leaves major issues open for continuing arbitration, compensation, and accommodation. Despite the misleading metaphor of "balance" and "equilibrium," it does not assume that we should attempt to reach a consensus about unambiguous principles for distributive norms or educational priorities. Recognizing that the priorities accorded to our various ends might properly vary contextually, it substitutes revisable rules of thumb for principles; it acknowledges the utility of ambiguity and vagueness in enabling people with different aims to have different reasons for cooperating. It recognizes that the mutual adjustment of general principles and considered convictions is suspiciously circular: today's considered convictions were formed by yesterday's general principles, and tomorrow's general principles bear a marked resemblance to today's considered convictions. Construed as directed to constructing a *system of practice* rather than a *theory*, the method of reflective equilibrium does not assume that political theory can replace or rationalize politics or that politics primarily involves applying the aims and principles demonstrated and articulated by political theory. The best balance and application of our aims is underdetermined by our moral theory. Sometimes it can emerge only as the result of dark and heavy negotiation and sometimes it does not emerge at all. But this dynamic, practice-oriented interpretation of the method of equilibrium need not belittle or deny the mediating, arbitrating role of reflective deliberation, guided by a range of regulative principles and rules of thumb, some substantive, others methodological and procedural, and many wholly accidental.

While moral systems incorporate and rely on theories of all kinds, they are directed at achieving a range of practice-oriented aims. They include a far wider range of regulative principles than do theories. Besides being regulated by ideals of rationality (which are, in any case, quite diverse[14]), they are also directed at promoting continuity of cooperation and allowing for contextual flexibility. Substantive disputes about norms of practice are likely to be reproduced as disputes about the priority of various regulative principles. Since there is unlikely to be useful (that is, policy-forming, action-guiding) consensus on the hierarchy of unambiguous regulative principles, hybrid systems concentrate on setting aims and principles in a dynamic, self-adjusting system of checks and balances. Systems allow for some indeterminacy and ambiguity, and they construe their investigations as combining discovery and construction.

One of the significant benefits of treating the method of reflective equilibrium as directed at adjusting systems of practice is that doing so calls attention to the need for educating citizens in a wide range of skills and abilities normally neglected if we concentrate solely on developing the abilities for debating-team justification: on demonstration, refutation, and defense. Practice-oriented moral pluralism directs attention at the need for developing the imaginative skills used in cooperative deliberation and the empathic abilities that promote mutual accommodation in situations of conflict. The practical aims and principles of moral education pull us in different directions; they can only be worked through by political processes whose procedures are themselves under constant critical examination.[15]

Notes

1. Ernst Tugendhat (this volume) characterizes a person as moral if he has the capacity to feel (moral) shame as an internalization of a social judgment of his guilt. But it is a curious analysis of morality to characterize it by focusing on the psychology of what (should) happen when we violate it; and a *capacity* lies dormant, useless unless it is developed as an active ability.

2. See Bratman, 1987. The domain of actions is quite broad: it includes morally significant psychological activities as well as behavioral patterns.

3. In speaking of traits, I am not committing myself to any particular analysis of disposition terms; my argument is compatible with the range of reigning accounts of traits and disposition. Many character traits are only analytically separable from one another, and many are strongly but contingently connected with some intellectual traits.

4. For instance, sound medical treatment depends not only on physicians but also on the cooperation of technicians and nurses, hospital hygiene, and adequate funding for research. Even the apparently solitary activities involved in scholarly research depend on the support of fellow scholars and librarians.

5. Although these traits are typically used in quite different ways in different cultures and political systems, at a general level of description they are needed and valued in every society. Nevertheless, it should not be surprising that lists of virtues also express cultural values. After all, we identify character traits as virtues just insofar as we think they serve social needs and instantiate social ideals. This is perfectly compatible with there also being culturally invariant virtues that can serve as critical and corrective boundaries to the self-defined interests and values of a particular social or cultural identity.

6. See Scanlon, 1982. This kind of explanation is behavioral as well as linguistic. Justifying one's principles to one's fellows in terms they can understand requires that one pay attention to appropriate *petites actions* for their tone of respect.

7. See "The Two Faces of Courage" and "Three Myths of Moral Theory," in Rorty, 1988.

8. See "Virtues and Their Vicissitudes," in Rorty, 1988.

9. Interestingly, these three emphases correspond to the traditional triadic division among psychological faculties: cognition, conation, and affectivity.

10. See the essays by E. Tugendhat, T. Wren, A. Blasi, and R. Döbert in Wren, 1990.

11. For distinctions between cultural, demographic, political, psychological, and interest pluralism, see Rorty, 1990, as well as Rorty and Wong, 1990.

12. See Richardson, 1990, especially pp. 293 ff. and n. 30; Bakhtin, 1981, pp. 51, 275–285; and Rorty, 1988, pp. 15–21, 324–329.

13. See Rawls, 1971, pp. 19–21. As Rawls remarks (p. 51, n. 26), this method "goes back in its essentials to Aristotle's method in the *Nicomachean Ethics*."

14. For instance, simplicity may limit fertility; the demands of direct relevance may constrain those of robustness.

15. I am grateful to Steven Gerrard and William Ruddick, as well as to the participants of the Ringberg Conference on Morality and the Self for lively discussion. This paper was originally written in 1990; I have since cannibalized a few paragraphs for Rorty, 1991, 1992, 1993a, 1993b.

References

Bakhtin, M. M. (1981). *The dialogic imagination*. Austin: University of Texas Press.

Bratman, M. (1987). *Intentions, plans, and practical reason*. Cambridge: Cambridge University Press.

Rawls, J. (1971). *A theory of justice*. Cambridge: Harvard University Press.

Richardson, H. (1990). Specifying norms as a way to resolve concrete ethical problems. *Philosophy and Public Affairs*, 19:279–310.

Rorty, A. (1988). *Mind in action*. Boston: Beacon Press.

Rorty, A. (1990). Varieties of pluralism in a polyphonic society. *Review of Metaphysics*, 44:3–20.

Rorty, A. (1991). King Solomon and Everyman: A Problem in coordinating conflicting moral intuitions," *American Philosophical Quarterly*, 28:181–195.

Rorty, A. (1992). The advantages of moral diversity. *Social Philosophy and Policy*, 9:38–62.

Rorty, A (1993a). Moral imperialism versus moral conflict. In L. Rouner (Ed.), *Moral Education*, South Bend, IN: Notre Dame University Press.

Rorty, A. (1993b). The many faces of morality. *Revue de Métaphysique et de Morale*, 98.

Rorty, A., and Wong, D. (1990). Aspects of identity and agency. In O. Flanagan and A. Rorty (Eds.), *Identity, character, and morality*. Cambridge: MIT Press.

Scanlon, T. (1982). Contractarianism and utilitarianism. In B. Williams and A. Sen (Eds.), *Utilitarianism and beyond*. Cambridge: Cambridge University Press.

Wren, T. E., Ed. (1990). *The moral domain: Essays in the ongoing discussion between philosophy and the social sciences*. Cambridge: MIT Press.

Self, Idealization, and the Development of Values

Ernest S. Wolf

My aim in this essay is to examine a contribution of the psychoanalytic psychology of the self to discussions of the development of an individual's values and ideals. Before turning to the development of values as seen from within such a frame, I will present some of the basic concepts of a psychoanalytic psychology of the self. I begin with some brief observations on classical Freudian psychoanalysis as the background out of which self psychology evolved.

Traditional Psychoanalysis

In traditional psychoanalytic theory the values and ideals that guide the personality are represented in the superego (which includes the ego ideal and is roughly equivalent to the conscience), a structure within the tripartite system of id, ego, and superego. Classical psychoanalytic theory posited that the superego develops when, under the pressure of castration anxiety, the child resolves the Oedipus complex by replacing sexual and aggressive impulses toward the parents by tender relationships with inhibited aims. In this process the child incorporates aspects of the father's personality into his or her ego via a process of identification. The now modified parts of the child's ego are recognized as a separate agency, the superego, within the psychic apparatus. Admittedly, this is an oversimplified version of how the superego forms, but a fully detailed version is not relevant to my purposes here (for a more detailed discussion of the formation of the superego, see Freud, 1923).

It is noteworthy that psychoanalysts as a rule consider only the thoughts, fantasies, emotions, and behavior, moral or otherwise, of individuals. Freud himself was interested in the superego primarily as a constituent of the mental apparatus derived from the Oedipus complex. Questions of morality per se did not seem to be of great interest. Toward his patients he maintained an attitude of concerned neutrality. From his colleagues he expected integrity: "As to morals, that goes without saying" (Freud, 1905, p. 267). To his friend Otto Pfister, a Protestant minister, he wrote, "Ethics is a kind of traffic regulation of human intercourse" (Freud and Pfister, 1963).

Post-Freudian Developments

In the half century since Freud's death there have been further developments of theory that have led to some distinctly different directions of psychoanalytic thought. The names of Melanie Klein, Bowlby, Winnicott, Mahler, Lacan, Erikson, Kohut, Stern, and others have become associated with efforts to modify and update psychoanalytic theory. We have become more cognizant of the decisive influence of the environment, especially during the earliest formative phases of an individual's development. We are also able to understand the urgency and drive that characterize so much apparently irrational behavior without assuming instinctual drives as the primary motivating forces. These modifications of psychoanalytic theory have significant implications for morality. Each of these theorists has put forward new conceptualizations of the moral domain and its evolution.

The modification of traditional psychoanalytic theory introduced by Heinz Kohut (1966, 1968, 1971, 1977, 1978, 1985) has become known as self psychology. Self psychology has emphasized the centrality of the self in development and pathology and the need for empathy in clinical work and data collection. The conceptualizations of self psychology reflect accumulating clinical psychoanalytic experience with its more prolonged and deeply empathic immersion into the life histories of our analysands. Also having a major impact on psychoanalytic thinking is the wealth of observations flowing from research on mothers and infants. Integrating clinical psychoanalytic data with the data from infant research has taught us much about the development of the self. However, a majority of psychoanalysts and psychologists have yet to accept the theories of psychoanalytic self psychology, and the work of Kohut and his colleagues remains controversial.

Selfobject Experiences

What differentiates contemporary psychoanalytic self psychology from traditional psychoanalytic thinking? I can mention here our recognition of the subjective nature of our data and the entailed need to have this subjectivity reflected in our theories. Our specific method for collecting data is prolonged empathic immersion in the inner life of analysands. Empathy is defined as "vicarious introspection," i.e., introspection from the viewpoint of the patient's experience.[1] Hand in hand with recognizing that empathy is central to psychoanalysis goes a shift from theorizing in terms of instinctual drives and psychological agencies (e.g., id, ego, super-ego) to attempting to theorize in terms of an overarching self and its psychological experiences. Instead of talking about id, ego, and superego, we talk about experiences of selfhood: about feeling whole versus falling apart, feeling empty, feeling scared of losing oneself, feeling proud or ashamed of oneself, etc. Though for convenience we may talk about the self as if it were an object, by the technical term "self" we always mean the subjective sense of selfhood through which one tries to express one's individuality. Instead of thinking about the classical mechanisms of defense (such as reaction formation, projection, etc.), we think of defensiveness as maneuvering to avoid fears of losing one's self, shame of the self's failures, etc. Instead of presupposing instinctual drives, such as sexuality and aggression, as the primary human motivators, I now propose that a biologically inherent tendency to organize orders sensory input into structured patterns and, among these, a structure we call the self. Those experiences that activate organization into the self and thus evoke a sense of selfhood have been designated selfobject experiences.[2]

In the following, I will briefly review the emergence of the self and its development. Then we will be ready to consider the role of values and ideals. After that I will discuss some of the vicissitudes that may befall the emergence and development of the self.

The Emergence of the Self

In speculating about the subjective experience of a newborn, we may reasonably assume that at birth there cannot yet be a distinction between self and nonself. With the emergence into the world from the womb, the neonate is suddenly exposed to all sorts of new sensory stimuli, probably in all modalities: sound, taste, touch, smell, sight, and proprioception. Freud postulated a stimulus barrier to protect the individual from becoming disorganized and traumatically overwhelmed by excessive stimulation, and perhaps there are times when the individual mounts such a barrier. But in general, infant researchers observe that, far from being merely a passive recipient, the baby actively seeks stimuli (cf. Lichtenberg, 1983, pp. 48–51). Most likely these stimuli activate developmental potentials with which the baby was born. One of these potentials, I postulate, is the ability to make sense of the apparent chaos of sensations. Perhaps this process resembles what has been described by people who regain their sight after having lost it during childhood through some accidental scarring of their cornea. When the scarring is surgically repaired, they suddenly can "see" again but can discern only a confusingly disorganized chaos of flashes, colors, spots, lines, lights, and darkness. Only gradually do they learn to make sense of what their retinas and visual apparatus perceive, and only gradually do they gain the capacity to really see again. A similar process of learning takes place when a student first peeks through a microscope at an anatomical specimen on a glass slide. Usually weeks pass before the student organizes the dots, spots, and colored areas into recognizable patterns of tissue. Analogously, I think, a baby gradually organizes its experiences so that they begin to make sense to it. There will come the moment when the baby identifies the repetition of a specific pattern of stimuli as the mother and the mother first notes her baby's smile of recognition when seeing her face. The baby probably recognizes the mother's smell even earlier, perhaps as early as after a couple of weeks.

With the necessary appropriate responsiveness of a nurturing, talking, caring, soothing, stimulating caregiver, the baby learns to organize its experiences into a self differentiated from the other. There thus emerges a subjective sense of "I" and, pari passu, a psychological structure that we can designate as the self.[3]

Spitz (1945, 1946) proved that depriving a baby of "maternal care, maternal stimulation, and maternal love" causes irreparable psychosomatic damage. He showed that orphaned babies raised in an institutional environment that supplied all the needed physical supports and nutrients but lacked a loving caregiver who supplied personal attention tended to be ill and died of marasmus. Survivors suffered irreparable damage. In contrast, a similar population of neonates raised in a physically less well supplied institution grew into healthy, lusty children if the participating caregivers lovingly interacted and responded to the babies.

The Self as an Organization of Selfobject Experiences

Observations such as these, together with close scrutiny of numerous "analytic couples" (analyst and analysand) in the intensely intimate situation of psychoanalysis, culminated in a fundamental hypothesis of psychoanalytic self psychology: the responsive interaction between baby and caregiver organizes the baby's innumerable disparate experiences into a cohesive self. To illustrate with just one example, the properly attuned mother will think of her newborn as a person, play with it, talk to it, address it by name. We might metaphorically speak of the baby's emerging self as made up of many constituents—partly of memories of images, thoughts, and feelings emanating from within, partly of other memories that have their origin from outside—all held together by the glue of the caregiver's responsiveness. In the somewhat awkward technical language describing this scenario, the caregiver is a selfobject who, by providing appropriate selfobject experiences, evokes the child's experience of being a self. Withdrawing the needed selfobject experiences before the child has irreversibly and cohesively established the evoked self results in a deficient structure or sometimes in fragmentation of the self. This technical language has some connections with the idiomatic expressions and colloquialisms of ordinary speech that express analogous experiences. We often hear people complain that they feel "like they are falling apart" or they are "disconcerted" by something. In Eugene O'Neill's play *The Great God Brown* we hear Brown say, "Man is born broken. He lives by mending. The grace of God is glue."

Indeed, I have been astonished to learn from the analyses of my patients in clinical psychoanalytic practice, as well as from the scrutiny of myself, that no one ever enjoys a completely cohesive and irreversibly solid self. Human beings universally and continually need selfobject experiences to maintain the integrity of their selves. From birth to death we need to be embedded in a matrix of relationships supportive of our selves. The comings and goings of daily life often make this matrix unable to sustain us. Consequently, we suffer a rainbow of psychological ups and downs that may range from minor fleeting moods, perhaps a feeling of having been slighted, to major psychotic illness associated with almost complete loss of a sense of self. Slight fragmentations manifest themselves as relatively minor psychological discomfort, perhaps some mild depression or anxiety, and they usually quickly heal when one is provided with appropriate selfobject experiences. Massive fragmentation is associated with major mental illness and even loss of self to an extent equivalent to psychosis. Severe anxiety accompanies massive fragmentations, and the fear of losing one's self often appears as a painful panic linked ideationally to the thought of death. Understandably, individuals will do almost anything to escape these unbearable anxiety states: the more exciting, dangerous, and death-defying an activity appears, the more suitable it is to distract one from the frightening internal experience of losing one's self. Some apparently irrational or immoral behaviors, immoral from the viewpoint of the community, are motivated by powerful desires to preserve one's self.

Head banging in some toddlers can be understood as an attempt to strengthen one's sense of being alive, one's self. Compulsive masturbation three, four, five times a day by some adolescents and adults can be similarly understood. Daredevil activities, particularly in some adolescents, often represent a need to experience one's self as invulnerable at the time when in fact the self is very fragile and on the verge of fragmentation. Reckless gambling often can be presumed to be similarly motivated. The inner experience of an enhanced self is familiar to most of us who have jumped from the high diving board, skied, or engaged in some other exciting action. We think of these as normal behaviors when the exciting danger to the self is mostly imaginary. However, those behaviors that involve real danger to the self or others, whether acknowledged or disavowed, we think of as psychopathological. Fragile, vulnerable selves need these latter self-enhancing actions because of the subjective experience of strength and greatness they provide.

The Development of the Self and Values

Contemporary infant researchers seem to agree that the newly emergent self first makes its appearance early in the first year of life. Observations by psychoanalysts oriented toward self psychology indicate that this emergent self normally reaches a relatively stable degree of strength and cohesion sometime during a child's eighth year.

What are its values, and how do they become part of its structure? To answer these questions I must again detour briefly to examine the selfobject experiences that evoke the self. We have learned to distinguish at least six types of selfobject experiences that are necessary for the development of a cohesive self: idealizing, mirroring, alter-ego, ally-antagonist, efficacy, and vitalizing experiences. All of these types of selfobject experiences are essential ingredients in the constitution and maintenance of a healthy, cohesive, energetic, and balanced self. All make a significant contribution to the development of values of the mature self, but the mirroring and idealizing experiences are the most important ones.

I have no doubt—and now 15 years of observation have made no dent in this basic conviction—these [mirror transference and idealizing transference] are two of the basic needs of the developing self. One needs to be accepted and mirrored—there has to be the gleam in some mother's eye which says it is good you are here and I acknowledge your being here and I am uplifted by your presence. There is also the other need: to have somebody strong and knowledgeable and calm around with whom I can temporarily merge, who will uplift me when I am upset. Originally, that is an actual uplifting of the baby by the mother; later it becomes an uplifting feeling of looking at a great man or woman and enjoying him or her, of following in his or her footsteps, of a great idea being uplifting, or a wonderful piece of music, etc. That is extremely important. And when I talk about cultural selfobjects, which is the replica of the culture for the group self of what occurs in individual development, I think that these two basic needs are also present, perhaps collectively. (Kohut, 1985, pp. 226–227)

A number of conditions are required in order for an infant to attain a sense of selfhood, i.e., for a subjective experience of self to come into existence. Critical are the perceptions that the infant has of its significant caregivers. Usually those are primarily the mother during the earliest weeks, and then later also other family members or their surrogates. The needed perception is that of the presence of another person functioning as a *selfobject* and thus providing a *selfobject experience.* A selfobject experience is the result of certain functions performed by an object—the selfobject (e.g., the mother)—that evoke in the subject the organization of its experiences into a sense of selfhood, that is, into a self. Six types of these functions, the selfobject functions, have been investigated. Apparently, a developing child needs to experience all six kinds of selfobject functions for a healthy, whole and cohesive self to develop. (1) The child needs to feel that another person acknowledges that it is a valued person, the so-called *mirroring* selfobject experience which thus affirms the child. (2) The child needs to feel that another person possesses special qualities of strength and knowledge, and exercises these powers benevolently, the so-called *idealizing* selfobject experience during which the child experiences itself as merged with the idealized selfobject. (3) The child needs to feel its essential likeness to another person, the so-called *alter-ego* selfobject experience which the child experiences as an approval of its being different from still other selfobjects. (4) The child needs to feel it can assert itself against another person's benevolently opposing intent, the so-called *adversarial* selfobject experience which the child experiences as a potential for self-expression (Wolf, 1980, pp. 125–126; Lachmann, 1986, pp. 341–355). (5) The child needs an experience of *efficacy*, i.e., of itself as an effective agent capable of eliciting a desired or needed selfobject response and thus having made a dent on the world. The associated efficacy pleasure appears to be derived from the enhanced awareness of the self having been strengthened through the experience of efficacy. (6) The child needs to have the vitalizing experience that the caregiver is affectively attuned to the dynamic shifts or patterned changes in its inner state, that is, across the specific categories of affect to the crescendos and decrescendos, to the surges and fades of the intensity, timing, and shape of its affectively colored experiences (Stern, 1985, pp. 156–160).

Reconstructions of a person's developmental history as it emerges in the course of a psychoanalysis allows some plausible inferences about the origin of the self. Such retrograde constructions from psychoanalytic data present evidence that a "nuclear self" normally has arisen out of the various selfobject experiences during the child's second year. However, recent findings resulting from research with infants suggest that a "core self" is "likely to form during the first half year of life as a primary social task" (Stern, 1985, pp. 69–123). Stern tentatively lists four types of experiences available to the infant that are needed to form an organized sense of a core self. These include self-agency, self-coherence, self-affectivity, and self-history. "These four self-experiences, taken together, constitute a sense of a core self. This sense of a core self is thus an *experiential* sense of events" (p. 71, my italics). It is noteworthy that the very different types of data in psychoanalytic self psychology and infant research lead to conclusions that, though they are not at all identical, do not significantly contradict each other. Both speak about the same basic unit of observation and study, the subjective self, even while the infant observations seem to discern a self earlier than psychoanalytic observations.

The following case vignette illustrates some of the vicissitudes of self formation and acquisition of values. "The idealizing experience" is our term for the universal need to experience oneself as associated with and accepted by others who are perceived to be strong, wise, calm, beautiful, just—in short, who are so wonderful that individuals idealize them and passionately want to be like them. They imitate their behavior and emulate their values and in doing so they shape their own personalities. It is as if they had taken the most valued part of the other into their selves and made it a part of their self-structures. Metaphorically visualizing our selves as structures we designate this part of the self that is derived from the admiration of another as the self's *pole of values and ideals*.[4]

A.C., a 39-year-old attorney came in for psychoanalytic treatment because he chronically felt uneasy about his professional competence. On the surface his anxiety seemed irrational in view of his achievements, his excellent academic record, and the high regard in which he was held by his colleagues. He worked hard, his efforts were appreciated by clients, and he was socially well liked in his extraprofessional life. He was happily married with two children. Yet he could not escape a constant feeling that he was not doing well, that he was not living up to expectations. Mild but chronic shame put a blight on his whole life.

He often talked about wishes to escape the pressure of his busy professional life and of going back to the peace and green fields of his home county in the mountains. He recalled his father with evident warmth and admiration for his simple "masculine" lifestyle of working hard, playing hard, and drinking hard in the company of his friends. His father, who liked to go hunting and fishing, was somewhat contemptuous of intellectual inquisitiveness, in contrast to A.C.'s mother, who encouraged his literary interests. His father had died suddenly of a cardiac illness during A.C.'s early adolescence. There was a period of turmoil, but under the influence of his mother, A.C. did well in school and subsequently in his professional education.

It seems that the early death of A.C.'s father disturbed and arrested the normal development of A.C.'s sense of values at a point when the cohesion of his self was primarily dependent on experiencing his father as an admired other, as an idealized selfobject, with whom he could merge. The development of his self was partially arrested at this level of identification with his father's apparent values.

By means of his intelligence, talents, and excellent education, A.C. eventually found himself in an upper-middle-class milieu without having made too much effort. He never felt at home there and felt out of place, with a strong sense of shame and guilt. He yearned to quit his professional life in the city and return to the physically harsher life of the mountains of his childhood. He wondered about being a sissy, though a number of extramarital affairs boosted his sagging self-esteem.

When he came in for treatment, both his marriage and his career were in danger of derailment. His extramarital escapades were perhaps an identification with the values of his father as he perceived them. But more importantly, they represented a desperate attempt to recover some of the self-esteem that he had lost with the fragmentation of his self as a consequence of his father's death. Going back to his old life in the mountains was a fantasy that represented a yearning to be reunited with his father and thus to emerge with an idealized self that would again provide a selfobject experience that would enhance and heal his fragmented self.

Values and Their Vicissitudes

Since the self of a small child derives its values by identification with the idealized caregivers (usually the parents), we must expect that the values guiding its behavior will be greatly influenced by the values of these significant others. Indeed, to win the needed approbation of the idealized other, a child often will imitate her or him. However, that does not mean that the child's behavior always will be in harmony with the values that form the self's pole of ideals, because this pole may have weakened and become ineffective. A weakening of the self's structure from whatever cause may make the self's values ineffective in guiding behavior and leave the person vulnerable to seeking immediate satisfactions rather than long-term, value-inspired goals.

In addition to idealizing selfobject experiences, other important experiences also constitute the self. For instance, the child also needs *ally-antagonist* selfobject experiences, i.e., experiences with a benign other who will maintain a warm positive attitude toward the child even when the child acts contrary. All parents are familiar with "terrible twos," two-year-old children who respond to every request with a decisive "no." Presumably, the child's negativism is caused by the child's newly gained sharp awareness of being truly a self, a separate person with a will of his own. Unconsciously, "being me" needs to be tested against the outside world for the child to gain sufficient self-confidence for further healthy development. Most parents intuitively grasp this and are able to manage terrible twos without damage to either themselves or their offspring. Sometimes, however, a child experiences inappropriately excessive or humiliating parental responses, and these injure the child's self. Perhaps some of these cases result from the child's being inherently more stubborn or provocative than usual; perhaps, through prior experiences, the child has learned to be especially fearful of losing the integrity of his self. But much more likely to cause the child injury is a parent's fragile self-esteem that will not allow the child even the minimally necessary experience of its own agency. The injured child may learn to protect itself from further injury by defensively hiding its humiliation and rage, and may carry this complex defensive psychological constellation into adulthood. It is easy to imagine situations where this overtly meek child-become-adult again feels threatened by something that is relatively trivial (to the outside world) but is a mortifying incitement for one whose fragile self requires a strong hostility against the offending agent to feel reasonably safe. That kind of action, of course, is usually not in harmony with either that person's own values or those of his or her parent's. One therefore expects much shame and guilt to follow such behavior.

Let me cite another case as an example. D., a thirty-year-old advertising executive, was referred for psychiatric consultation because of sudden, unexpected outbreaks of vituperation and rage at his co-workers. There seemed no reasonable explanation for these excesses until it became clear that the outbreaks of rage occurred when some suggestion by D. was rejected or even criticized by his co-workers. Further inquiry revealed that D. as a child had suffered from the ministrations of an excessively domineering, ruthlessly suppressive, and self-centered mother, which left him with an insufficiently mirrored and therefore chronically fragile self. It became clear that as a child his "no" was never tolerated, and his self-esteem was crushed. Even now as an adult, his fragile self required almost total submissive admiration from his co-workers, and he achieved this by intimidating them with his attacks of rage.

I have cited this case to indicate that even with the development of normal healthy values and ideals there can be other vicissitudes that derail optimal development of the self and leave a fragile self that engages in (socially) unacceptable actions.

Disordered Idealization

A pole of values and ideals is a necessary basic constituent of a healthy self. If this pole is missing or weakened by injury or is deficient because of interferences in normal development, the total structure of the self is weakened. A weakened self is prone to fragmentation, with loss of cohesion and increased vulnerability. It is important to grasp that a weakened pole of ideals not only contains uncertain values and ideals but thereby threatens the very cohesion, and sometimes even the survival, of the self. A self weakened at its poles is fragile and vulnerable and is forced to invoke emergency measures to protect its continuity.

A frequent cause for a weakened pole of ideals is sudden and severe disappointment in the idealized other, i.e., a sudden deterioration in idealized selfobject experience. For example, children frequently react to the sudden death of a parent with almost total denial. Often they act as if nothing had happened, and one notes the absence of mourning. The child feels a parent's death as a personal abandonment and as the dead parent's total weakness and unacceptable failure. In the normal course of events, parents are de-idealized gradually (except for the sudden de-idealization at the onset of adolescence) and therefore without traumatic effect on the child. However, studies of children with sudden early loss of a parent show that many of these children suffer lifelong detrimental effects on personality development. Fleming and Altschul (1963) found that object relations in adult patients who had lost a parent as late as adolescence remained arrested at the stage attained at the time of the parent's death. Wolfenstein (1966, p. 108) concluded that the child needs the continuing relation with the parent in order to advance its development. Shane and Shane (1990, p. 119) state that in order to mourn properly the child requires selfobject functions from the surround and that without such functions development will be impaired. As adults, they may continuously seek reliably idealizable selfobject experiences only to find again and again that there are no guarantees against disappointment and that they have to begin their search all over again.

More pernicious are the effects of subtle but chronic experiences of being rejected or unrecognized by a respected selfobject. Indeed, one can confidently state that single traumatic injuries to the self are less likely to leave a residue of psychopathology than the repeated small injuries that characterize a chronic environment of faulty selfobject experiences.

Generally, each instance of adult disturbed behavior has two constituent moments, of which participants are usually quite unaware: (1) an individual transfers from his childhood past needs, fears, and (for the child) appropriate protective maneuvers to an adult situation, which (2) evoke (for the adult) inappropriate behavior when occasioned by some action or inaction of others that the individual perceives as a disappointing selfobject experience. Thus the individual reenacts on the stage of adult life his or her outmoded history, with all its emotional force, representing values appropriate to the earliest months or years of life.

The Adolescent Transformation of the Self

Most of mankind did not have an experience of adolescence as we have come to know it. Until fairly recently, life for the average man or woman was not only short and brutish by our standards; it also lacked what we call adolescence. Youngsters at an age that we would judge to be still part of childhood were usually required to work and live like adults. Only a few privileged offspring had the means and leisure to postpone adult responsibilities. Most youngsters passed quickly from childhood to adults. Thus the peasant's sons and daughters became peasants like their parents, with the latter's values and ideals. Only the rare Prince Hal could enjoy the kind of leisurely self-education and self-development that nowadays most affluent teenagers enjoy in Western cultures. Psychoanalysts have traditionally thought of the often tumultuous psychological changes during adolescence as consequences of puberty and powerful new sexual impulses. Wolf, Gedo, and Terman (1972) proposed that adolescent psychological development is not primarily the result of sexual maturation but the consequence of changing relationships to parents and other authority figures brought about by cognitive maturation. According to this theory, a youngster's idealization of his parents, which had been an essential and sustaining aspect of the cohesion of his self, is suddenly undermined by a recognition of the parent's flaws. Having reached the intellectual capacity associated with Piaget's stage of formal operations or Kohlberg's conventional morality, young people suddenly notice that the old gods—the parents and teachers—have clay feet.[5] This sudden disillusion, this sudden de-idealization, confronts the adolescent with a genuine psychological crisis: the very continuity of the self is threatened by a loss of sustaining idealized selfobject experiences. In their crises, young people turn to each other for the needed experiences. The adolescent group offers an adolescent culture rich in ideals and idols. The common language, music, heroes, and villains of adolescent culture offer the needed idealizable selfobject experiences. New values and ideals become part of the self. As the years pass and the youth becomes integrated into a wider social network of selfobject experiences, his reliance on the peer group diminishes. The emerging adult has had an opportunity to create his or her own set of values that are only partially derived from parents. Much is owed to the peer group and its idols. As the new generation matures it becomes decidedly different from the preceding one. The transformations of individual selves that are characteristic of adolescence introduce the possibility of relatively rapid cultural changes. Whereas cultural change used to take centuries, it can now happen in a few decades. Thus, by giving its youth a respite from adult responsibilities, a society allows its youth to introduce new values and ideals.

I have stressed that the need for selfobject experiences is lifelong. But as our practical experience tells us, the ideal of psychological independence, self-sufficiency, and autonomy is illusory and unreachable. To be sure, some individuals appear to be totally independent of others. Yet a closer examination reveals that these persons have substituted symbolic representations for the live selfobject experiences on which they formerly depended. Most adults do not require the constant presence of the needed selfobject to maintain constant sustaining selfobject experience. Let me illustrate with a familiar scenario. Toddlers usually require their mothers' almost constant attendance to securely experience a selfobject environment that sustains the cohesive structure of their selves. When the child gets a little older, it is sufficient if the mother is heard stirring around the house. Occasionally checking to see that she is really there will be enough to maintain constant selfobject experience. A year or two later the mother can even say that she is going out and will return later. From the very beginning it is possible gradually to substitute other caregivers for the mother if the child is given a chance to get to know the substituting nurse or teacher. Yet it is never really an easy transition, for the neonate can already tell its mother from others by its sense of smell.

The direction of development is clear: a gradual lengthening of the time during which the person providing the selfobject experience can be absent, a gradual introduction of substitute caregivers, and finally, a gradual introduction of nonhuman objects, such as a blanket and a teddy bear (the transitional object of Winnicott) to serve as symbolic representatives of the original provider of selfobject experience. Adults predominantly use symbols to supply needed selfobject experiences. For example, early on the mother's voice has the power to soothe the small child's fragmenting self into a new cohesive calm. An adolescent may be able to create a related selfobject experience by going to a rock concert or perhaps by playing the guitar. For the adult, the possibilities are even greater. I myself often enhance my feeling of well-being by listening to music, and can trace the linkage of these experiences back to certain childhood memories. Some enhance their selves by reading a novel, others find that membership in a club provides their selves with needed cohesiveness, and still others find their needed selfobject experience from religious experiences. Psychologically, even the hermit in the wilderness is not really alone; he carries with him many of the symbols of society. Artistic creativity and the life of the spirit are not luxuries that we can dispense with. Rather, they are the very stuff from which we fashion our daily psychological sustenance. We thus assign a value to all sorts of cultural activities because they are needed to sustain the structure and functioning of our selves rather than for the moral content that these ideas and activities may represent.

Group Selves, Group Ambitions, Group Ideals

Human beings cannot live fully human lives in a psychological vacuum. We have learned that an environment of selfobject experiences, created by a matrix of selfobject relationships, is a sine qua non for a healthy, cohesive self to emerge, develop, and maintain itself. No matter how much a person may deny it, in his inner experience he is always a social individual concerned with his relations with other persons. Shared experiences, particularly shared selfobject experiences, define groups. Some groups are formed to achieve common aims that define the group's purposes. For example, a professional organization of psychiatrists may aim to advance the profession. But such aims are intimately related to the values of individual members and are based on shared idealizations. Quite apart from the conscious common aims that an individual may have in mind upon becoming a member of such an organization, there are other, less conscious but perhaps even more important benefits. Belonging to a group can affirm an individual's particular social role, one's identity, which in turn affirms the self. Such self affirmation that enhances one's experience of being somebody important, perhaps being someone special, is another type of selfobject experience, the so-called mirroring experience, which I will now discuss.[6]

Mirroring Experience and Morality

In contrast to idealizing experience, which focuses on the greatness of the other, Kohut designated as mirroring selfobject experiences the need to be recognized, acknowledged, and affirmed for one's own importance and greatness (Kohut, 1971, pp. 105–136). Membership in a group can confirm one's own value. Many adults derive their needed selfobject experience from membership in groups, including being a citizen of a nation or ethnic group. Shared ambitions and ideals provide group members with mirroring and idealizing selfobject experiences that strengthen their individual selves. However, such group membership can also be a source of weakness for an individual. The more an individual depends on the group for needed selfobject experience, the more one will have to disavow one's own values and ideals in favor of those shared by the group. While putting on a Nazi S.A. uniform gave greater cohesion to the selves of some weak characters, others found that imposed affiliations with such value-alien organizations generated internal conflicts that weakened their selves. Similar problems attend the organization of contemporary mass society. When individuals depend for their livelihood on a large corporation in which the morality of the bottom line and short-term profits reigns, at some time they will likely be caught between their own values of decent communal behavior and the values of the organization that feeds their families. Such conflicts fragment the self by threatening to give rise to a situation in which needed selfobject experience is denied.

I could go on multiplying such examples, but I think you can see that individual integrity is vulnerable to more than interpersonal relations with other individuals. Groups too can be thought of as having a group self, with group ambitions and group-ideals. Kohut (1976) pointed out some of the complexities in the relations of leaders and groups. When group selves are threatened, the groups may find healing selfobject experiences through charismatic or messianic leaders. Churchill, for example, was able, through his speeches, to convey his strength into a national selfobject experience that reversed the fragmentation of the British after Dunkirk. But the dangers of a group's depending on the strength and values of an individual leader are quite obvious. Churchill's leadership illustrates how a charismatic person may bolster the weakening pole of ambitions of a group self, messianic leaders like Ghandi and Martin Luther King illustrate how leaders may provide a group self with selfobject experiences that strengthen its pole of values and ideals, but Hitler illustrates how groups can be led into disaster by a charismatic leader whose pathologically distorted value system is imposed on the whole group.

Individual selves as well as group selves generally act to ensure the continuity of their existence. At least unconsciously, people seem to know that continuity of a healthy self existence depends on maintaining oneself within a minimum of continuous selfobject experiences. An individual may engage in all kinds of behavior— from kindness, compassion, and considerateness to the opposite extremes of indifference, hate, and destructiveness—to maintain the needed selfobject experiences. Regardless of whether such behavior is acceptable to oneself or to others, one is fundamentally motivated by self-centered self-interest. To admit to such selfish motivations is very difficult for many people, whose grandiose illusions about their moral virtue can make their self-centeredness unacceptable to them.

The values, let us say, of the need for a selfobject matrix throughout life by which we are, as it were, guided fit into our specific self-needs. Values of independence are phony, really. There is no such thing. There can be no pride in living without oxygen. We're not made that way. It is nonsense to try and give up symbiosis and become an independent self. An independent self is one that is clever enough to find a good selfobject support system and to stay in tune with its needs and the changing of the generations. To that system one must be willing to give a great deal. (Kohut, 1985, p. 262)

Kohut seems to be saying that all values are self-centered. Yet in his paper "On Courage" (Kohut, 1985, pp. 5–50), where he discussed the heroism of the anti-Nazis Franz Jaegerstaetter and Hans and Sophie Scholl, he observes individuals whose total personality is given over to their idealized values.

Under certain circumstances death is not feared at all. . . . If a person has given over his total self to an ideal . . . if a person is capable of doing that, then he will die without a trace of fear, die as a matter of fact proudly. He knows that he has supported his real self, which lives on. When the Spartans died at the Thermopylae, the famous inscription was: "Stranger, take word to Sparta: here we lie, obeying her orders." They lost their lives but only their lives. That was their feeling. If you're thinking in terms of biology, of course, then they lost their lives, but if you think in terms of psychology they didn't lose their selves. They lived on in the habits, the standards, the ethics of the Spartan city-state. That's one example where the inner commitment to the ideal outweighs the fear of death. (Kohut, 1985, pp. 263–264)

Kohut here begins to hint at what I would call the postnarcissistic state of the individual. Under favorable circumstances a strong, cohesive, mature self may expand its self-experience to encompass the world beyond its own physical boundaries. Such a postnarcissistic self is likely to have unusual qualities of empathy, humor, creativity, and wisdom. Unlike vulnerable and hence defensive selves that must always be on their guard, the mature postnarcissistic self has the energy and freedom to express the meaning it has created out of its relation to the world. Such expression may come in the creation of art or science, new ideas, or new values, with which the postnarcissistic self strives to give meaning to life.

Notes

1. "Empathy is the operation that defines the field of psychoanalysis. No psychology of complex mental states is conceivable without the employment of empathy. It is a value-neutral tool of observation. . . . We define it as 'vicarious introspection' or, more simply, as one person's [attempt to] experience the inner life of another while simultaneously retaining the stance of an objective observer" (Kohut, 1984, pp. 174–175).

2. The term 'selfobject' is an unfortunate neologism and somewhat misleading because the selfobject is neither self nor object but essentially describes an experience and its effects. Nevertheless, it is a well-established technical term. It would only cause widespread confusion to substitute another term now.

3. My use of the term "structure" here is convenient but archaic in that it represents a residual outdated way of thinking. "Structure" here means no more than that the experience of selfhood has the qualities of an enduring pattern.

4. The part of the self that is derived from mirroring experiences has sometimes been called "the pole of ambitions."

5. Noam et al. (1990) have found that most adolescents who are seen in clinics have not reached the social cognitive equivalent of the "formal operations" stage. Perhaps these youngsters have had such massive earlier trauma that they are retarded in the normal progression of their development by the time they reach adolescence. These "adolescent worlds" give rise to different forms of disillusionment and conflict resolution.

6. This is merely an example of a mirroring experience connected with group membership. Most mirroring experiences are aspects of interpersonal relationships: mother's admiring smile, the gleam in her eye when she looks at you, your father's pride in you as "a chip off the old block," etc. Mirroring experiences affirm the self.

References

Atwood, G., and Stolorow, R. (1984). *Structures of subjectivity*. Hillsdale, NJ: Analytic Press.

Basch, M. F. (1988). *Understanding psychotherapy*. New York: Basic Books.

Fleming, J., and Altschul, S. (1963). Activation of mourning and growth. Psychoanalysis. *International Journal of Psycho-Analysis*, 44:419–431.

Freud, S. (1905). On psychotherapy. In *The standard edition of the complete psychological works of Sigmund Freud*. Vol. 7. London: Hogarth Press.

Freud, S. (1923). *The ego and the id*. In *The standard edition of the complete psychological works of Sigmund Freud*. Vol. 19. London: Hogarth Press.

Freud, S., and Pfister, O. (1963). Letter of February 14, 1928. *Briefe 1909–1939*. Frankfurt: S. Fischer, 1963.

Kohut, H. (1971). *The analysis of the self*. New York: International Universities Press.

Kohut, H. (1976). Creativeness, charisma, group psychology: Reflections on the self-analysis of Freud. In J. Gedo and G. Pollock (Eds.), *Freud: The fusion of science and humanism*. New York: International Universities Press, 1976. Also in H. Kohut, *The search for the self: Selected writings of Heinz Kohut*, 1950–197. New York: International Universities Press, 1978.

Kohut, H. (1977). *The restoration of the self*. New York: International Universities Press.

Kohut, H. (1978). *The search for the self: Selected writings of Heinz Kohut, 1950–1978*. Vols. 1 and 2. New York: International Universities Press.

Kohut, H. (1984). *How does psychoanalysis cure?* Chicago: University of Chicago Press.

Kohut, H. (1985). *Self psychology and the humanities.* Chicago: University of Chicago Press.

Kohut, H., and Wolf, E. S. (1978). The disorders of the self and their treatment. *International Journal of Psychoanalysis,* 59:414–425.

Lachmann, F. (1986). Interpretation of psychic conflict and adversarial relationships: A self-psychological perspective. *Psychoanalytic Psychology,* 3:341–356.

Lichtenberg, J. D. (1983). *Psychoanalysis and infant research.* Hillsdale, NJ: Analytic Press.

Lichtenberg, J. D. (1989). *Psychoanalysis and motivation.* Hillsdale, NJ: Analytic Press.

Noam, G., Powers, S., Kilkenny, R., and Beedy, J. (1990). The interpersonal self in life-span developmental perspective: Theory, measurement, and longitudinal case analyses. In P. Baltes, P. Featherman, and R. Lerner (Eds.), *Life-span development and behavior.* Hillsdale, NJ: Erlbaum.

Shane, E., and Shane, M. (1990). Object loss and selfobject loss: A consideration of self psychology's contribution to understanding mourning and the failure to mourn. *The Annual of Psychoanalysis,* 18:115–131.

Spitz, R. A. (1945). Hospitalism. *Psychoanalytic Study of the Child,* 1:53–74.

Spitz, R. A. (1946) Hospitalism. *Psychoanalytic Study of the Child,* 2:113–117.

Stern, D. (1985). *The interpersonal world of the infant.* New York: Basic Books.

Wolf, E. S. (1976). Ambience and abstinence. *Annual of Psychoanalysis,* 4:101–115.

Wolf, E. S. (1977). Subjektivität und Ethik in der medizinischen Praxis—Die zentrale Rolle der Einfühlung. In J. Wunderli and K. Weisshaupt (Eds.), *Medizin im Widerspruch.* Olten: Walter-Verlag.

Wolf, E. S. (1977). "Irrationality" in a psychoanalytic psychology of the self. In T. Mischel (Ed.), *The self: Psychological and philosophical issues.* Oxford: Basil Blackwell.

Wolf, E. S. (1978). The disconnected self: Modern sensibility in the writings of Kafka, Sartre and Virginia Woolf. In A. Roland (Ed.), *Psychoanalysis, creativity and literature.* New York: Columbia University Press.

Wolf, E. S. (1980). On the developmental line of selfobject relations. In A. Goldberg (Ed.), *Advances in self psychology.* New York: International Universities Press.

Wolf, E. S. (1988). *Treating the self: Elements of clinical self psychology.* New York: Guilford Press.

Wolf, E. S. (1989). The self in psychoanalytic self psychology. In G. Lee and G. Urban (Eds.), *Semiotics, self and society.* Berlin and New York: Mouton de Gruyter.

Wolf, E. S. (1989). Das Selbst in der Psychoanalyse: Grundsätzliche Aspekte. In *Selbst Psychologie. Weiterentwicklungen nach Heinz Kohut.* Munich: Verlag Internationale Psychoanalyse.

Wolf, E. S., Gedo, J. E., and Terman, D. M. (1972). On the adolescent process as a transformation of the self. *Journal of Youth and Adolescence*, 1:257–272.

Wolf, E. S., and Wolf, I. P. (1979). We perished, each alone: A psychoanalytic commentary on Virginia Woolf's *To The Lighthouse. International Review of Psychoanalysis*, 6:37–47.

Wolfenstein, M. (1966). How is mourning possible? *Psychoanalytic Study of the Child*, 21:93–123.

The Open-Textured Concepts of Morality and the Self

Thomas E. Wren

In this essay I want to explore the way the concepts of morality and self operate in contemporary moral psychologies as well as in the philosophical traditions they consciously or unconsciously draw on. It is tempting, given the way most psychological studies of these topics proceed, to say that the terms "morality" and "self" designate two distinct conceptual domains, each of which can be understood quite well without reference to the other though they sometimes happen to overlap. If this really were the case, there would be much less confusion in the psychological literature (not to mention the philosophical literature), where researchers of widely different theoretical orientations tend to assume that their central categories have relatively stable meanings for everyone involved. This assumption has been fostered by the many analytical philosophers who have tried to isolate "the mark of the moral," "the human per se," and so on, as though such seemingly precise expressions comprised a definite set of semantic features serving as necessary and sufficient conditions for applying the terms in question to really existing things or practices.

Unfortunately, things are not nearly so simple. The meanings of "morality" and "self," like those of virtually all important socially defined terms, vary with the cultural or scientific context within which they are passed down to the next generation of language users. Living as we do in a complex society where one's linguistic coming of age takes place in several contexts at the same time, it is only to be expected that one term will have several equally legitimate meanings, not all of which may be compatible. Putnam

(1975) has made a similar point regarding the way we learn the reference of natural-kind terms such as "tiger," and I will not repeat his arguments here. What I will do instead is review several meanings that layfolk, philosophers, and psychologists associate with the two terms "morality" and "self," in an effort to show two things. First, I want to show that these terms are semantically *open-textured* (to use Waismann's [1952] suggestive term without its original positivist connotations) without being sheerly equivocal as are words such as "bank" and "will." And second, I want to show how taking account of this open-texturedness changes the way we address the profoundly important question of how the claims of morality and self-fulfillment can be, or seem to be, in conflict with each other. I will not settle that question, but what I have to say about its central concepts will, I hope, make it a little more answerable.

The Concept of Morality

Following a scheme introduced by J. L. Austin (1962) and H. L. A. Hart (1961) and used few years later by John Rawls as the basis of his *Theory of Justice* (1971), I propose that morality is best understood as a *concept* embodied in a number of alternative *conceptions*. The concept of morality transcends cultural traditions, but its conceptions do not. The concept is inherently transcultural for the simple reason that it is, or expresses, our general realization that there are good and bad ways to share the world with other persons, whose intentionality is like our own in that they too have worldviews, self-concepts, projects, needs, desires, claims, and so on. Conceptions of morality, on the other hand, vary from one culture to the next (and sometimes even within the same culture), for they are specific ways of filling out this general concept. They are sets of beliefs and motivations that more or less systematically cohere around a few central properties or "core features" that need not be the same for every person, place, or era. What the several conceptions necessarily have in common is not their core features (if they did happen to have some core features in common, this would be an empirical truth rather than a logically necessary one) but only the *overall function* filled by those conceptions. In the case of morality, this is the function of articulating the way people are to live with each other. Clearly, this specification is a cultural matter, and a list of all the conceptions of morality would not be limited to late twentieth-century Western ones. For now, however, I will only focus on the contemporary Western scene, which has more than enough diversity to demonstrate my claim that the concept of morality has many conceptions. To some extent, though perhaps not as fully as many philosophers suggest, contemporary conceptions of morality recapitulate the great traditions of moral philosophy, e.g., Aristotelian virtue theory, Kantian deontology, classical utilitarianism, and so on, as found in the table of contents of the typical college ethics textbook. However, it is more useful here to take a topical rather than historical approach, as in the following list which I have adapted from Abraham Edel (1964, 1968). This admittedly incomplete list portrays in a rough and ready way several major currents in contemporary moral philosophy and, by extension, moral psychology. Whether these currents also flow in the lives of ordinary people is an empirical question that cannot be resolved here, though it seems clear from the interview data collected by moral psychologists such as Lawrence Kohlberg that reasonably articulate people are quite able to use the categories of these conceptions (rights, duties, honor, love, common good, human dignity, etc.) in the course of expressing their personal views of how life should be lived. Note that each conception is itself a cluster of semantic features and that the core features of each conception can reappear as features of other conceptions as well, though not necessarily at the core. The list, which could be entitled "Some Current Conceptions of Morality," runs as follows:

1. The teleological conception of morality, which conceives of morality as an overriding concern for some objective, large-scaled good or value, such as the happiness of mankind, beauty, or the glory of God

2. The juridical conception of morality, which thinks of morality in terms of systematic laws, obligations, and universally reciprocal connections between rights and duties

3. The self-actualization conception of morality, which regards human life and social relationships in terms of the self and its qualities, be they stable (the static version, which stresses virtuous dispositions) or changing (the dynamic version, which stresses development)

4. The proceduralist conception of morality, which is keyed to structural aspects and procedures of either deliberation (the intellectual version) or choice (the voluntarist version) in moral decisions

5. The intuitionist conception of morality, in which moral values and principles are thought to be directly perceivable, in the same fashion that self-evident propositions or primitive sense qualities are immediately apprehended

6. The romantic conception of morality, which rebels against most or even all social institutions and other structures as enslaving, puerile, and ultimately immoral, and conceives of morality as liberation into a kind of cultivated artlessness

Each of these conceptions, as well as others not represented in this list, is an answer to the question of how individuals and groups are to live with each other. (Even the romantic conception deals with this question, though its answer usually promotes individualism at the expense of collective goods and to that extent can be thought of as not so much an answer as a defiant reconceptualization of the original question.) In what follows I will assume a fair amount of background knowledge on the part of the reader, since space does not permit a systematic analysis of each conception. For our purposes they can be thought of as forming two major groups, which, following current jargon, I will call the *deontic* and *ethical* forms of morality. The contrast between these two groups is an intramoral relationship reflecting the more problematic extramoral relationship between the moral and personal domains. The deontic group, which includes not only the juridical conception of morality but also the proceduralist and intuitionist conceptions as defined above, is so called because its central features are keyed to the notion of *right action* (relatively impersonal features such as justice judgments, criteria of fairness, duties, rights claims, and so on). The ethical group, which includes not only the teleological conception but also the various self-actualizing and romantic ones, is so called because its central features are keyed to various notions of *the good* (more personally nuanced features such as happiness, self-actualization, personal excellence, and other forms of human flourishing), notions that constitute the ethos or character of one's culture as well as of one's self.

Conceptions of morality, taken either separately or in the two groups I just delineated, are differentiated not only by the moral beliefs they incorporate but also by the motives associated with those beliefs. That is, each conception of morality and, a fortiori, each group of conceptions has its own distinctive motivational mix, comprising such specific motives as loyalty, reverence for the law, care, benevolence, pride, a sense of justice, and so on. If, as is usually the case in modern or postmodern cultures such as ours, a person's worldview includes not just one morality but rather a number of alternative, more or less balanced conceptions of morality, we may expect to find a considerable variety of moral motives in play in that person's self. At the day-to-day level, it is to be expected that these diverse motives usually will be mutually compatible and often will also causally interact, since, as cognitive dissonance theorists have shown, over an extended period of time a person can tolerate only so much conflict among his or her beliefs and values. However, it would be naive not to expect occasional, often intense experiences of conflicting ideals, values, and motives, even within cognitively sophisticated subjects for whom such conflicts are all the more painful for being intellectually intractable. For instance, it may very well be that when the Kohlberg-Gilligan controversy broke out with such vigor a little over a decade ago, many of the contending theorists were originally drawn to the controversy because of the dissonance created by conflicts they themselves had experienced between justice and care as sources of moral action—an experience possible only for moral subjects already personally engaged by the demands of both justice and care. Furthermore, in the subsequent exchange of assertions and counterassertions the partisans of these theoretical systems seldom completely rejected the motivational contents of the opposing system, preferring instead to show that a fully developed sense of justice includes care (see Kohlberg's final formulation of stage 6 in Kohlberg, Boyd, and Levine, 1990) or, conversely, that for mature adults care involves justice or justice-affiliated motives such as respect for persons (Gilligan, 1982).

Such considerations suggest that morality, however conceived, reflects basic divisions within the self, and does not by itself dissolve or otherwise do away with those divisions. Even when it is conceived deontically, as an inherently impersonal system or social code, morality is still understood (by the theorist as well as the moral agent) as being addressed to real-life persons who have their own ethical contexts and their own lives to lead. Personal values may or may not present themselves as moral values, depending in part on one's conception of morality, but moral values, if they are to be effective, must always present themselves as personal values, which is to say as motives wrapped up with one's sense of self. Common to all conceptions of morality is the assumption that we are enjoined not only to behave, think, and live in certain ways but also to cultivate the motives that produce such results.

Nevertheless, even when moral motives and values are not in conflict with each other, they can still be at odds with personal interests and under certain circumstances can eclipse the values associated with those interests even though those interests constitute one's sense of self. But before pursuing this point further, it is necessary to understand better just how wide is the referential range of the concept of the self.

The Concept of Self

When I introduced the distinction between the concept of morality and its conceptions, I said that what the latter conceptions have in common is not (except accidentally) any single feature or set of features but rather a general function, and that this is the manifestly normative function of articulating the way people are to live with each other. The concept and conceptions of self are similarly connected, except that here what is articulated is primarily how individual persons are related to themselves and only secondarily how they are related to others. Here too the concept and its conceptions are profoundly normative, though this might not be as obvious as it was in the case of morality. The evaluative force of the term "self" disappears when that term is used as part of such hyphenated expressions as "self-knowledge" or "self-regulation," but it is easily seen when "self" is used more or less synonymously with such terms as "person" or "identity," which is the way it is usually used in moral philosophy and moral psychology. A close look at these nonhyphenated terms reveals that they are what philosophers sometimes call success words, in that they suggest an achievement on the part of those of whom they are predicated—an achievement that is an ongoing process, ever tentative and admitting of degrees, rather than a once-and-for-all accomplishment. Admittedly, not all personality theorists use a developmental conception of selfhood in the strict sense of a sequence of hierarchical stages or structures. However, as far as I can tell all these theorists would claim not only that important changes occur in everyone's self but also that their own theories include or imply criteria for evaluating such changes as good (growthful, healthy, etc.) or bad (regressive, destructive, etc.).

I am not, of course, suggesting that every psychological conception of the self is a mental health program. Some are too speculative to be of much use to therapists, educators, or even just individuals concerned with their own psychic well-being. I am only saying that these psychological theories, including nontechnical formulations sometimes referred to as "folk psychology," are not value-free descriptions of natural phenomena, though of course they are just as accountable as any nonnormative theory is to charges of faulty methodologies, insufficient data, internal incoherence, and so on. Why there are multiple conceptions of the self is a basically historical question, as is the parallel question of why the concept of morality is mediated through many conceptions. In both cases, the question is probably best answered by a sustained historical-cultural analysis, such as Charles Taylor's aptly titled *Sources of the Self* (1989). Although that sort of analysis is impossible in this short space, we may briefly consider a list of several quite different conceptions of the self in order to see how they all endeavor to spell out the nature of successful human functioning.[1] The conceptions I have put on this list are found in the work of contemporary psychologists as well as that of philosophers of our own day and earlier times. In parallel to the list of moral conceptions, this list could be entitled "Some Current Conceptions of the Self," and runs as follows:

1. The substantialist conception of the self, which conceives of the self either as a primarily outward-looking entity that knows itself in terms of the external (natural or transcendent) world or as an inward-looking entity whose consciousness of the external world is somehow based on its own introspections

2. The bundle conception of the self, which conceives of the self as a set of contingent, more or less loosely connected cognitions, desires, and other psychological states and tendencies whose association with each other is utterly fortuitous, since they are the effects that social learning and/or genetic phenomena have on an essentially passive subject

3. The eidetic conception of the self, which conceives of the self as a construction or projection enabling a person to organize his or her multitudinous experiences under a "self-concept" that is both an object of knowledge and, under favorable conditions, the terminus ad quem of self-esteem

4. The noumenal conception of the self, which conceives of the self either transcendentally or naturalistically but in either case as a purely formal unifying principle of subjectivity

5. The dialectical conception of the self, according to which the self is conceived as a node in a web of social or interpersonal relations and not as an epistemically or psychologically self-sufficient subject

6. The identity conception of the self, which conceives of the self as a self-interpreting agent concerned with the way its own history is validated or invalidated by the cultural tradition it finds itself within

Each of these conceptions, as well as others not mentioned here, is a theoretical or metatheoretical attempt to show how personal experience can be rendered conceptually accessible for analysis and evaluation. As with my first list, space does not permit a close review of the various conceptions listed here, and so I must once again assume òn the part of the reader a general knowledge of major movements and figures in philosophy and psychology.

The substantialist conception (1) was originally formed by philosophers of a metaphysical bent (e.g., Plato, Aristotle, and Aquinas for the outward-looking version, Descartes, Leibniz, and Spinoza for the inward-looking one), but it lives on in our day-to-day folk psychologies of selfhood. In contrast, today's scientific psychological theories have their origins in the view I have named the "bundle conception" (2) in order to recall Hume's famous definition of the self as a bundle of perceptions. Although this conception once dominated Anglo-American psychologies of personality, its reifying implications have led empiricist psychologists to adopt what I have called the eidetic conception (3), according to which the self is an idea, and which has been elaborated by Gordon Allport, H. Markus, and others under the label "self-concept."[2] Their work has also influenced several analytic philosophers, e.g., D. Pears and R. Harré, and has interesting correlations with European phenomenology, especially the existential phenomenology of J.-P. Sartre. However, many philosophers prefer to emphasize the more elusive, subjective dimension of the self. I call this perspective the "noumenal conception" (4) to evoke Immanuel Kant's distinction between appearances (phenomena) and that which lies behind appearances, i.e., the so-called things-in-themselves (noumena). By this label I mean not that the self is considered a thing in itself, but rather that the self and its operations somehow provide the conditions under which phenomena can emerge from noumenal reality. This view was naturalized in cognitive-developmental psychology by Jean Piaget, for whom the self was a site for the cognitive construction of schemata under which reality is perceived, and later by Kohlberg, who applied this constructivist account to sociomoral meanings with predictably Kantian conclusions about the primacy of justice and other deontic concepts. But for the same general reasons used by G. W. F. Hegel to criticize Kant's view of reason as monological thinking, some self theorists have developed a dialectical conception (5), whose point of departure is not the individual self but rather the relationships in which selfhood emerges. This conception is found not only in Hegel's dialectical philosophy but also in the pragmatism of John Dewey, G. H. Mead, and J. Macmurray; it is also featured in the writings of a wide variety of psychologists directly or indirectly influenced by these philosophers. Here I have in mind such psychologists as J. M. Baldwin, R. D. Laing, and various symbolic interactionists as well as a few cognitive developmentalists who are also dialectically oriented. Finally, the identity conception (6) has recently captured center stage in contemporary moral philosophy, thanks to the work of C. Taylor, B. Williams, A. MacIntyre, and other so-called communitarians, but it has been a major part of the neo-Freudian literature ever since Erik Erikson's groundbreaking work on identity formation and has recently attracted the attention of social psychologists interested in the intersection of cultural critique and personality theory.

Successful selves

I said above that conceptions of self are normative, by which I mean that they provide us with ways of discriminating between successful and unsuccessful attempts by an individual to live as a human person. To appreciate this point, let us once again traverse the list of conceptions of the self, beginning with the substantialist conception (1). In this case, there are at least two quite different views of what counts as success, one classical and the other modern. The classical view does not speak of the self as such (medieval philosophers defined "person" as an individuated rational substance), since what is at stake in the human adventure is having a correct vision and the right relationship to the larger order of goods comprised by what the ancients and medievals simply called Being. The modern view, on the other hand, can be said to have invented the term "self," at least when it is used as a noun. The Cartesian *Cogito* is more than an epistemological ploy: it is the prototype of a radically new relationship to oneself, involving an equally radical shift in the role assigned to reason. This view of the self demands that the inquiring mind turn inward, away from the cosmos (which is now perceived as a neutral system rather than as a habitat of goals and values) as well as away from our own bodily natures. As Taylor (1989, chap. 8) explains, this double "disengagement" does not deny the existence or importance either of the world or of the body and its passions, but rather instrumentalizes them, with reason working on them until they are as it thinks they should be. What defines success for a self is, then, the rational power to remake not only the world but even one's own physical and psychological properties. This view of the self recurs in many ways over the next centuries, one of its most important later versions being Freud's conception of the self as a conflict-free zone mediating the libidinal, environmental, and internalized social forces that compete with each other. Freud's *Ich* or *ego*, like Descartes' *je*, reifies the perspective from which one objectifies oneself, not for the sake of truth (i.e., in order to know better how things are) but rather for the sake of mastery or at least smooth management of one's inner and outer worlds.

The Humean bundle conception of the self (2) continues the instrumentalism of the Cartesian view, even though for Descartes the passions were the servants of reason whereas it was the other way around for Hume. With this inversion of the master-servant relationship comes a new set of norms for human functioning, according to which reason does not set goals but rather reads them off from the individual's own motivational-affective features or tendencies. Furthermore, successful human functioning is assumed to be able somehow to bring these tendencies together. The self is a bundle, yes, but it is an intact bundle: my experiences are mine, yours are yours. Each self is understood to have its own frontiers and whatever interior coherence is necessary to maintain those frontiers, even though this conception refuses to posit innate ideas or other a priori structures as part of the human endowment (genetic endowment is another story, not told in detail until a century after Hume made his telegraphic remarks about elements of the serpent and the dove being kneaded into our natures). The bundle conception is normative in that, although the self is infinitely malleable (or virtually so, depending on how strictly this conception is interpreted), it should not be incoherent. Fragmentation, multiple personalities, psychosis, and other sorts of dissociation are regarded as malfunctions, a value judgment engendered not only by Hume's notion of the self but also by his moral view that people are responsible for their actions.

When we come to the eidetic conception of the self (3), it might seem that the empirical self-concept theories it comprises are exceptions to my claim that conceptions of the self are normative. To be sure, there is a problem here. In these theories the term "self-concept" refers not to a truth-valenced image discovered in the course of introspection but rather to a cognitive induction by the subject from the regular features of self-experience. Furthermore, as with any induction the important thing is that it be carried out correctly; if it is, the conclusion is unobjectionable no matter what it is. For these reasons, the empiricists' self-concept is a constructed figure that does not claim to point to anything real beyond itself or to any sort of ideal or value. If this were all there were to the eidetic conception of the self, it would be misleading at best to say that it is normative, i.e., that it offers criteria for evaluating a person or a way of life. But as Broughton (1978) has shown, an uncompromisingly empiricist self-concept theory is inherently unstable and leads the careful theorist beyond itself. To anyone not already in its grip, the obvious objection is to ask, If there is no real self, what is the so-called self-concept a concept *of*? Gordon Allport, one of the pioneers in modern self-concept theory, anticipated this objection and, in the course of blocking it, made the eidetic conception of selfhood normative after all. He postulated a "dynamic self-image" that generates a special sort of competence motivation, namely, the "propriative striving" of the actual self toward its ideal self. Since this striving, which Allport compared to the self-actualization discussed by J. H. Goldstein and A. Maslow, maintains the boundaries and internal consistency of the individual's personality and is a source of self-esteem, it seems fair to characterize Allport's and other eidetic conceptions of the self as attempts to answer the evaluative question of what should count as proper human functioning. If, on the other hand, the logic of a narrowly empiricist version of this conception blocks the very attempt to provide evaluative criteria, then so much the worse for empiricism (I have made a similar point in Wren, 1991).

The normative dimensions of the noumenal conception (4) are perhaps less clear than in the previous three cases, since in the original, transcendental version of this view developed by Kant, the self is a necessary condition for the possibility of *any* personal experience but is not itself known or experienced. Kant himself ascribed error and other sorts of human dysfunctioning to the failure to appreciate the gap between the noumenal and phenomenal worlds, a failure that is reflected in the heteronomy of the will. However, matters are more clear in the naturalistic version subsequently developed in Piagetian cognitive psychology, where the self is an epistemic subject whose proper activity is that of constructing more or less well-balanced systems whereby the natural and social worlds are organized. Even though, like the Kantian self, the self as epistemic subject is not itself an object of experience, it provides an unambiguous standard—admittedly, a highly cognitive one—for human success. The naturalistic version of the noumenal conception implies that intrapsychic (affective as well cognitive) equilibrium is good, disequilibrium bad—which is to say that our success as persons consists primarily in our ability to structure reality with maximum coherence, explanatory adequacy, and range of perspectives.

I will round out this review with only a word about the remaining two conceptions, in hopes that it is clear by now just what it would mean to say that they, as well as other conceptions not mentioned in this essay, are normative for human functioning. The dialectical conception (5) implies that a successful self is one that is related to other selves in such a way that what is most important is the relationship itself—a Hegelian and pragmatist view that is echoed in contemporary feminist theory. Finally and closely related to the dialectical view, the identity conception (6) suggests that a successful person has achieved a special type of integration and hermeneutical self-realization ("identity"), whereby one can understand and carry forward the cultural and autobiographical horizons of one's selfhood, simultaneously affirming and contending with one's own history in terms of whatever norms, principles, and ideals are its legacy.

Morality versus the Self

Let us now return to our earlier question of how moral motives and values can be at odds with personal interests and values. As I mentioned just before suspending that discussion to consider the concept of the self, under certain circumstances morality can seem to conflict with one's personal interests, even when those interests constitute one's deepest sense of self. Now it is important to realize that the personal interests mentioned in the last sentence are not selfish desires or passing pleasures, whims, and impulses, but rather are deep and complex human goods and activities such as friendship, self-esteem, creativity, and intelligence. They are the components of *eudaimonia,* the classical Aristotelian concept variously translated as "happiness," "the good life," and "flourishing." Aristotle himself had no great worries about the tension between the personal and moral domains, since in the moral psychology of his *Nicomachean Ethics* he regarded the moral life as instrumental to the good life and for the most part to be defined in terms of it.[3] Here Aristotle reversed Plato's conception, according to which morality is the fundamental notion upon which the notion of human flourishing or its cognates (happiness, living well, the good life) must be understood. For Plato, moral cognition not only reveals a core feature of human flourishing but also can be known only from the moral standpoint. The Platonic priority of the moral over the personal is not purely formal, as would be the case with axioms that are logical conditions for a conclusion, though this priority has its formal aspects. The priority is also practical, either in the sense that acting morally is a necessary and sufficient condition for living well or, more strikingly, in the sense that to act immorally is ipso facto to live badly. Thus Socrates countered Thrasymachus's cynical remarks about justice by saying that being just is an *oikeion* (intrinsic good), "one of those things which anyone who would be blessed must love both for their own sake and their consequences" (*Republic*, 358A, my translation).

In spite of their differences, the views of Plato and Aristotle both deny a priori the possibility of conflict between the moral and personal domains, or between the demands of moral rightness and the goods of what we call the self and they called human nature. It seems safe to say that their denial of this point is at odds with most people's experience, at least in today's moral cultures, where, to give but one example, Gauguin is not condemned out of hand for his decision to leave his family in order to pursue his personal goals. The possibility of genuine conflict between the two domains has certainly been a much-debated issue among philosophers after Aristotle, some of whom not only allow for this possibility but build guidelines for its resolution into their ethical theory. Thus articles have been published over the last few years with titles like "Admirable Immorality" (Slote, 1983), which start from the premise that it is an open question whether morality or moral conscientiousness is good for a person and conclude that when it is not, i.e., when a person's moral commitments actually interfere with his or her human development, then morality should be set aside. As the word "should" at the end of the previous sentence reveals, this conclusion is itself a normative statement, though it does not purport to be a moral one. It is made from a supposedly more comprehensive standpoint, the most famous of which is probably Nietzsche's "transvaluative" standpoint.[4]

The same thing holds for the opposite conclusion, namely, that on those unfortunate occasions when our conscience demands something *not* good for us, what should be set aside is not morality but personal flourishing. Like the former conclusion, this one too is a normative statement made, apparently, from some more comprehensive standpoint. It also proceeds from the premise that conflict between the moral and personal domains is a real possibility in the practical order, and so is different from Plato's view, in which the moral life is preferred because it is, in some fundamental sense, the humanly better one after all. The view that the conflict is real, which Kant held, is much more austere than Plato's, since it tells us that when we are faced with a choice between morality and personal well-being, we must choose the former, not because on the whole it makes a better, happier life but in spite of the fact that it does not.

What then are we to think about the relation between morality and the deep personal interests of our selves? Obviously, there are profound and longstanding metaethical issues here, wrapped up with other logical and psychological ones as well as with the problem of cultural diversity in how these two domains are conceptualized. The very fact that the positions sketched above are associated with philosophical traditions ranging from Plato and Aristotle to Kant and Nietzsche suggests that we are dealing with a perennial question, one whose nature precludes any once-and-for-all answer. But some progress can be made, I believe, if we adopt certain strategies. The first of these is the strategy of refusing to assume at the outset that either the moral domain or the personal domain automatically overrides the other, assuming instead that, in the absence of culture-specific evidence to the contrary, each domain is a repository of more or less strong reasons for action. To be sure, what makes such reasons "strong" or "weak" is no easy question, if only because the logic of each domain is that of an open-textured concept allowing for many conceptions. Though it is too facile to answer that a practical reason is strong solely because of its affective load, it seems truistic to say that when a practical reason is effective as well as affective, it is so because of its personal dimension, which is to say because of its linkage with the self.[5]

Combining this truism with what I said above about the concept/conception distinction, I would suggest that when the demands of morality and the self seem to collide, we also adopt the strategy of clarifying at the outset of the discussion just what the elements in conflict are. Such conflicts (or alleged conflicts) are almost certainly between specific *conceptions* rather than between the two domains or concepts themselves, and should be represented as such if we are to achieve meaningful and stable resolutions in both moral theory and real life. This means that we must recognize the perils involved in, say, contrasting the demands of a juridical conception of morality with a dialectical conception of the self, or setting a self-actualization conception of morality in contrast with a noumenal conception of the self. It would, of course, be presumptuous to declare a priori that conceptions cannot be contrasted unless they are in perfect counterpoint with each other, since moral reality and personal reality are not that neat. And so when I say that we must "recognize the perils" I am recommending a methodological strategy of conceptual vigilance; I do not mean that we should always flatly refuse to relate somewhat ill-fitting conceptions to each other.

As a final strategic suggestion, I propose that theorists and moral agents alike constantly be on the lookout for ways to revise their respective conceptions of morality and the self so as to minimize or reduce conflict between them. This strategy, modeled on Rawls's method of reflective equilibrium (Rawls, 1971, chap. 1), is by no means fail-safe: it can produce suspiciously easy solutions to moral problems, prodigious distortions of our intuitions, and sometimes sheer frustration. But these risks are less dangerous than those of dogmatically assuming there is only one correct conception of either morality or the self.

Can morality be bad for me? A final remark

In the preceding pages I have tried to leave open the complex issue of whether morality and self-fulfillment are truly at odds with each other, limiting myself to a conceptual analysis of some of the terms that give the issue its outlines. But I cannot forbear making one substantive observation, even though I cannot elaborate on it here. Most of the "trouble" that responsible people have with morality has to do with the impersonal perspective it requires us to take, even in moral decisions involving important personal goods and relationships. This perspective is what I earlier called a "core feature" of some conceptions of morality and, I think, is also a core feature of some conceptions of the self, e.g., Kant's view of the self as a member of a kingdom of ends. In other conceptions of the self, this feature is less central but nonetheless present as part of the idea of human fulfillment, as in Plato's and Aristotle's versions of the contemplative conception of the self. In still other views, such as the bundle conception, the impersonal perspective is not featured at all. Perhaps there are some versions of this or another conception where the impersonal perspective is not only absent but logically ruled out.

For what it is worth, my own view is that the tendency to decenter (Piaget, 1967), i.e., step outside one's own shoes, is part of the deep structure of human existence. No conception of the self can ignore this tendency and still claim to represent what we are as individuals or members of interpersonal networks. From this idea it follows that the seemingly impersonal demands of morality (to be fair, keep one's promises, etc.) are—paradoxically—deeply personal demands as well, and that to set them aside is to treat the impersonal perspective from which they are understood as though that perspective were not part of my self. On occasion I may, like Gauguin, find it necessary to do just this, to prefer a personal good to what is impersonally right. But such a choice tears my self apart, perhaps irreparably and certainly at great personal cost.

Notes

1. There is no one-to-one correspondence between the conceptions of morality listed above and the conceptions of the self listed here, nor is there any special significance in the fact that each list has exactly six entries.

2. The so-called "self-concept" is only verbally close to the above-mentioned "concept of self." The latter is a philosophical, semantical, or epistemological idea, whereas the former is both an autobiographical phenomenon and—because this phenomenon is the subject matter of personality theories—a psychological category. Putting the matter in terms of our original concept/conception distinction, the psychological category of the self-concept is but one of many conceptions embodying the concept of self. Because literature on the psychology of personality has been dominated over the last two or three decades by self-concept research, this quite narrow conception has tended to crowd the others out, functioning for many personality psychologists as though it were the very concept of the self.

3. Aristotle scholars sometimes argue that for him the good life is a cluster of human goods, including goods such as health and friendship but also human "excellences" such as the intellectual and moral virtues (see, for instance, Rorty, 1980). If so, it may be misleading though not exactly wrong to speak of morality,

as I have, as "instrumental" to the good life. However, even if Aristotle did think of morality as an ingredient of the good life, it is clear that he also thought of it as a means thereto.

4. Actually, in his *Genealogy of Morals* (1956) Nietzsche himself thought that morality was *never* good for us, though when he said this he had in mind a very narrow conception of morality.

5. I have criticized the classical conditioning paradigm and other noncognitive approaches to moral motivation elsewhere (Wren, 1991).

References

Austin, J. L. (1962). *How to do things with words.* Oxford: Oxford University Press.

Broughton, J. (1978). The development of concepts of self, mind, reality and knowledge. In W. Damon (Ed.), *Social cognition.* San Francisco: Jossey-Bass.

Edel, A. (1964). *Ethical judgment: The use of science in ethics.* Glencoe, IL: Free Press.

Edel, A. (1968). Scientific research and moral judgment. Paper presented to the Conference on Studies of the Acquisition and Development of Values, May 15–17.

Gilligan, C. (1982). *In a different voice: Psychological theory and women's development.* Cambridge: Harvard University Press.

Hart, H. L. A. (1961). *The concept of law.* Oxford: Oxford University Press.

Kohlberg, L., Boyd., D., and Levine, C. (1990). The return of Stage 6: Its principle and moral point of view. In T. Wren (Ed.), *The moral domain: Essays in the ongoing discussion between philosophy and the social sciences.* Cambridge: MIT Press.

Nietzsche, F. (1956). *The genealogy of morals.* Garden City, NJ: Doubleday.

Piaget, J. (1967). *Six psychological studies.* New York: Random House.

Putnam, H. (1975). *Mind, language and reality: Philosophical papers.* Vol. 2. Cambridge: Cambridge University Press.

Rawls, J. (1971). *A theory of justice.* Cambridge: Harvard University Press.

Rorty, A. (1980). *Essays on Aristotle's ethics.* Berkeley and Los Angeles: University of California Press.

Slote, M. (1983). Admirable immorality. In *Goods and virtues.* Oxford: Oxford University Press.

Taylor, C. (1989). *Sources of the self: The making of the modern identity.* Cambridge: Harvard University Press.

Waismann, F. (1952). Verifiability. In A. G. N. Flew (Ed.), *Logic and language,* first series. Oxford: Oxford University Press.

Wren, T. (1991). *Caring about morality: Philosophical perspectives in moral psychology.* London: Routledge, and Cambridge: MIT Press.

II

Building a New Paradigm

The Development of Identity: Some Implications for Moral Functioning

Augusto Blasi

Some years ago in an attempt to account for the relations between moral understanding and moral action, I formulated a rather sketchy model and called it the self model of moral behavior (Blasi, 1980, 1983a). This self model contained three main hypothetical statements: moral understanding more reliably gives rise to moral action if it is translated into a judgment of personal responsibility; moral responsibility is the result of integrating morality in one's identity or sense of self; from moral identity derives a psychological need to make one's actions consistent with one's ideals. According to this model, moral identity plays a central role, and self-consistency is the basic motivational spring of moral action.

This chapter can be seen in the context of this earlier work. Its central focus, however, is not morality but the development of identity, the successive forms that identity may take from age to age. I discuss the moral implications of these transformations briefly and more from a conceptual perspective than from an empirical perspective. One aim of my discussion is to shift the emphasis of the model from moral action to the moral personality.

The general view of moral functioning reflected in this self model remains the same. One of its advantages is that it is consistent with the common intuition that morality is a characteristic of the person and not simply a result of abstract understanding. Its most important characteristic, at least from my perspective, is that it does not attempt to replace moral ideas with a set of noncognitive personality characteristics: it sees personal identity as operating jointly with reason and truth in providing motives for action. Constructing identity around those moral ideals that one finds objectively convincing and valid would respect the cognitive features intrinsic in moral understanding. Two characteristics—the cognitive foundation of morality and its integration in personality—seem to be essential to any adequate account of moral functioning, but they are missing, as a pair, in all major psychological explanations of morality, from psychoanalytic models to Piagetian ones.

And yet this model cannot be correct in all cases. The main reason is that identity is a relatively late development, rarely occurring before the middle adolescent years, whereas genuine morality and even moral responsibility seem to be clearly present during childhood. Therefore, this self model needs to be extended to include, next to identity, other forms of moral integration in ways that respect the cognitive nature of moral reasons. None of these issues will be taken up here. With its clear focus on identity, this paper should be seen as a limited contribution to understanding adult moral psychology.

The Concept of Identity

The term "identity" does not cover one single concept: philosophers, sociologists, and psychologists tend to refer to different sets of ideas when they speak of identity. In psychology, mainly as a result of Erikson's work (e.g., 1968), it has become a widely accepted convention to speak of identity to refer to a special kind of sense of self (more conscious, more specifically individual, more "strenuous") that begins to appear in middle adolescence. I too will follow this convention. In fact, it should be useful for me to clarify the meaning of the concept from which my discussion begins by comparing my meaning to the meaning elaborated by Erikson, even though I distance myself from his theory.

Erikson (1968) distinguished three aspects or components of identity.[1] From a structural perspective, identity represents a basically *unconscious reorganization* of needs, motives, identifications, and characteristic strategies of coping; socially, identity involves a new kind of *integration in one's society*, including a more or less autonomous commitment to certain social roles and to the ideology of one's culture. On these two aspects depends what could be called the content of identity, namely, those specific characteristics with which one identifies and that establish one's *subjective sense of individuality*. Among these characteristics, psychological research has focused in particular on occupational choices and on political, religious, and moral ideals. Erikson has been interpreted as suggesting that identity, because of its essential relation to social and cultural integration, must be built on all of these issues, even though specific choices vary with each individual and culture. Therefore, at least from an Eriksonian perspective, this is the context from which one can approach the integration in one's personality of a culturally based morality and the motivational ground of moral ideals.

The third component of Erikson's concept refers to a special experience of oneself that should accompany the developmental vicissitudes of identity and should subjectively color its various outcomes. In its positive forms, this experience should include a "sense of sameness and continuity," a feeling of inner unity, a sense of individuality and uniqueness, a sense of general well-being, a sense of purposefulness and energy, a sense of being at home in one's body and in one's society.

Erikson did not seem to feel completely comfortable with the phenomenological aspect of identity. For instance, he found unnecessary and even mistrusted the explicit focus on the question, "Who am I?" In addition, he did not precisely know what to do theoretically with the subjective experience of self (1968, chap. 5). In any event, it is the genius of his theory to claim, without much evidence so far, that these three aspects are indissolubly related to each other: a subjective sense of identity is possible only through the unconscious reorganization of needs and identifications and an optimal integration of personal individuality and autonomy with society's expectations and demands. In this respect Erikson may be considered the last organismic optimist: he had no doubts, or so it seems, that the large majority of people could adequately satisfy their unconscious needs, maintain a sense of roots and belonging, feel a sense of purpose in their chosen occupation and in their ideals, and at the same time maintain a belief in their personal individuality and ultimate autonomy.

My own approach focuses exclusively on the phenomenological or experiential aspect of identity. Thus it neglects the dynamic and structural aspects, the aspects of psychosocial adaptation and cultural integration, and the specific contents by which individuals differentiate themselves. In fact, it is intentionally descriptive and refrains from setting the kinds of theoretical constraints that characterize Erikson's approach. In my view, identity must primarily be defined in subjective terms, as a special, identifiable sense of self. Only then can one begin to construct a psychological theory of the factors and the processes leading to the development of an identity and the consequences, for the person and for society, of different forms of identity. So I accept in principle the idea that an individual can adequately construct the experience of a deeper, truer, and unifying self around issues having little to do with occupational choices, political ideals, or sexual orientation. Similarly, I do not take the experience of a certain degree of alienation from one's society and culture, and even the unhappiness and low self-esteem that derive from it, as ipso facto indications that identity has not properly developed or has developed in a pathological direction.

In the approach I am proposing, the experiential aspect of identity is not only central but also specified in somewhat different terms than those used by Erikson. First of all, while I still generically define "identity" as the experience of a more central personal reality essential to one's sense of self, I also postulate that developmental differences along this very dimension are possible. Moreover, these differences are sought along the four basic dimensions that make up the experience of oneself as subject, namely, the sense of agency, the sense of unity as agent, the sense of otherness or differentiation, and the experience of distancing from oneself, for instance, as it appears in self-reflection and self-control (Blasi, 1983b, 1988).

As I argued elsewhere (Blasi, 1991), a number of important psychological variables could be conceptually organized under these four dimensions of self experience and their combination: a sense of control and responsibility, a commitment in investing one's efforts, a sense of uniqueness, an experience of autonomy, self-reflection, a sense of unity or of inner fragmentation. In sum, I assume that people do not differ from each other simply on whether they have developed identities or on the issues around which they have constructed their identities; people may also differ from each other in the way they experience their identities and subjectively relate to those identities, even when their specific contents are the same. For instance, several individuals may see morality as essential to their sense of self, of who they are. For some of them, however, moral ideals and demands happen to be there, a given of their nature over which they feel little control. In this case moral ideals exist next to other characteristics, all equally important simply because they are there. Others instead relate to their moral ideals as being personally chosen over other ideals or demands, sense their fragility, and feel responsible to protect them and to thus protect their sense of self. The search for differences of this kind was the object of the studies that I report below.

Identity Modes in Loevinger's Ego Development Categories

Among the most significant recent work in personality development are Loevinger's (1976) theory of ego development and her procedures for measuring it (Loevinger, Wessler, and Redmore, 1970; Redmore, Loevinger, and Tamashiro, 1978; Loevinger, 1979). She defined "ego" as that aspect of personality that establishes a basic unity by constructing the meanings that one gives to oneself, other people, and the surrounding world. By bringing together and reinterpreting the work of many other theorists and researchers, she outlined a series of stages of sequential development in this broad construction of meanings. Salient themes running through the stages concern impulse control and character development, interpersonal orientations, conscious preoccupations, and cognitive style.

More relevant to my discussion here is Loevinger's method for assessing ego development. Her procedure for gathering data relied on the completion of 36 sentence stems. To construct the coding system, thousands of responses for each stem or item were grouped into categories, exclusively on the basis of their similarity in surface meaning. Moreover, the response categories, always within each item, were assigned to one of the stages and were then ordered according to the sequence of stages. The decision to consider a specific category as belonging to a certain stage was made according to two main criteria, its match with the theoretical description of the stage *and* the empirical probability that the particular response would be given by people who, on the basis of their whole set of responses, were independently judged to be at that stage. In sum, when one reads the categories assigned to one stage of ego development and compares them with those assigned to other stages, one can begin to relate ideas, concerns, attitudes, and expectations to each other and reconstruct a more or less coherent turn of mind or mentality.

In my own work (Blasi, 1983b, 1988), my colleagues and I selected 8 out of the 36 items as eliciting frequent responses relevant to the self as subject. Some of these items were "The thing I like about myself is . . . ," "When I get mad . . . ," "What gets me into trouble is . . . ," and "When I am criticized . . . ." For each item and for the eight items as a group, we analyzed the response categories assigned to the same stage together and reinterpreted them in search for patterns of self experience. The questions guiding this analysis were, What kind of statements are typically given by people classified at a specific stage? What kind of experiences of the self do these statements suggest? How do these people experience themselves as agents, as unified wholes, as differentiated from others, and in distancing from themselves in reflection? How do these experiences seem to differ from those of people classified at other stages of ego development?

The results of this analysis were descriptions of self experience, each corresponding to one of Loevinger's stages or transitional levels. The descriptions derived from the four most advanced stages of ego development seemed to be very relevant to the subjective experience of identity.[2] These identity modes are briefly summarized here:

Social-Role Identity. One's sense of self is constituted by external appearance, social and family relations, simple socially approved feelings and traits. Neither subjectivity nor a sense of agency is an important aspect of these characteristics. In contrast with later modes, no specific aspect of oneself is isolated to establish a core self, a sense of inner unity.

Identity Observed. One discovers an inner quasi-substance made up of immediately experienced feelings, intuitions, and beliefs. This inner self is contrasted with the external superficial self and is considered one's true self. This discovery is accompanied by increasing importance attached to self-reflection, self-feelings, and sincerity. In contrast with later modes, the inner true self is understood as a ready-made given, not as a result of one's effort and the object of one's responsibility.

Management of Identity. Ideals for the self, standards, values, a philosophy of life replace immediately felt inner feelings in the constitution of the true self. Identity no longer is a natural given but something that must be worked out in daily action. Agent characteristics—achieving one's ultimate goals, resolving one's problems, improving oneself—become important to one's sense of self.

Identity as Authenticity. One's true self is no longer defined by a clear sense of goals and ideals to be achieved. Dominant characteristics instead become the discovery of inner conflicts and dichotomies; the affirmation of one's autonomy, particularly with respect to cultural and social stereotypes; one's relation to universal humanity and worldwide concerns; openness to truth and objectivity in determining one's life and identity.

The first identity mode, labeled Social-Role Identity, does not include any of the main characteristics that make up Erikson's concept. This type of sense of self probably developmentally precedes, at least in our culture, the sort of identity associated with adolescence. The other three seem to indicate that genuine Eriksonian identity, regardless of its content, can be experienced in very different ways and that these modes of experience may be ordered according to a developmental sequence.

These modes not only have a certain degree of psychological coherence around a basic experience of the self but also appear to organize and illuminate the development of self-consciousness and self-reflectivity, the origin of a split between the inner and outer selves and of the importance of sincerity, and the development of autonomy and of personal commitment to one's ideals. And yet for several reasons I could not take the descriptions derived from Loevinger's stages as having more than heuristic value. In fact, the purpose and conceptual framework that guided Loevinger's collection of data have little to do with my interest in the subjective experience of identity. In addition, while each of the characteristics that define an identity mode seems to be present in large groups of people at the same stage of ego development, our secondary analysis could not determine to what extent the *cluster* of traits characterizes each individual. Finally, on the basis of what we presently know, it is impossible to determine the relations of the identity modes to chronological age. In sum, additional independent evidence seems to be needed to support the reality of these descriptive categories.

Empirical Replication of the Identity Modes

My colleagues and I conducted two studies to answer the following questions: Do the various psychological traits that make up the description of each identity mode in fact tend to form empirical clusters, to be present together in the same individuals? Do the individual traits of each identity mode and the clusters that they might form differentiate people of various age groups? Our first study focused on the distinction between the modes of Identity Observed and Social-Role Identity and compared with each other a group of 24 sixth graders and a group of 24 high school seniors. The second study focused on distinguishing the Management of Identity mode from the earlier modes and compared two groups of women, 15 high school seniors and 15 adults mostly in their thirties.

We followed similar strategy in both studies. We used the description of the identity mode that was the focus of the study as the starting point in constructing the interview schedule and in determining the dimensions for analyzing the interviews. That is, the various characteristics that define the identity mode, as derived from Loevinger's categories, determined both the main themes of the interview and also the main topics or dimensions of meaning for organizing subjects' responses. Our analysis and interpretation was done separately for each dimension and, as much as possible, independently of the other dimensions.

For each dimension, we constructed categories of responses following a double criterion: primarily, the similarity in meaning of subjects' answers; secondarily, the similarity between subjects' answers and the characteristics based on our interpretation of Loevinger's categories. We never used the ability to differentiate age groups as a guideline in defining the categories. Finally, we formed scales by arranging the response categories that belonged to the same dimensions in an order that seemed approximately developmental. In analyzing individual protocols, we considered and summarized the responses given on a single theme or dimension (e.g., the nature of the true self) together and compared them with the categories of the corresponding scaled dimension. The category that best matched a subject's responses and the placement of that category in the scale determined the subject's score for that dimension.

As a last step, we correlated the scores of all subjects for each dimension with their scores on the other dimensions. Moreover, by bringing together specific categories across several dimensions, we constructed global indices to model the identity modes derived from Loevinger. Finally, we statistically compared age groups on each of the dimensions or scales and on the global index (referred to below as the Global Index of Self Experience).

The Early Development of Identity

Our first study is more fully reported in Blasi and Milton, 1991. In it, we understood identity, whose early appearance we tried to capture, not simply as self-definition (obviously present long before adolescence) but minimally as the experience of an inner self on which one's special individuality is established. The Identity Observed mode seems to correspond to this early identity stage. According to its description, the central experience consists of the discovery of an inner psychological quasi-substance that is taken to be one's true or real self. Several characteristics seem to follow from this discovery: dramatization of the separation between the inner and the outer, attaching importance to self-reflection and self-observation, a special understanding of the personal meaning of sincerity and phoniness. In this mode, however, one seems to understand the inner psychological substance or real self as a natural, basically unchangeable given, constituted mostly by spontaneous feelings and perceptions, for which one is not responsible.

Based on these ideas, the interview explored the following topics: the distinction between an inner private self and an external public self and the extent to which the former is accessible to other people (*Private Self*); the identification and the understanding of aspects of oneself that are considered to be more central and true than the rest (*Real Me*); the frequency, personal importance, and object of self-reflection (*Self-Reflection*); the understanding and personal importance of sincerity and phoniness (*Sincerity*); the affective importance that one's central characteristics have for the person (*Emotional Response to Self*); finally, the extent to which one can or wishes to change oneself, particularly one's true self (*Self Change*).

To give a concrete example, we asked the following questions concerning the real me: "Sometimes people say: This is the real me, this is my true self. What do they mean? Are there certain parts of your self that are more true and more real? Can you give me some examples? Why would these parts be especially real? Who decides what is the real you and what is not? How does one go about deciding?"

Some of the questions concerning sincerity were these: "Sometimes we say of another person, He or she is phony or fake. What does it mean to be phony? Can you give me an example? Could you be a close friend of someone who you think is phony? Why or why not? Imagine that one day you look at yourself and you think, I have become a phony person. What would go through your mind then? Would that be important to you? Why?"

Largely corresponding to the topics of the interview schedule, six *self scales* were constructed. Each scale included a set of content categories arranged in an order that seemed approximately developmental. The scales are Real Me, Private Self, Self-reflection, Sincerity, Self-change, and Emotional Response to Personal Characteristics. The categories of each scale, reported in Blasi and Milton, 1991, will not be described here. Much of the information carried by them is summarized by the Global Index of Self Experience.

We constructed the Global Index by clustering specific response categories across the individual self scales. In bringing these categories together, our purpose was to model the identity mode descriptions derived from our secondary analysis of Loevinger's data. This summary comprises five categories. In category 1 the self seems to be experienced as diffused in one's body and actions. Being sincere means to tell the truth about these actions. No inner true self has been constructed, so one's personal characteristics do not elicit any special emotional response. This picture largely corresponds to Social-Role Identity. In category 3, self experience is dominated by the inner world, namely, feelings, opinions, and beliefs. These make up the true self because they are spontaneous and are unaffected by other people. One cares about the true self and is committed not to betray it by insincerity. However, broad values or ideals to strive for are not included in the experience of the real me, which as a result is seen as rather static and unchangeable. These characteristics are very similar to the description of Identity Observed. Category 5 includes ideas that suggest the *beginning* of the Management of Identity mode: values and personal philosophy of life are included in the true self and become objects of reflection; there is concern with improving oneself according to one's self ideals. Categories 2 and 4 are intermediate categories, combining aspects respectively of categories 1 and 3 and of categories 3 and 5.

The results of our statistical analyses (reported in detail in Blasi and Milton, 1991) are straightforward. First, each of the self scales produced markedly divergent category distributions for the two grades, which overlapped, unevenly, only on the median category of the scales. The differences were significant consistently at $p < .001$.

Second, the six self scales highly correlated with each other, the average correlation being .72. Obviously, the scales tap the same underlying dimension.

Finally, as is shown on Table 1, all protocols could be classified under one of the main or intermediate categories of the Global Index, which sharply differentiated the two grades ($p < .00003$). In other words, the identity modes derived from a reanalysis of ego development categories could be empirically replicated with a high degree of fidelity.

This study not only confirmed the descriptions with which we started but also provided us with a richer, more complex picture of the two early identity modes. In addition, it presented some surprises, and it forced us to revise several of our expectations. For instance, not all adolescents classified in the mode of Identity Observed sharply differentiated their inner and outer selves and felt jealously overprotective of their privacy, as Broughton (1978, 1981) has suggested. Some did, but others did not. Similarly, not all adolescents in the mode of Identity Observed seemed to give great importance to or assiduously practice self-reflection. Again, some do, but others do not. In sum, this identity mode is compatible with considerable individual variations in attitudes about privacy and

Table 1
Study 1: Age Differences on the Global Index of Self Experience

Age group	Global Index Categories				
	1	2	3	4	5
Grade 6 ($N = 24$)	16	7	1		
Grade 12 ($N = 24$)	1	12	6		5

Mann-Whitney U (uncorrected) = 10.5, $p < .00003$

self-reflection. Finally, a significant number of high schoolers expressed an attitude toward self-change that was not expected: they considered change in their true selves as practically impossible and any attempt on their part to produce it as artificial, insincere, and therefore to be condemned. This attitude, of course, fits well with the picture of identity as a natural given, based on spontaneous feelings. It also suggests the potential difficulties these adolescents may experience in a psychotherapeutic setting.

The Sense of Identity in Adulthood

The descriptions of the identity modes derived from Loevinger suggest that identity, at least its subjective perception, does not remain the same after it originates in middle adolescence. A second study (Glodis and Blasi, 1991) raised the question of later changes in identity by focusing on the Management of Identity mode and attempting to differentiate this mode from earlier ones. According to the description, the Management of Identity mode retains a sense of a true inner self, the main feature of Identity Observed. The crucial difference is that the true self is no longer based on the sum of spontaneous feelings and thoughts that one experiences but instead is built on those ideals and goals that one has for oneself. Several implications follow: ideals and goals begin to be used as principles of selection and organization; one's true self is no longer a conglomerate of spontaneous experiences and emotions more or less passively accepted; rather, one begins to see some unity to the self (beyond what is provided by the subject being the same) and a more active approach to its construction. In addition, ideals are not objects of observation, like feelings, but guidelines for action. So identity should be experienced as something that one can change and shape to some extent, something to which one is committed and for which one feels responsible.

The search for these characteristics guided how we conducted the interviews. The first three parts of the interview explored topics already covered in the previous study, namely, one's understanding of the inner/outer distinction and of the private self, the nature of one's true self, and one's understanding of and attitude toward sincerity and phoniness. These three topics, we thought, should help us establish some continuity with the data from the first study. Three additional parts explored issues that should be central to the Management of Identity mode: one part focused on whether and how one's true self changed, and asked whether and in what way one is responsible for one's true self; the next part probed the participant's understanding of self-betrayal and inquired about her evaluation of and feelings about it, should she betray herself; the last section raised the issue of commitment to those aspects and ideals that each subject had previously recognized as important to her sense of self.

The following are examples of the actual questions. The first set concerns change of and responsibility for one's true self: "Do you think you can change your real self? How? Can you think of a time when you might want to change your real you? Some people believe that they are responsible for the kind of person they are. If you said this, what would you mean by it? Are you responsible for your true self? Would you be responsible for not living up to it?"

The next set of questions concerns one's commitment to one's true self: "Are there issues that have more objective importance than those you chose as being very important to your sense of self? Does it matter to you that your choices are objectively not the most important? Is what you chose so important that you would always want, under any conditions, to feel the same way about your choices? If you were to somehow lose these strong feelings, how would this affect you?"

As in the first study, here too the interview material was analyzed along a number of dimensions, within each of which response categories were constructed and arranged in an order that seemed to us approximately developmental. Five scales were constructed: the Real Me, Sincerity, Responsibility for the Self, Self-betrayal, and Commitment to One's Identity. One of the dimensions, the Private

Self, was left out of this study, as it did not yield individual differences that seemed relevant to our purposes. Subjects' sense of an inner/outer distinction and the importance they attach to private selves seem to be well established, at least in our samples, by the end of high school. This is not to say that later developments may not also be found in this area. For instance, there were indications in our data that more mature people may have a sense of a dialectical relationship between their inner and outer selves. Our questions, however, were not designed to explore this idea. The information carried by the individual self scales is largely included in the Global Index of Self Experience, and so I do not report their categories here.

We constructed the six categories included in the Global Index using a method similar to that followed in the first study; namely, we clustered categories across the five self scales together to match the descriptions of the identity modes derived from Loevinger. In category 1 the true self is made up of those activities one tends or likes to do. To be phony or to betray oneself means to tamper with the spontaneity of these activities by adjusting them to social expectations and pressure. This is where choice and responsibility to oneself can be exercised. The importance of these activities depends on their relation to external consequences and goals. Therefore, one's affective attachment to them is rather limited; their loss is either expected or is considered without any significant emotional response. In category 3 the true self is established on the inner world of feelings and perceptions, spontaneously experienced; they determine which issues and personal characteristics are important to one, and not vice versa. These feelings cannot be chosen or controlled, but one is responsible for outwardly expressing them in behavior. Failing to do so is to be phony and to betray oneself. Even though a clear and strong emotional attachment is expressed for one's valued characteristics, their hypothetical loss is felt not as a total loss of identity but rather as a change in personality traits. This category largely corresponds to the third category of the Global Index in the earlier study and to the Identity Observed mode.

Category 5 is distinguished from category 3 mainly on the basis of two characteristics: one's true self acquires a certain degree of unity, being based on feelings and values that are deeper and more central; for the first time one actively approaches one's identity, not only by selecting what is more central but also by controlling and shaping some of one's feelings.

Both one's sense of unity of the true self and one's sense of responsibility increase and become the constitutive characteristics of category 6. Here the direction of one's entire life becomes a central part of one's identity, while one's active commitments both establish and manifest it. The loss of this type of identity is said to be unimaginable or to produce a total loss of self. At the same time there frequently is a certain degree of tolerance for minor and situational betrayals of oneself.

Finally, the Global Index included two intermediate categories: 2 and 4. Category 2 reflects characteristics of categories 1 and 3, and category 4 reflects those of categories 3 and 5.

Statistical analyses produced results similar in pattern to those reported in the previous section. First, the two age groups revealed very different concerns and attitudes, as assessed by each of the self scales. All of the differences were significant at $p \leq .001$.

Second, the five self scales were highly correlated with each other, with an average correlation of .75. Once more, these scales seem to reflect a common underlying dimension. Moreover, considering the overlap between the self scales of the two studies, it is possible to argue that our method captures a basic continuity in self experience. Finally, the categories of the Global Index seemed to capture the identity modes derived from Loevinger, to accommodate reasonably well the protocols of all our subjects, and to sharply differentiate the two age groups (Table 2). In this study, in contrast with the first, the whole range of categories was represented in the older group. This observation is not uncommon in developmental psychology, and it suggests that as people get older, they begin to differ from each other on whether, and at what pace, they develop. As a result, the mode of experiencing oneself that appeared in the interviews of some adults seemed to be very similar to the mode conveyed by adolescents, even those who scored at the lower end of the continuum.

Perhaps the most interesting and pregnant finding of this study is that, while middle adolescents have a clear sense of an individual inner self and relate to it with affective attachment and even care, only when one's sense of self is constructed around active commit-

Table 2
Study 2: Age Differences on the Global Index of Self Experience

Age Group	Global Index Categories					
	1	2	3	4	5	6
Grade 12 ($N = 15$)	6	5	4			
Adults ($N = 15$)	1	1	3	4	3	3

$F = 24.99$, $p < .0001$

ments and responsibility for those ideals and characteristics with which one identifies does identity acquire the permanence and continuity that Erikson saw as its trademark. At least in our sample, this development only appears among young adults.

Response to Self-Betrayal: A Validational Study

Blasi and Oresick (1986) argued that self-betrayal and the response it evokes in some people can only be understood from the perspective of identity. In other words, a person can experience the kind of thoughts and emotions that we associate with self-betrayal only in connection with issues that she identifies as essential to her sense of self.

They also argued that not any form of identity but only an agentic approach to it would give rise to an experience of self-betrayal. It is not enough to feel responsible for the specific act of self-betrayal; one has to feel responsible for one's very identity, for constructing as well as for expressing and maintaining it. This type of relation to one's identity is absent in those people who consider identity to be a natural given more or less passively received, something to be discovered and explored. In my terminology, the typical response to self-betrayal should be found among those classified in the Management of Identity mode but not among those classified in the earlier identity modes.

Some rather indirect evidence that this might be the case came from a study on the development of responsibility (Blasi, 1984). When sixth and eleventh graders were presented with a fictional decision that was inconsistent with an agent's moral beliefs, only a small minority of the older group, about 15 percent, perceived the decision as self-betrayal, understood self-betrayal as some kind of spiritual death, and voiced strong negative emotions. That is, the appropriate response to self-betrayal seemed to be largely absent at an age when some form of identity should have developed.

Here a rather simple strategy was followed (for a more detailed report, see Blasi and Glodis, 1990): each one of the participants (the same 30 women of the previous study) was asked to select an ideal that was very important for her sense of self, one that she cared deeply about and to which she was totally committed (this formula was borrowed almost verbatim from Frankfurt, 1987). Subjects' choices included friendship, caring for others, morality and justice, self-reliance, and improving one's mind and knowledge. Some time later (the interval varied between 6 and 10 weeks), each participant was presented with a story in which a fictional character chooses a course of action that is advantageous financially and careerwise but compromises her ideals. While the stories had the same basic structure, they varied from subject to subject by focusing on the ideal that the participant had previously chosen for herself. Each subject was instructed to make an effort and imagine herself in the same situation, with the decision already made, and then to report feelings and thoughts as she experienced them. A few probing questions were also asked.

We analyzed responses to the self-betrayal situation according to the following scales:

Positive Emotion: the presence or absence of excitement, pleasure about the decision, and a sense of security and purpose

Conflict: the presence or absence of ambivalence, stress, preoccupation, and pressure

Strong Negative Emotion: the presence or absence of extreme distress, shame, intense guilt, and loss of integrity

Reference to Ideal: the degree to which the participant uses the previously chosen ideal to discuss and oppose the decision (a 3-point scale)

Practical Reasons: the presence or absence of justifications based on one's interests and future advantages

Moral and Altruistic Reasons: the presence or absence of justifications based on people's rights or one's desire to help others

Self-Inconsistency: the degree to which one recognizes the decision as contradicting one's integrity and sense of self (a 3-point scale)

In addition, we interviewed all subjects on their experience of self and scored them on each of the self scales and the Global Index described in the previous section.

Our statistical analyses proceeded in two steps. First, the various responses to the concrete self-betrayal situation were correlated with each other. These responses formed two distinct, psychologically coherent patterns: Some people tended not to see the situation as relevant to their ideals; they focused instead on the pragmatic consequences of the decision and expressed feelings of satisfaction and relief. Others, by contrast, voiced neither positive feelings nor pragmatic concerns; they tended to see the decision as a serious contradiction of their ideals and expressed such feelings as shame, guilt, and depression.

In the second step, subjects' responses to the self-betrayal situation were related to their scores on the self scales. All the correlations were in the expected direction, many statistically significant. That is, the higher a person's scores on the self scales (i.e., the closer she was to the Management of Identity mode), the more likely she was to mention her personal ideals, to speak of self-contradiction and self-betrayal, and to express strong negative emotions about herself and the decision.

It would be nice to report that the Management of Identity mode (as reflected in categories 4, 5, and 6 of the Global Index of Self Experience) is a necessary prerequisite for the full experience of self-betrayal. Even though this study clearly supported a relationship between the two variables, there were exceptions to this rule, and the exceptions go in both directions. It is not clear at this point how they can be explained.

Identity and Moral Motivation

The studies presented here directly concern the development of identity and a sense of self. But our findings are also indirectly relevant to the psychology of morality, particularly to the question of how objective morality becomes integrated in one's personality, how it acquires personal value and subjective relevance.

In this respect, a clear conclusion can be derived from our study of adult identity: the two aspects that make up a concrete identity, namely the specific contents around which one's sense of self is constructed (moral ideals are one such content) and the modes in which identity is subjectively experienced, seem to be largely independent of each other, though not exactly orthogonal.

About two thirds of the 30 women that composed the sample of this study chose either caring and compassion or morality and justice as one of two ideals that they saw as centrally important to their sense of self. When the sample is divided into two subgroups according to whether what subjects said of themselves corresponded to the Management of Identity mode (categories 4, 5, or 6 of the Global Index) or to one of the lower modes, the frequency with which moral ideals were chosen as a core part of one's identity does not statistically differentiate these two groups. The proportion of those who made this choice was indeed higher in the higher-identity-mode group (80 percent versus 55 percent). But obviously one does not need to function in the Management of Identity mode to consider morality as central to the sense of self, and vice versa, one can develop a higher identity mode without constructing it around moral issues.

This conclusion may seem obvious to anybody who has some experience with the variety of human concerns, but it raises the question of how and whence a strong personal concern with morality begins. It is not a necessary byproduct of the development of the subjective experience of identity. Very likely (clear empirical evidence is still missing) it is not even a certain consequence of more sophisticated forms of understanding moral principles. It is possible, and not incompatible with a cognitive-developmental view, that the issues around which one constructs an identity depend on specific life experiences, including the exposure to the views, ideals, and life in general, of one's parents, teachers, and friends. It is also possible that the choice (if one can speak of choice) is made relatively early, even before one's sense of identity begins to appear, and that one's central concerns remain more or less constant for the rest of one's life. What can change, then, is a person's subjective relationship to the ideals that anchor his or her identity, the specific meaning that "importance" and "concern" have for the person.

A more probable hypothesis is that specific experiences interact with developmental variables to produce both the contents and the modes of identity. To experience something akin to the Management of Identity mode, a person must see her central concerns as ideals to be pursued. For instance, one's body or one's sexuality, as fundamental as they are for a person's sense of self, do not seem to provide an adequate basis for generating lifelong projects or for constructing higher identity modes. By contrast, morality seems to offer an ideal ground for anchoring the successive forms of experienced identity. In any event, these considerations are purely hypothetical. The general questions of the origin of people's central concerns and of their continuity and change through life are still basically unanswered and require very different methods from those used here.

The fact that only some people in our samples placed morality at the center of their identity cannot be interpreted to mean that morality was not personally important to the others. Just the opposite conclusion seems to be supported by our findings, even though we undertook no precise analyses on this point. Morality appeared to be an important concern also to many of those who construct their identity around nonmoral ideals. In fact, it seems to be personally important to many of the sixth graders who had not yet developed a subjective sense of identity. The implication is that there must be other ways for morality to be important to people besides being important to one's identity. One way frequently mentioned by our interviewees has to do with the effect that moral behavior may have on one's social life, for instance, on others perception of, acceptance of, and friendly feelings toward the person. Another way, of course, concerns the objective consequences of moral or immoral behavior for other people.

On the basis of these considerations, one could argue that moral identity is not a more secure predictor of moral action than other forms of moral motivation. It is neither conceptually obvious nor empirically evident that the various reasons for morality to be important to a person have different relations to moral motivation and moral action, at least in the large majority of morally relevant situations. One exception would be the case when acting on one's moral beliefs is very difficult and requires subordinating all other motives, powerful as they may be. As Frankfurt (1987 and this volume) argues, centering one's identity around moral or other concerns produces a "volitional necessity" that renders certain actions "impossible" or "unthinkable" for the person. Several of our subjects, particularly those who seemed to experience themselves according to higher identity modes, appeared to look at self-betrayal in precisely these terms. Even so, it would certainly be too confining, for both morality and psychology, to measure the importance of moral identity in terms of moral behavior.

One final point is conceptual and relates to the nature of moral motivation. Some may think that if actions are motivated by a desire to protect one's sense of self and to support one's self-esteem, this detracts from the purity of moral motivation, even when the identity being protected is centered around moral issues. One could also tie this view to Kant's (1941) conception of a genuine moral motive (but, in my opinion, only through too narrow a reading of his work).

Be that as it may, it is important to distinguish the position presented here from the very different position exemplified by Wolf's discussion (this volume) of the role of ideals for the self. From his perspective, people acquire moral ideals and values, like all ideals and values, not because they understand the world and themselves in relation to it and therefore appreciate the objective importance of certain ideals but rather for the function that ideals and values exercise in sustaining one's sense of personal well-being (what Wolf calls narcissism). This view seems indeed to "functionalize" values, in Odier's (1947) sense of the term. What matters is the effect that one's values produce on one's sense of power, self-esteem, and psychological integration, not the specific nature of the values themselves. Instead, my understanding, and the understanding shared by our subjects, is that moral and other ideals are chosen as the core of one's identity, because they are understood to be objectively important. To some extent personality is shaped by what one knows to be worthy of dedication and commitment.

Concluding Remarks

Throughout its history, psychology's involvement with morality was consistently guided by one aim, the ability to predict moral behavior. Piaget's and Kohlberg's cognitive-developmental premises, as influential and important as they have been, can be seen as a parenthesis in psychology's pervasive interest in such prediction, accepted in part because it coincided with the general cognitive turn in the discipline. Even so, the most insistent critical question about the stages of moral understanding has been, Yes, but how do these stages relate to moral action?

The issue of whether there is a moral personality and of what it might be like was raised quite early and abandoned soon afterwards, mainly as a result of the disappointing findings of Hartshorne and May (1928–1930). But here too personality was defined in behavioral terms as people's consistently performing "moral" or "immoral" behaviors, morality being understood according to conventional and external categories.

The studies presented here concretely exemplify a different concept of moral personality and a different strategy for assessing it: the basic criterion becomes whether and to what extent a person constructs his or her sense of self around moral concerns. It seems clear that people vary in this respect. They also seem to vary on a different dimension, concerning the kind of relationship one has with one's identity and the way one experiences it. I described three such modes and related them to concrete expressions that people use in speaking about themselves.

It is not clear how these identity modes would help us to predict behavior. But it may be a mistake for psychology to focus on action as the final and incontrovertible criterion both of adequate moral functioning and of a satisfactory psychological explanation. Equally important are the different ways in which moral beliefs are integrated in personality. Of course, genuine moral integration will be expressed in action, but not necessarily in every single action that has moral implications. A more valid test may be how one conducts one's life in the long run. From this perspective, a person can be deeply moral even if he or she engages in actions that are morally ambiguous or outright immoral; in this case, the integration of morality in personality could be seen in one's response to one's own action, e.g., regret, guilt, and concrete attempts to repair the damage and reconstitute one's values.

There is no denying that psychologists would have difficulty in gathering reliable data, for instance, in distinguishing between genuinely moral responses and hypocritical answers or self-deceiving reassurances. But this kind of complexity and ambiguity is an intrinsic characteristic of what we are studying and cannot be exorcised by simpleminded, though straightforward, strategies.

Notes

1. One must be careful not to confuse Erikson's theory with any of the various cognitive-developmental theories. In spite of his emphasis on the ego and on social-cultural adaptation, Erikson remained a psychoanalyst, that is, skeptical about the possibility of establishing ideals through knowledge, independently of the affective demands of the psyche.

2. The precise stages of ego development on which the identity modes were based are, respectively, stage I-3 or Conformist; stage I-3/4 or Conscientious-Conformist; stage I-4 or Conscientious; and finally the combined stages I-4/5, I-5, and I-6, or Individualistic, Autonomous, and Integrated.

References

Blasi, A. (1980). Bridging moral cognition and moral action: A critical review of the literature. *Psychological Bulletin*, 88:1–45.

Blasi, A. (1983a). Moral cognition and moral action: A theoretical perspective. *Developmental Review*, 3:178–210.

Blasi, A. (1983b). The self as subject: Its dimensions and development. Unpublished manuscript, University of Massachusetts, Boston.

Blasi, A. (1984). Autonomie im Gehörsam: Die Entwicklung des Distanzierungsvermögens im sozialisierten Handeln (Autonomy in obedience: The development of distancing in socialized action). In W. Edelstein and J. Habermas (Eds.), *Soziale Interaktion und Soziales Verstehen*. Frankfurt am Main: Suhrkamp Verlag.

Blasi, A. (1988). Identity and the development of the self. In D. K. Lapsley and F. C. Power (Eds.), *Self, ego, and identity: Integrative approaches*. New York: Springer Verlag.

Blasi, A. (1991). The self as subject in the study of personality. In D. J. Ozer, J. M. Healy, Jr., and A. J. Stewart (Eds.), Perspectives in personality. Vol. 3, *Self and emotion*. London: Kingsley.

Blasi, A., and Glodis, K. (1990). Response to self-betrayal and the development of the sense of self. Unpublished manuscript, University of Massachusetts, Boston.

Blasi, A., and Milton, K. (1991). The development of the sense of self in adolescence. *Journal of Personality*, 59:217–241.

Blasi, A., and Oresick, R. J. (1986). Emotions and cognition in self-inconsistency.

In D. Bearison and H. Zimiles (Eds.), *Thought and emotion*. Hillsdale, NJ: Erlbaum.

Broughton, J. (1978). Development of concepts of self, mind, reality, and knowledge. *New Directions for Child Development*, 1:75–100.

Broughton, J. (1981). The divided self in adolescence. *Human Development*, 24:13–32.

Erikson, E. H. (1968). *Identity, youth, and crisis*. New York: Norton.

Frankfurt, H. (1987). Identification and wholeheartedness. In F. Schoeman (Ed.), *Responsibility, character, and the emotions: New essays in moral psychology*. New York: Cambridge University Press.

Glodis, K., and Blasi, A. (1991). The sense of self and identity among adolescents and adults. Unpublished manuscript, University of Massachusetts, Boston.

Hartshorne, H., and May, M. A. (1928–1930). *Studies in the nature of character*. Vol. 1, *Studies in deceit*. Vol. 2, *Studies in service and self-control*. Vol. 3, *Studies in organization of character*. New York: Macmillan.

Kant, I. (1941). *Critique of practical reason*. Trans. L. W. Beck. Chicago: University of Chicago Press. Originally published in 1788.

Loevinger, J. (1976). *Ego development: Conceptions and theories*. San Francisco: Jossey-Bass.

Loevinger, J. (1979). Theory and data in the measurement of ego development. In J. Loevinger, *Scientific ways in the study ego development*. Worcester, MA: Clark University Press.

Loevinger, J., Wessler, R., and Redmore, C. (1970). *Measuring ego development*. Vol. 2, *Scoring manual for women and girls*. San Francisco: Jossey-Bass.

Odier, C. (1947). *Les deux sources, consciente et inconsciente, de la vie morale*. Neuchatel, Switzerland: Éditions de la Baconnière.

Redmore, C., Loevinger, J., and Tamashiro, R. T. (1978). Measuring ego development: Scoring manual for men and boys. Unpublished manuscript, Washington University, St. Louis.

Morality and Personal Autonomy

Larry Nucci and John Lee

I do not like broccoli. And I haven't liked it since I was a little kid and my mother made me eat it. I'm president of the United States, and I'm not going to eat any more broccoli.
George Bush, April 1990

Autonomy . . . appears only with reciprocity, when mutual respect is strong enough to make the individual feel from within the desire to treat others as he himself would wish to be treated.
Jean Piaget, *The Moral Judgment of the Child*

Morality and personal autonomy have been inextricably linked in cognitive-developmental accounts of moral development. For both Piaget (1932) and Kohlberg (1969, 1976), individuals develop morally as they progressively replace convention and authority as bases for making moral decisions by constructing autonomously derived principles of justice. For Piaget (1932), this is an explicitly emancipatory activity, involving not only a set of cognitive transformations but also a shift in social relations from one of unilateral respect for authority to a social perspective based on mutual respect and reciprocity. In Piaget's theory, then, morality is autonomous not simply by virtue of its intellectual independence from social convention: it entails actual social autonomy in that it regulates the interactions of individuals with rights and personal freedoms. Similarly, in his depiction of moral development, Kohlberg (1969, 1976) assumes not only that morality requires an intellectual basis apart from convention but also that applying moral reasoning as principles of justice has meaning only in relation to a conception of persons as having rights.

Despite the importance attached to personal autonomy in these accounts of moral development, relatively little attention has been paid to children's conceptions of personal freedom per se. In this chapter we present recent research and theory on the development of children's concepts of areas of behavior they consider to be within their personal discretion, or what we have termed their personal domain (Nucci, 1977).[1] On the basis of this research we offer an account of children's emerging conceptions of personal rights. From this vantage point we reconsider the relations between children's personal autonomy and their capacity for interpersonal moral reasoning and action. Our discussion is admittedly speculative, since we have but an incomplete data base, particularly with regard to the latter set of issues.

The Domain Model of Social Development: General Issues of Theory

The general theoretical context for our discussion is what has been termed the domain approach to social cognitive development (Turiel and Davidson, 1986; Turiel, Killen, and Helwig, 1987). The domain model of social development posits that children construct social concepts within discrete conceptual and developmental systems that they in turn construct out of qualitatively differing aspects of their social interactions (Turiel, 1978). These domains correspond to what Piaget (1985) refers to as partial systems or subsystems with respect to the mind as a totality. Each partial system forms an internally equilibrated structure that in certain contexts may interact with other systems requiring interdomain equilibration or coordination. What distinguishes the domain model from prior structuralist accounts of moral and social development is the attempt to identify social-conceptual systems *independently* of their interdomain coordinations.

To date, three domains of social knowledge have been identified: moral (concepts of justice, welfare/harm, and rights), societal (concepts of social organization and social systems), and psychological (concepts of such intrapsychic processes as emotions, motivations, and intentions and psychological constructs such as the self, which are used to account for the actions of psychological beings). The primary focus of domain research has been on development within the moral and societal domains. In findings that bear directly on our discussion, research has shown that morality is conceptually independent of societal convention. More central to our present concerns, however, is the emerging body of work that investigates children's concepts of areas of personal prerogative. That research indicates that children's concepts of their areas of personal discretion are structured by underlying conceptualizations within the psychological domain. That is, children's conceptions of behavioral autonomy are tied to underlying notions of selfhood and personal identity. We will examine that research and its implications for reasoning in the moral domain after a brief review of research on the distinction between morality and social convention.

Morality, convention, and autonomous morality

One aspect of the societal domain is the child's concepts of social custom and convention. Social conventions—such as modes of dress, forms of address, sex roles, manners, and aspects of sexual mores—are the arbitrary and agreed-upon uniformities in social behavior determined by the social system in which they are formed. Through accepted usage, these standards serve to coordinate the interactions of individuals within social systems by providing them with a set of expectations about appropriate behavior. In turn, the matrix of social conventions and customs serves as one element that structures and maintains the general social order. Thus, the child's judgments about social convention are structured by underlying conceptions of social organization.

The domain model distinguishes convention from morality, which refers to concepts of interpersonal behavior entailing matters of justice and human welfare (Turiel, 1983). In contrast with conventions, moral considerations are not arbitrary but stem from factors intrinsic to actions (i.e., consequences such as harm to others). Although moral prescriptions (e.g., it is wrong to hurt others) are an aspect of social organization, they are determined by factors inherent in social relationships, as opposed to a particular form of social or religious structure (Nucci, 1985; Turiel, 1983;

Turiel, Nucci, and Smetana, 1988). Thus, while the child's concepts of convention are structured by underlying notions of social organization, the child's concepts of morality are structured by underlying conceptions of justice (Turiel, 1983).

The claim that morality and convention are discrete developmental systems poses a direct challenge to the view of Piaget and Kohlberg that it is only at the higher stages of moral development that morality (justice) is differentiated from and displaces convention as the basis for moral judgments. There are now, however, over 50 published accounts reporting research demonstrating that morality and convention are differentiated at very early ages and follow distinct developmental patterns. (Thorough reviews of that research may be found in Turiel, Killen, and Helwig, 1987, and Helwig, Tisak, and Turiel, 1990.) Thus, we conclude that children's construction of morality in the form of concepts of justice does not pass through a phase of heteronomy.[2]

What, then, are we to make of Piaget's position on this issue? Our interpretation, which we take up now, concerns the second, social aspect of autonomy. Our hypothesis is that autonomy in the interpersonal sense is integral to the formation of a mature moral system. Personal autonomy, however, is only indirectly related to morality. Its impact on moral reasoning and action is mediated through conceptions of personal rights. Whereas morality concerns itself with *adjudicating* rights among persons, the conceptual and psychological source of individual claims to rights lies elsewhere. That is, while moral structures of reciprocity require that rights and protections granted oneself be extended to others, moral conceptions of justice and beneficence do not in and of themselves provide us with the means to identify personal rights and freedoms. Such issues instead form a conceptual framework within the psychological domain, which Nucci (1977, 1981) has termed the *personal*.

The Personal

The personal refers to the set of actions that the individual considers to fall outside the area of justifiable social regulation. These actions make up the private aspects of one's life; they are subject not to considerations of right and wrong, but to preferences and choice.[3] Examples of personal issues within North American culture include the content of one's correspondence and creative works, one's recreational activities, one's choice of friends, and actions that focus on the state of one's own body (Nucci, 1981; Nucci and Herman, 1982; Smetana, Bridgeman, and Turiel, 1983). By their very nature, personal issues are a circumscribed set of actions that define the bounds of individual authority. In other words, they constitute rights, in the sense of freedoms to which one is entitled.

Characterizing a set of actions as personal implicitly carries with it the view that the actor is an agent possessing a degree of social autonomy and individuality. Psychological theorists of diverse perspectives have long understood the relationship between personal autonomy and individuation (Baldwin, 1897, 1906; Damon and Hart, 1988; Erikson, 1963, 1968; Kohut, 1978; Mahler, 1979; Selman, 1980). What we are now coming to realize is that children's psychological theories include an emerging understanding of the relationship between individuation and selfhood. As Damon and Hart (1988) emphasize in their review of research on children's self-concepts, children from very young ages define the self in terms of uniqueness. William James (1899) spoke of awareness of the "I," the aspect of the self that organizes and interprets experience as reflective awareness of one's agency, continuity, and distinctness. In research on the development of children's conceptions of personal issues, we have found that the child's concepts of personal issues are structured by underlying conceptions of self and psychological integrity. In particular, personal concepts are understandings of what is required for one to maintain the Jamesian "I."

Our linking concepts of personal issues with rights claims agrees with philosophical perspectives that ground the notion of rights in the establishment and maintenance of personal agency (Dworkin, 1977; Gewirth, 1978, 1982). For example, Gewirth argues that "agents value their freedom or voluntariness as a necessary good as long as the possibility remains of purposive action—that is, of action that is able to fulfill and maintain at least those purposes required for the continuation of agency" (1978, p. 53). And a few pages later he adds: "Since the agent regards as necessary goods the freedom and well-being that constitute the generic features of his successful action, he logically must also hold that he has rights to these generic features, and he implicitly makes a corresponding rights-claim" (p. 63).

Personal concepts form the aspect of the psychological domain that identifies freedom as a necessary good for maintaining agency and uniqueness. The content of the personal domain is the content of the individual's identified freedoms. Through interpersonal interaction people negotiate and coordinate individual claims to freedom of action to form rights. The concept of rights transforms these necessary personal freedoms into mutually shared moral obligations. What we are arguing is not that specific rights will be universal but that the source of rights claims—the psychological need for agency and uniqueness—is and transcends culture. Thus we agree in part with social theorists like Shweder who argue that cultural variation in morality stems largely from the social construction of boundaries that constrain or attempt to collectively define the personal (see Shweder, Mahapatra, and Miller, 1987).

Age-related changes in concepts of personal issues

As we noted earlier, children, perhaps even infants, express a need for control over a personal sphere of action (Mahler, 1979). These early inchoate strivings for individuation, we claim, form part of an emerging developmental and conceptual framework that enables the child to function as an agent in a social world. We now turn to a discussion of developmental changes in concepts of the personal.

We elicited changes in children's and adolescents' concepts of personal issues through semistructured interviews in which actions, previously identified by the subject as personal, were depicted in hypothetical scenarios as in conflict with social norms or authority. The focus of our interview questions was on why the acts should be considered personal matters and why it is important that the actors portrayed in the scenarios be able to govern the actions. Our analyses of subjects' responses revealed five levels of understanding about personal issues. These levels show that individuals' understanding of personal matters is related to their underlying conceptions of self and the person. At each level subjects focus on the importance that control over personal matters has for establishing and maintaining the self and personal autonomy. A synopsis of

Table 1

Description of Major Changes in Conceptions of Personal Issues

1. *Establishing concrete self/other distinctions.* The individual conceptualizes the personal domain as an observable body and an equally concrete realm of things and activities. The individual sees control over personal affairs as extending and enforcing one's sense of uniqueness, self-mastery, and personal identity by establishing observable difference between the self and others and by differentiating what is "mine" from what is "yours."

2. *Establishing a behavior style and concern about group opinion.* The individual extends the conception of the person to include the notion of personality, defined as a set of characteristic behaviors. The view of the group as mere "other" shifts to a view of the group as evaluator and comparer of individual personal qualities. Control over personal actions is seen as establishing a behavior style or personality while protecting the self from negative public labels.

3. *Establishing the self as an individual defined in terms of a unique set of ideas or values.* The individual begins to define the self in terms of internal cognitive processes. Control over personal matters is conceived as establishing oneself as an individual. Loss of control over the personal domain of actions is viewed as risking absorption by the group: to change one's ideas and values is seen as giving up one's distinguishing psychological features.

4. *Coordinating the self system.* The individual views control over events within the personal domain as essential to coordinating all aspects of the self into an internally consistent whole. Consciousness is understood as having depth. At the center of consciousness the individual has an immutable essence around which the self system is constructed. Control over the personal is seen as a means of coordinating one's actions with this essence and as a mechanism for probing aspects of the personal system.

5. *Transforming the labile self.* Instead of viewing the self as an essence the individual comes to view the self as labile, as a constantly evolving product of one's personal decisions. The individual sees control over actions within the personal domain as essential if decisions serving to create oneself are to follow the individual's subjectively valued course.

these five levels is presented in Table 1. (A more extensive description of these levels, with more detailed examples of subjects' responses, may be found in Nucci, 1977.)

As can be seen in the table, reasoning about personal issues closely follows the pattern of structural changes in individuals' conceptions of the self as reported in other research (Broughton, 1978; Damon and Hart, 1988; Selman, 1980). At level 1, thinking about personal issues is structured by concerns for establishing concrete distinctions between the self and others. Individuals here view all aspects of the personal, including such intangibles as privacy, in concrete terms of possession, access, and control. The personal domain is both an observable body and an equally concrete realm of things and activities which belong to, and are thus within the domain of, the person. In turn, one maintains personal identity by exercising control over what is one's own ("mine"). This reasoning is illustrated in the responses of a seven-year-old who rejected the notion that the local authorities should govern after-school play activities:

Question: Why shouldn't they have the rule about the recreation group?
Answer: Because they're forcing all the kids to go there. I like to do what I want to do, and not what other people tell me.
Question: Why do you think that is?
Answer: Because it's my life, and it makes me feel that I'm taking care of myself, and they're taking care of themselves.
Question: Is that important?
Answer: Yeah. Then you know who you are.

The concern for self in level 1 is distinct from a selfish lack of concern for others. Instead, it reflects a concrete understanding of control over personal affairs as a means of individuation. At level 2, the self/other distinction becomes elaborated such that the child's stylistic characteristics or "personality" evidenced in the person's typical behaviors, and relative competence become integrated into the conception of self. Within this emerging psychology, the individual sees the social group not only as distinct from the self but also as the contextual basis for qualitatively defining self (Ruble, Boggiano, Feldman, and Loebel, 1980; Selman, 1980). The self is not simply what you do but also how well you do it relative to others (Nicholls and Miller, 1984). When the child takes to heart this emphasis upon qualitative distinctions among people and understands that differences are assigned social value, he or she develops a concern for protection against negative social judgments and a desire for freedom to engage in activities important for developing a unique configuration of areas of competence. The child's search for uniqueness coupled with an awareness of audience lends new urgency at level 2 for a right to privacy as a means to avoid embarrassment.

At the third level, in early adolescence, these notions of personal control and privacy become consciously linked to one's internal, ideational structure rather than simply to one's behaviors or physical attributes. By exercising control in the personal sphere, the individual establishes and maintains a distinct set of opinions, preferences, and values that make one's self unique. Yet the individual still reactively defines this shift away from behaviors to ideas in terms of the referent group. From the perspective of level 3, loss of control over the personal domain contains the risk of absorption by the group; the individual fears that a change in his or her personal views will eventually eliminate all distinguishing psychological characteristics. The following excerpt from a 13-year-old subject's responses provides an illustrative example.

Question: Should Dana [the main character] follow the county law and join one of the recreation activities?
Answer: She should continue doing what she wants to do after school.
Question: Why is that?
Answer: She isn't hurting anyone, and besides, you shouldn't be organized totally. A person should have a choice of options.
Question: Why does a person need options?
Answer: Well, because people are individuals; not everyone likes the same thing as other people. To be an individual means to be yourself, to be not like everyone else, to be different, to have your own ideas and opinions about things and not just to go along with the crowd.
Question: How is this related to doing what you want after school?
Answer: It is an individual thing. A personal thing. You should be able to do what you want to do yourself, not what everyone else does. Otherwise, pretty soon you don't have a mind of your own. You are just what everyone else is. You aren't yourself.

The most salient feature of thought at level 3 is that the individual interprets events within the personal domain as expressing or maintaining self/group distinctions in terms of his or her own ideas or values. However, at this level one has but a superficial view of consciousness. Individualism at level 3 is more reactive than subjective; it depends on the contrast between one's own personal thoughts and those of others rather than being an in-depth probe of self per se. This reactive aspect comes through in the young adolescent's fervent concern with group absorption and the need to protect one's freedoms within the personal domain.

At level 4 the individual views freedom within the personal domain as essential to coordinating the self system, coming to know the real self, and the realizing of one's potential. Unlike level 3, this form of reasoning does not define concerns for personal autonomy in terms of contrasts with the group but instead features an understanding of consciousness as having depth. As described by Broughton (1978), adolescents at this level view consciousness as the center around which to construct the self system. Thus at level 4, adolescents view their decision making within the personal sphere as a means of coordinating their actions with their true selves and as a mechanism for probing and coming to know various aspects of their personal systems. The following responses serve as illustrations. The first excerpt is from an interview with a 19-year-old subject about a scenario in which a boy defies school policy by growing his hair long.

Question: Do you think he should keep his hair the way it is or do you think he should get a haircut?
Answer: He should leave it the way it is.
Question: Why?
Answer: That's the way he thinks and the way he acts and the way he wants to be and the way he wants others to see him and the way he sees himself. It seems like you should be able to be a whole person and have your outside look like your inside. And people can't determine what your inside looks like. The only person who can decide is you. So it seems like those should go together, and that would be why people should determine their own appearance.

The following excerpt is from an interview with a 16-year-old subject about a scenario in which club members are asked to share the content of their correspondence.

Question: Should Jonathan [the main character] follow the club rules and let them read his mail, or should he keep them to himself?
Answer: Well, if that's the club rule, he might have to. But if I were him, I wouldn't do it.
Question: Why not?
Answer: Well, it's carrying a group, a club, beyond the limits it needs in order to stay as a group. It's just a desire to overstep and go into personal things.
Question: Is it important to maintain the letters and phone calls private?
Answer: Yes. It's an invasion of you, you as a person. You are losing a component of yourself. It's tearing away at that.
Question: Why would a person want to keep things in a letter private if they aren't embarrassing or incriminating?
Answer: It just has its own importance. It's even one step further than being able to grow your hair the way you want. I guess your thoughts are as close to being able to describe the self that is possible. And then your physical freedoms, how long you grow your hair, just sort of build up yourself. They help contribute on the outside to the core of your thoughts and personal ideas.

At level 5 the personal system becomes truly subjective. The notion of the self as something that can be encapsulated and described has been replaced by conceptions of the self as a multifaceted evolving product of one's decisions within the personal domain. As one 20-year-old put it:

I don't think you ever have a true self, really. It's just something you are always positing in front of yourself. You make yourself as you go along by choosing to do those things that are coherent with what you think you are at the time or want to become.

When this thought is expressed in terms of control over one's personal activities, it takes the form of the following excerpt from the protocol of a 19-year-old subject.

Question: Should she follow the county rule and join the recreation group, or continue what she is doing?
Answer: She should do what she wants to do. That should be her time. Everybody needs some things, some activities, that are just their own for themselves. I think [by] being able to do what you want, then you in some sense create what you are, instead of having others create it for you.

Social interaction and the personal domain

Our analysis thus far has provided evidence that children treat a class of actions as personal. In some of our current work we are finding that children as young as three years of age can make conceptual distinctions among personal issues and issues of convention or interpersonal morality (Nucci and Weber, 1991). At this point we turn briefly to consider the social experiential origins of concepts of personal issues. By their very nature, personal issues lie at the border between individual and society. While it is now generally acknowledged that the self is socially constructed (Damon and Hart, 1988), it is less clear that self is societally determined. In contrast with some social constructivists (Shweder and Bourne, 1984), we view the child's establishment of personal borders as entailing a process of negotiation with society and its agents, rather than as mere reconstruction at an individual level of tacit and overt social messages that define the parameters of the personal. Cross-cultural work conducted from several perspectives is needed to shed light on this issue. At this time we can only report some preliminary findings on the pattern of parent-child interactions in the U.S. middle class.

In an ongoing study (Nucci and Weber, 1991) we are examining the at-home interactions of 20 mother-child dyads with children between the ages of 3 and 5. The parenting styles of the mothers fall within what Baumrind describes as authoritative parenting. The mothers have a set of firmly established behavioral expectations but are flexible in disciplining. Each family is observed during three activity periods throughout the day for three days. In addition, mothers tape-record interactions with their children during bath and at bedtime.

Trained scorers classify transcribed interaction sequences as personal, conventional, moral, or mixed. These interaction sequences are then coded for behavioral patterns. Preliminary analysis of these sequences has revealed distinct patterns of interaction for moral, conventional, and personal events. As Smetana (1989a) has reported, interactions in the moral sequences focus on the intrinsic effects of acts. Mothers convey to children that the act caused harm or injustice. For example, in one observed sequence an older child attempted to move a younger sibling by picking him up. The younger child responded by scratching his older sibling, to which the mother responded, "No scratching! That hurts!" Interactions in conventional sequences, in contrast, focus on the social order. Mothers respond by ordering, stating rules, indicating that an act is disrupting, or conveying contextual information (the act is appropriate in one social context and inappropriate in another). This is illustrated in the following example, in which a mother speaks to children who are becoming disorderly at the dinner table.

Okay, let's just lower the noise level. [The children continue.] Too loud, please. [The children continue.] JP, I asked you, please. You can be loud out there, but not here. [Children begin to eat quietly.]

In contrast with both moral and conventional sequences, where the mother expected and got compliance, personal sequences conveyed a different tone. Such sequences took two forms. In one form the mother conveyed a clear social message that the child was free to perform or not perform the act in question, as illustrated in the following exchange:

Mother: You need to decide what you want to wear for school today.
Child: [Opens a drawer.] Pants. Pants. Pants.
Mother: Have you decided what to wear today?
Child: I wear these.
Mother: Okay, that's a good choice.
Mother: How would you like your hair today?
Child: Down. [Child stands by the bed, and her mother carefully combs her hair.]

The interaction in the preceding example nicely corresponds to what Shweder, Mahapatra, and Miller (1987) call tacit communication. The mother conveys the idea that dress is a personal choice. The child might accordingly infer that such behavior is personal. In effect, this mother conveys the cultural norm that dress may be individualized. While we recognize such cultural messages, we hesitate to conclude that the child merely recapitulates society.

The second common pattern of interaction in personal sequences is resistance from the child and subsequent negotiation and compromise with the adult.

Mother: Evan, it's your last day of nursery school. Why don't you wear your nursery sweatshirt?
Child: I don't want to wear that one.
Mother: This is the last day of nursery school, that's why we wear it. You want to wear that one?
Child: Another one.
Mother: Are you going to get it or should I?
Child: I will. First I got to get a shirt.
Mother: [Goes to the child's drawer and starts picking out shirts.] This one? This one? Do you know which one you have in mind? You have to decide, because we have to do car pool. Here, this is a new one.
Child: No, it's too big.
Mother: Oh Evan, just wear one, and when we get home, you can pick whatever you want, and I won't even help you. [Child puts on a shirt.]

In this case we see a conflict between a dress convention (wearing a particular shirt on the last day of school) and the child's view that dress is a personal choice. The mother in the scene attempts to negotiate, finally offering the child a free choice once school is over. Discussions of this kind tended to involve issues such as dress or recreation where the child's interpretation of an act as personal conflicted with the adult's view of the same act as conventional or prudent or practical. The types of conflicts we witnessed were similar in many respects to issues identified by adolescent subjects as sources of conflict between themselves and their parents (Smetana, 1989b). What is important here is that to establish a personal domain of action a child must actively challenge authority and assert a claim to freedom of action within the personal sphere. Such claims, if valid, place moral restrictions on others to respect such actions as rights. Conversely, such rights claims place moral obligations on the person to respect the same claim when made by others. It is according to this formulation that we may read Piaget's statements on morality and autonomy. We may now return to consider the relation between the personal and moral domains.

Morality and Personal Autonomy in Context

Our analysis has stemmed from our recognition that the individual's social understandings are constructed within partial systems. These domains, as Turiel (Turiel and Davidson, 1986) refers to them, are dynamic, interactive systems of psychological equilibration (Piaget,

1985), and not static information-processing templates. Thus, changes in one system may have ramifications for the way in which issues are dealt with or understood within other conceptual frameworks. Our arguments concerning the relations between personal autonomy and morality are based on assumptions about the ways in which systems of social understanding may interact and influence one another in the course of individual development. We now take up a more detailed analysis of this proposal by examining the basic forms of interdomain interaction that we hypothesize result from attempts to coordinate conceptions of personal issues with concepts of societal and moral regulation. While we present the hypothesized domain interactions in dyads, we view these dyadic interactions as impinging on one another as well as potentially interacting with other conceptual systems (e.g., one's metaphysical conceptual scheme).

Personal × moral: Issues of personal freedom in relation to interpersonal rights and moral obligations

As we stated earlier, an individual's conceptions within the personal domain focus on the psychological function of personal freedom for establishing uniqueness and maintaining a sense of agency, both of which are essential to a sense of self and personal identity. We have also argued that this conceptual framework provides the underpinnings for the individual's conceptions of human rights by identifying freedom as a necessary good. This is not to say, however, that a claim to personal liberty in and of itself constitutes a moral conceptualization of rights. The function of such personal concepts in relation to morality is to provide the basic datum (i.e., the psychological necessity of a personal sphere) requisite to extend the moral conceptions of justice and beneficence to include a moral conception of rights. Thus, while we would not expect a tight structural or sequential relationship to exist between these two conceptual systems, we do assume that developmental changes in personal concepts influence structural changes in moral understanding and, as a corollary, that disruptions in an individual's formation of personal concepts, which might occur through suppression of personal choice or a pathological absence of social constraints necessary for the establishment of personal boundaries, would have important consequences for the course of one's moral development.

As has been repeatedly demonstrated, very young children display concepts of morality differentiated in terms of objective, universalistic, and categorical criteria. These early childhood expressions of morality are best thought of, however, as a set of intuitive understandings or inferences drawn from social interactions involving moral acts rather than as fully elaborated formal conceptualizations or structures of moral judgment (Shweder, Turiel, and Much, 1981). According to domain theory, moral development involves transformations in the elements (content) and regulations pertaining to concepts of welfare, justice, and rights (Turiel and Davidson, 1986). In research on age-related changes within the moral domain, Davidson, Turiel and Black (1983) found that up to about age 6 moral judgment is primarily regulated by concerns for maintaining welfare and avoiding harm and is limited to familiar and directly accessible acts. Not until age 10 do children develop concepts of fairness and consistently regulate competing welfare claims with concerns for just reciprocity. And not until about age 12 do moral concepts of fairness go beyond direct reciprocity and involve the coordination of concerns for equality with considerations of equitable welfare (Damon, 1977).

Our thesis is that personal concepts inform the construction of morality by extending conceptions of harm and welfare to include the psychological requirements of personal freedom. In young children this forms the basis of an intuitive moral sense of rights wherein children understand infringement of their personal freedoms as harmful or unfair. Only at a later point in moral development (middle childhood) do they incorporate these intuitions about liberty within a moral framework regulated by just reciprocity. Paradoxically, then, the child's early intuitions about moral claims to liberty without a conception of moral equality based on just reciprocity make her moral system unstable in that she appears to understand moral conceptions of harm and welfare and yet acts out of self-interest (see Nunner-Winkler's chapter in this volume). This instability in a child's moral framework, occasioned in part by extending issues of harm to include constraints on personal free-

dom, is amplified by instabilities in the child's underlying conceptions of the personal, which provide the basis for her claims to
freedom of action in the first place. Not until late childhood or
early adolescence does the child structure concepts of the personal
with a consolidated understanding of self as subject, and only at
that and later points in development can we say that moral conceptions of rights are truly based on a view of persons as agents.

As we have seen, the young child bases her intuitive sense of rights
as liberty on a very physicalistic sense of self. This is not to say that
the child has no conceptions of interiorized feelings or intentions;
our claim is rather that the primary and most stable elements of the
child's concepts of self are directly apprehensible. It is not until late
childhood or early adolescence that the child conceptualizes the
personal in terms of truly psychological, rather than physical or
behavioral characteristics of the self (see Table 1). It also seems that
it is only after children conceptualize the personal in these psychological terms that they enter the final phase of individuation, for
only then do they view their personal sphere as fully beyond the
legitimate intrusion of parents. Until about age 10 children seem
to hold two conflicting views of parental authority with regard to
their personal domains. On the one hand, children at levels 1 and
2 assert that they ought to have authority over issues they consider
personal, e.g., choice of friends, hair length, privacy of conversations (Tisak, 1986). On the other hand, they simultaneously maintain that their parents (and no one else) have the right to override
and determine such things for the child. Children maintain this
view even when they view the parents' reasons as whimsical (e.g.,
the parent simply dislikes the friend and forbids him or her to play
with the child). When asked to explain why a parent has the right
to override a child's decisions in the personal arena, children
provide justifications consistent with an underlying conception of
the self as physical rather than intrasubjective. They offer statements like the following comments made by a 10-year-old boy to
explain his claim that a child's parents "can tell him what to do
because they made him and they own him."

Question: Do they have the right to sell him or give him away?
Answer: Yes, because, like I said, they own him.

Question: Can they do anything they want with him?
Answer: No. They can't hurt him or anything, because, well, they don't own him exactly. It's like he's a library book on loan from God.

In effect children at this level view their personal domain as shared with their parents as if they were co-signers on a loan for a piece of property. This view of the parent-child relationship ends when children begin to conceive of the personal domain as an aspect of an internal self knowable only to the individual. The emergence in late childhood of a conception of the personal as fundamentally divorced from parental ownership (as opposed to parental influence) has important implications for interpersonal relations, since it marks an end to conceptions of a fundamental relationship (between parent and child) in which intimacy (the permeation of personal boundaries) is confused with possession. These developmental changes in conceptions of personal issues are also likely to have two primary influences on the development of moral reasoning. First, the development of an understanding of self as fundamentally rooted in consciousness provides depth to conceptions of rights by articulating a psychological need for liberty. Parenthetically, we view the emergence of such conceptions as a response to Dworkin's concern that "we lack a psychological theory that would justify and explain the idea that the loss of liberties...involves inevitable or even likely psychological damage" (1977, p. 272). A child's moral system now has impinging on it claims for freedom of action that are clearly differentiated from issues of physical harm and even go beyond the child's psychological pain of injustice or hurt feelings. The child begins to understand that one's self depends on the unique features of one's internal makeup and, accordingly, begins to structure the intuitions about liberty mentioned above.

Second, these developmental changes in concepts of the personal may affect moral understanding more generally by encouraging the child to view others as subjects. When one conceives agency as connected to freedom of choice and privacy of ideas, one cannot readily reduce personhood to "thingness," or resolution of interpersonal conflicts to pragmatics devoid of moral implications. As we noted at the outset, however, these hypothesized influences of personal concepts on the moral system, as well as others we might extrapolate from an examination of subsequent stages, should be interpreted not as determinants of moral development but as important sources of information that can extend the types of interpersonal dealings handled with moral reasoning.

Personal × conventional: Issues of personal freedom and the general social order

The contributions that changes in personal concepts may make to the development of moral understanding do not occur in a vacuum. The very identification of particular issues as personal takes place within a cultural milieu and requires an individual to differentiate between issues that pertain to the individual and those that belong to the social order. At the individual level, this distinction defines the conceptual boundary between the personal and the conventional. An unresolved aspect of research and theory is whether such constructs are unique to Western, so-called individualistic cultures, or whether the personal domain is a human (cross-cultural) epistemic category. While there is little research that directly bears on this issue, a wealth of clinical data has demonstrated that disruption in the formation of personal boundaries damages individuals' psychological health (Kernberg, 1975; Kohut, 1978; Mahler, 1979; Masterson, 1981), and suggests that there are basic psychological limits to the extent to which others (including society) can impinge on the private lives of individuals (see Wolf's chapter in this volume). In fact, contemporary anthropology has moved away from romanticisms about the "group mind" or collective consciousness of so-called primitive peoples (Shweder, 1979a, 1979b) and has instead focused attention on cultural influences in individuation (Crapanzano, 1990) and on the definition of personhood (Shweder and LeVine, 1984). The issue of culture and convention in relation to the personal is thus not so much a matter of whether the personal is a cross-cultural category but whether there are objective and cross-cultural aspects to personal issues. We say this while cognizant that obvious cross-cultural variations as hairstyle and marital customs and so forth superficially affect what constitutes a personal issue. As Shweder is wont to say, just cataloging these differences reduces cultural anthropology to a travelogue. Our concern, in contrast, is to identify the fundamental elements of the personal whose cultural variation amounts to differences in the nature of personhood itself.

As a starting point, we propose deriving basic elements of the personal from an analysis of the basic psychological requirements for establishing personal boundaries for the self as object and related requirements (for personal agency, continuity, and uniqueness) for establishing a sense of self as subject (Damon and Hart, 1988). These basic elements are one's body, ideas, and intimate associates. From these basic elements arise claims to privacy, control over one's own body, and claims to freedom of expression, communication, and association. These generic claims are obviously canalized by culture, and variations in the degree and form that these freedoms take in turn establish the observed cultural variations in moral content.

The process of individual development seen in our research recapitulates social discourse at the societal level. This results in the expected general tendency for increasingly older children to categorize events more and more like adult members of the culture (Shweder, Mahapatra, and Miller, 1987). But there are also areas of ambiguity, such as gender-role activities (Stoddart and Turiel, 1985), whose status as personal or conventional shifts at different points in development. This leaves opportunities for succeeding generations to change domain classification of particular issues. Moreover, the general tendency of adolescents to assert independence from adult authority in the personal area coincides with their constructing an understanding of societies as normative systems. These concurrent developmental changes mean, in effect, that each generation represents a new look at the social moral order and has an opportunity for shifts in the specific cultural content of what is personal versus societal. Parenthetically, precisely these kinds of content shifts have made up the generation gap between adolescents and adults in Western countries in the last part of this century (Conger, 1981). Youths in late adolescence develop what Kohlberg described as conventional moral reasoning. They thus have the capacity to coordinate their conceptions of the moral, personal, and societal so as to comprehend the formal political theory of rights held by their society.

In our analysis it is possible that the conventional social system will conflict with one of the basic elements of the personal. Such conditions, we believe, place stress on the social system, and this conflict can persist only through systematic political repression, as was the case in Eastern Europe until recently, or through metaphysical beliefs that either provide moral justification for subperson status in the present life (untouchable, sinner) or hold out the promise of personal autonomy in the afterlife (medieval Christianity) or next life (traditional Hinduism) (Shweder, Mahapatra, and Miller, 1987). Unresolved empirical questions are whether individuals with subperson status question their fate, how they conceptualize the notion of self and the personal, and how they conceptualize the moral concept of rights. Such concepts held by traditional Hindus of the untouchable castes seem to be more malleable than we have proposed (Shweder, Mahapatra, and Miller, 1987).[4] This study, however, did not directly examine the issues we have raised. Thus we do not know whether and to what extent such individuals employ compensatory mechanisms to maintain a sense of personal freedom and selfhood while adjusting to the larger social order.

Morality, Personal Autonomy, and the Self

The theme of the present volume is morality and the self. In our chapter we have not attempted to address the issue of how morality fits within the self system as a totality. We believe that attempts to capture the development of the self (as opposed to conceptions of the self) within a single global progression (e.g., Loevinger, 1976) are incompatible with the contextual nature of the interactions among the subsystems that make up the self at any one time. We are more sympathetic to perspectives that approach global personality and self development through personal biography (Noam, 1988a, 1988b, 1990; Sarbin, 1977, 1986), since such an approach is far more likely to portray accurately the multifaceted and situated nature of an individual's motivational and conceptual makeup. We have thus focused not on the agent's development but on the relationship between conceptions of morality and rights and the development of conceptions of agency itself.

As our research on children's concepts of personal issues shows and as preliminary study of social interactions suggest, establishing a personal domain of actions is closely linked to establishing personal identity and a sense of self as agent. In effect, these studies demonstrate what Dworkin (1977) and Gewirth (1982) have claimed: that establishing individual rights is fundamental to human psychological integrity. As our interaction data and interview responses make clear, such claims of rights, though generated within a cultural context, are motivated by psychological needs. Thus morality, as a normative guarantee of basic claims to freedom and well-being (Gewirth, 1982), requires agents with basic psychological integrity, that is, persons with a bounded sense of self or, in Piaget's terminology, autonomous beings.[5]

Notes

1. Though the term "domain" has been used with reference to personal issues since 1981, concepts of personal issues do not constitute a conceptual domain in the formal sense. Instead, concepts of personal issues form a set structured within the psychological domain. Our use of the term "personal domain" here is for historical reference.

2. We investigated this latter finding more thoroughly by posing a set of questions to 96 Jewish subjects and to 64 Calvinist Protestant children ages 10 to 17. We asked the children how they know that what God commands is the right thing to do, and whether God's commands can make morally right something, such as stealing that children treat as a moral transgression. Our questions were informed by philosophical (Nielsen, 1973) and theological (Ramsey, 1966; Bultmann, 1966) speculation, originating in Socrates' dialogue with Euthyphro. Put simply, these philosophical and theological arguments presume that for a person to evaluate whether the commands of God are moral, the person must invoke criteria of the good that are independent of God's word.

We found in our studies (Nucci, 1985; Nucci and Turiel, 1993) that the majority of children at all ages and from both religious groups rejected the notion that God's command would make it right for a person to steal. Over 65 percent of subjects at ages 10 and 12 responded in this way, while over 80 percent of subjects at ages 14 and 16 gave such responses. In exceptions to these general trends (those children who felt that God's commands would make it right to steal) children often attempted to coordinate notions of morality and God's perfection with conceptions of God's omniscience. These subjects assumed that God is good, and that his command to steal would reflect good intentions and an ultimately good outcome. Since God is all-knowing, only he can anticipate and comprehend an outcome which may simply be beyond the grasp of temporal consciousness. In sum, what we discovered through these interviews, is that we cannot account for children's conceptions of morality in terms of simple adherence to God's word. Instead, children attempt to coordinate their notions of God with what they *know to be morally right*.

3. A similar differentiation between the personal and the social-moral is contained in Durkheim's (1961) distinction between personal and impersonal values.

4. Shweder et al. (1987) consider the issue of who constitutes a person or moral agent to be a discretionary feature of socially defined moral codes. In support of this, they note the many distinctions societies make among persons (e.g., children versus adults) in according classes of individuals rights and privileges. At their most extreme, such schemes of social classification treat some human members of society as nonpersons, as in the case of slaves. We don't dispute the existence of such systems of social classification nor do we deny that members of the dominant class may accept them. Our claim is that basic psychological needs for a sense of self as subject provide the motivational force for individuals in the socially defined nonperson categories to resist the depersonalizing effects of such classifications through defense mechanisms (e.g., denial, rationalization), criminal or pathological behavior, or direct social resistance. Interestingly, the language of organized social resistance often employs terms expressing collective self-determination, autonomy, and rights for the selves suppressed by unjust systems.

5. We wish to thank Charles Helwig, John Nicholls, Judith Smetana, and Elliot Turiel for their helpful comments on earlier drafts of this chapter.

References

Baldwin, J. M. (1897). *Social and ethical interpretations in mental development.* New York: MacMillan.

Baldwin, J. M. (1906). *Thought and things.* Vol. 1. London: Swan Sonnenschen.

Broughton, J. M. (1978). The development of concepts of self, mind, reality, and knowledge. In W. Damon (Ed.), *Social cognition.* San Francisco: Jossey-Bass.

Bultmann, R. (1966). Reply to D. Heinz-Horst Schrey. In C. W. Kegley (Ed.), *The theology of Rudolf Bultmann.* New York: Harper and Row.

Conger, J. (1981). Freedom and commitment: Families, youth, and social change. *American Psychologist,* 36:1475–1484.

Crapanzano, V. (1990). On self characterization. In J. W. Stigler, R. A. Shweder, and G. Herdt (Eds.), *Cultural psychology: Essays on comparative human development.* Cambridge: Cambridge University Press.

Damon, W. (1977). *The social world of the child.* San Francisco: Jossey-Bass.

Damon, W., and Hart, W. (1988). *Self-understanding in childhood and adolescence.* Cambridge: Cambridge University Press.

Davidson, P. M., Turiel, E., and Black, A. (1983). The effect of stimulus familiarity on the use of criteria and justifications in children's social reasoning. *British Journal of Developmental Psychology,* 1:49–65.

Durkheim, E. (1961). Moral education: *A study in the theory and application of the sociology of education.* Glencoe, IL: Free Press.

Dworkin, R. (1977). *Taking rights seriously.* Cambridge: Harvard University Press.

Erikson, E. H. (1963). *Childhood and society.* New York: W. W. Norton.

Erikson, E. H. (1968). *Identity, youth, and crisis.* New York: W. W. Norton.

Gewirth, A. (1978). *Reason and morality.* Chicago: University of Chicago Press.

Gewirth, A. (1982). *Human rights: Essays on justification and applications.* Chicago: University of Chicago Press.

Helwig, C. C., Tisak, M. S., and Turiel, E. (1990). Children's social reasoning in context: Reply to Gabennesch. *Child Development,* 61:2068–2078.

James, W. (1899). *The principles of psychology.* London: Macmillan.

Kernberg, O. F. (1975). *Borderline conditions and pathological narcissism.* New York: J. Aronson.

Kohlberg, L. (1969). Stage and sequence: The cognitive-developmental approach to socialization. In D. A. Goslin (Ed.), *Handbook of socialization theory and research.* New York: Rand McNally.

Kohlberg, L. (1976). Moral stages and moralization: The cognitive-developmental approach. In T. Lickona (Ed.), *Moral development and behavior: Theory, research, and social issues.* Chicago: Holt, Rinehart and Winston.

Kohut, H. (1978). *The search for the self: Selected writings, 1950–1978.* New York: International University Press.

Loevinger, J. (1976). *Ego development: Conceptions and theories.* San Francisco: Jossey-Bass.

Mahler, M. S. (1979). *The selected papers of Margaret S. Mahler,* Vols. 1 and 2. New York: J. Aronson.

Masterson, J. (1981). *The narcissistic and borderline disorders.* New York: Brunner/Mazel.

Nicholls, J. G., and Miller, A. (1984). Reasoning about the ability of self and others: A developmental study. *Child Development,* 55:1990–1999.

Nielsen, K. (1973). *Ethics without God.* Buffalo: Prometheus Books.

Noam, G. G. (1988a). A constructivist approach to developmental psychopathology. In E. D. Nannis and P. A. Cowan (Eds.), *Developmental psychopathology and its treatment.* San Francisco: Jossey-Bass.

Noam, G. G. (1988b). Self-complexity and self-integration: Theory and therapy in clinical-developmental psychology. *Journal of Moral Education,* 3:230–245.

Noam, G. G. (1990). Beyond Freud and Piaget: Biographical worlds—interpersonal self. In T. Wren (Ed.), *The moral domain.* Cambridge: MIT Press.

Nucci, L. (1977). *Social development: Personal, conventional, and moral concepts.* Doctoral dissertation, University of California, Santa Cruz.

Nucci, L. (1981). The development of personal concepts: A domain distinct from moral or societal concepts. *Child Development*, 52:114–121.

Nucci, L. (1985). Children's conceptions of morality, societal convention, and religious prescription. In C. Harding (Ed.), *Moral dilemmas: Philosophical and psychological reconsiderations of the development of moral reasoning*. Chicago: Precedent Press.

Nucci, L., and Herman, S. (1982). Behavioral disordered children's conceptions of moral, conventional, and personal issues. *Journal of Abnormal Child Psychology*, 10:411–426.

Nucci, L., and Turiel, E. (1993). God's word, religious rules, and their relation to Christian and Jewish children's concepts of morality. *Child Development*, 63.

Nucci, L., and Weber, E. K. (1991). Social interactions in the home and the development of young children's conceptions within the personal domain. Paper presented at the biennial meeting of the Society for Research in Child Development, Seattle, Washington. April 18–20.

Piaget, J. (1932). *The moral judgment of the child*. Glencoe, IL: Free Press.

Piaget, J. (1985). *Equilibration of cognitive structures*. Chicago: University of Chicago Press.

Ramsey, I. T. (1966). Moral judgment and God's commands. In I. T. Ramsey (Ed.), *Christian ethics and contemporary philosophy*. London: SCM Publishing Co.

Ruble, D. N., Boggiano, A., Feldman, N., and Loebel, J. (1980). Developmental analysis of the role of social comparison in self-evaluation. *Developmental Psychology*, 16:105–115.

Sarbin, T. R. (1977). Contextualism: A world view for modern psychology. In A. W. Landfield (Ed.), *Nebraska Symposium on Motivation: Personal construct psychology*. Lincoln: University of Nebraska Press.

Sarbin, T. R., Ed. (1986). *Narrative psychology: The storied nature of human conduct*. New York: Praeger Publishers.

Selman, R. (1980). *The growth of interpersonal understanding: Developmental and clinical analyses*. New York: Academic Press.

Shweder, R. A. (1979a). Rethinking culture and personality theory, part 1. *Ethos*, 7:255–278.

Shweder, R. A. (1979b). Rethinking culture and personality theory, part 2. *Ethos*, 7:279–311.

Shweder, R. A., and Bourne, E. J. (1984). Does the concept of the person vary cross-culturally? In R. A. Shweder and R. A. LeVine (Eds.), *Culture theory: Essays on mind, self, and emotion*. Cambridge: Cambridge University Press.

Shweder, R. A., and LeVine, R. A., Eds. (1984). *Culture theory: Essays on mind, self, and emotion*. Cambridge: Cambridge University Press.

Shweder, R. A., Mahapatra, M., and Miller, J. G. (1987). Culture and moral development. In J. Kagan and S. Lamb (Eds.), *The emergence of morality in young children*. Chicago: University of Chicago Press.

Shweder, R. A., Turiel, E., and Much, N. C. (1981). The moral intuitions of the child. In J. H. Flavell and L. Ross (Eds.), *Social cognitive development: Frontiers and possible futures.* New York: Cambridge University Press.

Smetana, J. G. (1989a). Toddlers' social interactions in the context of moral and conventional transgressions in the home. *Developmental Psychology,* 25:499–508.

Smetana, J. G. (1989b). Adolescents' and parents' reasoning about actual family conflict. *Child Development,* 60:1052–1067.

Smetana, J. G., Bridgeman, D., and Turiel, E. (1983). Differentiation of domains and prosocial behavior. In D. Bridgeman (Ed.), *The nature of prosocial development: Interdisciplinary theories and strategies.* New York: Academic Press.

Stoddart, T., and Turiel, E. (1985). Children's concepts of cross-gender activities. *Child Development,* 56:1241–1252.

Tisak, M. S. (1986). Child's conceptions of parental authority. *Child Development,* 57:166–176.

Turiel, E. (1978). The development of concepts of social structure: Social convention. In J. Glick and A. Clarke-Stewart (Eds.), *The development of social understanding.* New York: Gardner Press.

Turiel, E. (1983). *The development of social knowledge: Morality and convention.* Cambridge: Cambridge University Press.

Turiel, E., and Davidson, P. (1986). Heterogeneity, inconsistency, and asynchrony in the development of cognitive structures. In I. Levin (Ed.), *Stage and structure: Reopening the debate.* Norwood, NJ: Ablex.

Turiel, E., Killen, M., and Helwig, C. H. (1987). Morality: Its structure, functions, and vagaries. In J. Kagan and S. Lamb (Eds.), *The emergence of morality in young children.* Chicago: University of Chicago Press.

Turiel, E., Nucci, L., and Smetana, J. G. (1988). A cross-cultural comparison about what? A critique of Nisan's (1987) study of morality and convention. *Developmental Psychology,* 24:140–143.

The Uniting of Self and Morality in the Development of Extraordinary Moral Commitment

Anne Colby and William Damon

"When you think about these goals and values and so on, how do these relate to your sense of who you are as a person and your identity?" "Well, it's one and the same. Who I am is what I'm able to do and how I feel all the time—each day, each moment. It's hard for me to separate who I am from what I want to do and what I am doing." Cabell Brand, American businessman and social reformer

In an individual's life, personal and moral goals can be coordinated in a number of ways. They can be segmented, as when we divide up our paychecks into amounts for ourselves and amounts for charity. They can be opposed to one another, as when someone jumps in front of a bus to save a child or, on the ignoble side, cheats an elderly widow and goes on a spending spree. Or they can be united. In this last case, people have the sense that their most powerfully motivating goals are indistinguishable from their moral convictions. So, in serving themselves, they serve morality, and vice versa.

Most people have some degree of unity between personal and moral goals, as when, for example, they act altruistically toward their own children or others they love. Most people, however, also have many areas of conflict between what they most want to do and what they feel would be best to do from the moral point of view. Although they may sincerely want to do what is right, they also want other things that conflict with pursuing the right. Though atypical, a high degree of unity between personal and moral goals bears special significance for both human development and social action, because conflict between personal and moral goals can prevent people from taking what they believe to be the more moral course of action.

In this chapter we will discuss an unusual sample of people who consistently experience a high degree of unity between personal and moral goals. These people are participants in our study of living moral exemplars, which is presented more fully in *Some Do Care: Contemporary Lives of Moral Commitment* (Colby and Damon, 1992). They are unusual in that they have demonstrated, in their lives and beliefs, an extraordinary commitment to moral causes and an extraordinary capacity for effective social action.

In our view, the unity or conflict between personal and moral goals is central to a discussion of morality and the self because goals are an important component in one's identity or self-concept. Many of the people in our sample explicitly say that there is a very close relation between their sense of personal identity and their (moral) goals, as exemplified in the opening quotation. It was no accident, we believe, that these exceptional individuals had unified goals and were effective in social action. Rather, this happy co-occurrence exemplifies, we believe, a more general relation between moral judgment and conduct: *When there is perceived unity between self and morality, judgment and conduct are directly and predictably linked and action choices are made with great certainty.* As noted above, we are assuming here that goals are a central component of self. Thus, when moral and personal goals are united, *moral* goals are central to the self.

The above principle can be seen most clearly in the cases of highly moral individuals, as we discuss later in this chapter, but it also applies generally in the course of normal human behavior and development (see Blasi, 1983; Noam, in this volume).

In a developmental analysis of self-concept, Damon and Hart describe periods in childhood and adolescence when the concepts of morality and self become joined (Damon, 1984; Damon and Hart, 1988). It is clear from this analysis that early in life, morality and self are separate conceptual systems with little integration between them. When children refer to who they are or what they are like, they typically make no reference to their moral goals or beliefs; instead, they focus on surface features of their physical, active, social, or psychological selves. Children often speak about what is fair and about what they would (or even should) do as wholly separate affairs. They overcome this segregation toward the end of childhood, and forge a closer link between their moral interests and self-interests. This results in greater predictability between children's moral judgments and their conduct. We have evidence for this both from Damon's studies of children's sharing behavior (1984) and from Burton's reanalysis of Hartshorne and May's data (Burton, 1963).

Still, most people exhibit many prominent schisms between morality and the self even in adulthood. In Damon and Hart's self-concept study (1988), only two subjects showed any marked tendency to define their identities in terms of their moral beliefs. Damon and Hart's longitudinal data went only through late adolescence, so they might have discovered a stronger developmental trend toward integration by extending the study into adulthood. But it seems safer to conclude that some individuals unite the moral and the self to a far greater extent than others. Moreover, the extent of a person's unity depends more on his or her sense of self than on the nature of the moral beliefs.

We would argue, therefore, that morality and the self are separate conceptual systems that grow somewhat closer during the course of normal development but that still tend to remain relatively uncoordinated for most (but not all) individuals. What is more, it is not possible to gauge the extent to which an individual has integrated the two systems simply by focusing on his or her moral judgements. This is because a person's moral judgments do not determine *the place that morality occupies in the person's life*. To know this latter key quality, we must know not only how people view morality but also how they understand the self in relation to their moral beliefs.

People with substantially similar moral beliefs may differ in their personal identification with those moral beliefs. Those for whom morality is central to their personal identities may be powerfully motivated by their moral beliefs and goals. Others may have equally elevated notions of the good but may consider these notions peripheral to many of their own life engagements.

This is not to claim that one's moral conceptions are wholly irrelevant to the issue of centrality. Certainly some moral positions make it more difficult to deny one's personal responsibility on crucial occasions. Colby and Kohlberg's (1987) characterizations of principled morality provide some examples of such action-defining positions. As they have described them, these principled positions can be segregated from the self (or separated from their action implications) only through rationalization and/or distortion of the facts in the case.

Nevertheless, even though the nature of one's moral beliefs may place conceptual limits on how one places morality within the frame of one's personal life, there is still considerable variation possible within these limits. In other words, moral beliefs in themselves often bear some implications for how individuals make use of them in their personal lives, but these implications do not cover every circumstance and at best offer only partial solutions to real-life problems. This is as true at the most elevated reaches of moral judgment as at the less sophisticated levels. In the end, moral behavior depends on something beyond the moral beliefs in and of themselves. It depends in part on how and to what extent individuals' moral concerns are important to their sense of themselves as persons. As we will show in this chapter, for some people, moral concerns are absolutely and undeniably important to their sense of who they are, but the reason for this does not lie in the specific nature of their moral concerns.

If, as we have claimed, the extent of unity between morality and the self is a personality dimension of its own, separate from the content of moral beliefs, then we should find such unity among persons with widely varying moral judgments. This, in fact, is exactly what we found. Moreover, in our sample of moral exemplars we also found evidence that such unity can create a firm bridge between moral judgment and action. This stands to reason simply because of the moral orientation that such unity provides: individuals who define the self in terms of their moral goals will more likely interpret events as moral problems and will more likely see themselves implicated in the solutions to these problems. Just as there is no separation between moral and personal goals in these people, there is no divergence between judgment and conduct. Their unity of goals provides a compelling call to engage as well as a sense of certainty about their course of action. Where one's personal choice seems predetermined, there is little room for hesitation or self-doubt.

The Psychological Study of Moral Exemplars

Throughout history, extraordinary individuals have personified moral values for the rest of the human race. From the time of the prophets to the modern age of Ghandi, Mother Teresa, and Martin Luther King, certain individuals have come to stand as "moral exemplars" for vast numbers of followers. One interesting feature of this phenomenon is that such individuals often represent ideas that are controversial and even unpopular in the broader context of the times. Despite this, the eventual impact of such people on the course of society is beyond question.

In fact, we contend, the moral behavior and moral beliefs of ordinary people are often influenced by those rare individuals who exemplify the highest moral ideals of their day. This is because people's moral choices are inevitably construed in the context of actual interpersonal relations, and moral ideas have behavioral meaning only insofar as they are actively interpreted in such contexts. Personifying moral ideals is a powerful and ready-made means of shaping such interpretations, since it brings with it direct specifications for what actions should follow in the dramatic form of life.

Most people are drawn more to concrete lives than to abstract ideals. When a particularly visible life represents an appreciated (though perhaps elusive) moral value, people may be influenced in a number of ways. Sometimes the extraordinary life influences by enlightening, making moral issues clear where they were previously unnoticed. Many of Jesus' acts (such as overturning the tables of the money changers in the temple) were instructive in this manner. Other times the extraordinary life influences through example, as when Bishop Tutu steadfastly adheres to a pacifist course under threats of physical harm and violence. Such examples may help others live up to ideals that they hold but have found difficult to put into action.

For capturing these kinds of profound social influence, we turn to social-psychological models that recognize the dynamic interplay between individual and social influence. Moscovici's writings on minority/majority relations offer us one such model. Unlike many contemporary social psychologists, Moscovici has emphasized the formative effects that strong individuals can have on society at large: "Original or extreme points of view, which are by definition expressed by individuals of minorities, are far more likely to exercise a strong attraction than to be rejected" (1976). Our interest is in cases where the "original or extreme point of view" is unusual because of its elevated morality. We believe that these cases determine the destiny and boundaries of moral living.

Even dynamic models like Moscovici's are insufficient for understanding such cases unless they include a developmental component. It is essential to ask not only how the individual and the group affect one another from situation to situation but also how they acquire longstanding patterns of thought and conduct. Answering the latter question requires a *developmental* model, a model that, like good social-psychological models, must recognize the dynamic interplay between individual and group. In contrast to strictly social models, however, developmental models emphasize what individuals retain from their experiences with groups.

This chapter addresses the question of how individuals form their patterns of moral beliefs and moral conduct over the course of their lives. We believe that we can usefully address this question through a model based upon the dynamic interplay of social influence and moral development. In our own current research we have been asking this question in our study of moral exemplars, highly moral people who themselves have exerted significant formative influence on the moral thought and behavior of others (Colby and Damon, 1992). We became interested in such persons partly because we believed that a study of their lives would give us access to the further important question of how certain extraordinary individuals influence the moral life of society at large. In this chapter we will present a brief account of our study of living moral exemplars.

Our analysis of the case material draws on a socially oriented model of developmental change. This model assumes that the individual is actively engaged in gradually transforming goals under processes of social influence. Its advantage over a Piagetian framework is that it provides for individuals' incorporating new systems of motives developed in communication with others, rather than merely for their acquisition of new knowledge. It also assumes that an individual cooperatively shapes new perspectives in the course of many negotiations between persons. This means that all new ideas owe their shape to some interaction between external guidance and internal belief.

We have called these notions "goal theory," and we believe that they offer us a more compelling starting point than do the cognitive-developmental assumptions that individuals form ideas by figuring out the way the world works and that they construct new ideas simply by revising old ones in the light of their observations of reality.

Moral Change in the Lives of Extraordinary Individuals

We will report here a study of morally exemplary individuals (described in more detail in Colby and Damon, 1992). We developed criteria for identifying individuals to be studied in consultation with twenty distinguished moral philosophers, scholars, theologians, and religious leaders from a wide variety of ideological persuasions. The resulting criteria are as follows:

•a sustained commitment to moral ideals or principles that include a generalized respect for humanity, or a sustained evidence of moral virtue

•a disposition to act in accord with one's moral ideals or principles, implying also a consistency between one's actions and intentions and between the means and ends of one's actions

•a willingness to risk one's self-interest for the sake of one's moral values

•a tendency to be inspiring to others and thereby to move them to moral action

•a sense of realistic humility about one's own importance relative to the world at large, implying a relative lack of concern for one's own ego

Our nominators identified 86 living Americans who they believe meet these criteria, and we arranged to interview 23 of these people. Our study group consisted of half women and half men, a broad mix of racial, ethnic, educational, and socioeconomic backgrounds, and a range of religious and political orientations. For practical reasons, all of the study participants were Americans.

Our interview included an extensive set of questions about the moral exemplar's personal experiences and beliefs. Here we probed for events and influences that may have shaped the exemplar's character, crucial life decisions that the exemplar made, and the exemplar's feelings and thoughts during these crucial decisions. The second part of the interview consisted of two of Kohlberg's moral dilemmas, followed by the standard probing questions.

We used case material from the life-history section of the interviews to try to understand the phenomenology of moral commitment and the meaning of these people's activities in relation to their values, beliefs, and the life experiences that seemed most salient to them. Among other things, we were interested in the cognitive strategies they used to sustain their commitment in the face of various obstacles. For these purposes, we thought it appropriate to use probing clinical interviews that draw out the subjects' perspectives on themselves and their work. We were not attempting in this study to establish empirical associations between behavior choices and personality factors or critical early experiences. For that we would need prospective data, verification of self reports by other sources of information, and so on.

Our use of goal theory to analyze case material is an attempt to demonstrate and elaborate a developmental theory of the transformation of goals. At this stage it is not an attempt to test the theory. Our purpose is to provide some insight into the lives of these people and to offer an analysis consistent with the way they conceptualize their own lives.

Case Example: Virginia Foster Durr

To illustrate our theoretical approach in the context of a case, we will describe the case in some detail. We will describe the life of Virginia Foster Durr, a woman from a prominent family in Montgomery, Alabama. She was 84 at the time of the interview, in 1988. Like most upper-class white children in the southern United States in the early twentieth century, she was very close to the family's black servants and their children when she was a young child but was separated from them as she grew older. Although she questioned this segregation to some degree at the time and during a number of later incidents, she basically held the prevailing views on racial segregation while she was growing up. Yet in adulthood she became a major figure in the black civil-rights movement in the United States. Beginning in her thirties, she became deeply involved in the struggle for voting rights and against racial segregation and the anticommunist movement in the 1950s.

As a young child, Virginia was devoted to her black nurse and played frequently with her nurse's daughter and the children of the other black servants. This harmonious situation ended for good on her seventh birthday when she was forbidden to include the black children in her party (being held on her grandmother's plantation) and the subsequent family argument resulted in the loss of Virginia's nurse.

I was told none of the black children could come to the party. Only white children—perfect strangers they had picked up in Union Springs. So I had a temper fit early that morning and they finally agreed that I could have a barbecue in the morning and the party in the afternoon. The barbecue would be in the backyard with the black children, and the party would be in the front yard with the white children. We had the birthday barbecue and everything was going fine. One of the little black girls was tearing up the chicken, and she offered a piece to Elizabeth [Virginia's cousin]. Elizabeth . . . said, "Don't you give me any chicken out of that black hand of yours. I'm not going to eat any chicken that your black hand has touched, you little nigger." I told Elizabeth to go to hell. I was just furious. You see, the black girl was Nursie's little girl, Sarah. She and I played together all the time. I was raised with her. When the afternoon came, I went to the birthday party with all these strange white children. I had another temper fit and screamed and yelled. I bashed the cake in and was put to bed again. That night at the supper table, my aunt said I was the worst child she had ever known. (Durr, 1985, p. 17)

The family fight led to an insult directed at the nurse by Virginia's aunt. The nurse, on overhearing the insult, quietly left and never came back. Virginia describes the incident as having been a terrible trauma in her life.

This incident reveals the strong will and independent mind that characterized Virginia throughout her life. Virginia nonetheless did internalize the prevailing views about race relations. A later incident when she was a college student illustrates how successfully she had been educated in racial prejudice by the culture in which she grew up. Upon entering her sophomore year at Wellesley

College in Massachusetts, Virginia moved into the dormitory and went down to the dining room that evening for dinner. "The first night, I went to the dining room and a Negro girl was sitting at my table. My God, I nearly fell over dead. I couldn't believe it. I just absolutely couldn't believe it. . . . I promptly got up, marched out of the room, went upstairs, and waited for the head of the house to come. . . . I told her I couldn't possibly eat at the table with a Negro girl. I was from Alabama and my father would have a fit" (p. 56). The head of the house calmly explained that the rules of the college required her to eat at that table for a month, and if she did not comply, she would have to withdraw from college. This was the first time that Virginia's values had ever been seriously challenged, and she stayed awake all night worrying about the dilemma. She was afraid of angering her father, yet she enjoyed Wellesley and very much wanted to stay. "Now I was having the time of my life at Wellesley. I had never had such a good time. I was in love with a Harvard law student, the first captain of VMI [Virginia Military Institute], and life was just a bed of roses. But I had been taught that if I ate at the table of a Negro girl I would be committing a terrible sin against society. About dawn, I realized that if nobody told Daddy, it might be all right. That was the only conclusion I came to. I didn't have any great feeling of principle. I had not wrestled with my soul" (pp. 57–58). Virginia stayed at Wellesley and spent a month eating at the table with the black girl, whom she came to like and respect. "That was the first time I became aware that my attitude was considered foolish by some people and that Wellesley College wasn't going to stand for it. That experience had a tremendous effect on me" (p. 58).

Although the dining room incident did not change Virginia's racial views overnight, it did sow the seeds of doubt about the beliefs she was raised with. But Virginia was not able to return to college after her sophomore year. Her family had undergone serious financial reversals and could no longer afford to send her to college. Virginia returned to Birmingham to make her debut and look for a husband. Soon afterward she met Clifford Durr, and they were married within a year. When President Franklin Delano Roosevelt took office a few years later, Clifford Durr, an attorney, was called to Washington to become the head of a program to recapitalize the banks under the Reconstruction Finance Corporation. The Durrs moved to Washington in 1933. After a year or two of domesticity, Virginia began to be involved with the political scene in Washington and started the work against the poll tax that was to consume her for the next fifteen years. She and Clifford were friendly with many of the key political figures of the time, and Virginia was very much influenced by the experiences she had with them. She also rekindled some college friendships at this time, most notably her friendship with Clark Howell Foreman. Clark Foreman was a Harvard student from Atlanta, Georgia, when Virginia was at Wellesley, and as two Southerners, they became very close friends. Foreman later became a central figure in Roosevelt's New Deal administration.

When Virginia renewed her friendship with Clark Foreman in Washington, she found that he had undergone important ideological changes since his college days. He had witnessed a lynching and had traveled and studied in England and Russia. He had come to believe very strongly in racial equality and was active in the effort to integrate Washington, D.C., which was still racially segregated at that time. Virginia Durr describes an incident with Clark Foreman concerning his relations with blacks that was clearly a turning point for her: "That Sunday afternoon when he came out to our house, he began telling us what he was going to do and what he was doing. Well, my Lord, I just fell into a fit! I couldn't believe it. We got into the most awful fight you have ever known in your life. Clark is not tactful at times. He said, 'You know, you are just a white, southern, bigoted, prejudiced, provincial girl.' Oh, he just laid me out. I got furious and I said, 'You are going back on all the traditions of the South. You, a Howell of Georgia, going back on all of it. What do you think of the Civil War? What did we stand for?' White supremacy, of course. When they left, Cliff said, 'Well, I don't think you'll ever see him again.' Amazingly enough, they called us up the next week and invited us to dinner" (p. 104). The Durrs proceeded to become very close to the Foremans and through them began to socialize with some distinguished African-Americans.

During the following 15 years in Washington, Virginia was consumed with the fight against the poll tax and related political activities, with an active family life, which now included three

children, and with a social life that revolved around her neighborhood and the Washington political scene. Clifford Durr became
commissioner of the Federal Communications Commission in
1941.

After the war and Roosevelt's death, the anticommunist feeling
in Washington began to escalate. Joseph McCarthy's House Un-
American Activities Committee had operated throughout the war,
and after the war President Truman instituted a loyalty order,
according to which everyone working for the government had to be
examined for possible communist ties. A loyalty oath was required
of all government officials. Clifford was in deep disagreement with
the loyalty order and felt that the procedures used to investigate
people were contrary to the most basic civil liberties. In these
investigations the accused were not told who had accused them,
and many people lost their jobs on the basis of unproven allega-
tions of communist ties. Clifford spoke out frequently against the
HUAC and the loyalty order, and decided eventually that he could
not continue to work for the government in the current climate of
fear and suspicion. When his term expired, he refused to accept a
reappointment.

Virginia did not want to go back to Alabama, so Clifford opened
a law office in Washington in 1948 and became one of a small
handful of attorneys who specialized in defending people accused
of having communist ties. The emotional tolls of this work were
heavy and eventually Clifford decided to leave Washington. He
took a position in Denver as general counsel for the Farmers'
Union Insurance Corporation. During the drive from Washington
to Denver, Clifford's longstanding back problem got so bad that he
had to have surgery when they arrived in Denver. He was hospitalized for over a month, and the Durrs had to spend all of the money
they had made in selling their Washington house to cover the
uninsured costs of his illness.

While Clifford was in the hospital, Virginia became involved with
an incident that was to cost Clifford his job. The Korean War was
escalating at that time, and Virginia received a postcard in the mail
from Linus Pauling and several other eminent scientists asking her
to indicate on a return card whether she favored or opposed
bombing above the Yalu River in Korea. Since bombing above the

Yalu was seen as risking a war with China, Virginia indicated on the card that she opposed the bombing. She signed it and sent it off.

Soon after Clifford returned to work, still on crutches, the *Denver Post* published a prominent story with a headline that read "Wife of General Counsel of Farmers' Union Insurance Corporation Signs Red Petition." In response, the head of the Farmers' Union Insurance Corporation demanded that Virginia sign a retraction of the statement, which would be published in the *Denver Post.* If she refused, Clifford was to lose his job. This presented a serious dilemma for Virginia. Whereas she did not want to jeopardize her husband's job and her family's welfare, she was well informed about the Korean War and opposed it strongly. Before Virginia had time to resolve her dilemma, Clifford walked in. He had been threatened with dismissal unless he talked Virginia into signing the letter. He told the head of the Farmers' Union that he would never allow his wife to sign such a letter and walked out of the office without a job.

Faced with no income, no savings, and Clifford's serious health problems, the Durrs decided to return to Alabama to live with Clifford's parents. When Clifford recovered from his illness, he opened a law office in Montgomery, and Virginia worked with him as his secretary. Clifford became known as someone who was willing to represent poor blacks, and very frequently the cases involved serious exploitation of blacks by supposedly respectable white citizens of Montgomery. His cases included police brutality, loan sharking, and insurance scams. During the early 1950s Virginia devoted most of her energy to her work in the law office and her family, yet she remained involved with civil rights issues and was centrally involved in the very early efforts to integrate Montgomery.

Within a few years the Supreme Court handed down its historic decision outlawing segregation of the schools, and "all hell broke loose. There was no choice. You had to stand up and be counted or move. We didn't move" (p. 272). Virginia became involved in the Council on Human Relations, the only integrated group in Montgomery, and devoted herself to the desegregation of Montgomery. As always, she valued very highly the opportunity to work closely with other people who shared her beliefs. "It was a tremendous relief to me to be able to join something like that, where I was with people who were against segregation" (p. 272).

The resistance to integrating Montgomery was intense, with bombings of the churches and houses of many black leaders and their white sympathizers. It was a difficult time for the Durrs, and they decided to send their two younger daughters to school in the North to remove them from the constant taunting that they endured from both teachers and other children. Although Clifford Durr received attractive job offers from universities and law firms in the North, he and Virginia felt that Alabama was their home, and they refused to leave. During the 1960s the Durrs remained very involved in the civil rights movement. Among other things, they housed and fed dozens of students and other protesters who passed through Montgomery on their way to Selma and other protests. During this period Virginia felt that she was living "in the middle of a storm." But in spite of the violence and turbulence of the times, the overriding feeling was that the battle for civil rights was slowly being won. Most of the important segregation cases that Clifford tried were eventually won. Virginia was left with a profound respect for the law, "when it works," and it seemed to her that by and large the law was working.

Despite this faith in some aspects of the American legal system, Virginia is not naive about the power of law as a complete solution to racism and poverty. In reflecting back on the gains, she is also acutely aware of how far we have to go and how difficult it will be. "I wish I could be more cheerful and end on an upbeat note and say, 'We're going into the land of Canaan now. We've been through the desert and we've crossed the Red Sea.' But I'm like Moses. I glimpsed the promised land, but I never got there, and I never will. It's sad, because I would like very much to live long enough to see a change come about, a really fundamental change. I don't think I ever will, because I think it's going to take an awfully long time" (p. 333).

Goal Theory as Applied to the Case

Let us now move to the analysis of this case and to generalizations we can draw from the larger sample. Our model combines a gradual transformation of goals through social influence, with the active engagement of the developing individual. Our model assumes that an individual cooperatively shapes new perspectives in the course of many negotiations with others. This means that all new ideas owe their shape to some interaction between external guidance and internal belief. That is, individual development is stimulated and guided, but not quite directed, by social influence.

One advantage of using goal theory to explain change in this manner is that it avoids the fruitless split between cognition and affect that has plagued other developmental explanations. A goal is an affectively charged motivator but is also part of an entire intellectual perspective. This is why it takes some time to genuinely substitute one goal for another, whether in childhood or adulthood. Substituting goals requires a gradual transformation, through social influence, of one's perspective on one's actions in the social world. Such change influences one on both the cognitive and affective fronts.

We do not know what allows some people to continue developing morally while others do not progress much after early adulthood. This is one of our interests in studying morally exceptional people. Certainly, in the case of Virginia Durr we see a history of openness to moral change. Although she did not fully initiate her emerging new values, they do reflect what we might call an "active receptiveness" to social influence of particular sorts.

Virginia's openness to change was not blanket receptiveness toward just any sort of influence. Witness, for example, her strenuous resistance to pressures to give in to the anticommunists or to go along with the prevailing racial views of her friends in Alabama. Instead, it seems to derive from a deep respect for honesty and truth and a desire for consistency between her beliefs and her most closely held values.

It is therefore important to emphasize that at each step in her evolving moral engagement with the civil rights movement, Virginia Durr actively chose to move forward rather than to withdraw. Consequently, we must conclude that the direction and shape of her moral growth were co-constructed by the continual interplay between her and her chosen community. The social influences in Virginia's life cannot be understood without knowing what she herself brought to the process.

Here we quote from the very beginning of her interview to illustrate the way in which her social experiences interacted with her values, beliefs, and character to result in the developmental path she took.

Anne Colby: Now, before I start asking the questions that I came with, I would like to hear a little bit more about your experience of not having made choices, as you put it. Maybe you could just talk about that a little bit. You've mentioned that a couple of times.

Virginia Durr: You make—I suppose you make choices every day of your life. But the thing is, as far as the decisions I made concerning my part, say, in the racial struggle in the South, it wasn't a decision, it was something that grew over a period of years, and one thing led to another. But I never (like Paul on the road to Damascus, was it?) thought that I saw a revealing light and just all of a sudden saw the light. But it was over a period of a number of years that I began to change my feelings. And the same thing was true about so many things. I changed as things happened. Rather, things happened, and I changed because they happened.

Later in the interview she says this:

V.D.: And actually I don't think that I really had much change in my attitude at all until I got to Washington in 1933. By that time I was thirty years old. . . . The thing that really changed me, I think, was the fact that I got into the Women's Democratic National Committee as a volunteer. You see, at that time, this is one of the things about being Southern that is also—even if you get to be a friend, you're exploiting them, blacks, all the time. My husband wasn't making but $6500 a year, but we had a cook, who I paid, I think, $12 a week to, and I had a nurse, and I had a yard man, someone to do the laundry, and the nurse made $12 or $15 a week. But the thing was that I had time to go in and be a volunteer at the Women's Division of the Democratic National Committee and that I'd gotten to be very devoted to the Roosevelts by that time. And, in the Democratic Committee I met black women on an equal basis. So that was my first meeting with black women on a totally equal basis. And Mrs. Roosevelt was there a lot. But the thing was, D.C. was segregated. People don't remember now that the District of Columbia was as segregated as Alabama. All the government buildings were segregated and D.C. was segregated. And so there was a movement started to desegregate the District of Columbia, and Mrs. [Mary Church] Terrell, who was a black woman whose husband had been a judge, brought the suit. She went into some lunch place, and they wouldn't serve her, and these two young lawyers were with her, and they took her case to the courts, and it was won. So segregation was abolished in D.C. And so you see, I saw it done in the District of Columbia. But, of course, I saw it done with the backing of the Supreme Court and the backing of the Justice Department, the backing

of Mrs. Roosevelt, the Democratic Committee, and so on and so forth.
A.C.: So that experience really changed you?
V.D.: Well, that did change me a great deal. And then the Democratic women started this fight against the poll tax because the Southern women didn't vote because of the poll tax. Of course, the poor whites didn't vote, and the blacks didn't vote at all, and only about 10 or 12 percent of the people were eligible. And so I got into that struggle, and then that brought me in contact with a lot of black men and women and so many people, and that also was very enlightening. But there again, I had the backing of Mrs. Roosevelt and had the backing of the White House, actually. But it took years and years for it to go through.
A.C.: When you were spending so much energy on the fight against the poll tax, what was driving that, do you think, from your point of view? What was really the energy behind it inside you?
V.C.: I thought the right to vote was something that everybody ought to have.

Goal theory as we use it does not presuppose a form or direction of change. In many cases, individuals follow paths better described as corruption than development. Social pressures are complex and multidirectional. Which of the various pressures are most salient and the nature of their influence depends very much on the individual's cognitive framework for interpreting morality and on her character and values. Virginia Durr's cognitive-moral framework (which was a classic stage 5 understanding of law and justice in Kohlberg's sense) may have predisposed her to be more susceptible to some influences than others. At least by the time of her serious involvement in the civil rights movement, she approached the moral issues she confronted with a cognitive-moral framework that stressed the value of law and due process in protecting fundamental civil rights, along with an awareness that many laws were unjust and had to be broken and then challenged through the courts. She clearly understands her work against the poll tax in this framework, and she strongly opposed Joseph McCarthy and other anticommunists in large part because the anticommunists continually violated basic freedoms and the right to due process of law. And, of course, her work in Clifford's law office frequently involved challenging the constitutionality of segregationist ordinances and laws. It is impossible to understand what Virginia Durr's work meant to her without seeing it in the context of this cognitive-moral framework. This does not mean, however, that she laid out all the assumptions of the framework when she was asked why she acted as she did. Her interpretation of the situation and what is right and wrong within it are closely tied to this cognitive-moral framework, but if asked why she took the actions she did, she would answer more simply, saying that she did it because it was right, because everyone should have the right to vote, or because people should not be segregated by race.

We find in Virginia Durr's story important threads of continuity connecting the different periods of her life and connecting her with her family and Southern heritage. But overall, her life is more dramatically a story of change than one of continuity. Perhaps the first really important period of change was the two years she spent as a student at Wellesley College. The incident in which she was forced to sit at the dinner table with the young black woman planted a doubt in Virginia's mind and shook the solid conviction of what she had been brought up to believe.

Virginia's dining room experience at Wellesley and later her involvement in the Women's Division and the fight against the poll tax are excellent examples of the transformation of goals in her development. Virginia's goal in agreeing to sit at the dining table with the black student was very clearly to be allowed to remain at Wellesley, in large part so that she could continue her active and entertaining social life. The result was not an immediate awakening to a new perspective on race relations and civil rights. The incident did move Virginia a perceptible step in that direction, however. She was forced to interact with an educated, middle-class African-American for the first time and realized that the girl was intelligent and civilized. She became aware that her views on segregation were not shared by the community she had joined, a community she prized very highly. She began to doubt.

The poll-tax fight provides an even more illuminating example, because it took place over such an extended period of time. Virginia's motivation for joining the Women's Division of the Democratic Party was to play some part in the exciting New Deal in Washington, to have an opportunity to work with Eleanor Roosevelt, and to meet some interesting women. She soon became intensely involved in the fight for women's right to vote but was not at first involved in racial issues. Because of the coalitions that formed around the voting-rights issue, Virginia soon began to work closely with black organizations and distinguished black women like Mary McLeod Bethune. The activities of the committee itself violated segregation laws. Together with an intellectual awakening on these issues stimulated by her more liberal Washington friends, such as Clark Foreman, this opportunity and need to work closely with black people led her to transform her goals in ways that changed her life dramatically, indeed, changed fundamentally who she was. As we have seen in all our exemplars, Virginia Durr was open to moral change, and her goals broadened and became ennobled as she engaged with the experiences and people she encountered.

Social influences played a central role both in transforming Virginia Durr's beliefs and goals and in sustaining her motivation and energy. We have already discussed the influence of her exposure to the liberal New England attitudes of the Wellesley College faculty and administration. While at Wellesley, Virginia chose Southerners as her closest friends, thus softening the impact of the "culture shock" she faced. These Southern friends were, of course, those who had chosen to attend such schools as Wellesley and Harvard and were themselves being influenced by the new environment. Her relationship with Clark Foreman illustrates the gradual nature of the transformation. She became close to Clark during their college days because both were from the South and considered their Southern heritage a very important part of who they were. After she returned to Alabama, however, Clark was studying in England and traveling in Europe and Russia, after having been greatly shaken up by witnessing a lynching in Georgia. When she encountered Clark Foreman again in Washington, he was able to influence her racial views as no Northerner could, because she knew that he came from a similar background and understood her point of view, having formerly shared its assumptions himself.

Without a doubt the most important social influence in her adult life was that of her husband, Clifford Durr. She deeply respected, even revered, her husband, seeing him as a figure of absolute integrity. Clifford's and Virginia's racial views changed together, and they supported each other fully at each step of their deepening commitment to civil rights and opposition to the anticommunist movement. In the Korean War incident in Colorado, Clifford fully supported her decision to sign the protest letter and to refuse to issue a retraction. He and Virginia shared equally the conviction that one does not go back on one's word or compromise one's principles for the sake of expediency. After Clifford resigned from the Federal Communications Commission, he had some trouble finding another position. Yet when he was offered a very lucrative position with a Wall Street firm dealing with communications, and that would thus use his political contacts, Clifford turned down the position without hesitation. In describing this incident, Virginia remarked, "The idea of Cliff's going back on his principles is just unthinkable. It never was a question. It was something he never even thought about. Cliff was a man of absolute principle, and he never cared much about money" (Durr, 1985, p. 218). Later, during the most turbulent times of the fight to integrate Alabama, it was often Clifford who insisted that they stay in Alabama and fight rather than retreating to the North. Clearly, in their long marriage, Clifford and Virginia each exerted mutual moral influence on the other, each positively reinforcing and supporting the other's highest values.

Interestingly, the social influences that shaped and motivated Virginia Durr came not only from her supporters but also from her opponents. She often talks about the importance of working closely with like-minded people in her poll-tax and desegregation work. Also evident, though less explicit, is the energizing effect of mobilizing against their opponents. Virginia often felt intense anger toward the conservative and anticommunist forces with which she had to contend. She felt their pressure to conform in a very personal way, and this pressure strengthened her will to resist. The emotions revealed are reminiscent of those aroused during Virginia's seven-year-old birthday party in which increased pressure to conform led her to respond with more and more disobedient behavior.

Findings from the Full Sample

On the basis of autobiographical interview material, we can trace the transformation of goals in each of our subjects in a way that closely parallels the analysis of Virginia Durr presented here. In addition, we found other striking similarities that cut across the very diverse group of people we studied. All of these similarities derive directly or indirectly from the unity of personal and moral goals and the centrality of these goals to the individual's sense of self, as we discussed in the opening section of this paper. The most striking cross-cutting themes are a certainty of belief (a lack of doubt, hesitation, or conflict), a relative lack of concern for possible dangers or negative consequences, the absence of an experience of moral courage, and a positive attitude toward life and deep enjoyment of one's work.

Moral affect

All of the moral exemplars in our study expressed great certainty about the moral decisions they made. Even during times of serious personal risk, they report having experienced little fear or doubt. Nor did they report sifting or weighing consequences when issues of principle were at stake. They cared little for moral courage, a notion in one of our questions that probed into their personal feelings. It seems that they do not see following principle as a matter of choice (that is, they don't seriously consider doing otherwise), and so they don't believe that they are courageous when making moral decisions. This was a striking finding, because many of these people had indeed placed themselves in danger by living out their values.

   This finding parallels that reported by Haste (1990) in her study of moral commitment. In a sample of dedicated social activists, she characterized her subjects as being certain, having conviction, and lacking doubt. They also showed strikingly little disjunction between their moral beliefs and their actions.

   Virginia Durr, throughout her interview, clearly expressed a strong sense of certainty about her beliefs and the central motivating role this certainty played. In this she is prototypical of our group. Like so many of the others, she denies having questioned or struggled with her beliefs. She knew what was right and knew that *she* was responsible for carrying it out. To a large extent, she disregarded the costs and dangers entailed, or at least did not weigh them strategically against the benefits, in making moral decisions. As a result, like our other exemplars, she did not experience herself as courageous. In this regard she is again prototypical:

A.C.: When you were working on all these things and so on, were there some times when you weren't sure what you should do? Many times it seemed very obvious what you needed to do and so on, but were there times when you really felt in a dilemma, you had trouble making decisions or you found it difficult?
V.D.: No, I can't remember that. I remember people saying, "You can't be self-righteous. You're so self-righteous. You know you're right." Well, I did know I was right, and I felt that denying anybody the right to vote was wrong. I felt to segregate people was wrong. I never had any doubts about it. You see, you're terribly criticized when you do these things that are against the majority. If you don't know you're right, you have nothing to fall back on. I knew I was right. I was actually certain of it. I never had any doubts.

Later,

A.C.: It seems that you attribute courage to other people a lot, but then you didn't attribute it to yourself. You would say that the little black children that were going to school, talking about them showing courage, and your husband and so on, and all these people, but you don't attribute yourself as having acted . . .
V.D.: Well, no, because I did what I felt I had to do, but I never felt that I was doing it from courage, that I was being so brave about it. It was just something I had to do. But I didn't feel any great sense of exultation about it.

To say that Virginia was certain she was right and did not consider backing off from her positions is not to say that she was immune to the pain of social disapproval and controversy. She was still very much a Southern lady, and the disapproval of her former friends meant more to her than it might to someone who had more fully renounced the culture. And in spite of her certainty that she had to act as she did, in looking back at age 84, Virginia Durr was not without regrets. She did not regret the lack of money or lack of ease in her life. She did not regret the turmoil of being "in the fray." But she did regret not having more time to spend with her children, and she regretted the pain the younger children had to endure during the hardest times in Alabama. In spite of this regret, when she thinks back on the urgency of the times, she realizes that if she had it to do over again, she would no doubt make the same choices:

V.D.: My children certainly don't look back on Montgomery with happiness. Too hard, and too many threats, and too poor, and didn't feel any sense of real pleasure. And that's sad, in a way, if your children have such a large number of years that they look back on as unhappiness. And you feel kind of guilty that you got them in that position.

A.C.: Remembering the urgency of what was going on, do you think you would have made different choices?

V.D.: Well, there were no choices to make.

In addition to this certainty, our moral exemplars demonstrate a highly positive attitude toward life and see themselves as having been very fortunate, even when their objective life circumstances have been marked by adversity, poverty, discrimination, untimely bereavement, and other forms of misfortune. They speak convincingly of the real enjoyment they have derived from such activities as raising troubled, inner-city adolescents or drug-addicted infants. As we have noted, Virginia Durr expresses a great deal of anger when she speaks of such issues as the exploitation of women, blacks, and the poor, and toward her political opponents. This contrasts sharply with the attitudes of some of our other exemplars, who stress the importance of love and forgiveness. In some sense, then, Virginia Durr did not have the same kind of positive attitude that we saw in most of our exemplars. The difference in orientation may have something to do with differences in the nature of their work. Virginia Durr's primary contributions involve *fighting against* a powerful establishment, whereas some of the others who most dramatically display a loving and forgiving attitude were extending charity to the poor. Although both tasks involve some relationship with both the oppressor and the oppressed, Virginia's primary focus is on the oppressor, and the primary focus of those working directly with the poor is on the oppressed. Another source of the difference may be in the role of religion in the lives of the exemplars. Many of our exemplars are deeply religious, and several explicitly aspire to be Christ-like, whereas Christianity plays a minimal role in Virginia Durr's life. On the other hand, Virginia was like the others in that she loved her work, "enjoyed being in the fray," did not pity herself with regard to the difficult conditions of her life and her modest financial circumstances, and was often able to turn a difficult situation into a positive one.

Moral judgment

On the standard moral judgment measures, the exemplars cover the full range of adult developmental levels. As noted above, those in our sample who reason at Kohlberg's stages 3 and 4 are as likely as those who evidence principled moral judgment to have unified personal and moral goals, have a close relationship between their moral convictions and their sense of self, and be deeply certain and free of conflict about their moral beliefs. This is not to say that our exemplars' cognitive-moral frameworks are irrelevant to their contributions. In fact, we see a close relationship between the exemplar's area of contribution and moral frame of reference. It is not surprising, for example, that Virginia Durr's moral reasoning was at stage 5, in view of the explicit focus of her life work on social justice and legal issues. This raises the question of the direction of influence and the sequence of development of her social-moral perspective relative to her involvement in the political activities we have described. It may be, for example, that her political experiences contributed to her cognitive-moral development, which then contributed to her further political engagement. Since we have only retrospective data, we cannot answer this kind of question. In other exemplars, we see stage 3 and 4 moral judgment in the context of lives characterized by selfless devotion to the poor. These exemplars are almost always deeply religious, and it may be that their religious convictions serve as the kind of anchor for them that moral principles serve for people like Virginia Durr. (Others in our sample are both deeply religious and at stage 5, so it does not appear that a scoring bias has underestimated the moral judgment stage of the religious people.)

In their explanations of their life decisions, moral exemplars at all stages of moral judgment tend to offer justifications based on actions, events, or circumstances rather than on generalizations or abstractions. It is as if they believe that the actions and situations speak for themselves, so there is no need to make explicit the values or principles underlying their moral choices. This again was a striking finding, because samples of adults who are no more intellectually sophisticated tend to be quite verbally explicit about their moral beliefs. But embedded within the action-oriented narratives that our exemplars tell are moral principles and values to which the exemplars are deeply committed. These values and principles can be abstracted from their narratives, and this, of course, has been one of the goals for our analysis of the interview data.

To quote again,

A.C.: When you think about the goals that you had—and I think we've talked a bit about what some of your goals were—do you think of those as basically being moral goals?
V.D.: I don't know if they were moral or democratic goals. The right to vote and the right not to be segregated are certainly moral goals in my opinion, but I never—in the middle of it I don't think I ever thought about any sense of moral goals. I just thought about them as something that had to be done.

Conclusion

Our intention in this chapter was to convey a perspective on the related phenomena of interpersonal influence, moral development, and the self. In approaching these problems, we employ a developmental model based upon the notion of reciprocal social influence. This model is compatible with social-psychological approaches that recognize the dynamic interplay of individuals with groups, but it focuses more on the lifelong development of individuals in the context of multiple, ongoing social experiences. A central underlying assumption of our model is that throughout the course of their development, individuals play an active part in determining their groups.

We call our blend of social-psychological and developmental perspectives a "transformation of goals" approach. In the case history that we presented in this chapter, as in others we have analyzed, one can trace the transformation and elevation of goals as the individual develops. In the course of the transformation, personal goals are transformed into moral goals and moral goals become more and more central to the individual's sense of self. In the process, the moral goals become less distinguishable from self-interest and thus ever more powerfully motivating. In spite of very great diversity in our sample of 23 people, we saw striking similarities across the group in this regard. This unity of moral goals and self-interest is, we believe, the best explanation for the internal unity and moral-centeredness that we observed in our extraordinary sample.

References

Blasi, A. (1983). Bridging moral cognition and action: A theoretical view. *Developmental Review*, 3:178–210.

Burton, R. V. (1963). Generality of honesty reconsidered. *Psychological Review*, 70:481–499.

Colby, A., and Damon, W. (1992). *Some do care: Contemporary lives of moral commitment.* New York: Free Press.

Colby, A., and Kohlberg, L. (1987). *The measurement of moral judgment.* New York: Cambridge University Press.

Damon, W. (1984). Self-understanding and moral development in childhood and adolescence. In J. Gewirtz and W. Kurtines (Eds.), *Morality, moral behavior, and moral development.* New York: Wiley.

Damon, W., and Colby, A. (1987). Social interaction and moral change. In W. Kurtines and J. Gewirtz (Eds.), *Moral development through social interaction.* New York: Wiley.

Damon, W., and Hart, D. (1988). *Self-understanding in childhood and adolescence.* New York: Cambridge University Press.

Durr, V. F. (1985). *Outside the magic circle: An autobiography of Virginia Foster Durr.* New York: Simon and Schuster.

Haste, H. (1990). Moral responsibility and moral commitment: The integration of affect and cognition. In T. Wren (Ed.), *The moral domain: Essays in the ongoing discussion between philosophy and the social sciences.* Cambridge: MIT Press.

Moscovici, S. (1976). *Social influence and social change.* London: Academic Press.

Morality, Self, and Sociohistorical Context: The Role of Lay Social Theory

Helen Haste

The Problem

There is a major debate in developmental psychology. It has been fueled in part by evidence of different conceptions of morality and self, found especially in cross-cultural studies but also in gender studies. The conflict is between those who search for the basic process inside the head of the individual and those who search for it in the interaction between persons. Many people see these as irreconcilable positions. In this chapter I argue for a model that bridges this gap. It is a model that I summarize as "taking Vygotsky seriously."

For the first position in this conflict, the starting point is the evidence for structural development, manifested in qualitative changes or stages in moral reasoning, in other areas of social reasoning, and in the individual's self concept. The concept of stage is embedded in a model of development that assumes that the individual constructs meaning and that developmental change reflects qualitative reconstruction of meaning in ever more integrated form. Though few would claim that this reconstruction happens in social isolation, the role of other individuals is mainly seen as catalytic intervention, providing challenges that, in Piaget's terms, generate disequilibration. The logic of stagewise development assumes progress moves toward increasing complexity and, by implication, increasingly adequate understanding. The structural pattern of development is presumed to be universal.

In contrast, those who take the second position argue that this model is embedded in a highly individualistic conception of development, that ignores the social and cultural context in which the child develops. Such critics cite the evidence for widely differing models of the self and of morality across and even within cultures. Their contrasting position is that the very concepts of the self and morality depend on social processes and are shaped through language and culture. Through discourse with others, the growing child learns what is morally salient and learns to invoke values and goals for moral solutions consistent with the expectations of the culture. He or she similarly learns appropriate ways of relating to others and of conceptualizing such relationships.

This situation seems to be a theoretical impasse: cultural variation is frequently cited as a terminal blow to individualistic conceptions of development, and there seems to be no place for stages or qualitative changes when the primary process of development is inculcating the growing child into a socially constructed world of meaning. The incommensurability of the two positions is demonstrated by the ways in which critics consider the very underpinnings of moral theory to diverge. Shweder (1990), for example, lumps Kohlberg with other cognitive developmentalists in the "Platonist" school, which includes mainstream empiricists and positivists who seek the "pure essential processes" of human thought and whose very methodology seeks to exclude misleading or "noisy" factors such as social context.

I want to explore a synthesis. In my view, the importance of Vygotsky is that he saw the individual as an active agent, making sense and constructing meaning within a social and a cultural environment. He thus distinguished between interpersonal interaction and the larger processes of the wider culture and sociohistorical context. Interpersonal interaction, especially in the "zone of proximal development" has generated much recent research in developmental psychology, but the issue of sociohistorical context has not penetrated the discipline so extensively. Research on the zone of proximal development recognizes the role of the peer or teacher in introducing the growing individual to new concepts; this is quite consistent with the "catalytic" model, which maintains that peer interaction facilitates development. Recognizing sociohistorical context is more radical; it involves taking seriously cultural variation in how experience is conceptualized, and not assuming, as in the Platonist approach, that there are universals (Bruner and Haste, 1987).

I will present a model that I term *lay social theory* and will consider how it bridges the gap. A lay social theory is a set of schemata and scenarios that explain or account for the origin of a desired goal or state, define what is salient, provide a structure for seeing relations between salient issues, and delineate appropriate responses to a situation. This model presumes that individuals actively make sense of their experience and apply their own repertoires of schemata and scripts in ways that much work in cognitive psychology describes. But it also presumes that making sense of something requires access to the repertoire of available lay social theories of the culture, a repertoire that both prescribes and proscribes "appropriate" solutions. Further, the model presupposes that invoking particular schemata and scripts depends upon interpersonal interaction and continuous discourse and cannot be explained solely in terms of the individual's own experience and thought.

Cultural Variation and Its Implications

A rich vein of anthropological material reveals how varied are human conceptions of selfhood, and how many conceptions are alien to the Western perspective (see, for instance, Geertz, 1975; Rosaldo, 1984; Shweder and Bourne, 1984; Shweder and Much, 1987). Embedded in these conceptions or models of selfhood are cultural assumptions about roles, relationships, and self-worth that underpin morality. Even before one begins to collect data, it is obvious that the Western model of the self (as described by Geertz, 1975) gives enormous weight to individuals' personal autonomy and freedom purely because they are persons rather than because of their role. It focuses on the self as the agent relating to others, rather than on the interconnection of persons. Self-worth is therefore seen in terms of the individual's being able to act freely and, within that, to act responsibly vis-à-vis others, who are free, separate, selves. Performing a "role" is not enough, for this is hiding behind a public face rather than acting as an individual. In contrast, for societies that locate the self in roles and think of the interrelationship of selves in functional terms, performing a role can be coterminous with morality and self-worth.

One might ask, however, why it matters that other societies have conceptions of the self and morality fundamentally different from our own, that society in which the science of psychology has largely developed. Can we not claim merely that our science is adequate to account for the members of our own culture and leave open the issue of what kind of psychology others might develop? Certainly one might feel that the criticism that Piaget's or Kohlberg's stages are not found among agrarian or hunter-gatherer societies is hardly an objection to their valid application in New York, Berlin, or London. There are two issues here: the assumptions underlying developmental theory and the implications of variations for the truth or value of any one position. These can both be subsumed under the distinction between universalism and relativism. Universalism implies that there are universals in development; that there are commonalities in conceptions of selfhood and moral codes despite local variations in the expression or boundary of values and concepts. Relativism implies that each society may generate very different ways of ordering human experience and of inculcating the growing child into the culture, so that concepts, values, and the processes of development cannot translate across boundaries and, indeed, may even be incomprehensible across cultures.

There is a large philosophical debate about this dichotomy, discussed in this volume by Amélie Rorty, but it translates into developmental theory as the question of individualism versus holism. Do we assume that development is primarily a matter of the individual mind engaging in construction and reconstruction, albeit facilitated by the cultural and social environment, and ultimately arriving at some common understanding that expresses universal requirements of the human condition? Or do we assume that not only *what* we know but also *how* we know derives entirely from our cultural heritage? In the latter case, the repertoires of experience and the meaning granted to that experience set the framework for the child's development, and growing "understanding" is in fact growth of an increasingly sophisticated appreciation of that meaning system. In other words, do we take cultural variation as prima facie evidence of the role of social context and of the primacy of social and cultural processes, or as evidence of some kind of "deficit" hindering normal individual development?

As an illustration of these alternatives, consider what happens if we assume that there *are* universals of human development. This generates a search for universals, usually after research has established the pattern of Western development. If universals are not found, there are problems of explanation. If the Bonga Bonga cannot do formal operational tasks or produce moral reasoning beyond stage 3, do we assign them to a "less developed" ontogenetic status, or do we try to find out what is wrong with (i.e., what is too narrowly Western about) our measures? The first conclusion assumes a deficit; it assumes that something about Bonga Bonga culture inhibits development. Shweder and Bourne (1984) describes this as the "evolutionist" model. A second possible conclusion is that there may be universals but we have not found them yet. If we then discover that the Bonga Bonga can do formal operations when they are cast in terms of the problems of their culture, or can resolve stage 4 and stage 5 moral dilemmas similarly, we may be reassured that there are structural universals but not necessarily content universals, and we have to find a way to incorporate the implications of this.

Things are much worse if we find that there is no place in Bonga Bonga culture for abstraction and complexity, that the culture, because it does not value complexity and abstraction, has no means to develop skills for dealing with them. If we decide that a deficit model cannot explain Bonga Bonga development, then we must conclude that our assumptions about universals are wrong.

There is a third option, which goes beyond the dichotomy of relativism and universalism: pluralism. If another culture (or subculture) treats the problems of our investigation in a different way, the relativist conclusion must be that this *undermines* the theoretical basis of our system. In contrast, the pluralist conclusion leads to an *enlargement*, rather than a rejection, of our position. One can argue, without being charged with evolutionism, that the abilities to utilize abstract concepts and to argue from the general to the particular as well as from the particular to the general are more useful than the absence of such abilities. It is more difficult, perhaps, to justify the argument that one particular form of abstract reasoning is always the most functional, whatever the situation. In the case of models of selfhood, it is certainly even less tenable to argue that the Western version is necessarily the most functional, integrated, or extensive.

Yet such differences are not only a matter of differences between societies; much parallel work points to *intracultural* differences. Ethnic groups and classes are differentiated by "cultural" beliefs, values, and ways of dealing with that knowledge which belie the universality of middle-class, white culture. These differences have been treated similarly to differences between societies: some researchers apply deficit models to argue that the deprived group underachieves because it fails to integrate into the dominant culture. But another argument is that working class (or black) culture provides an alternative set of values that gives its members a sense of self-worth even in the absence of "success," as defined according to middle-class norms. Both models imply that the route for upward mobility is by shedding or transforming value systems. The subcultural value system is a "deficient" system. It also follows that when social or legal changes remove institutional barriers or when particular persons gain equal status with the dominant group through achievement, they will perforce adopt the values and ways of knowing of that group.

The relativist view is that as well as providing a positive identity for ·an underprivileged group, the alternative value system has its own cultural history, and has validity in its own right. But it may still be a product of oppression; the alternative system may be functional for underclass status. This may be because it is a different route to self-worth, or because it is symbiotic with the dominant group's worldview. Recognizing the limitations of the dominant worldview leads to its rejection, but nevertheless, the alternative is in some sense an antithesis of it. A truly alternative system is not imposed on the group, nor is it merely a reciprocal version of the dominant system. The group "owns" it.

The relativistic conclusion that Shweder draws from his Indian data is that there are serious flaws in both a stage model and a model that makes justice central to morality. In studies with people in the province of Orissa he found that self-worth—*dharma*—was rated as more important than preservation of life for its own sake, and that autonomy meant not individualism but rather the surrender of material possessions and the pursuit of self-understanding (Shweder and Much, 1987; Shweder, Mahapatra, and Miller, 1987). Some Indians talk about moral issues in clearly postconventional terms, yet they would be coded in the Kohlberg system as at the conventional level because their reasoning is based on quite different premises about morality and a fundamentally different view of self. Shweder appears to query not stage theory as such but the preeminence of justice as the only basis of moral theory and the failure of Kohlberg's system to reflect postconventional Indian thought.

A pluralist perspective would conclude that there are several "latent moral theories," as it were, of which justice is but one. Shweder in his recent works talks of "divergent rationalities." A rational moral law has certain "mandatory" qualities, which are universal at least in form, but there are many discretionary elements. Similar conclusions have been drawn by Edwards in her review of cross-cultural research in moral reasoning. She identifies an alternative ethic of honor found outside northern European and Western societies, and the ethic of family loyalty pervasive in Chinese culture (Edwards, 1986). Members of other cultures, particularly if they are educated in a Western environment or system, may have access to an ethic based on justice and so be able to give responses to moral dilemmas couched in terms of justice, but it may not be a true reflection of their preferred mode of thinking about such issues. This point also applies to the question of sex differences in moral perspectives. As I have discussed elsewhere (Haste, 1987b; Haste and Baddeley, 1991; see also Gilligan, 1982, 1988), the evidence from work by Gilligan and others indicates that *within* Western culture there are two different ways of looking at moral issues, ways that depend on underlying differences in conceptions of relations between the self and others, namely, whether the self is seen as "connected" or "separate" from others. Whether these two ways actually map onto gender seems to me less important than the fact that two perspectives coexist in the same culture and can be elicited in different situations.

Culture and the Individual

In the rest of this chapter I shall address the problem of how to take on board the implications of cultural pluralism while still giving weight to the evidence for individual processes of construction. In the first section of this chapter I illustrated the kind of data that force us to recognize quite profound cultural differences in the concepts of self and morality. These differences challenge the assumptions of universalism underpinning those models of development that focus on individual construction of meaning. Such data require a model that does more than treat the social context as a catalyst facilitating or inhibiting the rate of development. What is needed is a model that recognizes the profoundly social nature of the construction of meaning.

There are, of course, a number of theoretical traditions in which there is no problem about conceptualizing the self or moral beliefs as products of socialization and in which there is no difficulty with accepting the pluralist position or even the relativist position. The standard position presents the relationship between individual thought and society as a hierarchy of unidirectional influence: society influences significant adults, who in turn influence the children. This model underlies various forms of functionalism, including social learning theory: different societies influence the (presumably passive) adult and the child in different ways. In a sense, neither culture nor the individual is problematic. In contrast, some theoretical positions (for example, those deriving from forms of Marxism) regard the culture as problematic, as subject to and a reflection of economic and historical forces. Yet these models tend to regard the individual's development as unproblematic. The social context, particularly class, provides frameworks for concepts and values, and this is regarded as sufficient explanation of an individual's development, with no need to address actual processes at the individual level.

Active, constructivist models of the individual, such as those underpinning cognitive-developmental theory, treat culture as unproblematic in the sense of assuming homogeneity across cultures. Only if they cannot explain cross-cultural differences by inhibition or facilitation is there any need to regard culture as problematic. Indeed, if the locus of developmental processes is primarily the individual, there is little need or space within the theory for considering the wider context.

The real recent tensions within psychology, I would argue, have not been the rather outmoded debate between social-learning theory and cognitive-developmental theory, both of which in fact concern themselves with the individual at the micro level. They are, rather, tensions arising from new forms of social psychology that emphasize the social processes of knowing, that a priori reject individual construction of meaning and the concept of stages, even to the point of arguing that a seven-year-old will produce, not just parrot, stage 6 moral judgments if the context is right (Rom Harré, personal communication). The counterargument often put by cognitive developmentalists is that such critics confuse structure and content, but this misses the point; these criticisms are based on a rejection of *any such thing* as individual cognitive structure. The extreme social-deterministic position has much in common with the dramaturgical model of selfhood: all the individual has are role repertoires, to be used as appropriate to social requirements. A milder position is that the individual's version of meaning does have valid status but that this derives solely from negotiation with others, and not from isolated cognitive activity.

To disentangle the debate, I argue that it is essential to recognize two distinct levels of social processes. One is the wider culture, the milieu or context within which people make sense of their experience. This is the level of cultural, class, and ethnic differences in belief systems, schemata of the self, and ways of approaching and defining problems. At this level there are taken-for-granted understandings: members of the culture share common schemata, common cues for interpretation, common expectations of action and response, and within these they communicate many layers of meaning.

The other level of social processes is the interaction between the growing children and others, either peers or adults. Here in face-to-face encounters the child learns what is *taken for granted* and what is *problematic*, is rewarded or sanctioned for actions and for the misunderstanding or misuse of concepts, and in a million small ways is led to tacit knowledge of the culture. For some social-psychological perspectives, this constitutes the whole explanation of individual development of understanding. From the perspective of cognitive-developmental theory, this is the level where one sees cognitive conflict arising from the gap between two people negotiating a task and, in doing so, revealing the limitations of their strategies and understandings. The role of such interaction has become increasingly integrated into cognitive-developmental approaches; researchers see it as one of the ways in which individual cognitive disequilibrium arises. In the moral domain, individual interaction is the locus of studies of "Socratic" discussions in the classroom and for the analyses of the Just Community. Other writers in the cognitive field have explored the role of the group as a facilitator of problem solving (Doise and Mugny, 1984; Doise and Palmonari, 1984).

So, how one views the role of interpersonal interaction depends on where one starts in conceptualizing the relationship between the social and the individual. For those who regard the larger context as problematic and the individual as unproblematic, the growing child is inculcated into the cultural values and beliefs by peers and adults presenting frameworks and schemata for interpretation and the contexts for their use—a process referred to as "scaffolding." The social process can be interpreted as facilitating the transmission of values through the negotiation of meaning. For those who regard the individual as the focus and the wider culture as unproblematic, the interaction process is also negotiation, but this negotiation is part of the individual's own process of making sense. The distinction between these two viewpoints is subtle but very important, because the main agent in the situation is crucially different. The difference is in *who constructs meaning:* is it ultimately the individual or society? No one denies that there is interaction, but when the debates begin, it is clear there is a fundamental, almost ideological, division between those who view the individual as the phenomenon to be explained and those who treat the individual as the end state of a social process.

The Vygotsky Triangle

To present a model that attempts to synthesize individual construction of meaning and the social context, I will describe what I term the "Vygotsky triangle." I use this model and image because it seems to me not only to express the essence of Vygotksy's theory but also to illustrate rather vividly the tensions described above.

Vygotsky has become important recently because in many ways he provides a resolution to the division between individualistic and social approaches. I need not recapitulate the details of Vygotsky's theory, but I will refer to its key ideas. I conceptualize Vygotsky's

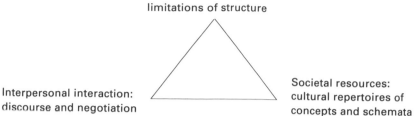

Figure 1 The Vygotsky triangle

theory as a triangle because this seems to me to represent his ideas and also the way in which they highlight, as well as potentially resolve, the division (Figure 1). This triangle contrasts with the linear model of causality and influence that I represented as the basis of functionalist approaches, most particularly because it conceptually separates "social" processes at the level of culture and "social" processes of interaction and does not see these levels simply as macro and micro levels of the same process.

Vygotsky maintained that the individual "makes sense" of the world and that individual thought processes and their structure are worth investigating. However, he differed from Piaget in the primary role that he assigned to language in the development of thought. He also made a celebrated, much quoted, and much researched statement that there is a "zone of proximal development," arguing that concepts first came to the attention of the individual through interpersonal action and discussion and only later are internalized by the individual. Finally and crucially, he argued, in line with Lenin and Engels, that knowledge is possible only within a given sociohistorical or sociocultural context.

What I have chosen to term the Vygotsky triangle consists of the individual (who has some agency in "making sense"), the interpersonal network (within which meaning is constructed, negotiated, or merely transmitted through discourse and performance of shared tasks), and the culture (the sociohistorical context that constitutes the repertoire of available frameworks and schemata within which both interpersonal discourse and individual cognition are constrained and constructed).

The triangle can be translated (with some oversimplification for clarity) into the debates outlined above in the following ways:

Traditional cognitive-developmental approaches are firmly within the individual corner but have lately moved to include the interpersonal corner, conceptualized as a catalytic process. The burgeoning work on the zone of proximal development (the interpersonal corner) has captured the imagination of many erstwhile cognitive developmentalists who have felt the limitations of purely individualistic approaches.

Much traditional social psychology, particularly work on small groups and influence processes, focused only on the relationship between the interpersonal and the individual. Recent European social psychology of the kind epitomized by Moscovici's work on social representations (Farr and Moscovici, 1984) links the cultural and the interpersonal, as does work on discourse analysis (for example, the work of Potter and Wetherell, 1987). In these approaches, a small group or dyad is the crucible of social meaning, but the culture is the main resource for frameworks of meaning. An important point of this recent work is that the interaction is *both ways:* the culture does not merely constrain what can be known; it is itself changed through the activity of the group, which generates new frameworks for meaning. Examples of this are oppressed groups who redefine the terms of reference for their positions and roles in society. The progress of feminist ideas is a notable instance of this.

Cross-cultural psychologists, who now call themselves "cultural psychologists" (see Stigler, Shweder, and Herdt, 1990), have made links between the interpersonal and sociohistorical points of the triangle. Their work shows how interpersonal processes act as the mechanism by which the culture is made explicit to the child, rather than only facilitating the child's own construction of meaning. The evidence of major differences in frameworks and schemata illustrates the role of the culture. What the child learns within a particular domain depends on how the culture defines the goal, role, and nature of that domain. Studies by Saxe and by Lave, for example, show that ways of conceptualizing even arithmetic can differ strikingly in different cultures (see Wertsch, 1985a, 1985b; Lave, 1990).

Vygotsky's theory, if taken seriously, as I have suggested, makes it possible to integrate the three points of the triangle, whereas currently much writing focuses on the relationship and interaction between two of the points while simply ignoring the third point. So, much of the discussion that starts from the position that social processes generate meaning has tended to play down, reduce to a passive state, or even reject, the role of individual construction, limiting development to an increasing "expertise" in expressing the culture's requirements. In contrast, much of the discussion that starts from an explanation of the individual's construction of meaning, especially if the explanation is conceived to be universal, has ignored the cultural context and considered interpersonal processes merely as facilitating the individual's reconstruction of meaning.

It has always seemed to me that recognizing a social context does not preclude recognizing intraindividual processes and that assuming that individuals actively construct meaning does not necessitate viewing culture as given, static, or universal. Vygotsky recognized a dialectical relationship between the social and the individual and between the individual and the culture. This is made explicit, for example, in his discussion of more advanced levels of conceptualization. His idea of "conscious realization" locates the individual's performance of higher level skills within a sociohistorical context. In generalizing such higher-level skills, the individual takes control of his or her own thought, which is no longer dependent on its context. Yet paradoxically, this abstraction is possible only because of a very culture-specific semiotic framework. Scientific concepts, for example, are necessarily learned in a formal institutional system that defines terms of reference very precisely; the very terminology and frameworks for dealing with scientific concepts are highly constrained by the culture in which they arise.

Thus the generalization of genuine mental processes that leads to their mastery lies at the foundation of conscious realization. Above all else instruction plays a decisive role in this process. [In contrast to everyday concepts] scientific concepts with their unique relationship to objects, with their internal hierarchical system of interrelationships amongst themselves are the area in which the conscious realization of concepts, that is, their generalization and mastery, emerges first and foremost. Once the new structure of generalization emerges in one sphere of thought, it is transferred, as any structure is, as a well-known principle of activity, without any training to any other area of thought and concepts. Thus conscious realization enters through the gates of scientific concepts. (Vygotsky, 1934, quoted in Wertsch, 1985a, p. 104)

As Wertsch says, this greater abstraction in fact means not a lessening of cultural effects but an increase. "This does not mean that such mental activity is somehow purer or less bound by constraints. After all, the structure of sign systems themselves are crucial in this respect. It does mean, however, that sociohistorically evolved semiotic mechanisms come to play an increasingly important role in mental functioning while concrete context plays a decreasing role" (Wertsch, 1985a, p. 104).

Thus, the more abstract and complex the concept held by the individual, the more it depends on the complex systems within the culture for sustaining the theory and on the culture-specific language for communicating such concepts.

To translate this into the moral domain, the paradox is that the more an individual is able to conceptualize moral boundaries or moral agency in terms of increasingly universal applications, the more these definitions of the universal or transcendent will depend on the abstractions and moral theories of the culture inhabited by the individual. This is well exemplified in Shweder and Much's (1987) study of the Babaji, one of the Orissan respondents. In terms of Hindu culture, this person was clearly using "postconventional" reasoning, in the structural sense of transcending the immediate, generalizing, and utilizing principles in his reasoning. Kohlberg and Higgins coded the interview, and Kohlberg recognized that the Babaji was *formally* operating as a postconventional thinker, but applying the strict format of the Standard Form coding system yielded only a score of a conventional-level stage (Colby and Kohlberg, 1987). This illustrates how Hindu culture offers a different moral language and different concepts of what is salient in moral considerations. Hindu moral language and concepts can be as complex as what emerges from American culture, but they are very different from the forms in which that complexity is expressed the Kohlberg scoring system; the Kohlberg system is the formalization of American reasoning. The point is that the higher the level of abstraction and universalizability, the more difficult it becomes to match two languages, because each is at that level a greater refinement of underlying assumptions and theory and is therefore even more embedded in the cultural framework.

Lay Social Theory

I want to present the concept of lay social theory as a way of using a Vygotskian framework to bridge the theoretical impasse I outlined earlier. As I am using the term, "lay social theory" means a set of schemata and scenarios that account for the origin of a situation, imply a desired goal or state, define what is salient in the situation, provide a structure for seeing logical or determining relations between salient issues, and delineate appropriate responses to the situation. My conception of lay social theory has much in common with "folk models" (D'Andrade, 1987) in the sense that it implies intersubjectively shared meaning, schemata, and scripts for action. Lay social theory presupposes commonsense assumptions about efficacy, about what works, and why.

Let us consider, for example, the lay social theory about crime and criminals. This lay social theory comprises schemata for what constitutes a crime, the law, a criminal, and so forth, which enables anyone in our culture to understand fully the statements "Marijuana should be decriminalized" or "Political prisoners are not criminals." The lay social theory of crime also contains beliefs about the causes and cures of crime. Thus the belief that strong punishment is important in the prevention of crime is both part of a schema about crime and a reflection of an underlying theory about mechanisms. In traditional attitude terms, this belief is seen as an attitude with an affective component: a desire for retribution combined with a belief about just desserts. But as a "theory" about what works, what is being invoked is a set of schemata about the effectiveness of deterrence, the justification of revenge, and the protection of society from further violence, each of which can exist as an explanation on its own and be applied in many different contexts.

In terms of cognitive social psychology, the concepts of schemata, scripts, and scenarios imply explanations and prescriptions for behavior or cognitive action, and they presuppose a series of events or related elements, rather than a single stimulus or focus. Thus issues are contextual rather than existing in isolation; their meaning depends on the context. In any situation, certain aspects or issues are salient because they easily fit into the familiar script or scenario (Schank and Adelson, 1977; Fiske and Taylor, 1984).

On the whole, such cognitive models focus on what happens inside the individual's head, but in fact, I want to argue, such schemata and scenarios cannot really be understood without attention to discourse. A classic example often cited is the restaurant script. This embodies a precise sequence of actions and interactions. The individual comes to know these and their meaning through personal experience and the initial guidance of an expert who is one's first host at a restaurant meal. Schank and Abelson stress the firsthand learning process, but people usually go to restaurants after some years of eating in the family and after exposure to secondary descriptions in the form of drama or stories. Furthermore, actual participation in the action takes the form of an apprenticeship, with continual commentary from the accompanying adult or peer. Thus the child is explicitly directed to take certain actions ("Sit here," "Put your napkin on your knee") but the child also hears talk that implies various aspects of the script ("What do you want to eat?" implies a choice, which is usually not part of the family meal script; "The steak is rather expensive, why not have the fish?" also departs from home eating by bringing in the idea of paying for food directly, and it also communicates the idea of thrift).

Comments like "The waiter is very slow" or "Those people over there don't seem the usual type for this restaurant" express norms not usually directly communicated, and only slowly does the child decode, for example, what his or her parents regard as a "good" restaurant. This hypothetical extension of the script model is consistent with extensive work by Shweder, Much, and Dunn on the ways in which teachers, parents, peers, and siblings continually comment on the child's behavior in ways that make assumptions (Much and Shweder, 1978; Shweder and Much, 1987; Dunn, 1987; Haste, 1987a). In decoding these assumptions, even more perhaps than through direct precept, the child learns what is taken for granted.

An individual's lay theory exists within a set of culturally available scenarios, schemata, or scripts that not only provide rules for action but also explain events and predict outcomes. Although the active individual does make sense of experience, making sense requires access to the lay social theories actually available within the culture and also presupposes that formulation, evaluation, and selection from that repertoire depend upon interpersonal interaction and continuous discourse. Individuals' lay social theories are integrally depend on the culturally available repertoires, which provide a resource for making certain things salient rather than others, for providing explanations, and for defining what is problematic and what is not. If what the individual can know and what he or she comes to know, believe, and value are constrained by the social, historical context in which the individual grows up, we must look for common frameworks, metaphors, and rhetoric within a culture to understand the possible ways in which the individual can make sense.

The first stage of integrating the individual and the social is to discover how individual understanding depends on what the cultural framework offers and what the actual mechanisms are by which the child is inculcated into such understanding and meaning. However, a full understanding of such processes requires an important shift in how we conceptualize the role of language. Recently theoretical understanding of how language operates has shifted away from seeing language merely as a tool for people to communicate their ideas monologically in the public domain after they have privately formulated them. Understanding language as being dialogic and rhetorical is crucial to a model of reasoning as a socially negotiated process, a dialectical process. A major exponent of this perspective is Billig, who argues that much of our thinking about social values and beliefs is a matter of public discourse rather than private reflection, and therefore that such thinking requires strategies for effective public communication. These strategies can be found in the ancient tradition of rhetoric, regarded with disfavor in recent times (Billig, 1987; Potter and Wetherell, 1987).

The tradition of private logic and the deductive search for "one solution" or consistency derives from Cartesianism and has its roots in Platonism. The modern version of this assumes that what is said expresses truth and validity and that language is merely a tool to transmit the logic of an idea. From this perspective, the concept of rhetoric has the unsavory quality of illicit persuasion and the distortion of "truth." But the alternative tradition of rhetoric has always existed alongside this tradition, even though lately it has been submerged, and it has a venerable history. The basic principle of rhetoric concerns the function of language in thought: we arrive at truth through *argumentation* and the conflict of different points of view—necessarily a social process, for the individual can only know through what is communicated and can only communicate through shared language and meaning. Discourse, therefore, necessarily has rhetorical characteristics: it is designed to persuade as well as to inform, it uses evaluative and logical concepts with linguistic and paralinguistic content in communicating meaning, and most particularly, it assumes a shared set of premises, rhetoric, between the speaker and the listener. Rhetoric is social speech, not merely logical speech.

In reclaiming a rhetorical model of thought and discourse for social psychology, Billig has highlighted another feature of making sense and giving meaning. This is the important distinction between whether something is seen as problematic or is taken for granted. Something problematic is explained differently from something taken for granted: the former demands explanation and justification, the latter, if questioned at all, requires merely the demonstration of its functional inevitability. In discussing the restaurant script, I noted how what is said reveals what is taken for granted as tacit, shared knowledge and how decoding this is a crucial part of how the growing child discovers what needs to be made sense of. An example of this process can be seen in the following common type of exchange:

A: It's ten o'clock.
B: I've been to the dentist.

B immediately decodes *A*'s statement as accusing *B* of being late, which was *A*'s intention. *B* responds with a factual statement that carries with it the shared understanding that going to the dentist constitutes an acceptable reason for being late.

An important aspect of the social nature of language is metaphor. Metaphor, like rhetoric, got consigned to the status of linguistic frill. A beacon in its revival was the classic work of Richards, published in 1936, but only in the last decade have psychologists begun to take metaphor seriously in trying to understand thought (Lakoff and Johnson, 1980; Lakoff, 1987). Metaphors are important to lay social theory for two reasons: first, they encapsulate concepts and schemata. Second, they make it possible to communicate ideas, including novel ideas, because they are shared; they provide frameworks and models within a common sphere of meaning. Geertz's (1975) metaphors of the stage in Bali and various Western metaphors (an island, a cocoon) all reflect models about the self.

A metaphor contains an implicit theory of how things work and what is salient. Shared metaphors enable members of the culture to allude to aspects of a model and suppose that the whole picture will be evoked in the other person's mind. There is now an extensive literature on the relationship between metaphor and concept. Consider some examples. The invention of the clock facilitated not only the advance of mechanical technology but also the mechanistic metaphors for human's relationship with Nature. This metaphor transformed the European model of science, replacing (or pushing to the background) the previous organic metaphor of the relationship between living things with a mechanistic model of the "objective" separation of the observer and the observed. The shift also made it possible to think of controlling what is observed, because it is mechanical (Merchant, 1980; Haste, 1988, 1993). The computer replaced the telephone exchange as the model for the human mind in the middle of this century, with enormous implications for the "cognitive revolution" (Gardner, 1986; Sternberg, 1990). Metaphors make certain ideas possible; even more important, they make complex ideas communicable by alluding to the familiar and the understood.

How do we translate lay social theory into the process of defining the self and morality? It gives us the basis for seeing how the individual makes sense of what he or she encounters in the social world, picking up in discourse concepts about what is problematic and what is taken for granted, what are the common and acceptable resolutions and what are the common explanations for the situation.

The constructivist perspective, the "individual" point on the triangle in Figure 1, assumes that the individual makes sense of experience within subjectively consistent "theories" about how things work, about the origins and goals or purposes of other people's behavior and ultimately of social forces. The perspective that links the individual and the "social" points of the triangle assumes that though the individual may actively "make sense" of experience, nevertheless this process is social; the individual's theories derive from culturally available repertoires, schemata, or scripts—the scenarios for explaining events or predicting outcomes. How the situation is interpreted and what is perceived to be salient reflect the familiar cultural script or scenario.

The link between the "individual" and the "interpersonal" points in the triangle is that frames and schemata for making sense emerge through the everyday discourse and negotiation of meaning with peers and because adults provide frameworks for the child's entry into particular frames of understanding and systems of meaning. This discourse takes place within the wider social context; culturally specific frames and schemata delineate what is available and salient for the discourse.

Thus, according to this integration of Vygotsky, the process is dialectical. It involves culturally available scenarios, normative expectations, and desired goals, which are accessed by the individual in part through the media (the individual-social interface) and in part through continuous social interaction (the individual-interpersonal interface). In my view, we can retain the conception of developmental stages within a model of discourse and cultural context. I argue that a child's development does reflect reconstruction processes in stages, which represent increasingly more complex structures for understanding the world (be it in the domains of logic, morality, or self-other relations), but the salient elements of those structures will depend on what schemata are culturally appropriate. Thus one must postulate stages *within* whatever happens to be the culturally prevailing "theory" of the self, or morality—be it justice, honor, responsibility, or whatever. This model requires us to extend our concept of the social process and to see social interaction and discourse as the crucible for negotiating meaning, rather than simply as a catalyst for individual disequilibration.

The Social and the Individual: Stages of Development

The model I have presented so far leaves us with two major questions about the relationship between self and moral theory. The first is the structural relationship between stages of the self and stages of moral reasoning. The second question concerns the deeper issue of how different conceptualizations of the self and self-other relations are likely to generate different lay theories of morality. Data for the first question are reasonably well established within the confines of Western conceptions of the self, but data for the second question depend on extrapolation from, at the moment, a limited range of studies.

Let us consider some of the logical ways in which we can look at the structural relationship between stages of the self and stages of moral reasoning:

Model 1   Stages of self-conception may be a necessary but not sufficient condition for the emergence of parallel stages of moral reasoning. This has been explored, with somewhat conflicting results, in discussions about the relationship between ego development and moral development.

Model 2   Stages of self-conception and stages of moral reasoning may both depend on a third dimension of development (for example, cognitive complexity); their commonalities therefore depend upon this underlying structural feature. An analogy would be to treat Selman's stages of social perspectives as the common basis for the self concept and moral reasoning stages.

Both of these models implicitly presume that the individual constructs the self, that the self progresses toward greater autonomy (Geertz's Western model), and that moral theory is based on justice. In my terms, they confine themselves to the individual corner of the triangle. The question is, How far do such models apply to other models of the self?

The answer logically seems to be that any theory of the self and any theory of morality can have levels of increasing complexity. Can we envisage levels of complexity in the Balinese self? Of course, for any theory of the self influenced by Buddhism has complexity built into it. Can we envisage levels of complexity within moral theories grounded on honor or family loyalty? Certainly, for we know that moral theory grounded on responsibility and care has identifiable levels of complexity. The common ground of these and other moral theories is likely to be their tendency to extend moral arguments and the range of moral scenarios to a wider, more inclusive set of categories, as well as increasing detachment from the particular so as to allow the application of general principles. In the case of a theory of justice, of course, such extension and detachment refers to the number of people or categories of people who must be included in moral deliberation or "moral musical chairs" (Kohlberg, Boyd, and Levine, 1990). This in effect means that the more autonomous the self, the larger the range of other autonomous beings that must be included in casting the moral problem. But Shweder observed that the Babaji did indeed manifest "structural" aspects of postconventional reasoning within the Hindu moral order; in particular, absent were hedonism, social consensus, and appeals to social norms and the presence of an independent moral order, a highly rational moral perspective, and transcendent principles (Shweder and Much, 1987). This example can be seen as evidence of a parallel system of increasing complexity in understanding self and morality. Only if one holds the position that a particular moral theory and a particular model of the self must be universal does the idea of stages of individual construction of meaning become grounded solely in a Western view. A pluralist perspective allows the theorist to substitute different theories of the self, or different moral theories, with parallel structural qualities.

Social determinists offer a more extreme criticism that sees stages purely as the product of social expectation:

Model 3 Stages are artifactual in the sense of being an inherent part of some systems but not others.

This position holds that once the individual has come to understand the self and moral theory of the culture to the extent that he or she produces the right responses, no further "development" takes place; there is no difference between a competent four-year-old and an adult. While logically tenable, this position seems absurd to anyone familiar with developmental theory. An attenuated version held by some developmental psychologists is that some cultural frameworks (such as those based upon scientific abstraction, justice, or autonomy of the self) are more likely to generate a developmental path of increasing complexity than frameworks based on other core elements. In other words, cultures differ in how much they value and facilitate abstraction per se.

Two other models suggest that levels of moral complexity exist within a culture as forms of understanding, into which the individual is led at appropriate points of development, rather than levels of understanding being the outcome of individual reconstruction:

Model 4   Stages or levels of complexity are in fact the outcome of entry into new levels of expertise. Inculcating a child thus does not facilitate individual growth but instead represents a socially-assisted transition to more complex levels and access to a more complex set of beliefs. The growing child is, as it were, "apprenticed" at a new level of expertise when mentors deem that he or she is ready for it.

Model 5   Stages of development are ontogenetic, but the social and cultural world facilitates access to particular "theories" of the self or morality. Because I can now deal with stage 4 moral reasoning, or the equivalent in Loevinger's ego stages, I can now enter the social discourse that takes place within that level of thinking. This again assumes that there are different levels of cultural schemata or scenarios that the child is helped to grow into.

Each of the above models accounts for evidence of different levels of complexity by pointing out different variations and groupings in the underlying moral or self theory and locating these in different social contexts. One does not need, however, to appeal to cross-cultural or even sex differences to find evidence of moral and self reasoning structured in different ways. Two individuals in Kohlberg's (1984) longitudinal sample held consistent but very different theories of the self and morality across a long period of time and through several stages of moral development (Haste, 1984). Lenny (case 23) maintained a rule-oriented, law-based model of justice throughout the period; Jack (case 7), throughout twenty years, invoked responsibility and roles and indeed sounded very much like Gilligan's female respondents. Within each orientation, and at different stages, they expressed different schemata, reflecting different salient issues. Lenny's case is particularly interesting because he maintained his general moral and self theories despite enormous changes in his political beliefs: he shifted from the extreme right to the extreme left during the relevant period. Different aspects of rule and law became salient for him, and these reflected the different moral systems he associated with the different political beliefs. Lenny was exposed to these different moral systems as he moved from the Goldwaterite militarism of his father's social milieu to the radical-left environment of the London School of Economics. What we see here is Lenny developing new schemata that are the products of increasing cognitive complexity and of exposure to different social contexts and integrating them into a stable moral theory at different levels. (I have discussed these cases in more detail in Weinreich-Haste, 1984, and Haste, 1990.)

A final possible model of the interaction of stages and social contexts is paradoxical:

Model 6 Abstracting postconventional reasoning (in whatever form) is possible only because it is rooted in a culturally specific semiotic. This is the moral equivalent of the point quoted earlier from Vygotsky: higher mental processes in scientific thought are free of their concrete support systems *only because* they are fully articulated within a specific cultural semiotic system.

There are two ways of conceptualizing "postconventional," or "abstract," levels of reasoning. One view is that postconventional reasoning is in fact the fullest flowering of culturally specific schemata. The other view, more generally assumed, is that in the earlier levels of development the individual is growing into successively closer approximations to the cultural norm, but at some point the process "takes off," and the individual is able to go beyond the culturally defined boundaries and consider novel possibilities. This is the characteristic of postconventional moral reasoning, or Selman's (1976) "prior-to-society" perspective-taking. Models of cognitive development tend to assume that at this postconventional level the individual is able to generate ab initio the principles for reasoning, whether on moral, logical, or self issues. At the very least, the individual at the level of postconventional reasoning can adopt a pluralistic perspective and consider other systems.

Such discussions leave open the question of where awareness of systems comes from. If the culture is monolithic, logically the only option is to refine the conventional system in more abstract ways. But few cultures are truly monolithic; there is quite a wide range of systems available. What constrains their accessibility is first, legitimacy. The dominant ethos of a culture defines the acceptable boundaries, acceptable forms of rationality, and acceptable explanations. The perennial debates about what constitutes "science" and what is relegated to "pseudoscience" are one manifestation of this. The second constraint is comprehensibility. Vygotsky argued that abstraction is possible because the higher levels of thought are a systematization of the semiotic tools of the culture. This means that the individual is ill equipped to operate with any other system. Objections to the legitimacy of alternative perspectives frequently reveal as much a lack of comprehension as a rejection on the basis of value. This, of course, is at the root of Shweder's argument that Kohlberg's (Western) moral order offers no basis for comprehending the Hindu moral order.

We must conclude, therefore, that to have access to an alternative system of thought in whatever domain, either the individual must be exposed to discourse within that system and have an opportunity to develop increasingly complex concepts within it, or the system must exist within the individual's culture but only become accessible after the individual has reached a level of complexity and abstraction to be able to transcend the terms of reference of the dominant system. The first model may apply in a pluralistic culture where individuals are exposed to several, in effect parallel, systems. This is perhaps what happens in countries where a Western (or other colonial) educational regime overlays the indigenous culture without replacing it, but it is certainly true of Western culture with regard to the different ethical systems of justice, responsibility, and perhaps honor. The second model seems to presuppose that postconventional reasoning is a necessary condition for discovering alternative systems. The paradox may be that pluralism is inherent in the fully abstracted postconventional system. This position is implied in Kohlberg, Boyd, and Levine's (1990) later refinements of their thinking about stage 6 reasoning.

Morality and Self

In this final section I shall consider in detail some of the evidence about the relationship between conceptions of the self and conceptions of what is salient in moral issues, illustrating the ways in which lay social theory operates and the ways in which individuals have access to different kinds of explanations within the culture. I argued earlier that the importance of Gilligan's findings of different moral and self orientations lie as much in what they reveal about the pluralistic moral orders in Western culture as in how such moral orders map onto gender. I have considered elsewhere (Haste and Baddeley, 1991) how gender operates as a subculture to facilitate the growing individual's expertise within one system rather than another. My concern here is how the evidence elaborates the model of lay social theories of self and morality.

In operationalizing her ideas in her scoring system, Gilligan and her associates utilize both self and ethical elements in differentiating the two orientations. In our own studies at the University of Bath, we have partially replicated Gilligan's work and extended it somewhat. An important feature of our approach was that we did not use the Gilligan's and Lyon's coding system but began with our own data and the differences that we found emerging within our own sample (Wingfield and Haste, 1987; Haste and Baddeley, 1991; Haste, 1992). We found interviewees adopting a distinctive "separate" or "connected" orientation in areas similar to those noted by Gilligan: friendship, responsibility, promise keeping.

These two orientations were reflected in the conceptions of self-other relationships that surfaced in our study. We asked our respondents a question about promise keeping: "Why is it important to keep a promise?" Those having a separate orientation saw promises as contracts between autonomous persons, implying that a contract requires the participants to be trustworthy persons. Trustworthiness is an attribute of the person; people adopting a separate orientation talk of "being that kind of person." Their emphasis is on the quality of the promisor rather than on the function of the relationship.

In contrast to seeing trustworthiness as an attribute of the person, respondents with a connected orientation focused on maintaining relationships as the primary goal of conflict resolution. For these individuals, breaking a trust involves letting others down and causing hurt, or betraying a relationship by no longer showing trust. Trust is the defining characteristic of friendship, an attribute of a relationship between persons.

In other words, the two orientations reflect different aspects of Western cultural norms about the self and about promising, and are embedded in different lay social theories of relationships. Another area that differentiated the two orientations especially well was loyalty. We posed a dilemma about two best friends. While one of them was on vacation, the protagonist (the friend who stayed behind) was invited by the other's boyfriend or girlfriend to go to a disco. Should they go? Should they kiss? For respondents with a separate orientation, the main feature of their responses was their territoriality: what did the protagonist consider as the rights of the absent best friend with regard to the latter's boyfriend or girlfriend, and what did the protagonist think about breaking a code of loyalty? This implies that there is a contract between best friends about property and rights and obligations based on the rules of friendship. In contrast, respondents having the connected orientation placed themselves in the roles of various members of the triangle, and they used the language of hurting or causing unhappiness.

Our evidence supports an interrelationship between one's model of self-other relations and one's primary concern in moral and social dilemmas. In terms of lay social theory, we, like Gilligan, are finding that conceptions of self-other relationships, models of connection or separation, make different things salient in the situation. What is problematic and what is taken for granted differs. Hurting and maintaining the relationship were salient for one respondent, Karen, in considering what is wrong. Another respondent, Adrian, saw the girlfriend as a possession of the friend. She is in the protagonist's "care" as part of his obligations to his friend, and this in effect removes her from the circle of persons whom he relates to.

Although we found that some individuals did move between orientations, for the most part throughout an interview we did find an individual invoking consistent schemata in very different situations, and this reflects a consistent lay social theory. Adrian was 17 years old. His view of people, and of himself, emphasized "character," discipline, and order. This came out in many of his answers. Karen, on the other hand, was 15. She adopted a connected orientation and continually invoked the schema of "hurting," as, for example, in the loyalty dilemma. A key element of Karen's connected orientation is the idea of *listening*; it recurs often in her language. Where Adrian was inclined to invoke rules, Karen invoked perspective-taking and listening. (These cases are considered in greater detail in Haste, 1992.)

Our findings are consistent with the distinctions that Gilligan found between the different orientations in responses concerning self and morality, but our data show that an individual's self-other orientation extends outside the strictly moral domain into lay social theories of social order. We presented to our respondents a modified version of Adelson and O'Neil's (1966) story concerning the "Pitcairn Island" situation of a thousand people who are marooned and have to develop a society. In the responses we identified different conceptualizations of the islanders' problems and resolutions. What we saw as separateness was reflected in the imposition of rules by a body of experts or people with power to deal with conflicts arising from lack of planning or from violence and greed. An ordered world of rules and roles provides clear expectations; boundaries to territory and behavior set limits. Order is achieved through a top-down organization run by experts accountable to the community, whether these work through democratic negotiation or through the imposition of power. What works is an ordered system within which people have tacit or explicit contracts and sets of rights and roles. Adrian saw the islanders needing order and expertise. The main problems he saw were the distribution of resources and the safety of people who might get lost and injured. The solution was structured leadership that drew on experts with the right background.

In contrast, a connected perspective focused on the development of social mechanisms to facilitate cooperation and resolution of conflicts through negotiation—a bottom-up model of community government. Karen illustrated this by stressing community, communication between the islanders, and the human side of organization.

Karen's underlying schema was that society requires the qualities, writ large, that work in individual interaction, such qualities as empathy, concern for others, and the social skills needed to create and maintain harmony. A community arises out of cooperation and collaboration. There is an implied interdependence and awareness of the needs of others. What needs to be established are mechanisms of contact, cooperation, and communication (Haste, 1991, 1992).

These examples happen to come from a boy and a girl, but even though we did find a sex-linked pattern in our small study, we also found some girls who used a separate orientation and some boys (though fewer) who used a connected orientation. But as I have discussed in Weinreich-Haste (1984), separation and connection, and different lay social theories, are also evident in Kohlberg's (1984) own longitudinal interviews.

The importance of these examples, all of which come from advanced Western cultures, is that they show remarkably different ways of dealing with issues of real life and hypothetical situations. Karen and Adrian are talking in very different ways across a wide range of issues. Yet each of them is quite embedded in British culture; each of their perspectives is entirely comprehensible to other members of the culture. They are drawing on different schemata, and applying different lay social theories with some quite profoundly different assumptions about what works and what motivates people. My analysis of what is going on is that each has found a different model congenial, not that each has invented or constructed a model in isolation. Internal evidence in these interviews shows that peer groups engage in a considerable amount of discourse in everyday life and that what these adolescents are reporting about their own perspectives and schemata is a common orientation for their group. In Haste (1991) I explored the relationship between different lay social theories and political understanding. My findings suggested that parent's political beliefs contributed somewhat to the available schemata used by adolescents, but it was also clear that the adolescents incorporated these schemata as their own lay social theory. Moral development, in other words, is a continual dialectic.

Conclusion

In this chapter I attempted the ambitious task of considering the evidence for intra- and intercultural differences in fundamental conceptions of the self, and the evidence for how this is related to the moral theories that individuals use in ordinary life. To relate conceptions of the self to moral theories, I provided a model that takes the dialectical perspectives of Vygotsky seriously, locating the process of making sense within a social and sociohistorical context while retaining the structural development manifested in individual thought. I argued that taking a pluralistic perspective allows us to integrate social and individual processes, rather than, as is often the case in current debate, seeing these as theoretically incompatible. I think that what is now needed is considerable research on interpersonal interaction and discourse and on the relationship between the schemata that young people use in their lay social theories and what is available to them through media and peer culture, including the subculture of gender. Some of this work is already being done. Interviews tap only the final outcome: what is in the individual's head, attenuated by the social processes of the interview.

I have argued that the prima facie evidence for some connection between a person's model of self-other relations and the dominant ethic of their moral theory begs major questions about the cultural basis of morality and self. Another basic question of this chapter is why particular models of the self seem to generate particular moral theories, although I concede that there is a natural logic to this, deriving from conceptions of self-other relations. But this "natural logic" is not merely the result of the individual making sense of morality on his or her own.

The cross-cultural material, Shweder's study in particular, forces us to ask how individuals reared with such different conceptions of the self generate moral systems (see Shweder, Mahapatra, and Miller, 1988). The answer we can gain from a more detailed comparison of the separate and connected orientations in Western samples is that different things are seen as salient in the situation, different issues as problematic, according to the individual's basic orientation toward relations with others. The concept of lay social theory, I have here argued, gives us a framework for seeing how the individual applies schemata, or scenarios, to make sense of situations defined by the culture, and experienced by the self, as problematic.

But a final question remains: is there a resolution of the divide between cognitive-developmental approaches (which take as given the individual's construction and reconstruction of the self and morality as manifested in stages of increasing cognitive complexity) and social-psychological approaches (which argue that once we accept social interaction as the crucible of understanding and concepts, there is no place for the concept of stages)? I contend that taking Vygotsky seriously in the way I have described enables us to see individuals as acting on their experience to reconstruct the self and morality within a social context that both limits and facilitates development. But to see people in this way, cognitive developmentalists have to become pluralists.

References

Adelson, J., and O'Neil, R. (1966). The growth of political ideas in adolescence. *Journal of Personality and Social Psychology*, 4:295–306.

Billig, M. (1987). *Arguing and thinking.* Cambridge: Cambridge University Press.

Bruner, J. S., and Haste, H., Eds. (1987). *Making sense: The child's construction of the world.* London: Methuen.

Colby, A., and Kohlberg, L. (1987). *The measurement of moral judgment.* Vol. 2. New York: Cambridge University Press.

D'Andrade, R. (1987). A folk model of the mind. In D. Holland and N. Quinn (Eds.), *Cultural models in language and thought.* Cambridge: Cambridge University Press.

Doise, W., and Mugny, G. (1984). *The social development of the intellect.* Oxford: Pergamon Press.

Doise, W., and Palmonari, A. (1984). *Social interaction in individual development.* Cambridge: Cambridge University Press.

Dunn, J. (1987). Understanding feelings, the early stages. In J. S. Bruner and H. Haste (Eds.), *Making sense: The child's construction of the world.* London: Methuen.

Edwards, C. P. (1981). The comparative study of the development of moral judgment and reasoning. In R. H. Munroe, R. L. Munroe, and B. B. Whiting (Eds.), *Handbook of cross-cultural human development.* New York: Garland Press.

Edwards, C. P. (1986). Cross-cultural research on Kohlberg's stages: The basis for consensus. In S. Modgil and C. Modgil (Eds.), *Kohlberg: Consensus and controversy.* Lewes, England: Falmer Press.

Farr, R., and Moscovici, S. (1984). *Social representations*. Cambridge: Cambridge University Press.

Fiske, S. T., and Taylor, S. E. (1984). *Social cognition*. New York: Random House.

Gardner, H. (1986). *The mind's new science*. New York: Basic Books.

Geertz, C. (1975). On the nature of anthropological understanding. *American Scientist*, 63:47–53.

Gilligan, C. (1982). *In a different voice*. Cambridge: Harvard University Press.

Gilligan, C. (1986). Remapping the moral domain: New images of self in relationship. In T. C. Heller, M. Sosna, and D. E. Wellbery (Eds.), *Reconstructing individualism*. Stanford: Stanford University Press.

Gilligan, C., Ward, J. V., and Taylor, J. M., Eds. (1988). *Mapping the moral domain*. Cambridge: Harvard University Press.

Haste, H. (1986). Brother sun, sister moon: can rationality overcome a dualistic cosmology? In J. Harding (Ed.), *Perspectives on gender and science*. Lewes, England: Falmer Press.

Haste, H. (1987a). Growing into rules. In J. S. Bruner and H. Haste (Eds.), *Making sense: The child's construction of the world*. London: Methuen.

Haste, H. (1987b). Why thinking about feeling is not the same as feeling about feeling, and why post-androgyny is dialectical, not regressive: A response to Philibert and Sayers. *New Ideas in Psychology*, 5:215–221.

Haste, H. (1988). Legitimation, logic, and lust: Historical perspectives on gender, science, and ways of knowing. *New Ideas in Psychology*, 6:137–145.

Haste, H. (1990). Moral responsibility and moral commitment: The integration of affect and cognition. In T. E. Wren (Ed.), *The moral domain: Essays in the ongoing discussion between philosophy and the social sciences*. Cambridge: MIT Press.

Haste, H. (1991). The dissolution of the right in the wake of theory. In G. Breakwell (Ed.), *Social psychology of political and economic cognition*. London: Academic Press.

Haste, H. (1992). Lay social theory. In H. Haste and J. Torney-Purta (Eds.), *The development of political understanding: A new perspective*. San Francisco: Jossey-Bass.

Haste, H. (1993). *The sexual metaphor*. London: Wheatsheaf Books.

Haste, H., and Baddeley, J. (1991). Moral theory and culture: The case of gender. In W. Kurtines and J. Gewirtz, *Handbook of moral development and behavior*. Vol. 1. Hillsdale, NJ: Erlbaum.

Holland, D., and Quinn, N., Eds. (1987). *Cultural models in language and thought*. Cambridge: Cambridge University Press.

Kohlberg, L. (1984). *The psychology of moral development*. San Francisco: Harper and Row.

Kohlberg, L., Boyd, D., and Levine, C. (1990). The return of stage 6. In T. E. Wren (Ed.), *The moral domain: Essays in the ongoing discussion between philosophy and the social sciences*. Cambridge: MIT Press.

Lakoff, G. (1987). *Women, fire, and dangerous things.* Chicago: University of Chicago Press.

Lakoff, G., and Johnson, M. (1980). *Metaphors we live by.* Chicago: University of Chicago Press.

Lave, J. (1990). The culture of acquisition and the practice of understanding. In J. W. Stigler, R. Shweder, and G. Herdt (Eds.), *Cultural psychology: Essays on comparative human development.* Cambridge: Cambridge University Press.

Merchant, C. (1980). *The death of nature.* San Francisco; Harper and Row.

Much, N., and Shweder, R. (1978). Speaking of rules: The analysis of culture in breach. In W. Damon (Ed.), *Moral development.* San Francisco: Jossey-Bass.

Potter, J., and Wetherell, M. (1987). *Discourse and social psychology.* London: Sage.

Richards, I. A. (1936). *The philosophy of rhetoric.* Oxford: Oxford University Press.

Rosaldo, M. (1984). Towards an anthropology of self and feeling. In R. Shweder and R. LeVine (Eds.), *Culture theory: Essays on mind, self, and emotion.* Cambridge: Cambridge University Press.

Schank, R., and Abelson, R. (1977). *Scripts, plans, goals, and understanding.* Hillsdale, NJ: Lawrence Erlbaum.

Selman, R. (1976). Socio-cognitive understanding. In T. Lickona (Ed.), *Moral development and behavior.* New York; Holt, Rinehart, and Winston.

Shweder, R. (1982). Beyond self-constructed knowledge: The study of culture and morality. *Merrill-Palmer Quarterly,* 28:41–69.

Shweder, R. (1990). Cultural psychology, what is it? In J. W. Stigler, R. Shweder, and G. Herdt (Eds.), *Cultural psychology: Essays on comparative human development.* Cambridge: Cambridge University Press.

Shweder, R., and Bourne, E. (1984). Does the concept of the person vary cross-culturally? In R. Shweder and R. LeVine (Eds.), *Culture theory: Essays on mind, self and emotion.* Cambridge: Cambridge University Press.

Shweder, R., Mahapatra, M., and Miller, J. G. (1987). Culture and moral development. In J. Kagan and S. Lamb (Eds.), *The emergence of morality in young children.* Chicago: Chicago University Press.

Shweder, R., and Much, N. (1987). Determinants of meaning: Discourse and moral socialization. In W. Kurtines and J. Gewirtz (Eds.), *Moral development through social interaction.* New York: Wiley.

Sternberg, R. (1990). *Metaphors of mind.* Cambridge: Cambridge University Press.

Stigler, J. W., Shweder, R., and Herdt, G., Eds. (1990). *Cultural psychology: Essays on comparative human development.* Cambridge: Cambridge University Press.

Vygotsky, L. (1978). *Mind and society.* Cambridge: Harvard University Press.

Walker, L. J. (1984). Sex differences in the development of moral reasoning: A critical review. *Child Development,* 55:677–691.

Weinreich-Haste, H. (1984). Morality, social meaning, and rhetoric: The social context of moral reasoning. In W. M. Kurtines and J. Gewirtz (Eds.), *Morality, moral behavior, and moral development.* New York: Wiley.

Wertsch, J. (1985a). *Vygotsky and the social formation of mind.* Cambridge: Harvard University Press.

Wertsch, J. (1985b). *Culture, communication, and cognition.*, Cambridge: Cambridge University Press.

Wingfield, L., and Haste, H. (1987). Connectedness and separateness: Cognitive style or moral orientation? *Journal for Moral Education,* 16:214–225.

"Normative Vulnerabilities" of Self and Their Transformations in Moral Action

Gil G. Noam

Moral Conduct: Do We Need a "Self"?

Vivid descriptions of morally evil leaders fill our history books. To help explain their actions, these men who have brought great suffering to their contemporaries are often depicted as struggling with injuries of the self. Hitler, the quintessence of immorality, was a man who endured many humiliations and traumas in childhood that contributed to his depravity. Napoleon's cold ambition, a typical outgrowth of a self made to feel insignificant, had such epic dimensions that popular culture has named a common psychological complex after him. But despite the many exemplars history provides where vulnerabilities of the self have resulted in murderous leadership, we possess no adequate account to understand the essential connections.

We also lack insight into the various relationships between the development of psychological strengths and moral commitment. Great leaders too have often suffered traumas to the self, yet they were able to create strengths and moral inspiration in themselves and their followers (see, e.g., Colby and Damon, this volume).

In my essay "Beyond Freud and Piaget" (Noam, 1991), I introduced a theory of the self that builds in part on constructivist moral principles and social cognition, while simultaneously exceeding the boundaries of cognitive and psychodynamic theories. I contrasted the perspectives of Habermas and Kohlberg on the self and distinguished between the development of schemata (a generalized pattern for constructing and transforming meanings about the self and relationships) and themata (the biographical path of these meanings). I further argued that Habermas, by retaining a theoretical commitment to psychoanalytic thought, was better able than cognitive-developmentalists to account for the essential dimension of life history in self development.

The power of biography has, of course, been postulated for a long time. Clinically, psychoanalytic psychotherapists have observed the influence of early experiences over the entire life cycle. But a new vision of development, one that sees the development of the self not only as childhood activity, necessitates an entirely new look at how biography becomes constituted and transformed over the course of life.

This question is at the core of all therapeutic activities. If we know how life history is transformed, not only as a revisitation through transference but also in the course of powerful shifts in thought and feeling in the actual present, we will finally be able to truly comprehend why therapy works. This is because therapy at its best is a process of cognitive, emotional, and interpersonal development. But beyond the consulting room, we need to understand the constant tension in development between powerful entrapment and emerging liberation of potentials.

Shedding light on this important and complex set of questions is a step in dealing with the issue of how moral action evolves and becomes centrally connected to personality. But because we have not recast our psychological theories, our theories about moral action are still not very advanced.

In this essay I will combine previous theory development and observations with necessary speculation. Little data is available that combines careful observations about moral action with a deep understanding of the self and personality. To gain more clarity, we need to know why a deeper understanding about the self and its vulnerabilities is essential in finding links between moral judgment and moral action. A strong self, I will argue, provides one foundation for shaping how moral judgments get transformed into actions. Because we have given so little attention to the development of the self, especially to the constraints created through difficult relationships that became part of the inner world, we have made little progress in understanding the nature of moral and immoral behavior. Stated most generally, I assume that morally evil or inactive people also lack a strong self and that establishing strengths in the self is often related to moments of moral conflict.

But what is a strong self? How and when do we create such strengths? Which strengths are especially important for moral action? To deal with these questions, I will show that the creation of a strong self is not restricted to childhood but continues to be on one's developmental agenda throughout life. Furthermore, a weakened self does not have to be a "lifelong sentence," for humans possess great abilities to self-right vulnerabilities in development— I mean here especially the ability to overcome the seeming inevitability of one's life history through self-reflection and the manifold interactions with the social world.

For this reason we should avoid discussing strengths and weaknesses in categorical terms, as entities or traits. Such approaches have not been very fruitful in the study of moral behavior. We will gain more insights, I believe, by reconstructing the dynamics of development, which allow for weaknesses to turn into strengths and for previous strengths to turn into vulnerabilities. Strengths and weaknesses of the self live together in each person, but for analytic purposes I will exaggerate their separate nature. My goal is to break open the assumption that in "normality" more complex moral judgments automatically lead to greater moral maturity. In so doing, I will create a language that will allow us to understand moral action in light of a developmental theory of self. And in turn we can follow our observations that a person overcomes earlier vulnerabilities in and through development especially in moments of moral choice.

Complexity and Maturity in Moral Development: The Problematic Fusion in the Cognitive Tradition

The theory of moral judgment did not require much of a self, even though Kohlberg first discussed morality and the social self as identical (Kohlberg, 1969) and later as parallel (Noam, Kohlberg, and Snarey, 1983). The self was not precisely defined and was not viewed in terms of specific strengths. It was a generalized epistemic organizing principle that corresponded to structures of moral complexity. Because the moral domain was the essential confirmation of the self, I will first deal with the basic architecture of development in this domain.

Kohlberg (1984) called the sequence and the measurement of moral development "moral maturity," a term that implies a combination of adaptive abilities and cognitive complexity. As in Piaget's work, every stage was defined by a new and more complex logic, in the sense of incorporating earlier structures into a more encompassing unity. This new gestalt functions not only as a more complex form of understanding of the moral world but simultaneously as a more adaptive way of referring to and interacting with the world. There was no question: higher stages are better stages in Piaget's and Kohlberg's model. But better in what way? What is a better moral judgment? Is it not only logically more coherent and complex but also better able to represent reality and to assimilate and accommodate it? But the paradigm of Piaget-Kohlberg is not only intrapsychic; it claims to be interactive, consisting of a constant exchange between actions in the world and internalizations. For that reason the split between thought and action, cognition and adaptation cannot be firm; they are two sides of the same coin. Because of this confirmation of greater abilities, higher stages are defined also as better adaptations, more mature forms of thought as well as responses to the world.

In an ideal (or idealized) world, moral complexity is moral maturity. Defining a world of the ought was one of Kohlberg's great contributions, not only the ought as the foundation of morality but also the ought as an imperative to a new, philosophically infused psychology where description should not be separated from the normative developmental endpoints we posit. It was badly needed medicine for a discipline that still pursued the ideal of value-free natural science in a domain where normative theories and tools were also essential.

But there were unforeseen costs to this seeming unity between moral complexity and moral maturity. Many examples in history, subjects in empirical research, and therapy encounters all point in the same direction: moral complexity can be used to justify immoral theories, systems, and actions. Kohlberg's own writings dealt with such an example: Adolf Eichmann had a set of somewhat complex moral judgments, yet he represented an archetype of evil, a repulsive example of some moral complexity without maturity.

This case and many others less extreme require our explanation. We cannot say that their judgments and actions are not in balance or that moral behavior is not the focus of the theory of moral judgment. The fact is that even on the representational level, the deeds are justified in complex and often even moral categories: "the fight against evil"; "A society needs to protect itself, etc." But also the strict distinction between moral judgment and moral action is problematic. Cognitive categories (and with them moral categories) develop in the exchange with actions in the world. Once internalized through accommodation, do they remain in the self separated from action? Such a view would lead to a strange form of interactionism, a one-way street from actions to thoughts. The spirit of interactionism is that thought and action are in continuously dynamic interplay. For that reason, a sign for moral maturity should be the adaptive quality of moral judgments. When we focus more directly on moral adaptation as an aspect of moral cognitions, we immediately find that evil conduct is performed not only by those who are morally, cognitively, and socially undeveloped. Rather, many of those who killed or contributed to mass killing in Nazi Germany or in other, more recent places of horror, such as Argentina, Cambodia, or Yugoslavia, are people often capable of complex understanding of social reality. Especially chilling is when the Eichmanns—who understand complex connections and are "adapted" from a certain perspective, yet are entirely pathological when it comes to basic human values—use their ability for immoral purposes.

For that reason, I propose that moral maturity needs to be judged by the relationship between the complexity of judgments and the capacity to transform judgments into positive adaptations. These adaptations do not need to refer immediately to moral action, and may remain at the cognitive level. But they imply an assessment about not only the structural complexity of the judgments but also the function and quality of moral thought. It is exactly here, around the concept of moral maturity, that we need a theory of the self and an understanding of all the factors supporting and inhibiting that affect moral adaptation. The person who has not developed empathy toward his self tends to be cruel and indifferent, or preoccupied. Yet another hindrance in the development of moral maturity (not necessarily moral complexity) comes from a deep insecurity, which leads to an obsessive back and forth, an ability to understand moral issues but not to use these insights to adapt or act. While complexity and maturity, cognitive organization and adaptive capacities, are already interwoven problematically in Piaget and Kohlberg, they have become ever more enmeshed in the theories of self and personality.

Complexity and Maturity in Self Theory

Building on Piaget's and Kohlberg's foundation, other theorists constructed narrower distinctions about cognitive categories for understanding the self, interpersonal relationships, faith, and many other developmental domains (e.g., Loevinger, 1976; Kegan, 1982; Fowler, 1981). Because the area of study had become so much broader than in the original moral judgment work, firmer distinctions about psychological functions should have been drawn when venturing out in such breadth. But instead, the same basic stage categories had to hold many more adaptive processes and cognitive functions. As I have shown elsewhere (e.g., Noam, 1991), the consequence of this strategy was that it became far less possible to distinguish between component parts of the theories, such as cognitions and affects, judgments and actions, adaptation and defense, mind and body, the self as subject and the self as object, etc.

Each new developmental position of the self became simultaneously a cognitively more complex form of perspective-taking and a more adaptive form of "being in the world." In other words, the more complex self was viewed as the more mature, integrated, adapted self. This idea was in part rejected (Loevinger, 1968), but one has only to read a variety of cognitive-developmental stage descriptions to see that earlier positions were viewed as weaker (e.g., impulsive, deceptive, projective, grandiose) and more mature stages were labeled in terms of strengths (e.g., capable of intimacy with boundaries, tolerant, empathic, accepting). Moral judgment theory created the basic architecture for these self theories, at first elegant and convincing, yet upon closer scrutiny, problematic and confusing. For one could not truly account for the fact that so-called mature levels of development could in reality be levels of entrapment of the self, procedures of hating the self more elaborately, and contexts for rejecting others on sophisticated grounds (see, e.g., Döbert and Nunner-Winkler, in press; Noam, 1988a).

An additional problem was written into these models as well: the conditions in which development occurs do not parallel the idealized reflections about development. Again, this problem was at first less visible because the focus was more narrowly on cognition and moral judgment, but in their full manifestation of the self and the ego, the problem became quite apparent. The social stresses and contradictions of complex societies are represented in family, community, and societal problems. These problems do not create optimal conditions for productive attachment, empathy, and morality. Nor do they provide optimal conditions for maintaining tolerance, holding contradictions, and encouraging supportive interpersonal relationships—all part of the idealized developmental sequences of morality, self, and ego.

This fact creates unsolved theoretical dilemmas: We need ideal end points in development if we want not only to describe but also to prescribe. But when our descriptions are based less on the real conditions in which development occurs and more on an idealized version of normality, the theories themselves obscure reality. The general social and relational situation in which children grow and adults continue to develop are full of strife, loneliness, and alienation. These experiences become represented in the structure of the self. We should stop viewing them as external constraints to an otherwise productive developmental path and see them instead as part and parcel of the formation and evolution of the self. What else can we mean when we posit that construction of reality is fundamentally an interactive process?

In this respect, cognitive theories of the self have fallen behind Erik Erikson's work (e.g., 1950). For Erikson, each developmental period or psychosocial stage is a struggle between new evolutionary strengths and virtues on the one hand and problems and maladaptations on the other. His insights still have not sufficiently changed theories about vulnerabilities of the self, such as Kohut's notion of self-pathology (e.g., Kohut, 1971; Kohut and Wolf, 1978). Since pathology is always contrasted with some notion of normality, one has to assume that the strong and healthy self in Kohut's work is the norm. And, as mentioned earlier, in the structural-developmental accounts, forward and upward movement is what normatively gives rise to the strengths of the self. But what if we were to postulate that the norm is a different one: that the conditions under which development occurs place so many people at risk for problematic self and moral development that it becomes rather arbitrary where to draw the line between strengths and weaknesses. Drawing the line is less difficult when it comes to a clear-cut psychiatric condition, such as schizophrenia or manic-depressive illness. Here, however, we are dealing with the more elusive categories of vulnerability.

Of course, Freud's pessimistic cultural philosophy might be detected here: neurosis is a condition not only of the ill; our civilization is by definition neurosis producing. Piaget and the cognitive-developmentalists have been far more optimistic. In their theories of the self and ego, this optimism, which one could refer to as "developmental upward-mobility," was in part a reaction to the traditional psychoanalytic worldview. "Adaptation" and "mastery" had become the big terms of the times, even in psychoanalysis, and helped to create a more positive and cognitive American brand of personality theory.

But maybe we can retain a balanced view that allows us to interpret the socialization conditions in complex societies as producing risk for the self without having to label culture and personality as pathological per se. Doing so allows a new understanding of normative development to become evident. We cannot just reconstruct typical progressions in the various developmental abilities but need also to understand the ways in which people try to overcome the internalized weaknesses created through participation in the various social systems and networks that mark the contexts of development. Only if we take such a perspective can we trace the difficult relationship between developmental complexity and maturity, judgment and action.

Self Processes in Moral Action

When we try to define those processes that contribute to moral conduct, we talk about the significant contributions of the self. Whether we focus on will and commitment, love and sympathy, decisiveness and leadership, empathy and responsibility, we end up tapping into domains viewed as involving the self. But in the literature dedicated to the bridge between moral judgment and action (for an overview volume, see Oser, Althof, and Gartz, 1986), most psychological processes revert back to strengths that exist as traits or to coping styles that support, or defenses that hinder, the transformation of moral judgment into moral action. None of the many interesting explanatory frameworks have tried to understand the self in dynamic categories that create the foundation for morality. One notable exception is found in the sophisticated longitudinal study of ego, cognitive, social, and moral domains in different ecological contexts (e.g., Edelstein, 1979; Keller and Edelstein, 1991). The self that will help us understand the maturity of moral judgments and actions is not an on-or-off ability. It is instead a process of developing meanings, and it gives rise to new abilities and vulnerabilities. For this reason we cannot overestimate the importance and difficulty of creating insightful ways of studying those elusive set of processes called the self.

Because the term "self" is so overused and ill defined—even now that it has become fashionable again in the social sciences—I will specify my use. I have already located my view theoretically: I build on constructivist and developmental principles and place them in relation to evolving biography. But I have not defined the term "self."

The self is a process of structuring thoughts, feelings, and behaviors about oneself, others, and the world at large. The process orientation takes account of the self's developmental character: creating and recreating meaning throughout the life span. The dimension of structure implies not necessarily stages but rather a continuous attempt to organize meanings, affects, and actions in some consistent and cohesive way. This internal attempt to create structure is paralleled by the researcher's attempt to find coherence of expression of these meanings. But this coherence is continuously in danger. The frame within which the self is represented derives from current interactions and from an internalized history of interactions. The history of experiences and less evolved forms of experience creates a reality at times in harmony, many times in conflict, with the more complex ones generated in present situations.

This somewhat abstract definition is still devoid of moral judgment or moral action. But we know from research that structures of moral judgment run parallel to meanings about the self and relationships (e.g., Noam, Kohlberg, and Snarey, 1983). We also know that a higher degree of consistency exists between moral judgment and moral action as level of moral judgment increases. But one is always struck by the fact that many people at these more mature levels of moral judgment are not acting according to their principles of proclaimed judgments.

Many factors have been proposed and studied as contributing factors to the bridge between moral judgment and moral action, such as context, culture, gender, and defenses (see, e.g., Rest, 1984). Through the above definition of the self we argue that while these dimensions have to be taken into account, we have to further our knowledge of the way in which relationships, experiences, culture, etc., are represented in the self. These internalized worlds support and/or hinder maturity and productive action when a moral response is called for.

To gain more insight into these questions, I will now elaborate three self dimensions usually involved in moral action.

•Moral action is typically not blind but a conscious choice for the good of friends or strangers, family or peer groups, or larger social systems. Moral choice usually has as its explicit goal to protect and support others, an activity that involves interest and empathy.

•In that moral action requires choice, it entails decision making. Complex knowledge about different paths of action certainly contributes to a sense of free will and autonomy. But increased vulnerabilities to indecision and obsessive ruminations are frequent results. Each fundamental choice entails giving up other possibilities, jeopardizing relational bonds or career aspirations, and the like. Moral action closes many doors. The more choices there are and the more we know about the implications of each possible action, the more we can become frozen in inaction or rationalize.

•Acting morally involves taking a stand, often an unpopular one. Not conforming to one's group or giving up the protection of the prevalent culture is always, even in little ways, an act of courage. Such actions often endanger the self without providing a guaranteed path to a good outcome. In extreme forms, moral actions can lead to death or serious suffering. To this day, prisons and labor camps throughout the world contain people who have acted out of moral motivations and reasons. But even under less extreme situations, moral action often occurs against the backdrop of social conformity and social sanctions, and thus demands strengths.

The abilities to be reflective and decisive, to weigh and judge, to delay and care, to keep narcissism in check and believe that one can make a difference—all these capacities contribute to moral judgment and moral action. The list can be (and has been) extended greatly. It should be apparent that these capacities are not only those of morality but are also core processes of the developing self.

Certainly one does not have to be a prototype of mental health to act morally, but a virtuous and moral life often signifies strengths that involve the self, commitments, recognition of choice, and an ability to act. If we turn for a moment to attachment theory as one important framework about the interpersonal foundations of the self, we can gain further important insights into the relationship between the self and moral action. Take the ambivalent and anxiously attached child who has great difficulties in exploring the world due to separation anxiety and self doubt. This child needs continuous affirmation and is overly dependent on security. We now have evidence from longitudinal studies that this kind of working model is fairly stable over time (e.g., Sroufe, Main). Will such a child learn how to stand up against peer pressure or confront adults when they make unfair decisions? Research findings suggest that these children are more prone toward bullying and submissive behavior, have lower self-esteem, and are afflicted with more behavioral and emotional problems than well-attached children.

Early relationships do not predetermine all strengths in one's life cycle, but it will be more difficult for the person who has internalized overly ambivalent relationships and incorporated them into his self to invest sufficiently in others, move forcefully when needed, and protect those who are weak.

Another example in attachment theory is the avoidant person who shies away from relationships and prefers isolation. Clinically, I have this seen this avoidant style grow to be, for example, the workaholic adult busily racing from deadline to deadline, not having time to think about the needs of others or the moral implications of his world. We find this type also in Kohut's descriptions, a tradition directly relevant to the development of the self.

Developing a theory similar to attachment theory, Kohut and his colleagues (see, e.g., Kohut, 1971; Wolf, 1988 and this volume) emphasized the early phases of the development of the self in order to elucidate narcissistic preoccupations and lack of self-cohesion. They view interference with the natural need for idealization and mirroring in the young child as giving rise to self disorders. Kohut was also impressed by the long-term effect of these early experiences and by the amount of energy these people use to try to maintain a cohesive self. While we are still lacking empirical research in this tradition, clinical evidence suggests that many people with narcissistic disorders are far too preoccupied with themselves to invest lovingly in others or to demonstrate strong and flexible moral commitments. They are often quite capable of complex moral judgments, but they rigidly apply principles to all situations without sufficient empathy for themselves and others.

They are also people who are more prone to becoming manipulated than those with more productive experiences in relationships. They have learned from early on to sequester parts of their selves, a process I term "encapsulation," and are unable to sufficiently internalize an empathic stance toward their selves. Why should they suddenly care enough to act courageously toward others? To pursue this topic, we have to deepen our understanding of the pathways of self-vulnerabilities.

Configurations of Self-Vulnerabilities

Finding the roots of evil in the early phases of the life cycle was also an important goal of another tradition dealing with weaknesses of the self: the "authoritarian personality" project (Adorno et al.,

1950). The relationships between courage and conformity, among sadism, authoritarianism, and socialization, between the family and social structure interested members of the Frankfurt School before, during, and after World War II. These issues are again becoming very important as group violence against minorities is on the rise. But from today's perspective one has to be more skeptical about finding the key to totalitarianism, moral inaction, or moral evil in personality structure of the early years in the family.

Of course, early socialization creates a foundation for later development. A child subjected to severe punishment will end up with a less organized and productive style of attachment. Similarly, an abandoned child will have a less secure self. Loevinger (1976) and Kohlberg (1984) and other developmental psychologists have made very important contributions to the topic of continuities and discontinuities in development by opening our vista to lifelong transformations of the self and personality. By focusing on later development, they found that the pull toward conformity, which can so easily be exploited for authoritarian rule, is especially strong at the "conformist" and "conventional" stages of development.

This recognition provided a major breakthrough—still largely unrecognized—for self-theory and our understanding of moral conduct. We now realize that this development is not only typical of adolescents but is also one where a great number of adults function throughout their lives. Of course, not every person functioning at this level of development demonstrates moral cowardice, but the conventional level, despite representing strengths (abilities for role-taking, understanding patterns of relationships and systems, etc.) involve a variety of risks. These include an overly strong desire for social conformity and the need to define the self through others' evaluations. Translations of such cognitions into personality traits make it more difficult for the individual to act against the group norm.

Some aspects of the authoritarian-personality project should remain a vital part of our present explorations: these include the study of how social conditions of alienation and division come to reflect the inner world of the family and the self. As mentioned earlier, modern psychology tends to individualize and pathologize these conditions, which Woody Allen humorously calls "being at two with nature." They are relegated to the nonnormative realm. We have seen that the normative position in developmental psychology is the ideal vision of the person who combines complexity and maturity by adapting to the world, the well-attached who has a place in relationships, the generative and caring who can altruistically give.

These idealizations of development now have to be enlarged by ideal types of vulnerabilities. These configurations are possible despite the fact that every biography is different, molded from specific experiences, motivations, and social situations. But patterns of lives can be generalized because experiences are also typical, condensed into forms that are socially given, contextualized by history and social trajectories. When we read biographies, we can identify with them because they represent something in us, or we learn not only about a person but also about a time. Biography, a very specific life unfolding, is at the same time an expression of the general. This tension makes it especially interesting as a field of study and useful in adding depth to the study of self and morality. In this chapter, I will introduce only two types of self vulnerabilities. More exist, but they are not needed here. The ones I chose, the *vacillating self* and the *alienated self*, build on the notions of encapsulation and problem pathways (Noam, 1988b, 1988c, 1991). These self vulnerabilities should not be viewed as mutually exclusive in any given person.

In our human inventiveness we explore the world, shape it, and reshape it. We think and rethink where we come from, how relationships work, what friendship and love mean. Piaget, Vygotsky, and others have tapped into this creative process, and many after them have shown how much each individual transforms the universe of experience and understanding. But what goes into this creative process, given that experiences are not only forward-looking and productive but also painful and overwhelming? Here I am concerned less about the one-time hurt (except when truly traumatic), and more about day-to-day, chronic interaction patterns with parents, siblings, teachers, peers, and so forth. In them we find ourselves, experience our worthiness, our vitality, and our exploratory powers. This insight is older than psychology, having already been stated by Goethe with typical simplicity: "In anderen erleben wir uns selbst" ("In others we experience ourselves").

But these others, even when not motivated by evil designs, construct their worlds, following paths of their individual choosing. Under the best of circumstances, one hopes for a continuous balancing act of individuals', mutually developing meanings across great gaps: generations, developmental levels, roles, cultures, institutions, etc. Inevitable breakdowns of communication need to lead to a reworking of the fractured understanding of these relationships and through them also to a reworking of the self. In fact, in a breakdown lies reconciliation, a process that can lead to knowledge, empathy, and security.

But relationships create patterns, often bad ones, in which empathy and understanding give way to preconceived notions and rigid circumscriptions. Systems theorists have taught us a great deal about relational scenarios in which everyone has a role to play. But we know far less about what the individual players make of these interactions, how others are internalized and thus become important building blocks of the self. As a psychotherapist, I am always amazed by the power of these internalizations; the therapist treats not only an individual patient but also the entire internal world of relationship. I am also very struck by the repetitive nature of these internalized patterns and individuals' capacity to transfer them onto new relationships. Such transfer is very common, but our theories are not sufficiently evolved, because internal objects, as they are called in psychoanalytical terms, are always viewed as early objects, mostly parents. As such, they are primitive remnants of a past that continues to shape the person.

But important others and relational patterns become internalized throughout life, and this creates fundamental changes not only in childhood but also in adulthood. Earlier internalized relationships, even when negative, can be transformed in view of these experiences. An analogy for the synthesis of cognitive, moral, and self functions comes from the historical and political realm. During the French Revolution, the organizing power of society went from a feudal to a bourgeois system. Counts continued to exist, not all people and relationships had changed, but the organizational principles, the laws, the institutions that executed the law, etc., had been transformed. In other parts of the world the transitions occurred with less revolutionary vigor, but the shift in structure did happen. Piaget's model of cognition bears similarities: through cognitive revolutions or evolutions, new systems supersede old ones and control the entire meaning-making structure in a new, cohesive way.

But as much as political and biological analogies are enticing, they do not account for important differences in the psychological domain. Evolutionary metaphors can be useful, but they should not be reified, which is exactly what happened in cognitive-developmental theory. Why should all earlier internalized experiences lose their structuring power and only serve as elements in a new structure? Darwin, from whom these ideas were taken, described the evolution of species over long periods and for very different domains. In contrast, in individual development, a person's cognition and self carry their own experienced history. Old meanings can be evoked at any time, can shape current experiences, and can live side by side with complex ways of understanding the world. But we know very little about how this multitude of meanings coexists. Nor do we know how to differentiate the flexible harmony of multiple structures from repetitive and destructive returns to more primitive thoughts, feelings, and behaviors.

These ideas, deceptively simple, are essential in understanding self vulnerabilities and morality. Obviously, these two types do not incorporate all existing forms of vulnerabilities. They do not reflect situational stresses of the moment, nor all forms of psychopathology. Rather I am attempting to trace two forms of internalization with two related internal self structures. For these kinds of structures to evolve, problems have usually existed for some time and have been woven into the person's self.

Both types of self vulnerability create divisions and splits, endless preoccupations with a self that has lost its abilities to flexibly adapt and explore. A great deal of psychological energy has to go into defending and supporting vulnerabilities, sequestering vitality away from love and work. In both cases, continued development occurs, so we cannot speak of a real developmental arrest. Even high achievement is possible, but accompanied by a great deal of suffering, rigidity, or fragmentation. Both types have problems with moral action because of their strong preoccupation with the self and the survival of its boundaries and integrity. And finally, that these are not rare types of exotic illnesses, but are prototypes of vulnerabilities of our times.

The Vacillating Self

Underlying structure

Assumed in Piaget's and Kohlberg's paradigm is that earlier structures become integrated into later ones. As a position between theories that focus primarily on the early, primitive dimensions of development and perspectives interested primarily in current structures, useful developmental processes are essential:

•Not all meaning systems necessarily become transformed in the forward movement in development. The way in which we subsume old meaning structures is far more complex than that suggested by Piaget's and Kohlberg's model. We know, especially from the neo-Piagetians, that development entails practice, skill, and action. For many developmental challenges, there are different fields of experimentation, and thus development is quite uneven.

•The further we move from cognition to social cognition to socioemotional and self processes, the more we have to assume that areas of practice and possibilities for exploration differ for different domains. An adolescent might have great support for accommodating mathematical understandings and very little opportunity to investigate how relationships work. The older one gets, the more differentiated are one's domains of knowledge and the more possibility there is for multiple developmental levels.

•Different capacities can exist not only in different domains of development but also within the same domain. Most relevant to my discussion here is the realm of relationships and the self. Significant disturbances in a child's relationship to a parent or a sibling can lead to a premature closing off of possible explorations. We find this frequently in abusive relationships, where the otherwise complex ways of organizing meanings have not generalized to the abusive relationship. Piagetians have been too eager in the past to interpret this phenomenon as a problem of acting not one of competence. My own observations have made me more sensitive to the additional nonevolved meanings that coexist with more complex ones (discrepancies of competencies). Since accommodation has occurred, in such cases, for only some parts of the self, I regard the continued ways of organizing experience within an old structure as instances of "overassimilation," assimilation that has taken place at the expense of accommodation (Noam, 1988a, 1992). In other words, the general capacities for further self complexity are in place but remain encapsulated, awaiting application to all domains of the self.

•It is tempting to organize cognition or adaptation around one evolving structure and to crown the advanced system as the executive function. It is equally seductive to view an earlier, fixated structure as the organizing principle in development. This is the psychoanalytic road of giving primacy to an early, unconscious meaning structure that determines one's life. But neither position is adequate. Human beings always explore reality on multiple levels, return and regress, pick up pieces that have never been acknowledged or understood, and combine moments of reconstruction as transformational moments in the present.

Imagine, for a moment, a person moving through a forest, enjoying the smell and the motion, the sound and the view. Suddenly one foot is caught between the roots of a tree, while the other foot continues to be free. Movement is still possible, but the freedom of one part of the body must be understood in terms of the unfreedom of the other, and vice versa.

In vulnerability, out of this multitude of meanings come preoccupations and confusions, not harmony and contrast. There are usually two reasons why meanings about self and other remain unevolved. Either thoughts and feelings have been experienced as so shameful or unresolvable that they have been kept from freeing interaction with others, or all attempts at engaging others have failed because of destructive patterns of interaction. In either case the person is thrown into him or herself and attempts at transformation fail.

Interestingly, those domains in which the person remains isolated are also the ones that require the greatest attention. This is true even when the great majority of one's meanings have developed. Every teacher knows that the children that feel disfranchised can destroy an entire group. They tend to reduce their acting out of grievances when they feel listened to and incorporated in the group. It is quite similar with the self.

Phenomenology

I now turn to the expression and phenomenology of layered meanings and "multiple selves." Since there are antagonisms between the different meaning systems in the self, the person frequently feels disjointed, disconnected, and confused. Though the internal preoccupation takes many forms, most important is that a great many inner resources are used to regain cohesion and consistency in the face of fluctuations and disorganizations. The person typically feels dizzy from all the motion, afraid that remaining strength will not be sufficient to "keep it all together."

Since the self is so vulnerable and forced to return to thoughts and feelings experienced as uncontrollable, certain feelings and symptoms are especially prevalent: serious and disorganizing anxieties are frequent, leading to a sense of disorientation. Derealizations serve to protect the self against the return of past meanings, but in the end they aggravate the problem because the discontinuity of self now feels like "nonexistence." The person can never quite trust in the self's own abilities. Too many realities impinge; too many past traumas and conflicts have retained their structuring abilities for the individual to attain a sense of integration.

Instead, a continuous question remains about who the self really is. Self-definition is tied to a sense of integration and consistency across time and context. In the vacillating self, the multiplicity of experience puts the self in continuous question. In the extreme, the physical and psychological survival of the self are at stake (this is supported, I believe, by recent findings about the relationship between anxiety disorders and suicide tendencies), but in more moderate forms the confusion is about identity.

This diffusion has serious interpersonal implications. Typically, the person cannot trust his perceptions of his self and thus becomes quite dependent on others. What at first looks like good abilities for closeness and intimacy usually evolves into a great need for guidance, tendencies toward submission, and a loss of mutuality. The internal splits in the self have their parallels in vacillating interpersonal relationships full of fear, separation anxiety, and unexpressed ambivalence.

The vacillating self is not necessarily an expression of one psychopathology. To some degree it represents a vulnerability of everyday life, in that traumatic experiences are so common, and little support exists for adolescents and adults to integrate their multiple worlds. But it is possible to view some of the more serious psychopathologies as powerful and extreme expressions of this vulnerability of the self. The borderline conditions that I have dealt with in other publications especially fall into this category. The self of a person is often represented by a continuous back and forth between mature and immature ways of understanding and adapting to the world. Borderline patients rapidly shift from developmentally complex meaning systems, with insight into some of their psychological makeup and relational patterns, to very unevolved, impulsive, and physical meaning systems, full of magical thinking and overstated dependency needs. The person with this prevalent set of problems is full of self-doubt and in continuous threat of "falling apart." Integration and synthesis are key developmental goals and hardest to achieve for such a person. But borderline conditions are only exaggerations of many disorders of fluctuation and subsequent overdependencies.

Helpful for gaining insight is the fact that many of those people I call borderline have continued to relive or repeat sexual or physical traumas that have supported their encapsulations (see, e.g., Herman, 1992). We are only beginning to recognize how prevalent these problems really are and are still mostly noting the extreme cases that end up in the health-care system. We can only image how many less severe problems exist in the general population of those afflicted with less severe cases of the vulnerability of a vacillating self.

The vulnerability of the vacillating self has many implications for moral action. First, the self is so preoccupied with its own survival and cohesion that the energy to think about others, a hallmark of morality, is quite diminished. Second, anxiety, depression, and a diffuse identity, traits I described above as relevant to moral action, lead to lack of decisiveness. Anxiety usually leads to retreat, depression to inactivity, and a diffuse identity to incoherent behavior.

Furthermore, the strong emphasis on powerful external figures in love relationships leads to special vulnerabilities concerning conformity. As we have seen, any individual choice bears with it potential exclusion from the group and a loss of friends and support. Without these bonds with others, the vacillating self is especially vulnerable. Moral action entails moral choice, often protecting outsiders and standing up against social pressures. The vacillating self is so continuously questioning itself and its integrity that group pressure can easily lead it to abandon any moral impulse. Even worse, it can lead to participating in group activities that are clearly immoral and aimed at hurting others who are less protected. These processes are complex and cannot be reduced to aspects of "the self." Rather, experiences, their internalizations, and the shape of the inner and interpersonal worlds of the self are importantly involved.

The Alienated Self

Structure and phenomenology

A different kind of split gives rise to what in clinical theory has been typically termed "the false self" (Winnicott, 1965) or the "divided self" (Laing, 1959) and what I discuss here from the perspective of alienation. But in contrast to clinical approaches that typically view this constellation as an unevolved expression or symptom of psychopathology, the alienated self actually consists of complex processes.

One important feature of a developmental analysis is that it allows us to pursue the hypothesis that symptoms are really complex attempts at adaptation. Why should all expression of maladaptation be primitive? As we have seen, each developmental progression of cognitive, social, and emotional function bears the seeds of new and more complex forms of weaknesses. This idea develops out of the earlier discussions in this chapter of complexity and maturity. New developments bring new vulnerabilities. Severe self-alienation is usually long-standing but has evolved into ever more complex forms. These vulnerabilities have been woven into the fabric of the self's more complex meaning system.

Empirical evidence exists for this position. Using Loevinger's model of ego development (1976), my associates and I found in psychiatrically hospitalized adolescents that the move to age-appropriate developmental stages (what Loevinger calls the conformist level) led to a reduction in externalizing, delinquent, and aggressive behaviors and syndromes. But the rates of internalizing disorders, such as depression and suicidality, increased significantly (Noam, Paget, Bartok, and Borst, 1990; Borst, Noam, and Bartok, 1991; Borst and Noam, in press). We concluded from these studies that one has to take a developmental orientation on risk and protective factors. Developmental delay has to be viewed in part as a protection against depression and suicide. Limitations in empathy and perspective-taking provide possibilities for blaming others and aggressing against them. When adolescents move toward a more psychological experience of the self and relationships, this self-protective "defense" is lost and the self is more prone to self-blame and self-aggression. These findings show that symptoms can change form in the context of the developing self.

But we cannot understand vulnerabilities of the self by exploring symptoms alone. As we have seen, depression and self-destructive behaviors can be part of the vacillating self as well, but the meanings and functions are different. Depression and self-destructive behaviors are more dangerous in the alienated self, because the vulnerabilities are usually ego-syntonic, in contrast to the vacillating self, where one encounters more ego-dystonic experiences. I mean here that problems in the alienated self have grown hand in hand with the rest of the self, that one finds little contradiction and dynamic back and forth between different developmental organizations. Being part of a psychological roller coaster, as the vacillating self can be described, has its own risks, but one at least finds confusion as a challenge, more mature meanings in some dialogue with less mature ones. In contrast, the alienated self tends toward totalitarian internal rule. The person has little empathy with vulnerabilities of self or others and interprets people as weak and out of control.

Since others are experienced as untrustworthy, the self has to overcompensate and be in charge of everything. Tears are weakness; self-discipline is strength. The self is disciplined by a rigid code; others continuously disappoint because they do not live up to overly high expectations, which leads to more isolation. In general, the self feels very much alone, suspicious of the motivation of others. The self is not moving forward and backward in dizzying motions. Instead, its motion is between expansion and constriction. When expansive, the person wants to gain control over the self by controlling others. Inner vulnerability is often expressed with anger and rage, rather than sadness and distress. But the more typical expression is that of constriction: tightening up and not letting others in. Alienation from others can become so complete, that suicide remains the final, logical consequence. But more typically, the self loses itself without fully knowing it. Behind the veneer of complexity and power lurks a wretched, abandoned soul. Tragically, incorporated into the current structure of thoughts and feelings, the self cannot be accessed directly. The paradox is that true transformation, where complexity goes hand in hand with maturity, requires a new view on the self's biography. There has to be empathy with the self that has been left behind, a self of vitality and self expression. But such empathy is in clear contrast to the prevailing perspective of the self, which views such pursuits as weak and pointless.

The reason why I focus here on the biographic aspect of alienation is that despite the complex form it has taken, it often originates quite early. Earlier, I elaborated on this observation by analyzing Kafka's famous letter to his father (Noam, 1988b). Clearly a document of great insight and complexity, his letter shows the early hurts that lead to self-negation and alienation. Long before the self is capable of complex understandings, it is subjected to severe rejections and incomprehensible actions on the part of adults. The result is a separation from essential vitality in life. The problem with this alienated self is that it is often extremely adaptive on the surface. The person has little recourse, because this way of being has become so essentially part of the self that trying to give it up feels like giving up the self.

The distinction between true and false self tries to get at the loss of vitality and wholeness involved in alienation. The false self is so entrapping because it often is not felt anymore in relationship to a potential true self, it is not known for its falseness. But the distinction is too dichotomous, as it carries with it a romantic notion of health and creativity (the true self) and lacks the insight that all of us are complex combinations of true and false self experiences and beings. How else could we understand Kafka's great creativity and self-expression?

Problems concerning moral conduct are part of this self vulnerability. First, the person sees much of life in moral terms, but this moral system creates a prison, not a flexibly applied set of principles. In psychoanalysis this phenomenon is described as a rigid superego. This structure gets established in the oedipal stage of development and changes only in terms of rigidity or flexibility. In the model I am proposing, the foundations for a rigid moralizing structure may be put into place early, but the organizing principles and the shape change over the course of one's life. The alienated self is more a developmental "accomplishment" of adolescence and adulthood. When this form has become established, the outcome seems to be one of moral integrity and unity but is actually quite unempathic toward the needs of the self and others.

Furthermore, the standards for the self and others are so high that disappointment and failure is often preprogrammed. Because the moral obligations are so extreme, inaction is often the unanticipated result. One typical example is a writing block, usually framed in moral terms ("I should produce something that is really correct and not tell lies"). Inaction is the brother of unempathic, grandiose self expectations. When true moral action is needed, perfection leads to passivity. Guilt is there aplenty, but it does not lead to an active response in a moment of need.

Complexity of self often produces a great potential for rationalization; everything can be reasoned away. A moral need of someone can be placed in some theory or system in which support would actually be regressive (e.g., a homeless person in need of protection from a cold night should not be helped, because that would make the person more dependent, or because the state should intervene, etc.). These arguments are often even sound, but structure and function cannot be distinguished any more; one does not know whether they are rationalizations to avoid acting compassionately.

Finally, more complex forms of thought create a keen awareness of the complexity of every moral situation. The multiplicity of arguments and perspectives can trap the self in a hall of mirrors, from which there is no path to moral action. Since the self is only seemingly decisive and strong but underneath is always experiencing slight, rejection, and displacement, the multiplicity of arguments creates a great deal of rumination and inactivity—again patterns that are not conducive to moral action.

Moral Action and Transforming Vulnerabilities of the Self

Few contexts are as informative for exploring vulnerabilities and their transformations as psychotherapy. Both types of vulnerability, the vacillating self and the alienated self, are quite stable across time. They are not momentary imbalances or derailments but established biographical paths that have entrapped the person for some time. This consistency of adaptational style can make one pessimistic about the potential for developing maturity. And yet most therapists have witnessed the amazing capacity for change inherent in human development. Developing a new relationship, creating trust, and, in a new partnership, working out the patterns by living and confronting them—how is such maturation possible?

We now have a fairly good clinical understanding, not as yet established with strong data, about factors that go into strengthening the self. Bowlby, Kohut, Sullivan, and Winnicott, among other psychoanalytic theorists, have painted different yet recurrent pictures about the need of the self to create strengths. These theoretical and clinical observations have more recently been supported by the creative work of a number of infancy and attachment researchers (e.g., Ainsworth, Stern, Tronik, etc.). Their work has shown how complicated the processes are that contribute to a strong self. But, for the purposes of this essay, some generalizations are possible. Importantly, social interactions create the foundation of self vulnerabilities, and the potential for transformation. For that reason, attachment relationships play a significant role in creating a strong self. The child begins to create models of expectation about the availability of others, the trustworthiness of people, and the loveability of the self. Bowlby (1969) has argued convincingly that the representations of significant others and relationships correspond quite well to the actual relationship experiences of the child.

We also know from longitudinal research that working models remain quite consistent over time by resisting change (e.g., Sroufe, 1979). Empirically, we know less about the self's capacity to mold a working model into more adaptive forms when the beginnings of relationships have been difficult. But most studies show a significant portion of subjects transforming from maladaptive to productive relational patterns. Bowlby and others have pointed to the healing power of new relationships, be they therapies, friendships, or marriage. The self always learns about itself through the eyes of others, through how significant others view the self. Not a childhood sense, but rather a lifelong experience of intersubjectivity, of selves merging and differentiating, protects the self from maladaptation. These lively interactions make the self feel alive at all times. Having missed out at first makes it harder later, but new opportunities arise to create new vitality.

Another essential ingredient in the creation of strengths where weaknesses prevailed has to do with self-reflection and insight. Here, we have the most reason to be optimistic that cognitive development creates potentials for recovery. Biographical knowledge, deciphering patterns, and understanding the limitations of significant persons are truly possible only in late adolescence and adulthood. These capacities can create cold, rationalizing knowledge that does not support health and maturity. But they can also create new abilities to combine self-reflection with reworking, and understanding with experience. Reflection with tears, exploration with mourning, are the stuff that insight into the self is made of. And it is never too late for such processes to commence.

Too many of our conventional ideas about resilience and recovery are purely psychological, concerned only with the self, life phases, or relationships. But what if we took the perspective that moral choices and actions are centrally involved in the transformation of vulnerabilities of the self? A strengthened self, less vacillating and alienated, is free to act more morally. Of course, psychological freedoms can be used primarily for hedonistic purposes. But still, the likelihood is greater that a more mature self will lead to more empathy, to deeper commitments to relationships and causes, and thus to potential moral engagement. But moral choice and moral action can also lead to significant moments of both self and moral transformations. By acting morally, we discover our own strengths and forge deeper bonds with others.

When I ask people about key moments in their lives in which they were able to discover and build strengths, I often hear stories of moral courage and action. Confrontations with situations of great unfairness make some people rise to the challenge of moral action. Taking the side of those who are needy, fighting for those who experience discrimination, and participating in movements for just causes are examples of such moral commitments. These moral actors usually provide us simultaneously with models of evolved morality and self, for moral action is often the outgrowth of will, courage, compassion, empathy, and many other strengths of the self.

But these strengths are not just present in a person, a reservoir of capacities from which the person can draw. These strengths are continuously evolving. We all need to be challenged in social interactions to create such strengths. Positive attachments lead to commitments, which in turn produce the foundations for moral strengths such as a sense of fairness, a sense of loyalty, engaged judgments.

But experiences that challenge moral sensitivities and call for moral action can also serve to instigate the development of strengths of the self. One simple mechanism is that moral action often brings with it a great deal of social approbation and enhances a sense of self and relationships.

In times of moral crisis, the vacillating self can learn to focus by becoming fully engrossed in the requirements of the moment. Principled action is an antidote to fluctuations. The self begins to experience itself as consistent, committed, and reliable. The new capacities do not guarantee a transformation of encapsulations, but by combining relational needs with moral action, a foundation is laid that pulls the person away from the internal confusion. Focused judgments in concert with actions create internal organization, a sense of purpose, and a way to prioritize among the multitude of desires and demands. Through this emerging ability to prioritize, which was first experienced in the clarity and power of moral actions, the self learns to delay, to concentrate, and to experience agency and will. Few experiences can be more healing for the vacillating self. In addition, since moral commitments often bring the individual into closer contact with other people and groups, essential support for the maturation (and not only the complexification) of the self evolve.

The alienated self, too, can use moral action to move toward maturation. The typical role of moral action is different, however, than in the vacillating self, since, as we have seen above, the alienated self tends toward judgment, not only in the moral sense but also in the sense of being judgmental. This evaluation is often exaggerated into hate toward the self and great suspicion of the motives of others. The isolation of the alienated self makes one tend more toward moral thought than moral action. Thought often reproduces "the hall of mirrors," the labyrinth of possibilities that render the self immobile. Moral action is often the first possible act the self is capable of, as it is tied more closely to ideation than most other actions. It is also closely tied to the enormous expectations of the self and defines a commitment toward others without the need for too much intimacy (e.g., "I was called to do this by a moral imperative"). When action is taken, the self thus can often overcome its negative focus on itself.

In a moral act often lies a deep-seated wish to overcome the alienation. The wish is never admitted and usually not even known to the self, yet through the moral act the self makes an affirmative statement about its validity and vitality. What begins as a rigid application of moral rules can lead to explorations with more flexible evaluations of internal reality and to new relational capacities. The alienated self's moral system supports not only moral action but also boundaries against repeated hurt that created the alienated self in the first place. For that reason moral action holds great potential for the alienated self to mature and develop toward a self that is more flexible and actively moral and toward a morality that is truly human.

References

Adorno, T. W., Frenkel-Brunswik, E., Levinson, D. J., and Sanford, R. N. (1950). *The authoritarian personality*. New York: Harper & Row.

Borst, S., and Noam, G. (In press). Developmental psychopathology in suicidal and non-suicidal adolescent girls. *Journal of the American Academy of Child and Adolescent Psychiatry*.

Borst, S., Noam, G., and Bartok, J. (1991). Adolescent suicidality: A clinical-developmental approach. *Journal for the American Academy of Child and Adolescent Psychiatry*, 30:796–803.

Bowlby, J. (1969) *Attachment and loss*. Vol. 1: *Attachment*. London: Hogarth Press.

Döbert, R., and Nunner-Winkler, G. (In press). Common sense understandings about suicide as resource for coping with suicidal impulses. In G. Noam and S.

Borst (Eds.), *Child and adolescent suicide: Clinical-developmental perspectives*. San Francisco: Jossey-Bass.

Edelstein, W. (1979). *Project child development and social structure*. Reykjavik, Iceland.

Erikson, E. (1950). *Childhood and society*. New York: Norton.

Fowler, J. W. (1981). *Stages of faith: The psychology of human development and the quest for meaning*. New York: Harper & Row.

Herman, J. (1992). *Trauma and recovery*. New York: Basic Books.

Kegan, R. (1982). *The evolving self*. Cambridge: Harvard University Press.

Keller, M., and Edelstein, W. (1991). The development of socio-moral meaning-making: Domains, categories, and perspective-taking. In W. Kurtines and J. Gewirtz (Eds.), *Handbook of moral behavior and development*. Vol. 2. Hillsdale, NJ: Erlbaum.

Kohlberg, L. (1969). Stage and sequence: The cognitive-developmental approach to socialization. In D. Goslin (Ed.), *Handbook of socialization: Theory and research*. New York: Rand McNally.

Kohlberg, L. (1984). *Essays on moral development*. Vol. 2: *The psychology of moral development*. San Francisco: Harper and Row.

Kohut, H. (1971). *The analysis of the self*. New York: International Universities Press.

Kohut, H., and Wolf, E. (1978). The disorders of the self and their treatment. *International Journal of Psychoanalysis*, 59:414–425.

Laing, R. D. (1959). *The divided self*. London: Tavistock.

Loevinger, J. (1968). The relation of adjustment to ego development. In S. Sales (Ed.), *The definition and measurement of mental health*. Washington, DC: Government Printing Office.

Loevinger, J. (1976). *Ego development*. San Francisco: Jossey-Bass.

Noam, G. (1988a). A constructivist approach to developmental psychology. In E. Nannis and P. Cowan (Eds.), *Developmental psychopathology and its treatment*. San Francisco: Jossey-Bass.

Noam, G. (1988b). The self, adult development and the theory of biography and transformation. In D. Lapsley and C. Power (Eds.), *Self, ego, and identity*. New York: Springer.

Noam, G. (1988c). The theory of biography and transformation; foundation for clinical-developmental therapy. In S. Shirk (Ed.), *Cognitive development and child psychotherapy*. New York: Plenum.

Noam, G. (1991). Beyond Freud and Piaget: Internal worlds—interpersonal self. In T. E. Wren (Ed.), *The moral domain: Essays in the ongoing discussion between philosophy and the social sciences*. Cambridge: MIT Press.

Noam, G. (1992). Development as the aim of clinical intervention. *Development and Psychopathology*, 4:679–696

Noam, G., Kohlberg, L., and Snarey, J. (1983). Steps toward a model of the self. In B. Lee. and G. Noam (Eds.), *Developmental approaches to the self.* New York: Plenum.

Noam, G., Paget, K., Bartok, J., and Borst, R. (1990). Conduct and affective disorders in developmental perspective: A systematic study of adolescent psychopathology. McLean Hospital Report, 5.

Oser, F., Althof, W., and Gartz, D., Eds. (1986). *Moralische Zugänge zum Menschen— Zugänge zum moralischen Menschen.* Munich: Kindt.

Sroufe, L. (1979). The coherence of individual development. *American Psychologist*, 34:834–841.

Winnicott, D. W. (1965). *Family and individual development.* New York: Basic Books.

Wolf, E. (1988). *Treating the self.* New York: Guilford Press.

Balanced Identity: Morality and Other Identity Values

Mordecai Nisan

The following dilemma was presented to 150 Israeli students:

Dr. Barnea was invited to spend his sabbatical year as a senior researcher at a well-known research institute in the United States. The institute has a unique research laboratory, where Dr. Barnea has aspired for years to work. He realizes that this is a rare opportunity to carry out his research and realize his plans—an opportunity that may never present itself again. However, Dr. Barnea is an only child, and his elderly parents cannot accompany him. He knows that if he leaves, he will cause them considerable grief.[1]

In a previous study, we found that the above dilemma was perceived by our respondents as realistic and plausible. The first question presented to the respondents was: "From a moral point of view what is the correct thing to do in this situation?" The respondents were offered a choice between two responses: (1) "To go away and carry out the coveted research," and (2) "To stay in Israel so that the parents are not alone." Approximately 70 percent of the respondents thought that the correct thing to do from a moral point of view was to stay with the parents. When asked why, they explained, as expected, that Dr. Barnea has a moral obligation to support his elderly parents. Most of the respondents felt a need to explain why this obligation is so important and mentioned the parents' investment in bringing up their child, the grief that will be caused if they stay alone, the obligation to respect one's parents, etc. The respondents were then presented with the following question: "You were asked what was the right thing to do from a moral point of view. Now what would you do if you were actually faced with this situation?" Of the respondents who felt that from a moral point of view the parents should not be left alone, 30 percent indicated that if they were faced with the same situation they would go abroad. A similar distribution was obtained when the second question was "What would you advise Dr. Barnea to do?" or when the questions were asked in a different order, i.e., when respondents were first asked what they would do themselves (or alternatively what they would advise Dr. Barnea to do) and then about what is the right thing to do from a moral point of view. When asked to explain their choices, these respondents (i.e., those who exhibited a discrepancy between moral judgment and behavioral choice) mentioned considerations of self-actualization (realization of plans, aspirations, self development) and usually made it clear that such considerations are valid even if they cause the parents grief. (Other types of rationalizations were also offered, e.g., that the parents themselves are interested in their son's development.)

When three additional dilemmas were presented to the respondents, a similar discrepancy was found between moral judgment and moral choice, i.e., "What would you choose to do in this situation?" One of the dilemmas was as follows:

Arie was driving over the speed limit in his father's car. A police car began following him, and he managed to get away. After parking the car on a side street, Arie went back home and told his father what had happened. Such behavior is not characteristic of Arie, who is a law-abiding citizen. His father, who anticipates being summoned for a police investigation, is faced with a dilemma: If he tells the truth, Arie may be sentenced to prison. If he says that someone apparently stole the car Arie will be exonerated. The father knows the police will not find out if he lies and is not afraid of being found out. The question is whether to tell the truth to the police or lie.

A full 85 percent of the respondents believed that from a moral point of view the father should tell the police that his son was guilty. Of these respondents, however, 40 percent said they would choose to lie to the police rather than confess that their son was to blame. These choices were based on such justifications as love for the son, fear of what might happen to the son, attachment to the son. Many respondents mentioned that these factors override the moral judgment.

On the basis of these findings we can argue in several ways: First of all, the findings reveal a distinction between the judgment regarding what is right to do in a given situation and moral choice. Subjects who judged that the moral thing to do in Dr. Barnea's situation is to stay with the parents, responded immediately afterward that they would advise Dr. Barnea to go away and do his research, contrary to the recognized moral claim. The discrepancy between the two questions suggests that judgment and choice are not guided by the same principle or by the same considerations. This argument is strengthened by the fact that the choice was made immediately after the judgment was expressed and rationalized. Thus it is plausible to assume that the respondents were aware of the discrepancy, were willing to accept it, and—in some cases— even rationalized it. In such cases judgment and choice must constitute two separate decisions. Given the basic tendency, at least in Israeli culture, toward consistency between judgment and choice, we can assume that even respondents who did not indicate a discrepancy between the decisions made them separately but gave similar responses.

At this point I should mention some interpretations of the distinction between judgment and choice that do not hold. The distinction is not between judgment in principle as opposed to choice in an actual situation with intervening conditions. The judgment pertained specifically to Dr. Barnea (or to Arie's father), and no information was added between the judgment and choice questions.

Similarly, the discrepancy under discussion is not the well-known discrepancy between judgment and behavior. It does not derive from denial of moral obligations, as in "I am aware of the moral obligations in this situation (just as I am aware of the customs of the Eskimos), but they don't mean anything to me." Similarly, the discrepancy does not derive from weakness of will, i.e., "I know that one should do such and such, but I can't live up to those standards." Analysis of the explanations clearly shows that the respondents who indicate a discrepancy between judgment and choice feel the parents' pain (in the case of Dr. Barnea), are sorry to have to leave

the parents behind, regret the moral shortcoming, and would seek
to rectify the situation to the extent possible (visits home, phone
calls, arrangements for home care). Nevertheless, these respondents chose to leave their own parents because (as one of them
wrote), "Even though it weighs on my conscience and I am aware
that my parents will suffer, I must take advantage of this unique
opportunity to develop myself." The choice is viewed as justifiable
and the respondents in fact offer reasons for it. Thus the choice is
guided by a certain principle, which I will discuss later in more
detail.

Second, in justifying a choice that deviates from moral judgment,
certain counter-voiding considerations come into play. These are
perceived as distinct from moral considerations but are given equal
status, which enables them to compete with moral considerations.
As one respondent expressed it, "Even though from a moral point
of view I should stay with my parents, in this case the consideration
of fulfilling my aspiration is more important." Even though a small
number of respondents mentioned that from a moral point of view
people have an obligation to fulfill themselves, most of them
believed that self-actualization and personal development are not
moral considerations. Nevertheless, this type of consideration is
close to a moral consideration in that it invokes a sense of "ought."
Indeed, hardly anyone explained the choice to leave one's parents
(as in the case of Dr. Barnea) or to lie to the police (as in the case
of Arie's father) as deriving from wishes, desires, or considerations
of immediate benefit and gratification. All of the explanations were
presented and viewed as valid justifications, which implies not only
a right but in some cases even an obligation to choose the nonmoral
alternative. For example, "It would be a crime for a person [such as
Dr. Barnea] not to take advantage of such an opportunity to engage
in the research he has aspired towards all his life."

Thus both the moral and nonmoral considerations refer to what
ought to be done, and the choice is perceived not only as conforming with the individual's plans but also as something the individual
has a right to do and even ought to do. Nevertheless, respondents
differentiate between moral considerations in a limited sense and
"ought" considerations in a broader sense. Later we will examine
this distinction.

Third, the respondents' moral choice, which they explain and perceive as justified, shows that, in contrast to a prevalent philosophical conception (e.g., Baier, 1958), nonmoral considerations of what one ought to do can be perceived as overriding moral considerations. It must be emphasized that the distinction relates to the way the respondents themselves perceive the considerations.

Clearly one can argue, as I believe Hare (1952) would have, that the overriding consideration is, by definition, the moral one, since it is the one that is perceived as decisive. I will not discuss this response, since it does not pertain directly to my purposes. However, my findings have shown that this is not the case from a phenomenological point of view. Many respondents accept the idea that moral considerations may be overridden by other considerations. The subjective distinction between moral and nonmoral considerations thus does not rest on the found feature of overridingness.

This argument corroborates and complements my previous ones. The argument that moral choice is guided by a different principle than that which guides moral judgment is related to the fact that the choice is influenced and can be decided by considerations perceived as extramoral but nevertheless desirable, as valid and justified. The influence of these considerations, or the need to weigh such considerations against moral ones, necessarily generates a need for a principle other than the moral one, a principle that will make it possible to decide the dilemma of moral versus nonmoral considerations. The dilemma of moral choice thus appears to differ from that of moral judgment. Although the principle guiding moral judgment is not clear to us (perhaps it involves a certain combination of several principles, deontological, utilitarian, and others), it seems to have a feature that distinguishes it from other considerations. This feature, which plays a central role for philosophers and is also clearly evident in the phenomenology of reflective respondents, is the impersonal nature of moral judgment, that is, the belief that it is valid for every person in a similar situation. Indeed, this characteristic was mentioned in many of the arguments offered in response to the dilemma of Arie's father. Respondents submitted that from a moral point of view the father must disregard his special relationship to his son and tell the truth to the police. The personal considerations that arise in the dilemmas under discussion, such as self-actualization and the father's relationship to his son, are perceived explicitly (in the case of Arie's father) or implicitly (in the case of Dr. Barnea) as extramoral considerations. However, when making a moral *choice*, the individual weighs both types of considerations. In so doing, one needs to rely on a principle that will enable one to decide between the two options. This is the unique principle underlying moral choice. In the following sections I will make several proposals regarding this principle, based on an analysis of the nature of nonmoral considerations.

The Varied Forms of the Sense of "Ought"

The psychological study of morality has been based on a dichotomous distinction between moral and nonmoral considerations. Nonmoral considerations are those related to the individual's desires and preferences, as well as to his or her long-term benefits. As opposed to moral considerations, nonmoral considerations do not involve claims or obligations. Moral considerations are not up to the individual's preferences, and often even obligate one to act against those preferences. Indeed, moral considerations can only be conceived in relation to nonmoral ones as restraining and limiting them. In most, if not all cases, moral considerations are perceived as connected with relationships between the individual and others and between the individual and society.

This dichotomous distinction, which would appear to be a product of Judeo-Christian culture, guided the psychology in morality in its heyday. A clear manifestation of this distinction is found in the Freudian division between the superego and other structures of the personality. Indeed, Freud resorted to the concept of identification to explain the development of strong moral claims that stand in opposition to personal preferences. However, this dichotomous distinction also underlies Piaget's and Kohlberg's cognitive theories, which hold that the same logic that led Kant to perceive morality as having absolute claim guides the individual along the stages of his or her moral development. This logic is based on an impersonal position, what Kohlberg (1973) called "moral musical chairs." Hoffman (1984) and Gilligan (1982), who contend that this position cannot serve as the only basis for morality, added elements relating to personal feelings: empathy and sympathy, consideration and responsibility. Such elements would make it possible to soften both the moral claim and the dichotomous distinction mentioned above. However, there is little evidence of such softening in their own arguments. In fact, in terms of content, Hoffman's and Gilligan's approaches would seem to strengthen the idea of dichotomy: the moral feelings they discuss pertain to the relationship between the individual and others, and this is the clearest content feature of moral as opposed to nonmoral considerations.

The above-mentioned dichotomy has led to a diluting of moral choice, as distinct from moral judgment. The dichotomy between moral and nonmoral choice allows for two types of moral conflicts: between a moral consideration and a nonmoral consideration, and between two moral considerations leading in different directions. Psychoanalytic and learning approaches to morality have dealt with conflicts of the first type. These constitute a behavioral conflict, involving a choice between acceptance or rejection of morality. This is not, I would claim, the typical moral conflict experienced by people, which entails a choice between two justifiable considerations.

The second type of conflict, generally labeled a moral dilemma, has been dealt with in the cognitive developmental approach. This type of conflict, which seems to have become more prevalent in modern times, does not allow for moral choice. It calls the individual to think out and discover the one correct solution to the dilemma rather than to choose from a number of acceptable solutions.

Unlike the two types of conflict mentioned above, the dilemmas faced by Dr. Barnea and Arie's father seem to involve a choice between two alternatives each of which can be justified. Although from a moral point of view there may be only one correct answer, the alternative answer also has an acceptable justification; there is no one "correct" solution and so the individual must make a choice. This sense of moral choice is reflected in the answers to questions presented in the study. Respondents were asked to reread the first dilemma and put their responses in writing. Afterward they were asked, "Do you believe that everyone presented with this situation should respond in the same way?" Approximately 50 percent of the respondents answered this question negatively and explained that different people can make different choices, depending on how they feel, what their situation is, and how they wish to lead their lives. Interestingly, in all of the dilemmas presented, the large majority of respondents believed there was one moral answer. In the case of Arie's father, for example, the "moral" answer was to reveal the truth to the police. At the same time they believed that the dilemma does not have one correct solution and that there is room for choice. The choice was between a decision for the moral consideration versus a decision in the direction of the nonmoral, where the latter is viewed as justified and decisive even when weighed against the moral consideration. Indeed, the nonmoral considerations guided the choice of many respondents *contrary* to their moral judgment.

These findings, together with examination of the perceptions and choices of individuals, suggest a type of reasons for action that lies midway between moral claims and personal preference, reasons that involve a claim, but not a strong one. I will refer to these as value considerations, to use a term accepted in the social sciences. Such considerations are related to perceptions of what is desirable (as opposed to what is desired), as well as to the understanding that one should act in a certain way even if one does not wish to do so and even if it contradicts what one would really like to do. This concept of value is distinct both from personal preference (Nucci, 1981) and from moral obligation. It is distinct from preference in that it presents the individual with a claim, and it is distinct from morality in that the claim does not obligate the individual. This meaning of "value" is more limited than in some other contexts. For instance, a more general use of the term "value" also includes moral values, i.e., conceptions of obligatory behavior, and in an economic context "value" refers to aspirations guided by conceptions of what is desired and not only what is desirable.

The distinction between morality, values, and personal preference manifests itself as early as age 10 (Nisan, 1988, 1989a). At that age, when children are asked about certain behavior (such as reading books, making friends, and becoming independent), they indicate that children should be educated and encouraged to do those things, although they should not be obligated to do so or punished for failure to do so. This can be contrasted with such behavior as watching television, which children believe requires no education, and with such behavior as hitting or lying, which one is obligated to avoid and should be punished for. When children were asked to explain why one should or should not be educated for the behavior in question, their arguments related to three types of reasons. Values are generally explained in terms of one's development and long-term utility. Morality is explained in terms of the welfare of others and of society. And preferences are explained in terms of the individual's personal likings. Thus differences among "ought to," "must," and "depends on the individual's preference" are parallel to differences in types of reasons: the other person's welfare, the individual's development, and matters of personal preference.

Needless to say, the distinction between these three types of perceptions is not clearcut. There are gray areas, supererogation being a particularly striking example. While supererogation is related to morality since it involves the welfare of others, in terms of the nature of the claim it is closer to the area of values, since it is viewed as desirable but not obligatory.

Like moral behavior, the value-related behaviors mentioned above are perceived as having intrinsic value that is neither dependent on the child's desires nor on culture. Thus the children interviewed believe that people should be educated to read books even if they live in a culture where most people do not do so. Respondents perceived the value of reading books as deriving, as it were, from human nature and the nature of the world. Indeed, as mentioned, the respondents' reasons for saying that reading books or making friends should be encouraged indicate that their perception of values is based on what they view as universal conditions for a long-term welfare and development.

While morality and values are perceived as having intrinsic value and thus as not contingent, other conceptions of what one ought to do are perceived as contingent on the individual. This characterizes conceptions related to the individual's personal projects (Williams, 1981). When respondents were asked whether children should be encouraged to participate in an extracurricular astronomy course, almost all responded that this is not necessary. Interest in astronomy is perceived as a personal preference, and it is up to the child to choose whether or not to pursue it. However, this was not the case when astronomy was said to be a priority in the child's life. In one study (Nisan, 1986), a group of Israeli respondents was presented with the following character description: "Danny is 17 years old. Danny is very interested in astronomy. The subject of astronomy plays an important role in his life, so important that Danny cannot envision himself without pursuing his interest in the subject." Another group of respondents was presented with a different description: "Danny is a 17-year-old boy who is somewhat interested in astronomy." Then both groups were presented with the following situation: "One day a lecture was being given on an important topic relating to astronomy. That same day there was going to be a soccer game that Danny really wanted to see." Afterward the respondents were asked a number of questions, including "To what degree do you think Danny ought to go to the lecture?" The question was answered (on a 9-point scale from 1 = "not at all" to 9 = "very much") by 120 respondents, half of whom were between the ages of 16 and 20 and the other half between the ages of 30 and 50. The results showed that when the boy was described as considering astronomy a central part of his life, he was more likely to be perceived as having to go to the lecture (average = 6.5) than when he was described as being "somewhat interested" in astronomy (average = 5.7). Similar results were obtained for other stories with a similar structure. It thus seems that an individual's personal project creates a perception of ought: a person should be dedicated to his or her personal project even if the activity involved is not perceived as having intrinsic value, i.e., as being desirable for everyone.

Another contingent perception of ought is that generated by commitment to a group or cause. If a personal project is usually directed toward self-development, commitment is usually directed toward a group or goal that transcends the individual. In the study described above, the following characterization was presented: "Yosi is 17 years old. For Yosi, the fact that he is Jewish is extremely important. Yosi feels that his being Jewish is a central factor in his life, and he cannot describe himself without relating to this part of his personality." This contrasts with the following characterization, which was presented to another group of respondents: "Yosi is 17 years old and has taken a certain interest in his being Jewish." After the respective description of the boy, the following paragraph was added: "One day Yosi was told that on a certain evening there was going to be a fund-raising event for Jewish culture in the Soviet Union. However, a soccer game that Yosi really wanted to see was scheduled for the same evening." Then the respondents were asked, "To what extent do you think Yosi ought to attend the fund-raising event?" On a 9-point scale, different responses were obtained, according to the extent of Yosi's involvement in the subject. When he was described as being extremely involved in Judaism, he was perceived as having a stronger obligation to attend the fund-raising event (average = 6.8) than when he was described as having little involvement in the subject (average = 5.1). The results thus suggest that one expects people to do what is consistent with their values and emotional commitments and not only what furthers their personal projects.

Several types of considerations were found to lie between personal and moral ones. Of these, some were perceived as having intrinsic validity and others as contingent on the individual's projects and commitments. The important point here is that there is a category of considerations that neither belong to the realm of morality nor involve strong claims but nevertheless are viewed as involving a claim of some sort. The fact that they involve a claim distinguishes them from considerations of personal preference and lends them a validity that, as it were, transcends the individual. Moreover, the claim gives these considerations a normative status, and, even if it is weaker than a moral claim since it does not obligate the individual, it at least gives the individual an "extra right" to behave in the way dictated by it. We can at least say that value considerations are partners with moral considerations, and that in a conflict between moral and value considerations, the latter are not dismissed outright.

Affirmation of Identity: The Source of Moral Motivation

Moral obligations and values of the first type involve claims perceived as having intrinsic validity and as not being contingent on desire, individual tendencies, or social conventions. Their validity is perceived as deriving from the power of reason: on reflection, everyone must come to accept morality and values of this type. This validity holds for those who consider the issue from an impersonal perspective, those who judge from the "original position," as Rawls (1971) expressed it. In other words, it holds in the eyes of the person who makes *moral judgments*. Such judgments are indeed decided on the basis of moral obligation. Analogously, one can speak of *value judgments*, which dictate how one ought to act when faced with a choice between pursuing values versus following desires. Value judgments are also made from the vantage point of the overall development of the individual beyond considerations of the here and now. We can assume that a value judgment will be determined by the value claim. Yet, the question remains, what validity do moral obligation and values have for the acting person (as distinguished from the judging person)? Why should one feel that the dictates of reason indeed obligate oneself? Why do considerations made from an impersonal, atemporal position, a position alien to the individual, create and set in motion an operative sense of obligation? This is, in essence, the question "Why be moral?"

At first glance the question seems more complex when it relates to the two types of personal values mentioned above. Why should people feel that they "ought" to pursue their personal projects and personal commitments when these reasons do not have objective validity? The commitment is *theirs* and the project is *theirs*. If they do not want to act accordingly, they have every right to do so. Why do they feel they "have" to?

Examination of this issue in relation to personal values, projects, and commitments provides us with a clue that may help us understand the motivational basis for behaving according to what is desirable. Respondents had difficulty explaining why one "has" to act according to commitments and projects, but the reasons they gave include variations of the following: "If it is so important for the person, then he should do it," or "If he does not do what is so crucial to him, he is a weakling." It should be noted that these reasons do not apply to the expectation that a person should always follow his or her preferences. If Danny likes to watch television, we do not think he must do that instead of going to a soccer game. However, Danny is expected to pursue projects that are very important to him and to fulfill deeply rooted commitments. If astronomy is a major concern for him and a major project in his life, then he is expected to pursue that project. Similarly, if Yosi feels a strong commitment to the Jewish cause, then he is expected to attend the fund-raising event for Soviet Jewry. If they do not do so, they are not being loyal to themselves, since astronomy and commitment to Judaism are important parts of their selves. This might be phrased thus: Failure to pursue projects and commitments cannot be perceived as neutral behavior, since these are part of the self. Failure to pursue projects and commitments that the individual still holds near and dear means disregard and even denial of a part of the self. If this failure derives not from inability but rather from personal choice, then it can be viewed as hindering and restraining the self.

The expectation that one should pursue personal projects and commitments derives from their unique position vis-à-vis the self. They form part of one's personal identity. Many scholars have written about the problematics of the term "identity" (Blasi, 1984). However, as R. Brown writes, "We can move ahead anyway because everyone roughly understands what is meant" (1986, p. 551). According to various usages in social psychology (see Stryker, 1987), one's identity is made up of self-definitions, i.e., the essential characteristics perceived as making an individual the unique person he or she is. These "components of identity," as I shall call them, have different degrees of essentiality. We may say that a component of identity is more essential to the extent that a person believes that change in this component will more extensively change his or her self. In this sense, personal projects and commitments are highly essential components of identity, and expecting that a person will act according to them means that one should "be oneself." Perception of behavior as desirable and motivation for acting accordingly thus derive from the same source: perception of the behavior as an essential element of personal identity. It is also possible, although not necessary, that motivation and perception of what is desirable be two sides of the same coin.

This explanation of the claim and motivational force of personal projects and commitments in terms of striving toward self-preservation and self-actualization seems reasonable since they are indeed part of the scheme of a person's intentions and desires. It is easy to concur with social psychologists who postulate such a tendency in order to explain projects and commitments, and our own research supports that assumption. For example, Horenczyk (1989) found that in a situation where Jewish identity was aroused, male and female teenagers who were given an opportunity to actualize their Jewish identity (for example, by writing an essay on the subject) exhibited a higher degree of self-esteem and self-satisfaction than did a similar group not given an opportunity to do so (the latter group wrote an essay on American identity). Moreover, comparison of this group to a control group whose Jewish identity was not aroused at all showed that failure to provide an opportunity for actualizing identity led to a decline in self-esteem. These results indicate that when a component of identity is aroused in an individual, a need to actualize or express the component is also aroused. This need derives not from a wish to enhance self-esteem, as suggested by Tajfel (1981), but rather from a need to maintain one's identity and self-esteem. This need is analogous to the individual's sense that he or she ought to affirm and express his or her identity. When prevented from fulfilling this need, the individual will feel dissatisfaction and a decline in self-esteem.

At first sight, this explanation would not seem to apply to moral motivation. In contrast to personal projects and commitments, moral considerations appear as hostile and foreign to the individual. In the dichotomous distinction between personal and moral considerations, moral considerations are presented as harnessing personal ones, or at the most as an expression of a cold, removed "reason." Is it really possible to explain moral motivation in terms of personal identity? I suggest that it is, and that the prevailing conception that the basic motivational force for moral choice is reason and/or empathy should be revised.

It is difficult to dispute the contention that morality is perceived as an essential element of identity. In a study by Nisan and Horenczyk (1988), youths and adults were presented with various components of identity (e.g., morality, gender, nationality, ideology, facial features) and asked to indicate the extent to which a change in a component would (or would not) make them different people. Of all the components, morality received the highest mark. The youths and adults alike felt that if they were to become immoral, they would to a large extent become different people. If morality is such an essential element of identity and if, as I proposed above, the individual seeks to affirm and actualize his or her identity, then we can expect people to feel not only that they *ought* to act morally but that they *must* behave that way. As indicated by the previously cited findings regarding national identity, one expects that moral behavior will lead to a sense of personal gratification and fulfillment, while immoral behavior would lead to a feeling of anger and loss of self-esteem.

This perception of moral motivation suggests a different picture of the psychological nature of morality from the one prevalent in the psychology of morality. Morality is not a hostile agent, as suggested in the psychoanalytic approach, or a "persuasive philosopher," as suggested in the cognitive approach. Nor is it an empathetic agent, as suggested by Hoffman (1984), or the concerned and responsible spectator, as suggested by Gilligan (1982). Rather, morality relates to the very essence of the individual, what he or she really is.

Balanced Identity

The idea that maintaining and actualizing identity is what motivates people to behave according to their perception of how they ought to behave suggests a principle for choice in moral and value dilemmas: maintaining personal identity. Before entering into a discussion of how this principle actually works, let us consider some of the implications of the preceding argument.

First, the principle of maintaining personal identity suggests a yardstick the person uses in conflicts of morals and values. When guided by this principle, one does not ask whether one did the right or wrong thing—whether such behavior is allowed, prohibited, or required—but rather *to what extent* an action harms one's personal identity. It is true that some acts harm identity so badly that the individual does not assess them in quantitative terms: they are simply unthinkable. Such acts generally involve serious moral transgressions or violation of central human values. Performing such acts means becoming inhuman. At the same time, however, there are values and even moral dictums whose violation is considered in quantitative terms, i.e., on the basis of the extent to which they harm identity. This argument seems to correspond with everyday experience.

Second, the principle of maintaining personal identity provides a standard of comparison for choosing between different values, including moral values. The problem of comparing values that are qualitatively different and hence irreducible to a scale of utility is one of the most complex problems in the domain of values. The fact is, however, that people *do* choose between qualitatively different values and seem to believe that the choice is not arbitrary but has a basis. The argument presented here proposes one such basis: the extent of harm to personal identity. Apparently, it was this kind of comparison that our respondents made when they said that abandoning morality would change them "very greatly" whereas change of gender would just change them "greatly." Comparisons made on this basis seem to be relevant to moral choice but not to moral judgment.

Third, my proposal suggests that moral and value choices are personal rather than impersonal. In contrast to moral judgment, which is regarded as "correct" and "objective" (so that anyone who thinks correctly is supposed to arrive at the same judgment), an individual's moral (and value) *choices* aim at maintaining his or her personal identity, with its unique structure. One would therefore expect such a person to accept not only that people differ in their evaluations of specific acts and in the way they choose to behave, but also that different choices may be correct, depending on the personal identity of the person making the choice.

These implications constitute the basis for my proposals regarding the principles that guide the choice between considerations of value. Let us first consider the "simple" case of a choice between value-based behavior and behavior based on personal preference (i.e., based on utility). The question in such a case is, To what extent does a person have to fulfill his identity, given that actualization of personal identity has no limit? This question indicates a similarity between some supererogatory behavior and behavior that fulfills a component of personal identity. If some of the former behavior is, as Kant would put it, an imperfect duty, then the latter is an imperfect value. As in the case of supererogatory behavior, I propose that the individual strives to maintain a certain balance in actualizing a component of identity, expressing it to a satisfactory extent but not necessarily to a maximum extent. This principle clearly does not provide a complete answer to the question posed before. It does, however, suggest a direction for future research.

If value choices are guided by the principle of maintaining a satisfactory balance of an identity component then when one has recently behaved in a way that fulfilled an identity component, the need to do so again will not be as strong as it would have been if one had not expressed that component for a long time. This hypothesis rests on the assumption that balance is calculated over time. Horenczyk (1989) indeed found this to be true in studies that examined the tendency of 17-year-old students at Jewish high schools in New York to actualize Jewish identity. The respondents received questionnaires that included stories consisting of two parts. The first part described people who had actualized (or not actualized) their Jewish identity (such as fund-raising for poor Jews). The second part described a situation of several days later in which each of the two people described in the first part of the story faced a conflict between another claim to engage in activity on behalf of Jews (such as distributing a Jewish newspaper) and a temptation (such as going to a party). The respondents were asked, among other questions, "To what degree would you have been ready to say that it would be OK not to help with the distribution of the Jewish newspaper and go to the party?" In another version of the questionnaires, it was mentioned that both of the people described had decided not to accede to the claim of Jewish identity, and the respondents were asked, "To what extent ought Jeff to feel guilty about this?" The results showed evidence of a Jewish-identity balance. Respondents were more willing to allow the person in the story not to actualize his Jewish identity when he had recently engaged in such activity than when he had not recently done so. They also believed that in the former case he should feel less guilty about not volunteering at the present time.

Another study examined the effect of balance on actual behavior of two groups of 16-year-olds at Jewish schools in New York. In the first part of the study, to arouse their sense of Jewish identity the subjects were told about an educational program aimed at enhancing Jewish identity. One group was then given an opportunity to actualize their identity by writing an essay relating to it ("Is it important for me to remain a Jew? If yes, why?"). The second group was not given such an opportunity. Rather, they were asked to write a similar essay relating to American identity ("Is it important for me to remain an American? If yes, why?"). In addition, there was a control group of students who neither had their Jewish identity aroused nor were given an opportunity to actualize their Jewish identity. All of the respondents were then asked if they would agree to be interviewed in the framework of a project examining issues relating to Jewish identity, and if so, how much time they would be willing to devote (anywhere between 15 and 45 minutes). The results showed that the respondents in the actualized first group were less prepared to be interviewed than those in the other two groups. Moreover, those in the unactualized second group were willing to be interviewed for a longer time than those in the control group. Thus we can surmise that members of the group that had been given an opportunity to actualize their identity had achieved a satisfactory balance and did not feel a need for further actualization. In contrast, members of the group whose identity had been aroused but were not given an opportunity to actualize it arrived at a negative balance (in comparison with the control group), which they felt a need to rectify by volunteering to be interviewed for a longer time.

These findings are corroborated by studies on morality (Nisan, 1985; Nisan, 1991; Nisan and Horenczyk, 1990) showing that people are prepared to *allow* some moral deviation—for themselves and others—more after performance of good deeds and less after performance of bad deeds. The distinction between one's moral balance and identity balance is related to the difference between expectations for positive behavior (actualizing an identity component, as well as supererogatory behavior) and expectations that negative acts (harming others or society) will be avoided. In the case of positive acts, we might say that the balance should reflect the "minimum credit" an individual is prepared to allow him or herself, and in the case of negative acts, the balance should reflect the "maximum debit" allowed.

The principle of satisfactory balance relates to "simple" situations in which an individual must choose between actualizing and not actualizing an identity value (where personal preference takes precedence). A more complex situation is one in which the individual must choose between two alternatives, both of which are supported by (either moral or value) considerations of what one ought to do. The accepted approach to such dilemmas is that values are arranged in a hierarchy that serves as a basis for the individual's choice (as assumed, for example, in Rokeach, 1973). When a moral consideration is involved in a conflict, accepted philosophical assumptions lead one to expect that moral considerations override nonmoral ones. This would indeed seem to be true of judgment (given certain modifications that I will not discuss here). However, as shown at the beginning of the chapter, this is not true of choice, which is guided by a different principle than judgment. I propose that the conflict between two or more "ought" considerations is decided on the basis of a principle of "balanced identity." According to this principle, an individual will choose the alternative leading to an optimal state of balanced identity, covering all of the components of his or her identity.

When two values relating to what ought to be done conflict with each other, preference for one consideration means denial of the other and harms that aspect of identity corresponding to the denied value. In Dr. Barnea's case, if he chooses to go on sabbatical he is violating the moral consideration of honoring one's parents, which is an important element of his identity. If he chooses to stay with his parents, however, he is violating the value consideration of actualizing a personal project, which is also an important aspect of his identity. I propose that the individual will choose the alternative perceived to do least harm to the general balance of his or her present personal identity. Thus, according to this proposal, the choice is not being made by evaluating and comparing separate alternatives (which is supposed to take place at the stage of judgment), but rather on the basis of their current meaning for the individual from the perspective of his or her personal identity.

This argument assumes that the significance of an act for the identity of the person engaging in the act is not the same as an objective evaluation of the same behavior. The significance of a certain behavior for one's identity is related to the unique structure of the individual's identity (what one considers more important or less important), as well as to the current balances of one's identity, i.e., the extent to which different components have been actualized in the time span that affects the balance. This leads to the hypothesis that if an individual has recently actualized a certain component of identity, he or she will more willingly give up actualizing that component and prefer to focus on another component of identity that has not yet been actualized.

The principle of balanced identity fits my finding that in some cases a person will choose nonmoral over moral considerations (as in the case of the dilemmas faced by Dr. Barnea and by Arie's father, presented in the beginning of this chapter). In the proposed theoretical framework, I would say that the choice was guided by the principle of balanced identity, and those respondents who preferred nonmoral considerations apparently believed that if they chose the moral alternative, their overall identity would be harmed more than if they chose the nonmoral alternative. Such a situation can result from the weight of different considerations and actions in an individual's identity. Or it can result from situational factors, like behavior in the recent past, that give the individual moral credit so that he or she can allow a certain amount of deviation, even though the balance for the other value under consideration would not allow it.

Another hypothesis deriving from my argument is that people will justify the different choices of another individual according to the actor's unique identity structure. If the choice is guided by the principle of maintaining a balanced identity and if it is acknowledged that personal identity is unique in terms of its structure, then it will also be acknowledged that people have a justified reason and a right to make different choices according to their identity. The more central an issue is to the individual's identity, the more that person will feel he or she has a reason and a right to give priority to the issue over moral claims.

These hypotheses were examined in several studies. In one study (Nisan, 1989b), students were presented with three dilemmas, each of which involved a conflict between two different values. The first, Dr. Barnea's dilemma, was between a moral claim and self-actualization, i.e., an obligation not to upset one's parents versus an opportunity to spend a sabbatical at a unique research laboratory. The second dilemma was between a national claim (participation in research important to the country) and self-actualization (accepting an offer to work at a university). The third dilemma was between a moral claim and a national claim (along lines similar to the above). Two versions of each of the above situations were presented to the respondents. In one version, the person had devoted considerable time to realizing the first value, while in the second version, the person had devoted considerable time to realizing the second value ("Up to now Dr. Barnea had devoted a lot of time to taking care of his parents at the expense of his scientific work . . .”). The findings were mixed, partly because of different interpretations of the sentence relating to behavior up to the present (“The fact that he spent so much time taking care of his parents shows that they must be more important to him than his research,” or “If he hasn't devoted so much time to his parents up until now, they must not need him so badly”). In any case, a large number of respondents showed a clear inclination to choose according to the principle of balanced identity: if the individual in the story focused on value x up to a given point in time, there was a tendency to advise him to choose value y. Some of the explanations offered by respondents were explicitly based on the principle of balanced identity (“Up to this point [Dr. Barnea] has mainly fulfilled obligations towards his parents. Now he deserves to fulfill an obligation to himself”).

In another study, Hacohen (1992) examined the conflict between loyalty toward one's family or nationality and the moral consideration of being impartial or of not discriminating on the basis of family or nationality. She sought to examine the effect of several variables on the resolution of this conflict, as well as whether the respondents would be willing to justify different decisions by others on the basis of their unique personal identities. The respondents (Jewish 16-year-olds living in England) were presented with four stories. In one story, the protagonist had promised two friends he would take them to a musical show, and it turned out that he could only take one of them. One of the children is either a family relative of the protagonist or a member of the same nationality, and the other has no such connections. The respondent was first asked to indicate which other child the protagonist should choose to take to the show, whether to favor the family or group member or to flip a coin. After making their decisions, respondents were told that the protagonist had decided to take the family or group member and were asked to evaluate the protagonist and his act and to indicate how he should feel and why. Two of the stories dealt with negative behavior, as described in the example above, and the remaining two dealt with positive behavior, such as donation of a rare type of blood to a patient.

For our purposes, the important questions are, do subjects perceive favoritism as justifiable and what factors affect this justification? A considerable percentage of respondents (about 30 percent for the negative stories and 64 percent for the positive stories) chose to favor the family or group member. Moreover, and perhaps more interesting, of those who chose *not* to favor the family or group member, about half evaluated the *act* of favoritism as being "good" or "OK," and 70 percent evaluated the *person* who favored as being "good" or "OK." Among the other findings was that favoritism was perceived as being more justified when it is based on family membership (55 percent) than on nationality (40 percent), and more justified in the case of positive behavior (such as donation of blood) than in the case of negative behavior (breaking a promise). Finally, favoritism was perceived as being more justified for a protagonist characterized as considering his family or nationality as very important in his life, than for a protagonist who does not consider these factors to be important.

An important point in the present context is that favoritism can be perceived as acceptable. This is the case when the discriminating person is viewed as strongly connected or involved with the group that person is favoring. In other words, favoritism is perceived as more justifiable when it is related to an important component of a person's identity. In the research under discussion, this perception was based on an explicit statement (e.g., that the family is very important to the person). The role of personal identity is also revealed in the discrepancy, mentioned earlier, between evaluation of the act and evaluation of the actor. Again, of the respondents who chose *not* to favor, approximately 50 percent believed that the act of favoritism was "good" or "OK," and 70 percent believed that the person who favored was "good" or "OK." The difference between these two results is statistically significant and suggests a distinction between evaluation of the act (to a large extent on the basis of moral judgment) and evaluation of the person (mainly on the basis of identity).

Not only were a considerable percentage of the respondents willing to let national identity override the moral claim; such willingness was also strongly influenced by the respondent's national involvement. The higher the degree of involvement, as measured by several behavioral indicators, the greater one's willingness to let moral national identity override the moral claim. We can assume that people with a higher degree of national involvement believe that national solidarity is important to others too;

that is to say, they project onto others their own feeling that belonging to a nation is an essential element of identity. However, respondents considered national identity not absolutely valid but rather valid only according to the individual's personal identity.

Similar findings were obtained for involvement related to personal projects. As mentioned, when Yosi was characterized as being very interested in astronomy and as considering the subject an essential part of his life, respondents were more willing to accept his lying on a test (in order to get into a coveted workshop on astronomy) than they would have been had he only taken a superficial interest in astronomy. In this case, the element of identity is essential not in the sense that it is inevitable (as family is) but rather in the sense that it forms an integral part of the individual's identity.

Since these findings corroborate my hypotheses, they indirectly support my contention that the conflict between different considerations of what ought to be done is determined by the principle of balanced identity. Needless to say, the principle and the overall scheme elicit numerous questions that cannot be addressed here. Such questions range from specific ones (e.g., What determines a satisfactory level of an identity component and the weights of specific activities?) to more general ones (e.g., What elements will be included in a person's identity, and is there a compensatory relationship between different components?). And ultimately there are questions relating to the specifics of when the principle should be applied and when it is valid. These issues involve the distinction between moral judgment and moral choice, as well as cultural correlates of the principle (I assume that we are dealing with a cultural perception).

Conclusion

An important test of the proposed model is its ability to explain, in an intrinsically consistent framework, perceptions and feelings relating to features of moral choice. In this concluding section I will indicate several such features that seem to fit well with my proposed model.

A prevalent phenomenon that should puzzle psychologists dealing with morality is people's willingness to accept different choices or behaviors in dilemmas between morals and values. In my studies, as in everyday life, different choices are viewed as legitimate, and even when a respondent does not agree with the choice made by another, that choice is not condemned. This is puzzling, considering that nothing arouses more criticism than immoral behavior: how can a respondent who has made a particular choice, implying that this is the correct one, accept another?

A second feature to be explained, one that was already mentioned at the beginning of this chapter, is the feeling that we do indeed have moral choice. Moral judgment does not involve a sense of choice. Rather, it seeks *the* correct solution, and this applies also to complex dilemmas, such as those presented by Kohlberg. It is generally after making a judgment as to the morality of an act that one feels it is necessary to make a moral choice. Moral choices can be of different types. One would be of the sort: "Should I be moral or evil?" Such a choice may be involved when someone is considering cold-blooded murder to satisfy an urge. However, for one who adopts a moral position, there is no choice of this type. Another meaning of moral choice takes the following form: "Can I afford a minor transgression that would not render me evil?" This is a choice involving the *level* of moral balance that individuals demand of themselves (Nisan, 1985). Such a choice is one-dimensional (*how much* I demand of myself) and by no means exhausts the full range and depth of moral choice. A true moral or value choice would appear to be multidimensional, i.e., to be a choice between various alternatives, each of which presses for a satisfactory balance. An appropriate description of moral choice must provide a reasonable explanation of this sense of moral choice.

A third feature that requires explanation is the fact that moral choice is often largely influenced by gut feelings and not necessarily by clear, rational consideration. The interesting point here is that in many cases we do not feel disturbed by this; reliance on gut feelings is considered appropriate. The statement "That's the way I feel," for example, is often accepted as reasonable. Another side of the same coin is the feeling that some behavior is beyond consideration, that there is nothing to talk about, that the behavior is out of the question.

Still another feature that requires explanation is the feeling of regret and guilt following a certain choice and behavior. Once the individual has considered a matter, decided that he or she ought to behave in a certain way, and done so wholeheartedly, he or she may still feel uncomfortable. What I have in mind is not regret for the choice or remorse for the harm caused to somebody. If a person knows that he or she had a choice between options and feels satisfied with the choice made, what reason does that person have to feel uncomfortable?

All of these features combine with several others mentioned in the body of this chapter, for example: the fact that a moral choice is considered justifiable despite the discrepancy between one's moral judgment and moral choice; the fact that people compare and choose between qualitatively different kinds of values that seem incommensurable and incomparable; and the fact that, in contrast to moral judgment, moral choice is not viewed as guided by an alien principle.

The framework proposed here suits these features and thus in an important sense can explain them. According to my proposal, value conflicts and moral choice relate to components of identity, components determined not by virtue of their intrinsic features (as in moral *judgments*) but rather by virtue of the individual's history and personal projects, although because of certain intrinsic features, some components of identity will exist for all or most of the members of a culture. Moral choice is based on the principle of maintaining a balanced identity. Since people differ in their identities in terms of the content and weight of their components, they can be expected to differ in their choices, and this is how it ought to be (in most people's eyes), since it is the only way in which they can maintain their identities and remain loyal to them. Tolerance and acceptance of different choices thus reflect the belief that different people have different identities and that they should be loyal to their identities.

Furthermore, divergent moral choices made by the same person at different times may also be viewed as acceptable. The balance of the components of one's identity can change in accordance with one's recent activities, with the claims placed on oneself, and even with various situational factors. A personal event (such as the death of one's father) or a national event (such as war) can increase the salience of a specific identity component and elicit a profound need to express it. A person's choice will be made according to the balance of the various components of his or her identity at the time the choice is made. It will aim at achieving an optimal or satisfactory identity balance at that time.

This kind of choice cannot be made solely with rational judgment and consideration. Rather, to a great extent it is made on the basis of an individual's feelings. When a person faces a value conflict, he or she must choose one component of identity to prefer over another. This is a true choice, since it pertains to components of identity rather than external alternatives. When the person makes a choice, it is based on an evaluation of the balance of his or her identity, and not on a hierarchy of values. The principle of balanced identity thus allows for preference of nonmoral considerations over moral ones, where under the given conditions such a choice will cause less harm to one's identity balance than will preference for the moral considerations. This kind of choice cannot be viewed as "alienated," since it is the individual's choice between components of his or her own identity. The individual is the one who decides, the one who will act, and the one who will take the consequences of the act, including the consequences for his or her value balances after the choice is made. I submit that this is why a person may feel uncomfortable after making a choice, even if he or she is satisfied with it. By choosing in favor of one component of identity, an individual may have upset another component, and it is only natural that this upset in the identity balance would make him or her feel uncomfortable.

Not every moral choice is guided by the principle of balanced identity. Oftentimes value dilemmas can be circumvented and "solved" on the basis of social conventions. In many cases, for example, people decide to move their elderly parents to institutions because this is an accepted norm and not as a result of a considered choice guided by the principle of balanced identity. In other cases, people choose on the basis of moral judgment, that is, they compare the alternatives but do not consider their balances of values with regard to each alternative. This happens mainly in hypothetical situations or situations that are not important to the respondent. In some cases, however, as I have proposed here, people will consciously choose according to the principle of balanced identity (although some are more likely to do so than others). A striking example is the following response to the famous dilemma described by Jean-Paul Sartre involving a choice between staying with one's mother or going into the French underground, a response that brings up some of the points mentioned above: "Woe to him if he chooses to stay with his mother, and woe to him if he chooses to go with the underground. So that he will feel satisfied, I would tell him that if he has been with his mother until now, the time has come for him to fulfill his duty to his country. Personally, I would choose to stay with my mother, but in this case everyone has to act according to his feelings. Whoever does so is OK, and it doesn't matter what decision he makes."[2]

Notes

1. This and other quotations from the study are translated from the original Hebrew.

2. This work was supported by a grant from the United States—Israel Binational Science Foundation, in Jerusalem. I would also like to thank Gus Blasi, Tom Wren, Barbara Applebaum, and Gabi Horenczyk for the helpful discussions and cooperation they provided, and Helene Hogri for her editorial assistance.

References

Baier, K. (1958). *The moral point of view*. New York: Oxford University Press.

Blasi, A. (1984). Moral identity: Its role in moral functioning. In W. Kurtines and J. Gewirtz (Eds.), *Morality, moral behavior, and moral development*. New York: Wiley.

Brown, R. (1986). *Social psychology* (2nd ed.). New York: Free Press.

Gilligan, C. (1982). *In a different voice*. Cambridge: Harvard University Press.

Hacohen, C. (1992). Factors affecting partiality in moral choice. M.A. thesis, School of Education, Hebrew University of Jerusalem.

Hare, R. M. (1952). *The language of morals*. New York: Oxford University Press.

Hoffman, M. (1984). Empathy, its limitations, and its role in a comprehensive moral theory. In W. Kurtines and J. Gewirtz (Eds.), *Morality, moral behavior, and moral development*. New York: Wiley.

Horenczyk, G. (1989). Actualization of national identity. Ph.D. dissertation, Hebrew University of Jerusalem.

Kohlberg, L. (1973). The claim to moral adequacy of a highest stage of moral judgment. *Journal of Philosophy*, 70:630–646.

Nisan, M. (1985). Limited morality: A concept and its educational implications. In M. W. Berkowitz and F. Oser (Eds.), *Moral education: Theory and application*. Hillsdale, NJ: Erlbaum.

Nisan, M. (1986). Personal project and commitment to a group as sources of a feeling of ought. Unpublished manuscript.

Nisan, M. (1988). The child as a philosopher of values: Development of a distinct perception of values in childhood. *Journal of Moral Education*, 17:172–182.

Nisan, M. (1989a). The child's distinction between value, morality, and personal preference. Unpublished manuscript.

Nisan, M. (1989b). Studies in balanced identity. Unpublished manuscript.

Nisan, M. (1991). The moral balance model: Theory and research extending our understanding of moral choice and deviation. In W. M. Kurtines and J. L. Gewirtz (Eds.), *Handbook of moral behavior and development*. Vol. 3. Hillsdale, N.J.: Erlbaum.

Nisan, M. and Horenczyk, G. (1988). Centrality and essentiality of components of identity. Unpublished manuscript.

Nisan, M. and Horenczyk, G. (1990). Moral balance: The effect of prior behavior on decision in moral conflict. *British Journal of Social Psychology*, 29:29–42.

Nucci, L. (1981). Conceptions of personal issues: A domain distinct from moral or social concepts. *Child Development*, 52:114–121.

Rawls, J. (1971). *A theory of justice*. Cambridge: Harvard University Press.

Rokeach, M. (1973). *The nature of human values*. New York: Free Press.

Stryker, S. (1987). Identity theory: Development and extensions. In K. Yardley and T. Honess (Eds.), *Self and identity: Psychosocial perspectives*. Chichester: Wiley.

Tajfel, H. (1981). *Human groups and social categories*. Cambridge: Cambridge University Press.

Williams, B. (1981). *Moral luck*. Cambridge: Cambridge University Press.

III
Empirical Investigation

The Growth of Moral Motivation

Gertrud Nunner-Winkler

Cognitive moral development theory, as it has developed over the last decades under the influence of Lawrence Kohlberg, is based on the assumption of a fundamental unity of moral motivation, judgment, and action, with preconventional morality following an instrumental understanding of morality and postconventional morality following a Socratic understanding. Within that theory, the self is but a label for this basic unity that changes in a universal manner as development proceeds. However, recent research suggests a new model, in which the self is reconceptualized as an active agent building up second-order desires that commit one to value orientations that guide life choices and determine personal projects. Though selfhood or personhood is always constituted by the fact *that* commitments are made (see Frankfurt, this volume), people may differ widely on the specific *content* of the values chosen, some making morality their personal project (see Colby and Damon, this volume).

The research presented below follows this second understanding of selfhood. Moral motivation is understood as a second-order desire—in this case, a commitment to morality—which is analytically independent of moral knowledge. Children's growth of moral motivation is herein reconstructed. As we will see in the following pages, even at a preconventional age some children, those who are morally committed and have built up moral selves, already have a Socratic understanding of morality. They have an understanding of the intrinsic validity of moral rules and have developed an intrinsic commitment to follow them: they want to do what is right *because it is right*. If this claim of the early existence of moral understanding is true, then what does moral development consist in? On this account, it consists mainly in sociocognitive development: a deepening understanding of motives and intentions of people, of the meaning and functions of institutions, of consequences and costs of changes in individual behavior or institutional arrangements. Such deepened understanding will allow an increasingly contextualized and flexible application of morality, whose core—the commitment impartially to avoid doing harm or even to be good—is already well understood and given personal importance.

My argument will proceed as follows. In an introductory statement, Kohlberg's description of preconventional moral understanding is contrasted with contradictory evidence leading up to the central hypothesis: the analytic independence of moral knowledge and moral motivation. The first step of my argument is the claim that moral motivation can be operationalized by assessing children's ascriptions of emotion to hypothetical moral wrongdoers. In an opening section the theoretical rationale underlying this claim is briefly explicated (for a fuller theoretical account, see Montada, this volume); then I describe the details of the procedure and present experimental results that support the hypothesis that emotion ascriptions can indicate moral motivation. In the second step I analyze the justifications given for the emotion ascriptions with the intent of reconstructing the content of moral motivation. After a brief account of different types of moral motives as discussed in the philosophical and psychological literature, the empirical findings are presented. These show that even at a preconventional age a genuine moral motive can be found: the desire to do what is right because it is right. In the next section I argue that this moral motive differs from spontaneous altruistic inclinations and can best be understood as the result of building up a second-order moral desire. In a concluding section I describe moral development as a two-step learning process: children universally acquire moral knowledge yet differ in the extent to which they make following out their moral insights a personally relevant life goal.

Independence of Moral Knowledge and Moral Motivation

Kohlberg's theory of moral development is based on the Piagetian assumption of a cognitive-affective parallelism: in each stage the same type of reasons are used both to justify and to motivate doing what is right. At the preconventional level, both moral knowledge and moral motives are instrumental: "Right is literal obedience to rules and authorities . . . , avoiding punishment . . . ; the reasons for doing right are avoidance of punishment and the superior power of authorities" (Kohlberg, 1981, pp. 409–410). This description of preconventional children's instrumentalism, although confirmed in several studies (see Damon, 1982; Blasi, 1984), has been criticized from different perspectives. For example, in a series of carefully designed explorations in children's understanding of rules, Turiel (1983) has shown that even young children differentiate moral (universal) from conventional (culture-specific) and prudential (goal-contingent) rules, using the same criteria philosophers use: categorical and universal validity (see also Nucci and Lee, this volume). Children consider moral rules that forbid doing harm to be binding in all cultures, at all times, independent of authorities or punishment. Thus, even young children seem to have adequate moral knowledge, that is, an understanding of the intrinsic validity of moral rules. From another perspective, the characterization of preconventional children as instrumentalists has been criticized by results from observational studies that amply document that even very young children spontaneously display altruistic behavior: they generously share with, help, or console other children in need or distress (Eisenberg, 1982, 1986). In their longitudinal study Keller and Edelstein (1986) found that preconventional children argue in an altruistic manner in a friendship dilemma. Keller and Edelstein, on the basis of their empirical data, and Döbert (1987), on theoretical grounds, have integrated evidence showing that young children are not instrumentalist and—again assuming cognitive-affective parallelism—have constructed a portrait of the young child as a morally competent actor, equipped with intrinsic moral knowledge and moral motivation (for criticism, see Nunner-Winkler, 1989).

In the following, I will dispute the assumption of cognitive-affective parallelism and, on the basis of my own research data, argue instead that moral learning involves a two step process: the first step is the early and universal acquisition of moral knowledge; the second step is a differential process of building up moral motivation. Moral understanding and moral motivation are, then, seen as analytically independent variables. Children do not complete this second step in a uniform manner: some will complete it quickly, others will take long time; some end up with a deep-seated, encompassing moral motivation, others with a more superficial and narrowly circumscribed commitment to the moral domain, still others remain morally disinterested; some may be motivated by empathy, some by respect for the law, others by the desire to achieve personal integrity. Thus, children differ in developmental speed, breadth, and type of moral motivation. A description of the development of moral motivation and the analysis of its nature are the main focus of the research I will discuss.

The Measurement of Moral Motivation

Theoretical considerations

As mentioned above, a central hypothesis of the work I will discuss is that moral motivation is indicated by children's attributions of emotion to hypothetical moral wrongdoers. This hypothesis is derived from two theoretical assumptions about the meaning and function of emotions. The first assumption is that emotions include cognitive (albeit often global and rash) judgments; the second is that these judgments concern those aspects of a situation that are of high personal relevance (see Solomon, 1976, 1984). An everyday example may illustrate the plausibility of these assumptions: If I observe my lover walking on the other side of the street with his arm around a lovely young woman, I will feel a sudden and intense pang of jealousy. This is the correlate of an intuitive and implicit judgment that I am being deceived by someone who is highly important to me. The emotion will subside immediately if the cognitive content of the judgment is changed—for example, if I learn that this woman is my lover's sister. Similarly, the emotion will not arise if the observation is of little personal significance to me—for example, if I have already grown tired of my lover and have found another. Thus, the direction, intensity, and justification of an emotion can indicate a person's understanding and evaluation of a situation. To apply these considerations to assessing children's moral motivation, a procedure (described in further detail below) was devised in which children are presented with picture stories portraying a protagonist (of the same gender) in a conflict between a moral norm and a personal desire. After the children's understanding of the moral norm is checked, the protagonist is portrayed as having transgressed the norm to fulfill a personal desire. The children are then asked to give an emotion attribution, that is, to say how they expect the protagonist to feel. In responding, they must focus on either of two simultaneously true aspects of the situation: the protagonist's norm transgression ("She feels bad, because she did something wrong") or the protagonist's fulfillment of a desire ("She feels good, because she got what she wanted"). According to the rationale of the research strategy for this procedure, whether the children give higher importance to moral norm conformity or to need fulfillment is a measure of their moral motivation.

The interpretation of emotions as judgments about relative importance can be illustrated by two responses given to the question of how the protagonist would feel after having declined another child's legitimate request for help in solving math problems or baking cookies. In the first case, the subject replied:

It doesn't really matter how many items you've solved. After all, it is *important* that all the students know how to do them. [The protagonist] will feel *great because she could help*. (Emphasis added.)

In the second case, the subject explicitly stated that the protagonist ought to help, since "surely [the other child] also wants to have some cookies." However, when asked how the protagonist, who did not help, would feel, the subject replied:

Great, because he did not have to help. He *does not care* whether [the other child] can make cookies or not. (Emphasis added.)

Empirical procedure

The data I will discuss were gathered as part of a longitudinal study directed by F. E. Weinert (see Weinert and Schneider, 1986). We presented children at ages 4–5 ($N = 213$) and ages 6–7 ($N = 203$) with picture stories in which a protagonist transgressed a negative or a positive duty in order to satisfy a personal desire (she stole sweets; she did not share or help), or fulfilled a positive duty (she did help). (See Table 1 for a more detailed description.)

To avoid confounding moral orientation with the children's understanding of authority or friendship relations, the stories involved peers or playmates only, rather than adults or close friends. The measures gathered from the moral development tasks are listed in Table 2. These included knowledge and understanding of moral rules, ascriptions of emotion to protagonists, and justifications for these emotion ascriptions.

Results

I begin with results on children's *moral knowledge and understanding* (for details, see Nunner-Winkler and Sodian, 1988b, 1991). Even the youngest children knew that it is forbidden to steal and most also held the positive duties to be obligatory. Almost all children gave intrinsically moral reasons when justifying the validity of the moral rules. Most referred to the fact that there is a moral obligation to respect the rights and fulfill the needs of others ("If it belongs to another, you must ask first," "One ought to share/ help"), or that the protagonist wanted to be a moral person and not do something mean ("Stealing is mean," "Otherwise she will be a thief," "She'll have a bad conscience"); some referred to the needs of the other child ("[The victim] will be sad, is thirsty, wants the prize"). In contrast, reference to friendship considerations ("One ought to help friends") or to external sanctions by peers, adults, or societal institutions ("The others won't like her," "Mother will scold," "The police will come") were rare. Some children did give a second justification, in which sanctions were mentioned more frequently. However, it should be noted that this reference to sanctions was often used to demonstrate the existence, rather than the legitimacy, of a norm. Durkheim explicated these different understandings of sanctions quite clearly: "If we define the moral rule by the sanction which is attached to it, it is not as if we were considering the sentiment of obligation as a product of the sanction. On the contrary it is because the latter derives from the former

Table 1
Moral development tasks

Story	Transgression type	Content
Story 1: stealing	Negative duty	A child stole sweets from another
Story 2: sharing a drink	Positive duty	A child refused the request of a thirsty child to share his or her own drink
Story 3: sharing a prize	Positive duty	A child did not share an unfairly won prize with the disadvantaged peer
Story 4: giving help	Positive duty	A child did not help another child who needed help in fulfilling a task but rather fulfilled her own achievement need; a third child did help

Table 2
Measures in moral development tasks

Measures	Task
Knowledge of moral rule	
"Is taking the sweets allowed or is it not?"	Story 1
"Must one share/help or does one not have to?"	Stories 2, 3, 4
Understanding of moral rules	
"Why is it not allowed to take something?"	Story 1
"Why does one have to share/help in the given situation?"	Stories 2, 3, 4
Ascription of emotion to protagonist	
Moral wrongdoer: "How does the child [who transgressed the rule] (stole, did not share, did not help) feel?"	Stories 1, 2, 3, 4
Moral hero: "How does the child [who conformed to the moral rule] (helped) feel?"	Story 4
Justification for ascription of emotion	
"Why does the protagonist feel the way he or she feels?"	Stories 1, 2, 3, 4

that it can symbolize it" (1966, pp. 425–426). On the basis of an analogous distinction by Piaget, Döbert (1987) has suggested that the failure to make this differentiation between a constitutive and an indicative function of sanctions may be one of the reasons why an instrumentalist understanding of moral rules has been attributed to young children (see also Keller and Edelstein, 1986, 1990). I agree with Döbert on this point, and take our data on children's rule understanding to be in accord with Turiel's (1983) and Nucci and Lee's (this volume) more carefully probed and experimentally controlled finding that most young children do understand the intrinsic validity of moral rules.

I will now turn to the central issue: *ascription of emotion*. Given that most children have a good knowledge and adequate understanding of moral rules, how do they expect a protagonist—who, as we explicitly mentioned, knew the rules—to feel after having transgressed them in order to satisfy a personal desire? About half the children at ages 6–7 (and about 60 percent at ages 4–5) expected the moral wrongdoer to feel "great," "funny," "good"—because she has the sweets, can keep the drink or the prize to herself, or finish the task without being disturbed (see also Barden, Zelko, Duncan, and Masters, 1980), with no significant difference in IQ in children giving justified amoral versus justified moral ascriptions of emotion. This is a surprising finding: adults expect a wrongdoer to feel bad and expect children to agree (see Zelko, Duncan, Barden, Garber, and Masters, 1986). Together with B. Sodian, I have explored the stability of this finding in a series of cross-sectional experiments (see Nunner-Winkler and Sodian, 1988a). In these studies we showed that young children expect a protagonist to feel good even if she has severely transgressed without gaining any tangible profit (e.g., has physically hurt another child she wanted to annoy), and to feel bad if she has resisted the temptation to transgress. These attributions of what I shall call amoral emotions are not due to a lack of understanding of moral emotion terms: children expected a protagonist (even one with bad intentions) to feel bad if she hurt another child by mistake or saw another child hurt herself. Nor are ascriptions of amoral emotions due to children's failure to realize that rejoicing upon transgression is worse than feeling sorrow. Thus a majority of the younger children expect a protagonist to feel good whenever she successfully does what she wants to do, even if this involves transgressing a moral rule (e.g., stealing desired sweets, hurting the child she wants to annoy) and to feel bad whenever she does not do what she wants to do (e.g., not taking the desired sweets) or does what she does not want to do (e.g., hurting another child by mistake).

These results thus show that there is a discrepancy between younger children's adequate understanding of moral rules and their morally inadequate expectations about how a protagonist transgressing these rules would feel. On theoretical grounds, it was hypothesized that these attributions of amoral emotions indicate young children's lack of moral motivation: a failure to abide by norms that are already known and understood to be valid. This hypothesis is empirically testable. If attributions of emotions to a hypothetical wrongdoer are in fact an indicator of the strength of moral motivation, children should behave differently in real situations of moral conflict according to their attributions of moral (or amoral) emotions. This hypothesis was tested in two experiments conducted on part of the longitudinal sample described earlier (Asendorpf and Nunner-Winkler, 1992). In the first experiment, 88 children (ages 5–6) were individually involved in a guessing game (animals from a covered basket were hidden under a scarf) with an experimenter. Children were promised a reward for guessing correctly, and they experienced failure in their first guesses. Then the experimenter left each child alone in the room for a while, providing an opportunity to cheat in the guessing game. The child's behavior in this temptation situation (to cheat or not to cheat) was videotaped from behind a one-way mirror. In the second experiment, 42 groups of three children had to come to an agreement among themselves on how to share scarce resources (one child could watch a funny movie, one could look through a kaleidoscope, the third could only watch the other two). Amoral behavior in the first experiment consisted of lifting the scarf or touching the hidden animals, and, in the second experiment, it consisted of attempts to physically assert one's own interest (stepping in front of the movie box, grabbing the kaleidoscope, pushing another child aside). The results from both experiments confirmed the hypothesis: the number of attributions of moral emotions and social inhibition or shyness (a personality characteristic that Asendorpf carefully investigated in the sample; see Asendorpf,

1990) made significant independent and (in the second experiment) joint contributions to the explanation of behavior. Moral children as well as shy ones cheated significantly less often in the first experiment. In the second experiment, the number of amoral acts was minimal in groups containing two or three children in the highest quartile of either attributions of moral emotions or social inhibition, but increased disproportionately with the number of children in the triad who were neither shy nor moral. That is, even among "preconventional" children there were quite a few who, for truly moral reasons, refrained from immoral behavior.

Types of Moral Motives

Theoretical considerations

If ascriptions of moral emotions to a wrongdoer indicate moral motivation, then children's justifications for these ascriptions might indicate the types of motives young children expect to produce moral behavior. But what is moral behavior? Behaviorist approaches relying only on observable criteria identify moral behavior as that which conforms with dominant norms and immoral behavior as that which deviates. Norm conformity is seen as a product of specific reinforcement histories and as only strategically motivated, that is, motivated by the desire to avoid sanctions or gain rewards (see Skinner, 1974; Bandura, 1977). Ethical consequentialism agrees with behaviorism inasmuch as it too bases the classification of moral/immoral on objective, external observation of behavior and its results. Behavior is moral if, from an impartial point of view, its positive consequences outweigh its negative ones.

Other approaches maintain that one cannot decide from an external observer's perspective whether an action qualifies as moral or not, because morality depends on the type of reason that motivated the behavior (for a careful analysis of this issue, see Sytsma, 1990). To give an example, altruistic behavior can be defined objectively as behavior that serves the interests of the alter ego at a cost to the ego. In fact, this definition is used in sociobiology, a field where observation from an outside perspective is the only possible approach (see Boorman and Levitt, 1980). Yet overt behavior may serve many motives. For example, if I give financial support to a colleague in need, this seemingly "altruistic" act could be motivated by quite different types of considerations, some of which are clearly amoral: I may wish to acquire the image of a generous person, to humiliate my colleague (immoral behavior), to make him dependent on me, or to buy his friendship (strategic behavior); conversely, I may want to alleviate his plight (altruistic motive), to do what I feel obliged to do (respect for norms), or to keep my self-respect by doing what is right (personal integrity).

Strawson (1962) has argued that in their spontaneous emotional reactions people show they are interested not just in the consequences of the behavior of others but also in their attitudes. In short, the everyday understanding of morality includes reference to intentions and motives as well as outcomes. For example, although the pain I feel may be physically the same regardless of whether you stepped on my toes by mistake or by negligence or even from bad intent, I will react with resentment toward you only in the latter two cases. Or although the benefit I may draw from your behavior may be the same regardless of whether you intended it or it just happened coincidentally as a byproduct of your actions, I will feel gratitude in the first case and not in the second. Strawson maintains that human relationships as we know them would not be possible without these types of emotions (resentment, gratitude, egalitarian love) that are reactions not to the behavioral output but to the attitudes of others (see also Habermas, 1983). A similar conclusion can be derived from a more sociologically oriented analysis of the presuppositions behind enduring social relationships. Because I am interested in my future well-being as well as my present wellbeing, I wish, not only that you will not do me harm right now or when it happens to coincide with your own interests, but also that you have a standing moral motivation not to harm me in the future or in situations where refraining from harming me might be costly to you. A minimum amount of reciprocal trust is a necessary condition of social life.

Yet there is no unanimity as to the type of moral motives considered to constitute moral action, even among those philosophical theories which agree that only motivated action (and not merely externally observable behavior) can be classified as moral or immoral. For Kant (1788/1956), only acts motivated by respect for the law or a sense of duty are moral. For Schopenhauer (1968), behavior is moral only to the extent that it is motivated by an immediate concern for the well-being of others. An Aristotelian answer to the question of moral motivation refers to an interest in personal dignity and integrity. In psychological theories, too, different types of motives for moral behavior have been advanced. Kohlberg's description of the early moral stages resembles the behaviorist account of moral motivation: preconventional children are assumed to obey moral commands in order to avoid punishment or satisfy personal interests. Freud saw moral behavior as motivated by fear of internal superego sanctions (which represent internalized parental commands). In psychoanalytic ego psychology, the adolescent in crisis may revise a rigidly internalized superego and be motivated by more ego-syntonic ego ideals (Jacobson, 1973; Blos, 1962). Hoffman (1982), like Schopenhauer, sees the basis for morality in an inborn tendency for spontaneous empathy that is transformed into genuine sympathy. Similarly, Keller and Edelstein (1986, 1990) consider the development of friendship bonds as the decisive experience for building up moral motivation. Blasi (1984) suggests that a desire to achieve personal integrity is the origin for moral motivation, and Wren (1991) uses a philosophical concept of constitutive desires to develop an internalist theory linking moral cognition, motivation, and personal identity.

Thus, there is no lack of theoretical accounts of the type of concern assumed to motivate moral action. The following empirical analysis of the everyday understanding of moral motives may help connect these accounts to real life.

Empirical results

An analysis of the justifications for attributions of moral emotions to a wrongdoer may show what type of concerns young children assume motivate norm-conforming behavior. In the longitudinal sample about one fourth of the children at ages 4–5, and about one half of the children at ages 6–7, expected the wrongdoer to feel bad for having transgressed. Table 3 shows the justifications children gave at ages 6–7.

As can be seen from Table 3, sanctions are seldom mentioned except with story 1, which involves the transgression of a negative

Table 3

Percentage of children attributing and justifying wrongdoer's emotion
(N = 203; ages 6–7)

Wrongdoer's emotion	Story 1, stealing	Story 2, sharing drink	Story 3, sharing prize	Story 4, helping
Outcome-oriented	**49**	**46**	**56**	**63**
Without justification ("feels good"—no reason given)	7	3	7	1
Naive ("feels good because she got the sweets, the drink, the prize," "feels bad because she's got no more sweets left, because her stomach hurts")	34	12	39	33
Explicit ("feels good because she stole, did not share, did not help")	8	31	8	4
Reference to protagonist's achievement ("feels good because she made so many cookies")				24
Unclassifiable		2		1
Ambivalent or disjoined ("feels good and bad," or "feels good, but did something bad")	**5**	**2**	**3**	**5**
Morally oriented	**46**	**49**	**34**	28
Without justification ("feels bad"—no reason given)		4	4	1
Rule orientation ("feels bad because she stole, did not share, did not help")	12	18	15	16
Victim orientation ("feels bad because victim is sad, thirsty")	2	4	6	3
Sanction ("feels bad because mother will scold, police will come, others won't like her any more")	15	4	1	1
Moral evaluation ("feels bad because she did something mean, is a thief")	11	10	6	4
Friendship ("feels bad because friend feels sad, because one should not take from friend")	2			
Unclassifiable	4	8	2	3
Don't know		3	7	4

duty. This may seem surprising in view of the fact that in story 1 the transgression was committed secretly, while in the other stories transgressions took place publicly, with the protagonist openly refusing the victim's explicit request, but it probably indicates that children (like Kant) consider negative duties to be more binding. Most children expected the moral wrongdoer to feel bad because she transgressed a moral rule (rule orientation) or because she did something mean or behaved like a mean person (moral evaluation). Only a few children referred to the needs or sufferings of the victim, and even fewer to friendship concerns. These findings have several implications:

First, Keller and Edelstein's (1990 and in this volume) claim that the growth of children's understanding of friendship relations is an important source for moral development was not supported. Their results may be due to the fact that the dilemma they used involved not only the universal duty of keeping a promise but also special duties owed to friends. Children's understanding of these special duties may in fact correlate with changes in their conceptualization of friendship. (The influence of actual involvement in real-life friendships is a separate issue; see Krappmann, this volume.)

Second, Kohlberg's (1981) claim that preconventional children have a purely instrumental understanding of moral motives has to be differentiated. An instrumental understanding describes only those children who ascribe amoral emotions to wrongdoers. These children focus on their own interests and therefore will respond instrumentally to Kohlbergian dilemmas (asking for action recommendations in situations involving adult authorities and the risk of institutional sanctions), weighing the risk of punishment against the benefits to be gained. However, once children ascribe moral emotions to wrongdoers—and, as has been shown, may even do so at a "preconventional" age—they assume that the protagonist is motivated by moral rather than strategic concerns. Their main reason for norm conformity is neither fear of sanctions (by peers or adults) nor desire for reward, but rather the desire to do what is right. Even when children did mention sanctions, most saw them not as the only or primary motive but rather as an additional aspect or a further consequence of transgressing. Thus one subject expected the wrongdoer in story 3 to feel "bad conscience and fear:

bad conscience because (the victim) is sad and fear that (the victim) will tell the others, and she'll get into trouble."

Third, only a few children mentioned altruistic concerns, e.g., referred to the needs or suffering of the victim, when explaining the wrongdoer's remorse. This may suggest that Schopenhauer's postulate, that only behavior motivated by an identification with another's welfare counts as moral, is unduly restrictive. Also, Hoffman's claim that moral motivation springs from empathy finds little support.

Thus it seems that, rather than referring to concrete (egoistic or altruistic) concerns, children assume that a formal motive guides moral behavior. This motive consists of a generalized desire to do what is right. What is right has to be determined by a moral judgment applied anew to each concrete situation.

From a societal perspective, such a formal concept of moral motivation is functional in that it provides the flexibility necessary for adjusting to the contextual complexities of concrete moral dilemmas, as well as to changes in knowledge and values that arise from individual development or social change. Rather than providing the child with concrete need dispositions to obey specific commands, the development of a more formal commitment to do what is right releases moral judgment from specific content restrictions and allows the child to consider all the morally relevant aspects in concrete moral conflicts. Furthermore, this formal commitment does not limit the moral domain to acts motivated by a direct concern for the welfare of others. This is important, because in modern society many moral transgressions do not directly harm concrete others (e.g., tax evaders and other sorts of free riders).

The Structure of Moral Motivation

In the following, I would like to argue that whether behavior is motivated by spontaneously good desires or by moral concerns makes a difference. This discussion ties in with Kant's identification of moral behavior with behavior performed from a sense of duty. Kant has been vehemently criticized for this presumably rigid, abstract, and narrow delimitation of the moral domain. Friedrich von Schiller, an early and particularly eloquent critic, complained that on these terms altruistic acts performed from spontaneous inclinations would not count as moral. M. Baron (1984), however, has convincingly argued that there has been a misunderstanding of Kant's conceptualization of "acting from duty." Acting from duty, Baron claims, "can operate together with sympathetic concern" (1984, p. 210); acting from duty implies that "one's conduct should be governed by one's unconditional commitment to doing what one morally ought to do. To say that one should always act from duty is not to say that one should always act from duty as a primary motive. One's sense of duty will serve generally as a limiting condition" (p. 209). That is, "a sense of duty" can be seen as a filter through which other motives must pass. If moral duty and spontaneous inclinations converge, no problem arises. Problems arise only in cases where spontaneous desires and moral commands conflict. These cases show that spontaneous altruism is not a sufficient basis for morality.

For an empirical corroboration of this claim, I will use children's reactions to story 4. This story had two protagonists: one refused to help (the moral wrongdoer), and one did help (the moral hero). Each child had to attribute an emotion to both protagonists. When these two attributions are combined, the patterns shown in Table 4 emerge. Almost half the children attributed either a moral or an amoral emotion pattern: they expected the wrongdoer to feel bad and the hero to feel good (moral emotion pattern) or vice versa (amoral emotion pattern). A few children fell into what may be called a moral trap: they expected both protagonists to feel bad, the wrongdoer for having transgressed a norm, the hero for having failed to satisfy a personal desire. This pattern may reflect a transitional step in the long and arduous process of developing moral motivation, a hypothesis I intend to examine longitudinally. The pattern most relevant to the understanding of moral motivation is the pattern I term the "happy world." Almost a third of the children expected both the wrongdoer and the hero to feel good. Both are said to feel happy with what they did, because, one may add, each did what he or she wanted to do: the hero wanted to help and did help, the wrongdoer wanted to continue working on the task at hand and did so. A child manifesting this attribution pattern, I maintain, has not yet built up moral motivation.

Table 4

Percentage of children attributing emotion to moral wrongdoer and hero ($N = 203$; ages 6–7)

Emotion pattern	Story 4, helping
Amoral: wrongdoer feels good, hero bad	26
Happy world: both feel good	32
Moral trap: both feel bad	4
Moral: wrongdoer feels bad, hero good	19
Unclassifiable: either no emotion is attributed to one (or both) of the protagonists, or else the emotion is ambivalent, disjoined, or basically unclassifiable	19

The distinction between first- and second-order desires, so clearly analyzed by Frankfurt (1988 and in this volume), may help to clarify this last point. Children displaying the happy world pattern assume actions to be guided by spontaneous first-order desires, regardless of whether these are altruistic impulses or egoistic interests. Whenever these desires are met, the person is expected to feel good, regardless of whether the behavior did or did not agree with moral demands. The development of second-order desires presupposes that a person has acquired an ability to distance herself from, and reflect on, first-order desires and can take a stance toward her first-order spontaneous desires on the basis of reasons; in the case of moral second-order desires, these are moral reasons (see Tugendhat, 1979 and in this volume). This ability to distance oneself from one's immediate needs has cognitive and motivational prerequisites. For example, if one is presented with the choice of receiving a small piece of chocolate now or a larger one an hour later, opting for the larger piece presupposes at least a rudimentary understanding of physical quantities and time units. As Mischel Nerlove and Mischel (1983) have shown, in a hypothetical situation both younger and older children will prefer the larger piece: that is, they already possess the cognitive requirements. When actually confronted with the chocolate, however, younger children are unable to delay gratification whereas the older ones know how to cope with the urgency of immediate desires: they look away and try to think of other things. Cognitive and affective self-distancing (see Blasi, 1984) is a necessary condition for the building up of a second-order moral desire. It is not, however, a sufficient condition, for one may opt for other second-order desires, such as the acquisition of knowledge or a care for beauty. Moral motivation is a second-order desire with a specific content: wanting to do what is right or wanting to be a virtuous person. A first-order altruistic desire, though undoubtedly good, does not as such qualify as moral motivation, because it is not maintained in a conflict with an egoistic first-order desire. Moral motivation implies that one is willing to do what is right not only when one feels like doing it but also when doing it necessitates sacrificing personal desires.

One further implication of the happy world pattern should be noted. Philosophical and psychological theories differ in their understanding of the nature of man. Some assume that man basically is an egoist in need of societal constraints. Thus Hobbes saw the State functioning as a necessary bastion warding off the otherwise inevitable war of "all against all," and Freud saw the individual's internalizing the superego as a necessary prerequisite for social life. Kohlberg's description of moral development seemed to give empirical support to this position. In contrast, Rousseau assumed that man is by nature good but may lose this innocence by bad social influences. Gilligan and Wiggins's (1987) view that "early moral wisdom" consists of feelings of empathy and compassion (literally, "co-feeling") that originate from the primary experience of relatedness yet are endangered by later detachment is in line with Rousseau. Empirical research on young children's spontaneous display of altruism seems to corroborate this position. However, the findings presented above suggest that the young child is neither good nor bad but has both egoistic and altruistic inclinations and spontaneously acts on both. In developing moral motivation, the child will learn to filter spontaneous inclinations by subjecting them to the test of moral justifiability.

Moral Understanding, Moral Motivation, and the Self

From these findings I wish to suggest that moral development in young children is best conceptualized as a two-step learning process. In the first step, knowledge of moral rules and an adequate understanding of their intrinsic validity is acquired. This step is mastered successfully by practically all children quite early in life, though learning will undoubtedly occur concerning the ability to apply these rules to increasingly complex situations involving not only personal but also societal concerns (see also Döbert, 1987). In the second step, moral motivation is built up. This step involves a differential, not a universal, learning process. Children differ widely in the age of onset and in the degree of mastery finally attained. This description of moral learning is in accord with the fact that although nearly all adults understand simple moral rules they differ widely in the importance they accord to the moral domain, that is, in the way they integrate morality and the self. On the one end of a hypothetical continuum of intensity of moral motivation, there is the sociopath, who may deal with other people exclusively in a strategic manner yet manifests good knowledge of moral norms by doing so in a hidden way. In the middle there is the normal adherent of the modern conception of a minimal morality that requires fulfilling negative duties (avoid doing harm) and strict positive duties (fulfill contracts and role obligations). Finally, at the other endpoint of the continuum there is the moral virtuoso (or to use Damon and Colby's term, the moral exemplar) for whom morality has become a personal project (Williams, 1976; see also Heyd, 1982; compare Nisan's [1990] concept of "moral balance").

If cognitive and motivational learning are indeed separate processes, as is suggested by the fact that the first is characterized by universal and early learning, whereas the second is characterized by differential and slow learning, then it is plausible to assume that different learning mechanisms are at work. Cognitive moral learning, one might speculate, may be accomplished by learning the moral "language game," to use a concept of Wittgenstein's. Evaluation is one of the main dimensions of semantic meaning (Osgood, Suici, and Tannenbaum, 1971), and categorical condemnation is an indispensable part of the very meaning of such terms as "theft," "murder," "lying." By learning a language, children thus acquire an understanding of the intrinsic badness of immoral acts. However, building up moral motivation implies more than merely acquiring knowledge of the factual existence of moral norms: it requires the development of a commitment to make following these norms an important personal concern.

There are different explanations of how this result is to be achieved. Psychoanalytic and behaviorist approaches, as far apart as they may be in other respects, agree in that they conceptualize the child as an object passively exposed to external socializing influences. In behaviorist approaches, the child is shaped by parental disciplining techniques and processes of identification. In Freudian theory, moral motivation is seen as the consequence of a successful solution of the oedipal crisis, when parental commands become internalized in the form of a rigid superego or, to put it in Parsonian terms, when instinctive needs are culturally transformed into need dispositions.

Cognitive socialization theories, in contrast, see the child as active in structuring reality, reading the implicit rules of intra-familial interactions, and making life choices. This approach has not explicitly focused on the growth of moral motivation, because moral motivation has been assumed to mirror cognitive moral understanding and, in the preconventional stage, to reflect instru-mentalist orientations. The data presented here, however, suggest that although children have an early understanding of the intrinsic validity of moral rules, they are not yet ready to make following them a personal concern. In fact, before they do so they will resemble Kohlberg's preconventional calculator. Yet sooner or later most children begin to build up moral motivation: they come to expect a wrongdoer to feel bad after a transgression, which implies that they come to expect a wrongdoer to want to follow a norm even when it conflicts with personal desires. A different picture may emerge among the moral late bloomers, but for most (especially morally precocious children) the main reason is neither fear of external sanctions (punishment, blame) nor fear of internal sanctions (bad conscience), but rather a desire to do what is right or to be a moral person. Such a second-order moral desire, assuming as it does a person's free will to make life choices, is the type of moral motivation that fits best into a cognitivist approach to morality.

References

Asendorpf, J. B. (1990). Development of inhibition during childhood: Evidence for situational specificity and a two-factor model. *Developmental Psychology*, 26:721–730.

Asendorpf, J. B., and Nunner-Winkler, G. (1992). Children's moral motive strength and temperamental inhibition reduce their egotistic tendencies in real moral conflicts. *Child Development*, 63:1223–1235.

Bandura, A. (1977). *Social learning theory*. Englewood Cliffs, NJ: Prentice Hall.

Barden, R. C., Zelko, F. A., Duncan, S. W., and Masters, J. C. (1980). Children's consensual knowledge about the experiential determinants of emotion. *Journal of Personality and Social Psychology*, 39:968–976.

Baron, M. (1984). The alleged moral repugnance of acting from duty. *Journal of Philosophy*, 81:197–220.

Blasi, A. (1984). Autonomie im Gehorsam: Der Erwerb von Distanz im Sozialisationsprozeß. In W. Edelstein and J. Habermas (Eds.), *Soziale Interaktion und soziales Verstehen*. Frankfurt: Suhrkamp.

Blos, P. (1962). *On adolescence*. New York: Free Press.

Blos, P. (1980). The second individuation process of adolescence. *The Psychoanalytic Study of the Child*, 22:162–186.

Boorman, S. A, and Levitt, P. R. (1980). *The genetics of altruism*. New York: Academic Press.

Damon, W. (1982). Zur Entwicklung der sozialen Kognition des Kindes: Zwei Zugänge zum Verständnis von sozialer Kognition. In W. Edelstein and M. Keller (Eds.), *Perspektivität und Interpretation*. Frankfurt: Suhrkamp.

Döbert, R. (1987). Horizonte der an Kohlberg orientierten Moralforschung. *Zeitschrift für Pädagogik*, 33:491–511.

Durkheim, E. (1966). *The division of labor in society*. New York: Free Press.

Eisenberg, N., Ed. (1982). *The development of prosocial behavior*. New York: Academic Press.

Eisenberg, N. (1986). *Altruistic emotion, cognition, and behavior*. Hillsdale, NJ: Erlbaum.

Frankfurt, H. G. (1988). *The importance of what we care about*. Cambridge: Cambridge University Press.

Gilligan, C., and Wiggins, G. (1987). The origins of morality in early childhood relationships. In J. Kagan and S. Lamb (Eds.), *The emergence of morality in young children*. Chicago: University of Chicago Press.

Habermas, J. (1983). *Moralbewußtsein und kommunikatives Handeln*. Frankfurt: Suhrkamp.

Heyd, D. (1982). *Supererogation: Its status in ethical theory*. Cambridge: Cambridge University Press.

Hoffman, M. L. (1982). Development of prosocial motivation: Empathy and guilt. In N. Eisenberg (Ed.), *The development of prosocial behavior*. New York: Academic Press.

Jacobson, E. (1973). *Das Selbst und die Welt der Objekte*. Frankfurt: Suhrkamp.

Kant, I. (1956). *Critique of practical reason,* tr. and ed. by L. W. Beck. Indianapolis: Bobbs-Merrill. (Originally published in 1788.)

Keller, M., and Edelstein, W. (1990). The emergence of morality in personal relationships. In T. Wren (Ed.), *The moral domain: Essays in the ongoing discussion between philosophy and the social sciences.* Cambridge: MIT Press.

Kohlberg, L. (1981). *Essays on moral development.* Vol. 1, *The philosophy of moral development.* San Francisco: Harper and Row.

Kohlberg, L. (1984). *Essays on moral development.* Vol. 2, *The psychology of moral development.* San Francisco: Harper and Row.

Mischel Nerlove, H., and Mischel, W. (1983). The development of children's knowledge of self control strategies. *Child Development,* 54:603–619.

Nisan, M. (1990). Moral balance: A model of how people arrive at moral decisions. In T. Wren (Ed.), *The moral domain: Essays in the ongoing discussion between philosophy and the social sciences.* Cambridge: MIT Press.

Nunner-Winkler, G., and Sodian, B. (1988a). Children's understanding of moral emotions. *Child Development,* 59:1323–1338.

Nunner-Winkler, G., and Sodian, B. (1988b). Moral development. In F. E. Weinert and W. Schneider (Eds.), *The Munich longitudinal study of the genesis of individual competencies (LOGIC). Report no. 4: Results of wave two.* Munich: Max Planck Institute for Psychological Research.

Nunner-Winkler, and Sodian, B. (1991). Moral development. In F. E. Weinert and W. Schneider (Eds.), *The Munich longitudinal study of the genesis of individual competencies (LOGIC). Report no. 7: Assessment procedure and results of wave four.* Munich: Max Planck Institute for Psychological Research.

Osgood, C. E., and Suici, G. J., and Tannenbaum, P. H. (1971). *The measurement of meaning.* Urbana: University of Illinois Press.

Schopenhauer, A. (1968). *Kleinere Schriften.* Darmstadt: Wissenschaftliche Buchgesellschaft.

Skinner, B. F. (1974). *About behaviorism.* New York: Knopf.

Solomon, R. C. (1976). *The passions.* Garden City: Anchor Books.

Solomon, R. C. (1984). Emotions and choice. In C. Calhoun and R. C. Solomon (Eds.), *What is an emotion?* Oxford: Oxford University Press.

Strawson, P. F. (1962). Freedom and Resentment. *Proceedings of the British Academy,* 48:187–211.

Sytsma, S. E. (1990). *Ethical internalism.* Ph.D. dissertation, Loyola University of Chicago.

Tugendhat, E. (1979). *Selbstbewußtsein und Selbstbestimmung: Sprachanalytische Interpretationen.* Frankfurt: Suhrkamp.

Turiel, E. (1983). *The development of social knowledge: Morality and convention.* Cambridge: Cambridge University Press.

Weinert, F. E., and Schneider, W. (1986). *The Munich Longitudinal Study on the Genesis of Individual Competencies (LOGIC), First Report.* Munich: Max Planck Institute for Psychological Research.

Williams, B. (1976). Persons, character, and morality. In A. O. Rorty (Ed.), *The identities of persons.* Berkeley: University of California Press.

Wren, T. E. (1991). *Caring about morality: Philosophical perspectives in moral psychology.* Cambridge: MIT Press.

Zelko, F. A., Duncan, S. W., Barden, R. C., Garber, J., and Masters, J. C. (1986). Adults' expectancies about children's emotional responsiveness: Implications for the development of implicit theories of affect. *Developmental Psychology,* 22:109–114.

Understanding Oughts by Assessing Moral Reasoning or Moral Emotions

Leo Montada

Psychological Indicators of Moral Oughts

As an empirical science, moral psychology does not claim to establish a universal ethic. Instead, it investigates differences between groups, cultures, or individuals, as well as changes within these entities. Differences and changes are observed and analyzed with respect to the contents and structure of moral norms, their generality or specificity, the flexibility or rigidity with which norms are applied, their development, processes of moral socialization and internalization, reasons given for norms, reactions when they are violated, and their influences on experiences, judgments, and actions. Before we investigate these questions, we need to understand how moral rules are represented psychologically. What does it mean to say that we should act in such and such a way or that we are not allowed to act thus and so (Tugendhat, 1984, p. 3)?

Here we may recall Kant's (1959) distinction between the three kinds of rules (maxims or imperatives) that are the basic forms of human action: technical rules (skillfulness), pragmatic rules (prudence), and rules of morality. Technical and pragmatic rules are not ends in themselves but are relative to the goals of the subject. Therefore, they are more or less functional or dysfunctional for a goal, which means that they will be good or bad only conditionally or hypothetically with respect to the goals of the subject. In contrast, moral rules are ends in themselves, they are good in themselves, which means that their value is not derived from their utility for some external ends. They are good categorically, not conditionally or hypothetically.

What psychologically represents this quality of being categorically good and bad? What are the psychological indicators that a moral rule exists in a person? We can read what a philosopher considers to be universally valid oughts, and we can see from the legal code of a society what legal norms are enforced under penalty. But how do we learn what moral rules a person "really" has? What are the oughts a person considers categorically valid?

In psychology, moral norms have the status of "theoretical constructs," which means they are not directly observable or assessable by asking people. Instead, their existence and their content must be inferred from observable indicators resulting from the moral norms people have adopted, internalized, or built up. There is some debate about the question of what is an adequate indicator of an effective or operative personal morality. Is it knowledge about the existence of moral or legal norms in society? Is it behavior or action according to norms? Is it moral reasoning in Kohlberg's sense of that term? None of these alternatives seems adequate. Knowledge about the social existence of moral (and legal) norms is not an adequate indicator, since knowledge does not imply a personal approval or acceptance. Criminals, for instance, know about the established social norms, but this does not mean they approve of them or consider them obligatory for themselves.

Norm-abiding behavior is not indicative, for two reasons. First, the very same behavior can be morally motivated or can have technical or tactical reasons. Only an analysis of a person's motivation will give us a valid diagnosis. We may abstain from killing our enemies because we obey a moral norm, or because we don't know how to do it, or because we are afraid of revenge or legal punishment, or because we want to represent ourselves as magnanimous, or because we need them, and so forth. Second, deviant behavior does not prove that moral convictions do not exist. Before we can consider deviant behavior to indicate missing moral norms, we have to clarify at least (a) whether there was a moral dilemma and whether the subject decided to act according to a second norm to which he or she gave priority, (b) whether or not deviating from the norm has aroused guilt feelings in the subject, and (c) whether the subject feels responsible for the behavior in question and whether he or she makes excuses or denies responsibility.

From Kohlberg's perspective, the subject's level of moral reasoning is no indication, since even contradictory norms can be justified by arguments of the same level, and since the same moral norm (in terms of its behavioral realization) can be argued for on different levels in different ways, and, above all, since reasoning to ground a norm does not imply a personal obligation: we can understand the arguments and present them without accepting the norm as obligatory.

Whether a person has psychically internalized effective or operative moral rules is not based on their ethical foundation; it does not presuppose reflections about whether they universally apply to all rational beings or whether they impartially regard all those concerned as having equal rights. Consequently, a personal moral norm may prove to be wrong in an ethical discourse. Nonetheless, it may function as a categorical imperative that is perceived and experienced as being obligatory for oneself and for others. How moral norms can be grounded is certainly an important question not only for moral philosophy but also for moral psychology, since any moral norm should be objectively true, and what is true must be grounded by reasons and arguments. A moral norm that the subject cannot convincingly justify is a candidate for change. However, at a given point in time a norm may be operative without the subject's having reflected about its reasons.

What should we use, instead, as indicators that a moral rule is psychologically operative? I propose considering "moral emotions" as indicators of operative personal moral norms. The term "moral emotion" may be misleading. I do not mean to classify emotions as moral or immoral. What I mean is that some emotions indicate the existence of moral oughts.

Moral Emotions

Salient emotional reactions to deviations from moral norms include guilt feelings when the subject has violated one of his or her personal moral norms, and moral outrage or resentment when another person has violated a duty that the subject normatively expected that person to meet. There may also be emotional responses when actions are performed in accordance with moral norms: moral satisfaction about one's own acts (or omissions) and moral admiration for the acts of others.[1] Satisfaction about atonement, deserved punishment, restitution, or apologies by the deviator also indicates existing moral norms: it shows that the violation of moral norms creates a need for atonement and justice, which might continue until satisfied.

Before discussing moral emotions, let me briefly recall Kant's view of emotions and feelings. Kant argued (1) that emotions and feelings are transitory, changeable, and capricious, (2) that emotionally motivated conduct is therefore unreliable, inconsistent, unprincipled, and even irrational, (3) that to clearly see the rights and wrongs in a situation, we must abstract or distance ourselves from our feelings and emotions, (4) that we are passive with respect to our feelings not under our own control and therefore beyond our responsibility, and (5) that emotions are directed toward particular persons in particular circumstances and therefore do not have the generality and universality required for rational morality: they are not based on principles, and thus they involve "partiality" (Kant, 1959).

I mention Kant's conception to avoid a misunderstanding. I do not want to base moral norms on emotions, as, for instance, Blum (1980) convincingly did for altruism, which he based on feelings of empathy and friendship. I only want us to consider emotions as indicating the existence of moral norms, the rationality, impartiality, and universality of which remain open to question. From a psychological point of view, it is not useful to speak of moral norms only in cases when they are rationally reasoned and universally valid. Most people have operative personal norms that they have never impartially and rationally reflected on before. Nevertheless, these personal norms function as categorical imperatives.

Besides this, I do not agree with Kant's conception of emotions. I see emotions not as being capricious, inconsistent, and unreliable but instead as predictable and understandable evaluative responses to cognized or imagined "facts." During the last few years the cognitive core of emotions has become more and more recognized (Epstein, 1984; Lazarus, Averill, and Opton, 1970; Montada, 1989; Solomon, 1976). We can conceive of emotions as a specific category of evaluations based on specific cognitions of an object or a situation. The object may be an event, an achievement, an act, a person in a specific situation, and so forth. Each emotion will be aroused by a specific pattern of cognitions, which I will sketch for guilt and resentment.

Cognitive Models of Guilt and Resentment

Guilt feelings arise when subjects think they have violated a personal moral norm by action or omission and view themselves as responsible for the violation. Responsibility presupposes freedom of choice between the alternatives, as between action and omission. Objectively, subjects bear no responsibility when internal or external conditions such as psychopathology, inability, or physical coercion cause their behavior. In such cases the "subject" is not an agent but an object of causes. Responsibility is a necessary prerequisite of guilt but not a sufficient one. Responsible deviation from a moral rule does not provoke guilt when it is justified by good reasons, for instance, to prevent an even greater wrong.

How intensely one experiences guilt will depend on several facts that are morally marginal or even irrelevant, for instance, on whether or not someone will suffer by the immoral act or omission, and who will suffer. Everyday observations show that people experience more guilt when another person is suffering and the other person has a close relationship to the subject (agent). When subjects themselves are victims of their own deviant acts, they may perceive their action as more or less expiated by the suffered harm or loss, and this often reduces guilt feelings. Imagine a drunken driver who causes an accident. It makes quite a difference whether or not someone is injured and who is injured: a stranger, a loved one, or the driver himself.

There are cases of guilt feelings that Schneider and I (1989, 1990) called "existential guilt." In these cases, guilt feelings are aroused not by one's own reproachable actions but by experienced lucky advantages. Not everybody can feel happy about being the one who survived a disaster, who escaped persecution, or who lives on the sunny side of the world. Some of these lucky people feel guilty, as can be observed, for instance, with survivors of concentration camps (von Baeyer, Haefner, and Kisker, 1964) or of the Hiroshima bomb (Lifton, 1967). They saw their relative privilege as infringing on solidarity and justice, and they could not enjoy it. Following Hoffman (1976), we used the term "existential guilt" to describe the feelings of people who suffer a bad conscience because they find themselves in undeserved advantaged positions or life circumstances in comparison with the disadvantages of others.

When others violate a moral rule, one's emotional response might be resentment, moral outrage, or anger. Again, for this to happen, one must view the perpetrator as responsible. Excuses from responsibility alleviate one's moral outrage. Responsibility does not imply blameworthiness when reasonable justifications are offered and accepted. As with guilt, it is relevant who the victim is: the subject will more likely experience resentment when the deviant act or omission has caused negative consequences for the subject or for others with whom the subject sympathizes. Resentment motivates a desire to punish the perpetrator, which might even be stronger than one's desire to compensate the victim (including oneself) and impose justice in that way.

Moral emotions are embedded in a network of antecedents and consequences. Using such cognitive models, we may suggest hypotheses about antecedents and motivational consequences of emotions. Antecedents, like biases, contribute to the formation of relevant cognitions on which the emotions are based, and motivational consequences like reproaches or retaliation in case of resentment. I will outline this network later in more detail. For the time being, let me point to the crucial role that perceived responsibility plays for the emotions of guilt and resentment. Whether we attribute responsibility may depend on the perpetrator's attitudes, apologizing arguments, and so forth.

Our attributing responsibility follows certain rules that we have become aware of (Tedeschi and Ries, 1981; Semin and Manstead, 1983). We may deny responsibility using the following arguments:

•Denial of causation ("It wasn't me.")

•Denial of agency ("What looks like an action was only the effect of physical causes, fatigue, drugs, inability, and so forth.")

•Denial of foreseeability ("I couldn't foresee the outcome.")

•Denial of intent and volition ("I didn't intend these outcomes of my activity, and I did not want them.")

But even if an agent accepts responsibility, this does not imply that he is blameworthy, since he may have justifications. Justifications do not deny responsibility; they deny blameworthiness. We may distinguish two categories of justifications (see also Semin and Manstead, 1983; Tedeschi and Ries, 1981):

•Pointing to the responsibility of others, such as authorities

•Justification of an action by pointing to more important values and goals, such as justice (e.g., actions serving as punishment or acts of atonement or retaliation), survival, or political, moral, and religious values

In moral dilemmas we need to distinguish two further categories of justification. In the first, one justifies violating a moral rule by pointing to a second moral rule given priority in the specific case. In the second, one restricts the field of applicability of a moral norm: one puts moral obligations into perspective to "justify" self-interests aimed at protecting one's own security, self-image, and so forth.

Resentment may also arise when the victim refuses to accept claimed excuses and justifications, and it can be reduced by proffering a complete apology (Goffman, 1971). For an apology to be complete, the perpetrator must (1) express emotional distress because he or she violated a moral norm, (2) accept responsibility for the violation and liability for blame, (3) express willingness to observe the moral rule in the future, and (4) acknowledge that it is up to the victim to accept or refuse the apology and that forgiving is a grace granted by the victim.

The Authenticity of Emotions as Indicators of Moral Rules

The subject experiences an emotion as a state provoked or aroused in him or her, as an uncontrolled, involuntary reaction to an inner or outer reality. Again, the subject experiences an emotion not as active conduct but as aroused and instigated by a given fact or reality. The subject might have contributed to this reality, as, for instance, in cases of guilt, but once the fact exists, the subject perceives it as causing the emotion. And again, the subject perceives him or herself as passive with respect to the emotion.

Descriptions of emotions—such as "You are making me angry," "He is falling in love," "She is consumed with envy"—point to this passive, reactive experience of emotions. We do not say, "I want it to make me angry," or "I will now start to feel guilty," or "I have some time left to feel sympathy with the victims of the earthquake." All through penal law, affects are accepted as causal explanations of behavior that are not under the control of the subject and, therefore, as excuses that reduce responsibility and blameworthiness when they result in law violations.

According to the common view, moral emotions are authentic indicators of a person's moral rules since people usually do not pretend to have emotions. The common belief that emotions are passively experienced, that they just happen to a person, may contribute to this view, although I suspect this belief might often be a biased attributional view.[2] Focusing on the control of intense affects and their reduction or modification, I have elsewhere stressed how the views a subject has taken and that he or she principally can change contribute to the arousal of emotions (Montada, 1989).

A second feature of emotions contributes to their authenticity. Emotions are instigated by, or imply, specific views of the reality that occasion them. An emotion is not a hypothesis about reality but an assertive cognition. The man who feels guilty assertively knows that he has violated a valid norm, that he is responsible, and that he does not have convincing justifications. The adolescent girl who resents her parents' demand to be back from a party by 11:00 P.M. will not ask whether they have good reasons for their demand: she assertively knows that it is her right to decide autonomously, that her parents' reasons are irrational, and therefore that she might even refuse to listen to them. I have proposed that one can reduce the intensity of an emotion by replacing the implied assertive judgments with hypothetical judgments or questions (Montada, 1989). The above mentioned girl would reduce the intensity of her resentment by asking whether her claim for autonomy is justified and whether her parents' reasons may have some validity.

A third feature of emotions, important in this context, is that emotions presuppose or imply cognitions but are not identical with cognitions. The usual question in this respect is, How will cold cognitions turn into hot emotions characterized by raised physiological arousal? From a cognitive point of view, the usual answer is that one is responding to a reality of personal concern and importance (Arnold, 1960). Lazarus's concept of primary appraisal in the emotional response means that the given situation concerns oneself, that the situation is relevant and important to oneself. Primary appraisal is followed by a secondary appraisal of the possibilities for dealing with the situation (Lazarus, Averill, and Opton, 1970). Thus, emotional responses indicate that one's very own self is concerned and that the concern is an important one.

These three features of emotions make them indicators of operative personal moral norms. Experiencing guilt or resentment implies that the subject's own moral rule has been violated, and the subject experiences this fact as an important issue. The emotional reaction proves the personal involvement, which in turn provides evidence that the violated norm is a relevant part of the self, that the subject is really affected and concerned.

An emotional response is more than lip service or mere intellectual approval of a moral rule: it indicates that the subject has internalized and integrated the rule into his or her moral self, and reveals various commitments that go beyond mere intellectual approval. It is for this reason that many schools of psychotherapy adopt the rule of focusing on the emotions of clients, since they indicate the really significant issues and problems. In sum, moral emotions imply that the subject's self is significantly affected.

A person's morality necessarily involves self involvement and commitment. Having a morality means experiencing it as obligatory. And experiencing it as obligatory means that one experiences or observes deviations as affecting one personally. Otherwise, it would not be *my* morality; maybe it is someone else's, but not mine. The operational definition of "obligatory" is that the subject is liable to blame and sanctions when he or she deviates from the rule (unless the deviation is excused or warranted). Feelings of guilt mean self-blame; resentment means to blame others.

Moral Emotions as Cues for Moral Norms of the Self

Moral emotions serve only as cues for the operative existence of norms. The observation of moral emotions, if it is a valid observation, only proves that moral norms exist. It does not reveal their contents and structure, however, or the structure of the arguments grounding them. The norms themselves have to be assessed and analyzed in a different way. Frequently subjects do not know their moral norms, in the sense of possessing a verbal knowledge of their content, or the scope of their applicability, and having reasonable arguments for grounding them.

Emotions are based on cognitions or contain them as preconscious constituents. Moral emotions consist of cognitions about one's own moral rules, cognitions about which actions conform to or violate which norms, and cognitions about an agent's responsibilities. These cognitions are not always considered, verbalized, and conscious. There is a general consensus among scholars on this point. Epstein (1984) and Ellis (1979), for instance, speak of preconscious cognitions, Solomon (1976) of pre-reflections, Beck (1976) of automated cognitions, and Arnold (1960) of intuitions. By bringing preconscious cognitions to the fore, the experience of moral emotions offers a subject a chance to enhance the knowledge about one's own morality. The analysis of emotions, Epstein (1984) and I agree, is the royal road to preconscious cognitions of the self. Using observed moral emotions as a starting point for exploring a person's moral norms has definite advantages.

By focusing on moral emotions a researcher can inductively identify the operative moral rules of a person. When a person is directly asked for his or her moral maxims, the answer will be at a rather abstract level, whereas moral emotions are evaluations of concretely realized, described, or imagined situations. Moral emotions prove that a moral maxim is operative in a given situation, while statements about moral maxims on an abstract level do not allow predictions about which situations they will apply in.

When a spectator in a soccer game is outraged about a referee who did not punish an obvious foul, we can formulate several hypotheses about the moral rules of the spectator. To give a few examples: the referee should impartially punish every violation of the rules of the game; the referee should not disadvantage the spectator's favorite team; the referee should punish a player who has repeatedly fouled; the referee has the duty neither to privilege nor to disadvantage one of the teams. Our predictions of the spectator's resentment in a second case will vary a lot, depending on which of these hypotheses we choose. According to the hypothesis we choose, we may predict on the basis of who was fouling, the previous fouls of the offending player, the previously avenged fouls of the other team, or the proportion of punished and unpunished fouls by both teams.

Of course, identifying moral rules by observing emotional responses presupposes their repeated observation in different situations. On the other hand, I doubt that asking people abstractly, by which I mean whenever they are not involved in a concrete situation, would lead to identification of their operative moral rules: respondents will tend to formulate general rules without being able to specify occasions for their application, exceptions, warrants, excuses they would be willing to accept, the impact of attitudes toward the actors and the victims, and so forth.

Moral emotions not only indicate the existence of moral rules. They are evaluations of a complex constellation encompassing more components than a moral rule alone. This shows that besides the moral rules themselves, there are rules for applying them in specific cases. Let me take moral outrage about a slanderer as an example. What further appraisals are relevant besides knowing that another person has violated a moral rule by defaming me? Here are a few: The other person is sane and responsible (that is, not mentally ill, e.g., not suffering a paranoic delusion). The other person's act was not caused by an internal condition (e.g., hate) or an external condition (e.g., extortion) but was freely chosen; a bad outcome of the action for me was intended, or was at least foreseeable. There are no warrants for the act, as there would be if, say, I had previously insulted the slanderer. The outcome is or could be really bad for me: if, for instance, nobody believed the calumny and everybody blamed the slanderer as being a liar who invented the story out of envy or revenge, gloating would be a more likely emotional response than resentment.

Thus resentment implies more appraisals than only the one of violating a moral rule (to respect my social integrity), and not every violation of a moral rule will incite resentment. Moral emotions are evaluations not of abstract rules but of rules within the context of action and interaction. These contextual aspects are manifold: perceptions of people, attributions of causes and responsibilities, hypotheses about the effects of the violation, attitudes toward actor and victim, one's self-concept, aspects of the social system, and so forth. While the violation of a rule is necessary for resentment, lack of resentment does not indicate that there is no violation: perhaps one of the other prerequisites is absent, and this results in a reduction of the moral relevance of the case.

The "or" in the title of my chapter does not mean that cognitive judgments and moral emotions are mutually exclusive. I am convinced that emotions have cognitive judgments as prerequisites. As I already stated, these judgments need not be explicit, they need not be objectively apparent, they need not be verbalized, conscious, and communicable. Nevertheless, they are functional in producing emotional responses. Explicating the cognitions implied in emotional responses may be a way to rationally specify them, to test whether they are realistic, whether they are shared with others, whether they are verified or should better be given the status of unproven hypotheses, whether there are equally or even more reasonable alternative views, and so forth.

Moral emotions have an experiential authenticity: they are assertive (not tentative) evaluations of an experienced event, action, or situation. This does not prove or mean that operative moral rules are right or good in an objective or intersubjectively consensual way. Only subjectively are they claimed to be right and obligatory. The neurotic described by Freud may have an immature morality; the member of a deviant subculture, as well as the member of the majority, may have moral rules that would be evaluated as immoral in an ideal power-free discourse.

How to develop and change the operative moral rules of a person is an interesting question. Various strategies of formation and change may result in different types of morality along the dimensions of strict versus flexible, reasoned versus unreflective, heteronomous versus autonomous, and so on.

How to change moral emotions is a second question. We can do it not only by changing moral rules but also by changing the rules for their application or by changing cognitions about specific cases. Again, we can choose various approaches to do this. Many cognitions contribute to the arousal of an emotion, and many factors contribute to the formation of cognitions (including personality traits, attitudes, worldviews, and heuristics for making judgments). Some are mentioned in Table 1.

Table 1
Frame for generating and specifying path models for the multivariate empirical study of "operative" moral rules

Background variables (distal predictors)	Cognitions about a specific case (proximal predictors)	Moral emotions	Resulting motivations and commitments
Verbally expressed moral convictions	What are the moral oughts in a given situation?	Moral outrage	To blame, to punish, to retaliate against the actor
Personal views about justice in general	Who has violated a moral norm?	Guilt	To blame the victim
Personal value orientations	Is the actor responsible?		To help the victim
General views about the world, human nature	Are there justifications?		To claim help for the victim
	Who is the victim?		To enforce the violated moral rule
Attitudes toward the actor	What are the bad outcomes?		To blame authorities for not having prevented rule violations
Perceived traits of the actor	Is the outcome unjust, or is it deserved?		
Attitudes toward the victim	Is the victim responsible?		To change moral emotions. either by changing cognitions about the case (e.g., by attributing responsibility to the victim), or by changing relevant background variables (e.g., by changing one's attitude toward the victim, or by liberalizing one's attitude toward justice)
Aspects of self, e.g., centrality of fairness, social responsibility, self concept of competence, locus of control, conception of social duties	Is the victim repenting? Does the actor apologize?		
Traits of the subject, e.g., moral anxiety, authoritarianism, civil courage			

Note: To avoid an impenetrable web of arrows, I have omitted hypothetically expected paths.

Studying Moral Emotions Empirically

Because operative moral rules are not directly observable, we must infer them. Inferences from any single variable are more prone to error than inferences from a network of relationships among observable variables, for instance, among moral rules, moral emotions, norm-violating actions, attributions of responsibility, excuses and justifications, apologies, and various efforts to cope with norm-violating actions. We may use various sources of data.

The validity of any single variable is far more open to doubt than a meaningful pattern of relationships among variables. To give one example, the statement of a person that charity is an important personal norm may be subjectively true or false. If it is subjectively true, it does not specify the cases in which this norm applies and those in which it does not. These specifications may include such dimensions as group memberships, social attitudes toward the needy, the needy's own causal contributions to the current state, third parties' liability to help and support, one's own abilities and resources to support the needy, conflicting motivations and duties, and so on.

Few people can validly make these multiple specifications on an abstract level. Hence, asking for intentions to act and for actual charitable engagements in concrete cases, or observing these in concrete situations, will give us information that might be relevant for evaluating the truth of the initial statement. Also relevant are moral emotions and actions, because they are related to personal norms within a multicomponent theoretical network of thoughts and oughts.

We should also observe the motivational impact of moral emotions. Resentment may dispose one to blame the perpetrator, to punish him or her, to reinforce the rightness of the violated norm in general, to claim compensation for the victim, and so forth. Guilt may dispose one to apologize, to compensate the victim, or to perform good deeds for the benefit of third parties in order to atone for one's guilt. Both emotions are aversive and therefore may dispose one to various coping strategies.

What if moral emotions are lacking? This may indicate that relevant personal norms are lacking, that a personal norm has not been violated in the specific case, that moral emotions have been reduced by appropriate acts (including atonement in the case of guilt and retaliation in the case of moral outrage), or that they have been reduced by appropriate coping strategies. The list of coping strategies is a long one that includes changes in personal norms, in specifications of applications, in attributions of responsibility, in thinking about justifications of norm violations, in forming good resolutions, and so forth. All these activities indicate that we are dealing with a psychological situation, which corroborates the personal importance of moral emotions.

We have conducted several questionnaire studies to test specific path models derived from the conceptualizations portrayed in Table 1, including cognitive judgments about specific cases, general moral convictions, and morally relevant dimensions of the self as well as moral emotions of guilt and resentment. We also assessed actions and commitments, discovering that moral emotions were significant predictors of actions and commitments and that they were based on morally relevant cognitions, general beliefs, convictions, and facets of the self (Montada, 1989, 1991; Montada and Boll, 1988; Boll, 1991). To generalize on the basis of these studies, it seems evident that the assessment of moral emotions significantly improves the predictability of morally driven actions and commitments.

Conclusion

Thus, the empirical study of morality should not be restricted to the study of moral reasoning and its development. Research in the tradition of Piaget and Kohlberg provides knowledge about the "naive" moral philosophy of people, especially about its ontogenetic development. There is, however, a hiatus between moral philosophy and moral actions (Oser and Althof, 1992). One way to explain this hiatus is by the fact that moral cognitions and moral motivations are often incongruent, meaning that insights about what would be the morally best solution are not always experienced as obligatory imperatives (Kohlberg and Candee, 1984; Nunner-Winkler and Sodian, 1988). Two sorts of discrepancies between moral reasoning and moral emotions should be distinguished. In the first case, a moral insight is not motivationally supported, meaning that violations or deviations cause no moral emotions. In the second case, a moral rule is not considered rationally justified but remains nonetheless operative and emotionally relevant. These discrepancies may be due to the fact that the moral self is the result of socialization experiences as well as of rational thinking.

The inner experience of the obligatory validity of moral insights and solutions of conflicts psychologically represents what Kant called the categorical imperative and I have called the operative or effective moral rule. Moral emotions imply the component of obligation because they only emerge when the subject is really affected by a violation. The attribution of blame (to oneself in case of guilt, to another agent in case of resentment) reveals the obligatory character of the violated rule. The readiness to engage in retaliatory, compensatory, or expiatory activity demonstrates the motivational power of these emotions.

Moral insights and solutions are not operative or effective if their violations do not initiate moral emotions. They are, rather, moral hypotheses that the subject does not regard as imperative oughts. My own view is that the moral self is made up of imperative oughts, even though I am aware that many scholars accept moral relativism as a way of having a moral self. As I have used the concept of morality in this chapter, a consistent relativistic position (where "anything goes") is not a moral position at all. Morality involves imperative oughts, and imperative oughts are the basis of moral emotions.

Notes

1. Both emotions are more likely when there is a conflict between a moral obligation and a strong motive against fulfilling it: the dangerous rescue of a persecuted person and the refusal of an attractive offer that is incompatible with existing duties are prototypes of such conflicts. The greater the motivation for the moral alternative, the greater the moral achievement. Often, emotional reactions to (im)moral behavior are more salient in cases of violations of moral norms than in cases of norm- or law-abiding behavior. When an individual observes moral norms as a matter of course, he or she might entirely lack emotional evaluations. If, however, a subject obeys a moral norm in spite of immense inner resistance, risk, cost, temptation, and so forth, we naturally expect moral satisfaction or moral admiration and respect. Anybody who does not betray political friends in spite of torture will experience moral satisfaction and is worthy of moral respect. The alcoholic who, after swearing to stay dry, successfully resists a temptation might be morally satisfied too.

2. Jones and Nisbett (1971) describe attributional biases. A so-called dispositional error or fundamental attribution error means that observers tend to attribute behavior to others "internally": to personal attributes, competencies, and dispositions, etc. Subjects themselves, however, tend to explain their behavior by referring to the external situation. Subjects who have emotions have a strong bias to explain their own emotions by factual circumstances.

References

Arnold, M. B. (1960). *Emotion and personality.* Vol. 1, *Psychological aspects.* New York: Columbia University Press.

Beck, A. T. (1976). *Cognitive therapy and the emotional disorders.* New York: International Universities Press.

Boll, T. (1991). Emotional reactions to the loss of a driver's license. Paper presented at a meeting of the International Society for Research on Emotions, Saarbrücken, July 1991.

Blum, L. A. (1980). *Friendship, altruism, and morality.* London: Routledge and Kegan Paul.

Ellis, A. (1979). *Die rational emotive Therapie.* Munich: Pfeiffer.

Epstein, S. (1984). Controversial issues in emotion theory. In P. Shaver (Ed.), *Review of Personality and Social Psychology.* Beverly Hills: Sage Publication.

Goffman, E. (1971). *Relations in public.* Harmondsworth: Penguin.

Hoffman, M. L. (1976). Empathy, role-taking, guilt, and development of altruistic motives. In T. Lickona (Ed.), *Moral development and behavior.* New York: Holt, Rinehart, and Winston.

Jones, E. E., and Nisbett, R. E. (1971). *The actor and the observer: Divergent perceptions of the causes of behavior.* Morristown, NJ: General Learning Press.

Kant, I. (1959). *Foundations of the metaphysics of morals.* Indianapolis: Liberal Arts Press.

Kohlberg, L., and Candee, D. (1984). The relationship of moral judgment to moral action. In L. Kohlberg (Ed.), *Essays on moral development.* Vol. 2, *The psychology of moral development.* San Francisco: Harper and Row.

Lazarus, R. S., Averill, J. R., and Opton, E. M., Jr. (1970). Toward a cognitive theory of emotion. In M. B. Arnold (Ed.), *Feelings and emotions.* New York: Academic Press.

Lifton, R. J. (1967). *Death in life: Survivors of Hiroshima.* New York: Random House.

Montada, L. (1989). Bildung der Gefühle? *Zeitschrift für Pädagogik,* 35:293–312.

Montada, L. (1991). Life stress, injustice, and the question "Who is responsible?" In H. Steensma and R. Vermunt (Eds.), *Social justice in human relations.* Vol. 2. New York: Plenum Press.

Montada, L., and Boll, T. (1988). Auslösung und Dämpfung von Feindseligkeit. *Untersuchungen des Psychologischen Dienstes der Bundewehr*, 23:43–144.

Montada, L., and Schneider, A. (1989). Justice beliefs and emotional reactions toward disadvantaged and victimized people. *Social Justice Research*, 3:313–344.

Montada, L., and Schneider, A. (1990). Justice and prosocial commitments. In L. Montada and H. W. Bierhoff (Eds.), *Altruism in social systems*. Toronto: Hogrefe.

Nunner-Winkler, G., and Sodian, B. (1988). Children's understanding of moral emotions. *Child Development*, 59:1323–1338.

Oser, F., and Althof, W. (1992). *Moralische Selbstbestimmung. Modelle der Entwicklung und Erziehung im Wertebereich*. Stuttgart: Klett-Cotta.

Semin, G. R., and Manstead, A. S. R. (1983). *The accountability of conduct: A social psychological analysis*. New York: Academic Press.

Solomon, R. C. (1976). *The passions*. New York: Anchor Press.

Tedeschi, J. T., and Ries, M. (1981). Verbal strategies in impression management. In C. Antaki (Ed.), *The psychology of ordinary explanations of social behaviour*. London: Academic Press.

Tugendhat, E. (1984). *Probleme der Ethik*. Stuttgart: Reclam.

Von Baeyer, W. R., Haefner, H., and Kisker, K. P. (1964). *Psychiatrie der Verfolgten*. Berlin: Springer.

The Development of the Moral Self from Childhood to Adolescence

Monika Keller and Wolfgang Edelstein

The research we present here was designed to reconstruct the development of moral responsibility in the context of close friendship relationships. By "responsibility" we mean a person's commitment to moral and interpersonal obligations in making decisions in situations of moral conflict. This involves a self who, as an agent, accepts responsibility for his or her actions and the consequences of these actions for others. One central indicator of moral responsibility is a person's feeling that it is necessary to establish consistency between moral judgment and action. Consistency is central both from the perspective that others have on the self and from the self's own view of itself (Epstein, 1973). Unity across interactions as well as unity among thoughts and actions make for regularity and predictability of behavior, the basis for interacting. The traditional moral labels of reliability, dependability, and trustworthiness are attributes of consistency in moral transactions, and thus also of moral responsibility.

From the viewpoint of cognitive development, feeling the need to establish consistency between action and thought is a rather late achievement in development. It is based on the development of a self that accepts responsibility for its actions and defines itself in morally relevant categories (Blasi, 1984; Blasi and Oresick, 1986; Damon and Gerson, 1978). The development of a moral self has cognitive and motivational prerequisites. While basic knowledge about moral rules appears to be available already to young children (Turiel, 1983), the motivation to accept these rules as strictly binding for the self lags behind in development (see, e.g., Blasi and Oresick, 1986; Nunner-Winkler and Sodian, 1988; Piaget, 1965). Thus young children do not seem to feel a need to establish consistency between their moral judgments and actions.

With regard to the development of a moral self, it is theoretically fruitful to differentiate yet another aspect of moral consistency. On the one hand, the relationship between moral judgment and action serves as a criterion of consistency. On the other hand, in cases of inconsistency between judgment and action, moral feelings of guilt and shame, moral justifications, excuses, and compensations indicate the presence of a moral self. Interpersonally, these reactions to inconsistency serve to restore moral balance in relationships. Internally, they serve to maintain the person's view as a moral agent. For example, moral feelings and strategies of compensation can be a way of establishing moral consistency.

Elsewhere we have argued that the development of interpersonal moral understanding depends on the development of complex social knowledge structures about persons, relations, and the social and moral rules governing relations (Keller and Reuss, 1984; Keller and Edelstein, 1991). The categories of knowledge refer both to social facts, i.e., descriptive social knowledge about what is the case, and to moral facts, i.e., prescriptive moral knowledge about what ought to be and where one's responsibilities lie. Descriptive social knowledge refers to explanatory knowledge about subjective motivations in terms of intentions, preferences, hopes, interests, expectations, and feelings; to knowledge about the consequences of actions for others and oneself and their relationships; and to knowledge about strategies to achieve certain goals. Prescriptive moral knowledge refers to the moral desirability of actions, i.e., whether actions and their psychological components are responsible or irresponsible in view of normative standards. This type of knowledge refers to shared, or intersubjectively valid, norms and values according to which the members of a group, or people in general, ought to organize their behavior. These norms provide people not only with "reasons for action" in the sense of descriptive social cognition but also with interpersonally and morally justified reasons (Keller and Reuss, 1984; Keller and Edelstein, 1991). In the process of development and socialization, individuals come to reconstruct the meaning of such normative standards, and they reconstruct the meaning and evaluation of actions, people, and relations in light of such normative standards.

Perspective-taking plays a central role in the development of such social knowledge structures. Following Mead (1934), we see the development of a self as complementing the development of social and moral knowledge. Through interaction and through the self-reflective nature of perspective-taking, the person becomes the recipient of his or her own actions as mirrored through the meanings these actions acquire for others. Thus the social construction of the self is based on recognition of the self as agent in interaction with significant others, and the meaning that important others attribute to the self's actions are a significant force in the construction of the self. As social knowledge structures develop over time, individuals become increasingly aware of obligations and responsibilities. They come to understand that certain goals, means to pursue goals, and (subjective) reasons for actions are illegitimate or immoral in the light of normative standards.

In interacting with others, the individual experiences the fact that the violation of normative standards has consequences not only for others and for the relationship between self and others but also for others' perception and evaluation of the self and for the self's own perception of itself. This is the meaning of Cooley's (1966) concept of the "looking glass self." Thus the person is aware that violating normative standards gives rise not only to external sanctions, such as punishment or blame by others, but also to internal sanctions like moral feelings and the self's view of itself as a moral agent. In the course of development the person experiences the fact that to establish and maintain relationships, the self must take into account both the consequences of its own actions on others as well as others' evaluation of it. Thus, insofar as the person wishes to be part of relationships, he or she must regulate actions in accordance with these standards.

In a first step of the development of a moral self, the child becomes aware that the self's actions have consequences for others which it may or may not intend or desire. This experience has both cognitive and affective aspects. Through perspective-taking the self comes cognitively to share the world of others. Through empathic feelings, the self comes emotionally to share the world of others. This emotional sharing of consequences of the self's actions on others is an important motivational source to avoid negative consequences for others or to make up for them through compensatory strategies that serve to reestablish a moral balance in relationships, such as showing regret or making excuses (Hoffman, 1984).

In a further developmental step, the self begins to realize that its actions and the effects of its actions on others give rise to others' evaluations of the self. The child gradually becomes aware that this evaluative process not only includes the moral quality of self's actions but also the moral quality of the self as a person. In the course of development, persons increasingly come to take into account the effects of their actions on others as well as the evaluation of the self's actions by others. Moreover, the individual comes to develop a system for evaluating the self's actions and the self.

This system of self-evaluation includes the development of moral ideals that motivate moral action. Moral feelings of shame or guilt arise if the person has acted in a way inconsistent with moral ideals or self ideals, and feelings of pride and contentment arise if the person lives up to these moral ideals. Thus, moral feelings are tied to an image of the self that the person wants to establish or seeks to maintain. They function as motives to act on one's obligations and responsibilities and to establish consistency between what is judged to be right and responsible and what is done in situations of conflicting interpersonal and moral claims. When moral standards are violated, such feelings have the function of reestablishing the self's status as a dependable moral actor, both in the eyes of the self and in the eyes of others.

Developing interpersonal and moral responsibility also means that the person experiences an increasing need to morally justify the self's actions. The justification establishes self-consistency in two ways: Externally, justifications refer to others who are affected by the self's actions and thus maintain or reestablish others' view of the self as a moral agent. Internally, justifications and excuses establish moral consistency when obligations or responsibilities are violated (Döbert and Nunner-Winkler, 1978; Sykes and Matza, 1957; Keller, 1984) and thus maintain a conception of the self as a moral agent. The experience of a self-referenced need to justify the self's actions presupposes the development of a system of self-evaluation where the self has internalized the evaluation of significant others or is oriented toward moral principles equally binding for the self and others.

Thus, the development of sociomoral knowledge structures and the development of a moral self that accepts responsibility for one's actions and seeks to establish moral consistency are two complementary and interconnected aspects of sociomoral development. On the one hand, in the course of development the person gains access to a variety of social and moral knowledge categories for understanding actions, persons, and relations as well as the rules governing relations. On the other hand, in practical decision making and the moral evaluation of actions in the context of a particular situation, the person makes motivated use of social and moral knowledge in designing and justifying lines of action. The research reported in this paper provides data that show the developmental regularities in both the development of sociomoral knowledge structures and the development of interpersonal moral responsibility.

The Development of Moral Responsibility in Close Relationships

Affective bonding in relationships plays a central role in the development of a moral self. By feeling part of relationships, individuals not only become cognitively aware of obligations and responsibilities but also come to regulate their actions in ways consistent with obligations and responsibilities. In the cognitive structural tradition there has been a marked emphasis on the role of peer relationships in social-cognitive and moral development. Several authors have pointed out that peer relationships are relationships of equality in which children come to construct the meaning of norms of reciprocity under the regulatory principle of autonomy, whereas authority relationships tend to be regulated by power and obedience (Damon, 1977; Krappmann, 1989; Piaget, 1965; Youniss, 1980). In modern psychoanalytic traditions, the special role of close friendship for emotional and identity development has been emphasized. Some psychoanalysts have argued that through emotional bonding to a peer, a sense of self is established. Early adolescence is seen to be a critical phase in the development of the sharing of emotions and intimate bonding (Sullivan, 1953) and the development of a self. The experience of affective bonding can be seen as an important motivation for the development of moral responsibility.

Friendship is a particularly relevant context that discloses how cognition and affect are related in the development of a moral self. Researchers have argued that in adolescence the self is predominantly experienced as a member of relationship (Selman, 1980; Selman and Schultz, 1990). On the basis of these findings one can hypothesize that strong affective bonds to the relationship are indicated by the intimate sharing of emotions and life worlds that characterizes adolescents' friendships. Obligations and responsibilities toward a close and intimate friend are particularly significant and become a strong motivational force in regulating decision making in a situation of conflicting interpersonal and moral claims between friends. Thus the development of moral responsibility must be seen as closely interconnected with the development of intimacy in personal relationships.

In the empirical study presented below, we will analyze cognitive and affective-motivational components of the development of a moral self. First we will show how the development of moral responsibility is evidenced in general reasoning about moral obligations and responsibilities toward a close friend. Then we will approach the question of personal commitment to obligations and responsibilities by analyzing a situation-specific use of moral and friendship reasoning in the interpretation of a morally relevant dilemma for action or "action dilemma" in a close friendship. We chose three aspects as evidence for a moral self that experiences obligations and responsibilities as personally binding:

•The cognitive awareness of morally and interpersonally relevant aspects of a situation in the interpretation of the conflict for action

•The awareness of moral feelings related to the violation of obligations and responsibilities

•The motivational relevance of interpersonal and moral reasoning in decision making in the action dilemma evaluated with regard to two aspects of establishing consistency between judgment and action: (1) Action consistency is established by regulating action choices in a way consistent with what is perceived to be right or responsible in terms of interpersonal and moral standards. (2) Cognitive consistency is established by justifications and excuses if moral standards have been violated.

Method and sample

We assessed sociomoral reasoning in a longitudinal study of 121 subjects (57 female, 64 male) at ages 7, 9, 12, and 15. In interviews with the subjects we assessed various aspects of general and situation-specific moral and relationship knowledge:

•General reasoning about the contractual norm of promise-keeping: What does it mean to promise something? Why, in general, must a promise be kept? What are the consequences of not keeping a promise?

•General reasoning about the meaning of close friendship in terms of the expectations and feelings on which such relationships are based: What makes friendship really close? What does it mean to be (how are you) really close friends?

•Situation-specific reasoning about promise keeping and close friendship in a situation involving conflicting claims about promise keeping between best friends.

The dilemma was based upon Selman's (1980) friendship dilemma. The protagonist promised to meet his or her best friend on their special meeting day. Later the protagonist receives a more attractive invitation (a movie or pop concert, depending on age) from a third child who has only recently moved into the neighborhood. This invitation happens to be for an event at the same time the protagonist had promised to meet the best friend. Various psychological details complicate matters further, for example, that this is the friend's special meeting day, that the friend has problems he or she wants to talk about, and that he or she does not like the new child.

The interview involves descriptive social and prescriptive moral reasoning. First, the subject has to define the action problem in a preliminary way. Second, the subject has to make a (hypothetical) choice for the protagonist and to give reasons for the choice as well as for the alternative option. Third, the subject has to anticipate consequences of choices from the perspective of those concerned (the protagonist, best friend, and new child). Fourth, the subject has to explore strategies to avoid or compensate unintended and undesired consequences for self and others. Fifth, the subject has to evaluate the choice of action in terms of moral rightness.

Scoring

We determine developmental levels for the arguments given in each content category. Theoretically, the definition of levels draws on the definition of levels of descriptive social and prescriptive moral reasoning in the sociocognitive and moral literature (see Colby and Kohlberg, 1987; Damon, 1977; Gibbs and Widaman, 1982; Selman, 1980; Youniss, 1980). Levels vary from the lowest level 0 to the highest level 3, with transitional levels in between (i.e., 0/1, 1/2, 2/3). Percent agreement for sublevels in the different age groups varied between 75 and 90 percent for the various categories (Keller and Edelstein, 1990). Examples of the definition of full levels are presented in the next section.

Results

The development of general social and moral reasoning

In the following, we will first present the developmental levels of the general understanding of the contractual norm of promise keeping and the general understanding of close friendship. Second, we will give examples of how normative and relationship knowledge becomes salient in reasoning about the hypothetical friendship dilemma.

The development of reasoning about the contractual norm of promise keeping
We defined four developmental levels, which are partly consistent with Kohlberg 1984 (see Keller and Edelstein, 1991).

At the lowest level 0, subjects are confused about the meaning of promise keeping and cannot give reasons why one ought to keep a promise and do not see promise keeping as obligatory. No consequences are seen to arise if a promise is not kept.

At level 1, subjects understand that one ought to keep one's promises and can give reasons to support this obligation. The obligation to keep a promise is seen at this level as a question of obedience to a rule (one has to keep it) or a superordinate authority that cannot be further legitimized. In contradistinction to Kohlberg's (1984) findings, punishment is mentioned not as a reason for the obligation to keep promises but rather as a consequence of not keeping promises (see Keller, Eckensberger, and von Rosen, 1989; Keller, 1990).

At level 2, promise keeping is seen as obligatory, but special situations justify exceptions (e.g., in case of the death of a grandmother, a promise to meet someone may be broken). Not keeping one's promises is judged as betrayal. The person who does not keep promises is judged as a traitor or promise breaker. The obligation to keep a promise is derived from the person's commitment as expressed in the act of promising and from the anticipation of concrete consequences that the act of violating the norm has for those concerned. Consequences predominantly concern others' feelings and reactions to the norm violation (e.g., feeling sad, disappointed) but also concern negative feelings for the self (e.g., feeling bad about not keeping a promise). In contradistinction to Kohlberg's (1984) findings, we did not find that moral reasoning has the character of instrumental exchange at level 2. Rather, already at this level genuine normative and interpersonal arguments are in evidence (Keller, Eckensberger, and von Rosen, 1989; Keller, 1990).

At level 3, the obligation to keep a promise is seen to result from a generalized conception of how people ought to treat each other under the norm of reciprocity and how one ought to act in order to be a reliable and trustworthy person. Violation of the obligation to keep a promise is interpreted as a betrayal of trust. The effects that a violation of a norm has on the self become salient. In terms of moral feelings, a guilty conscience is anticipated.

The development of reasoning about close friendship
Selman (1980) defines four levels:
   At level 0, there is no real understanding of the concept of close

friendship. A friend is everyone with whom the child plays.

At level 1, a close friend is someone with whom the child likes to play, plays more often with, or shares toys or goods. While there may be one very close friend, preferences for friends are still interchangeable.

At level 2, close friendship is interpreted as a relationship that develops over time. While liking to play with each other is still an important aspect of friendship, this alone is not sufficient to define a close friendship. Close friends usually have known each other for a long time, share secrets, and help each other. Close friends have an obligation to keep their promises to each other and keep secrets for each other.

At level 3, close friendship is interpreted in terms of intimacy and mutual dependability. A close friend is someone whom the self knows well and who knows the self well. Close friends share not only common interests but also personal experiences and inner feelings. They have a deeper understanding of each others' personalities. At this level the moral implications of close friendship become salient. Close friends must trust each other, be able to completely rely on each other, and be available for each other in times of need.

The development of situation-specific reasoning: Awareness of moral and relationship norms in the context of interpreting the action dilemma
Subjects reconstruct their knowledge about promise keeping and friendship in the context of specific topics or issues in the interview about the action dilemma. Three levels of conflict understanding were defined. These levels provide a general impression of the qualitatively different interpretations of the conflict situation that arise in the course of development.

At level 0, subjects have no understanding of the interpersonal dimension of the conflict. The self's subjective hedonistic interests are attributed to the friend as well without any transposition of actors. There is no clear awareness of self as an intentional agent. The psychological effects of the self's action for others are interpreted in terms of self's interests. Thus there is no real awareness of the dilemma.

Level 1 can be characterized as prenormative, in the sense that subjects do not spontaneously refer to the promise mentioned in the story. The predominant focus is on the protagonist's desires and interests. Subjects refer either to the pleasurableness of the offer made by the third child or to the pleasurableness of the relationship in terms of self's interests to play with the friend. A first notion of regularities of interaction in friendship is expressed as "playing with each other often." A type of quasi obligation results from the fact that "the friend has offered the invitation" or that the friend wants to play with the protagonist. However, violating the friend's interests or expectations is connected with the anticipation of negative consequences for the friend (e.g., that the friend has prepared everything, is waiting, is alone, or is angry and will not want to play anymore if the protagonist does not visit). These consequences are also used as criteria for moral judgments (e.g., it is right to go to the friend because otherwise the friend will be angry). Regulative strategies include veridical and nonveridical strategies of communication with the friend. Thus the hedonistic interests of the protagonist may be pointed out to the friend as a reason for not coming (e.g., he or she wanted so much, or wanted more, to go to the movie). But there may also be an attempt not to mention the hedonistic desires or even to hide the alternative action from the friend (e.g., not telling anything or offering excuses for not coming).

At level 2, the normative aspect of having given a promise to the friend becomes a central focus of concern. Not keeping the promise is judged as betrayal, and the friend who breaks a promise is judged to be a traitor, a promise breaker, and/or a bad friend. The time dimension (e.g., having been friends for a long time) and the special regularities of interaction (e.g., always meeting on Sundays) mark the special features of the friendship and constitute reasons for choices of action as well as moral reasons. There is empathy with the friend's feelings if he or she is left out, left behind, or betrayed. At this level, genuine moral feelings are emerging (e.g., that the protagonist feels bad about not keeping the promise to the friend). These feelings are derived from the moral facts (e.g., the obligatoriness of the promise) but also from the relationship itself (e.g., having been friends for a long time and meeting on a special day imply a special concern for the other's welfare and thus arouse special emotional reactions in cases of violation of responsibilities). Regulatory strategies serve to avoid an imbalance or to reestablish a balance in the relationship in cases of violation of moral and interpersonal claims. After the fact, subjects at this level may seek the friend's understanding by explaining their motives to go to the movie with reference to the special opportunity (e.g., that the movie was so good or that it was the last show). Also, the friend may be asked forgiveness and offered special compensation. Subjects may also try to reach a consensual agreement with the friend by explaining the situation before deciding, for example, by asking whether the friend would mind. In the case of after-the-fact regulation, explicit lying is one strategy used to avoid negative consequences that result from the violation of obligations and responsibilities. Only rarely is the situation of the new child pointed out as a reason for the choice to go to the movie.

At level 3, a more general notion of moral and interpersonal responsibility has been established, one that involves feeling strongly bound by one's moral and friendship commitments. The need to keep one's promises is derived from a generalized norm of reciprocity involving trust and trustworthiness. But at this level, informal expectations and responsibilities of friendship achieve special salience. Responsibilities toward the friend result not only from the promise given and the fact that one is obliged in general to keep one's promises but also from the relationship itself (e.g., that one ought to be especially sensitive to the friend's welfare). Friends have to take each others' feelings into account and assist each other in situations of need. Thus the friend's problems mentioned in the story have specific moral valence. Obligation appears to be derived from a conception of the self as part of a relationship in which the self feels closely connected with the friend and wants to be a trustworthy, reliable, and dependable friend.

The development of interpersonal moral feelings

The ascription of negative emotional states to the protagonist as a consequence of an anticipated choice of action that interferes with others' concerns was taken to indicate awareness of the violation of interpersonal and moral responsibilities. Depending on the choice of action by the subject, feelings refer either to consequences of the chosen action (e.g., how does the protagonist feel when he or she is at the movie with the new child) or to anticipated consequences related to the alternative choice (e.g., how would the protagonist have felt if he or she had gone to the movie).

Nearly all subjects from age 7 on concluded that the protagonist would feel (at least partly) bad if he or she went to the movie. Three types of negative feelings were differentiated:

•Nonmoral feelings: Negative feelings arise from egoistic considerations related either to the quality of the choice of action (e.g., one feels bad or not so good because this is not such a good movie or one thinks that the friend's toys are nicer) or to the anticipation of negative consequences of the choice action for the protagonist (e.g., one feels bad because the friend will never play with one again).

•Interpersonal empathic feelings: Negative feelings arise from an empathic sharing of the friend's situation (e.g., one feels bad because one thinks that the friend is waiting or is home alone or will feel left out).

•Interpersonal moral feelings: Negative feelings are interpreted in terms of guilt and shame that arise from the violation of moral obligations or friendship responsibilities (e.g., one feels bad because one has not kept the promise or has not kept the special meeting date or has betrayed a longtime friend or has a guilty conscience about betraying the friend).

Figure 1 shows the distribution of three types of negative feelings across the age groups. The three categories are rather equally distributed in the group of 9-year-olds. Subjects at this age also show the highest incidence of nonmoral self-centered feelings, while this category decreases over time and has dwindled to insignificance at age 15. Purely empathic feelings show a similar decrease over time. Moral feelings related to the violation of friendship responsibilities and moral obligations represent the developmentally most important category. This category increases over time and at age 15 is the only important category left. In sum, the data show clear developmental effects. Nonmoral and purely empathic feelings lose importance, and moral feelings become increasingly important, over time. This result is corroborated by reflections on feelings that relate to meeting the friend, which were not assessed systematically.

Keller and Edelstein: Development of the Moral Self

percentage

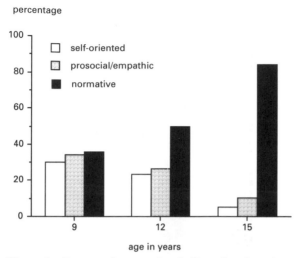

Figure 1   Reasons for negative feelings for choosing to see the movie, by age

Here we find an increase in positive moral feelings, such as contentment and pride over living up to one's commitments and standards for relationships.

The establishment of moral consistency: A quantitative analysis of situation-specific moral judgments

Age, choice of action and developmental level of reasoning
The first analysis shows a statistically significant relationship between decision making in the friendship dilemma (how does the protagonist decide in this situation) and the age of subjects. In the course of development, increasingly more subjects decide that the protagonist will opt for the friend (chi-square = 74.10, p < .0001; see Figure 2). Only in the group of 7-year-olds did a majority of subjects opt for the movie. In all other age groups, a majority opted for the friend. In the group of 15-year-olds, this is about 80 percent. No gender differences obtain in the distribution of choices of action across age groups. The dilemma thus represents a situation that in adolescence produces strong convergence toward a normative choice of action.

We also found a statistically significant relationship between the developmental level of reasoning and the direction of choice for

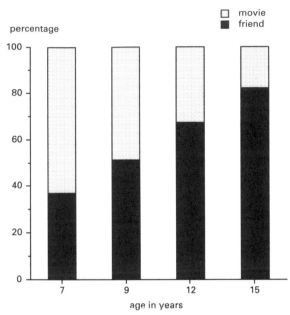

percentage

☐ movie
■ friend

age in years

Figure 2 Choice of action by age

both general and situation-specific reasoning about the dilemma. All coefficients are significant at level of $p < .001$. The results show that with higher developmental level, subjects increasingly opt for the friend. The relationship is most salient at level 2/3 or 3, where between 80 and 90 percent of the subjects chose this alternative. Multiple regression analysis shows that the developmental level of sociomoral reasoning is a stronger predictor of the choice than is age.

To sum up these results, both understanding the contractual norm and understanding the meaning of friendship function as predictors of decision making in the action dilemma. Thus we can conclude that interpersonal moral reasoning is an important factor in decision making in the moral conflict presented to the subjects.

Direction and content of moral judgment
The following analysis takes into account the content aspects of the conflict situation in the subjects' moral judgments. Three content

aspects of the dilemma were chosen to represent the interperson-ally and morally salient features of the conflict:

•Nonmoral reasons referring to the protagonist's subjective inter-ests (desire)

•Interpersonal moral reasons referring to the promise and the friendship (friendship)

•Interpersonal moral reasons referring to the concerns of the third child (altruism)

We defined five different types of moral judgment in terms of which of these aspects were mentioned in subject's moral judg-ment. Three of these represent unambivalent moral judgment types, while two represent ambivalent moral judgment types:

1. Desire. The choice to go to the movie or to meet the friend is judged to be right because of the desire of the protagonist (e.g., it is right to go to the movie because it is such fun, such a good opportunity, the last showing, or it is right to meet the friend because he or she has such nice toys, it's fun to play). Self-centered concerns may also be morally justified (e.g., it ought to be possible to go to the movie once, or it is right to go to the movie because breaking the promise does not matter in this one case).

2. Friendship. The choice to meet the friend is evaluated as exclusively right because of empathic feelings and/or obligations toward the friend (e.g., it is right to meet the friend because he or she would otherwise feel left out, because it is unfair to break a promise, because one should not betray a best friend).

3. Altruism. The choice to go to the movie with the new child is evaluated as exclusively right because of prosocial concerns (e.g., it is right to go to the movie with the new child because he or she has no friends, because one should help someone who is new).

4. Friendship versus desire. Moral ambivalence stems from the fact that the choice to go to the movie is evaluated as wrong because of feelings or obligations toward the friend but is also evaluated as right from a self-centered hedonistic point of view (e.g., it is wrong to go to the movie because the friend is left out, because it is breaking the promise, etc., but it is also right to go to the movie

because it is such a unique opportunity, because this is the last showing, because it should be possible at least once).

5. Friendship versus altruism. Moral ambivalence results from feelings or responsibilities toward the friend and altruistic feelings or responsibilities toward the new child (e.g., it is wrong to go to the movie because one has promised the friend, etc., but it is also right to go to the movie because the other child is alone, has no friends, one should not leave out someone who is alone).

Category 1 represents exclusively self-centered desires, and it may seem doubtful that the moral meaning of the question is properly understood. Moral understanding in this category can be taken for granted only in subjects who at least implicitly acknowledge an existing obligation (e.g., it should be possible to go to such a good movie this one time). On the other hand, it might be argued that only in category 5, which represents conflicting interpersonal concerns or obligations, is the situation construed with its full interpersonal or moral meaning.

Figure 3 shows the different patterns of moral judgments within age groups. The results show that within all age groups most subjects judge it to be morally right, and exclusively so, to opt for the friend because of friendship and moral obligations (friendship). This category becomes even more pronounced among the 15-year-olds in comparison with the 9- and 12-year-olds. On the other hand, only a few subjects judge it to be exclusively right to go to the movie or to meet the friend by referring to the self-centered desires of the protagonist (desire). Analysis of the reasons given in this category shows that 15-year-olds reveal their moral awareness by using self-centered concerns like justification, while younger subjects make straightforward use of desire as a reason for action. A further developmental trend is observed in the category of conflicting obligations (friendship versus altruism), which, surprisingly, shows a decrease with age. Thus younger subjects are, to a greater extent than older ones, ambivalent in their moral judgments because of their awareness of conflicting obligations toward the friend and the new child. No developmental trend is observed for the category of desire versus friendship, which has a peak in the 12-year-old group. Overall, these results indicate that from a moral

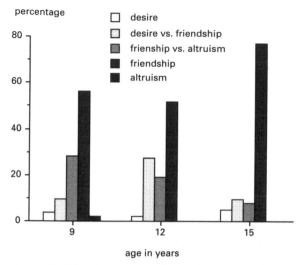

Figure 3 Moral reasoning about choice of action, by age

point of view, obligations and responsibilities toward the friend are the most salient categories and become increasingly more so with age. Altruistic concerns toward the third child seem to play a role only for the 9-year-olds and are of little importance to the 15-year-olds. Thus it seems that the developmental achievement of adolescence is a commitment to the friendship rather than a more generalized sensitivity to another person's welfare.

The last analysis focuses on the question of whether and how consistency between moral judgment and choice of action is established. Subjects deciding that the protagonist should opt for the movie have to judge this choice as morally right to establish consistency between moral judgment and choice of action. On the other hand, opting for the movie and judging the option to meet the friend as exclusively right indicates moral inconsistency. Moral ambivalence in this case might be interpreted as an attempt to establish consistency between choice of action and moral judgment by judging the choice of action as (at least partly) right. In contrast, deciding that the protagonist should meet the friend and judging this choice to be exclusively right establishes consistency between moral judgment and action. Moral ambivalence in this case might indicate not inconsistency but moral conflict because of an awareness of conflicting obligations.

Figure 4 shows the distribution of types of moral judgments for the group of subjects who decide that the protagonist should opt for the friend. Two trends are salient. One is the developmental increase in the definiteness of moral judgment, i.e., the practical decision is increasingly judged as exclusively morally right because of friendship obligations. Correspondingly, there is a decrease in moral ambivalence over time. It is notable that moral ambivalence refers mainly to a conflict of interpersonal obligations (friendship versus altruism), while the two categories that refer to self-centered desires of the protagonist (desire and desire versus friendship) are of little importance to this group. Thus there is a developmentally increasing consistency between moral judgment and choice of action.

In the group of subjects who opt for the movie (Figure 5) the most salient trend is a substantive decrease over time in the friendship category, i.e., judging it to be exclusively right to meet the friend. On the other hand, there is an increase in the category of self-centered concerns (desire). No developmental trend is evidenced relative to the two types of moral ambivalence. But it is interesting that moral ambivalence refers more often to the conflict between desires and obligations than to conflicting interpersonal concerns.

In summary, these results can be taken to indicate a developmental trend in the establishment of consistency between moral judgment and choice of action. Subjects who opt for the friend are increasingly convinced that this option is the only morally justified choice. In contrast, subjects who opt for the movie increasingly argue that the choice to meet the friend is not the only right one from a moral point of view. They increasingly offer arguments that their choice to go to the movie is morally justified or justifiable. However, it has to be kept in mind that only 20 percent of the subjects ($N = 20$) opt for the movie at age 15. Most subjects at this age establish moral consistency by opting for the friend.

It is interesting to note, moreover, that subjects who opt for the friend appear to be morally more aware of the concerns of the third child, while those opting for the movie are more aware of the self-centered desires of the protagonist. Thus it seems that, in general, subjects who opt for the friend are more sensitive to the interpersonal moral aspects of the situation.

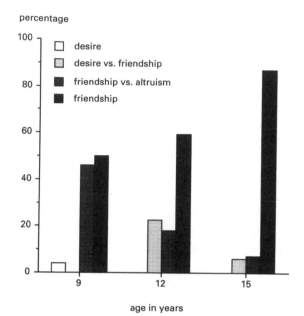

Figure 4 Moral reasoning for choosing to meet the friend, by age

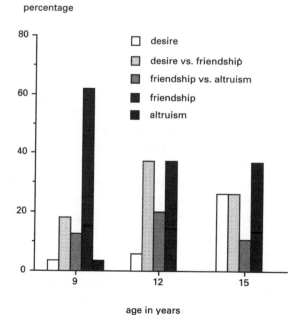

Figure 5 Moral reasoning for choosing to see the movie, by age

Discussion and Conclusion

The results of this study illustrate cognitive and motivational aspects of the development of a moral and interpersonally conscious self. Cognitively, the development of a moral self includes the development of knowledge about moral rules: why it is important that promises should be kept and what are the consequences for self-other relationships of violating this rule. The concepts of trustworthiness and reliability indicate the developmentally most elaborated cognitive structure. Motivationally, this development includes a commitment to rules in the sense of experiencing them as binding for the self and includes a sense of responsibility for the consequences of one's actions if and when they violate moral obligations. In developing an interpersonally conscious self, the individual comes cognitively to understand the meaning of closeness in relationships in terms of intimacy, trust, and loyalty. Motivationally, individuals feel committed to relationships in such ways that actions are regulated to establish and maintain mutual trust. The violation of moral and interpersonal responsibilities increasingly leads to the experience of moral feelings of guilt and shame.

In the course of development, individuals increasingly establish consistency between their moral judgments and their choices of action in a morally relevant situation. Two forms of consistency were distinguished. Cognitive consistency is an attempt to avoid contradictions between moral judgment and action through justifications or excuses. Action consistency avoids moral contradictions by regulating actions in a way that is consistent with obligations and responsibilities. From our data we have some indication that both forms of consistency are developmental variables.

Regarding cognitive consistency, we observe that definiteness or ambivalence of moral judgment varies with choice of action: subjects whose choice of action is consistent with obligations and responsibilities toward the friend are increasingly more certain about the moral rightness of their choice. Subjects whose choice of action violates obligations and responsibilities toward the friend are increasing moral ambivalence, defending their choice as justifiable, or at least as understandable, from a moral point of view.

Establishing action consistency is related to age and the developmental level of sociomoral reasoning. But in spite of the significant correlation between developmental level and the choice of action, the distributions show that already at the lower levels of reasoning, a substantial number of subjects decide in ways consistent with what they judge to be right. Therefore, developmental level of sociomoral reasoning is by no means an exact predictor of choice. We may assume that interindividual differences in rule-orientedness as well as in empathy or emotional bonding to a friend play a role in decision making in a morally relevant situation (see Rest, 1983). We may also assume that complexity of moral reasoning and moral self is no guarantee for more mature adaptations, but can instead lead to higher-order rationalizations (see Noam, in this volume).

Our data show that even though young children may have basic notions about the obligatoriness of promise keeping, they do not necessarily take this knowledge into account in the interpretation of a situation. Thus, at the first level of reasoning about the action dilemma, subjects do not mention the moral facts of the situation. Only at the second level do they interpret the given promise as a personal commitment to an action and not keeping a promise, from a normative viewpoint, as betraying. Individuals become sensitive to the past duration and the special regularities of interaction involved in a close relationship. Violating obligations and responsibilities resulting from a promise or friendship leads to negative moral feelings. The experience of these feelings indicates an internalization of moral standards, which has been described as an important aspect of a moral self (Hoffman, 1984; Melden, 1977; Montada and Schneider, 1989). The experience of moral feelings when one violates moral or interpersonal standards may be comprehended as an attempt to reestablish moral consistency by blaming the self and making it feel the need to provide justifications, excuses, apologies, or other compensations to rebalance the relationship (Keller, 1984). At this developmental level, basic aspects of a moral self are thus established.

However, our results also show that it is only after a level 3 structure of interpersonal moral reasoning emerges that friendship obligations and responsibilities are experienced as strictly binding for the self, and only then do most subjects regulate their choices of action in a way consistent with these obligations. The strong commitment and affective bonding to the friend, as well as the importance of the (moral) evaluation of the self by both self and others, leads to an experience of the need to base choices of action on the moral evaluation of these choices. This result is clearly dependent on the type of situation presented to the subjects, which in the present case strongly pulls for the normative and friendship components. One evidence of this is the fact that obligations toward the new child carry even less importance in adolescence than among 12-year-olds. Thus the result appears to mirror the importance and value of friendship in the life of adolescents.

Established consistency between an adolescent's judgments and actions seems to indicate a moral and interpersonally conscious self that perceives obligations as personally binding. Cognitively, the development of the moral self has been shown to be dependent on the growth of complex sociomoral knowledge structures regarding actions, persons, and relations. With regard to moral motivation, the development of a moral self implies an awareness that the self is part of relationships and that close and intimate friendship is most salient among these relationships. The development of a conception of trustworthiness, dependability, and faithfulness appear to be of major importance in the development of a moral self. Younger children are already aware of interpersonal and moral obligations and may even experience internal sanctions like shame or guilt when they violate obligations and responsibilities. But only when a person wants to be perceived as trustworthy, dependable, and faithful both in the eyes of others and in the eyes of the self is consistency between moral judgment and choice of action experienced as a need. Apparently, conceiving friendship in terms of intimate sharing of each other's worlds is a major component of establishing a moral self characterized by trust, loyalty, and dependability.

There appear to be two lines in this developmental process. On the one hand, the obligation to keep a promise is increasingly understood as universal, as a moral duty that, other things being equal, applies to everyone. On the other hand, a motivational pull toward actually keeping one's promise in the given situation is derived from the strong affective bonding in the particular friendship. The formal norm of promise keeping plays a greater role in younger children's reflections than in those of older ones. Adolescents base their decision and the moral evaluation of an action both on the promise given and on the informal responsibilities of friendship that compel the subject to exhibit special concern for the friend's needs. It seems clear that adolescents closely identify with their friends and that a moral self is also an interpersonally conscious self.

The mechanism of developing a moral self accountable for the self's actions can thus be summarily reconstructed as follows: An increasing awareness of the conditions that maintain an ongoing relationship requires an increasingly reflective and differentiated ability to take the perspective of the other in a dyadic relationship. Thus individuals experience increasing internal pressure to take their moral obligations and interpersonal responsibilities into account. This is complemented by anticipation of inner sanctions for failing to comply—the emergence of moral feelings of shame and guilt. At the same time, the other's concerns about the self's actions in a relationship is increasingly understood to be reciprocally valid. Hence mutual trust, mutual dependability, and mutual faithfulness are increasingly understood as conditions for maintaining a close relationship. Because of this development, the norm of promise keeping is both generalized and differentiated, that is, universalized as a contractual norm, in principle binding to everyone in all nontrivial situations, and differentiated as a psychological condition for maintaining trust between friends in situations of subjective relevance. The more differentiated the understanding of the friendship, then, the more this understanding is present to reflective consciousness in the form of a normative structure, the stricter the standard of interpersonal dependability, and the greater the claim for intrapersonal consistency between judgment (being aware of the parameters of the situation) and action (consummating the moral implications thereof). The actor who perceives the relationship between his understanding of a situation and the claim for a given course of action to be normative, and thus morally necessary, by this very insight is constituted as a moral self.

As we have described elsewhere (Edelstein, Keller, von Essen, and Mönnig, 1986), moral consistency represents a trajectory from hedonistically disregarding norms or rigid obedience to moral rules to an internally sustained conformity to mutually agreed-upon regulatory principles of interaction. In the first step of this achievement it seems that priority is given to others' concerns and to the mutual concerns for the relationship. The next step may be a reemergence of legitimate concerns that the self must negotiate in a situation of conflicting self-other concerns without violating its obligations toward others. Thus, consistency does not imply overconformity to moral norms and obligations but rather the ability to reflect on one's obligations in light of the particulars of situations and relationships.

The action dilemma we used appears to be well suited to provide an understanding of how a person establishes a moral self in relationships. In future research it will be interesting to examine situations of conflict, including real-life dilemmas, between friendship norms and moral norms in order to attain an understanding of the functioning of peer loyalty and general moral responsibility or moral autonomy.[1]

Note

1. We wish to thank Tobias Krettenauer for his help with the scoring and analysis of the data.

References

Blasi, A. (1984). Moral identity: Its role in moral functioning. In W. Kurtines and J. Gewirtz (Eds.), *Morality, moral behavior, and moral development*. New York: Wiley.

Blasi, A., and Oresick, R. G. (1986). Emotion and cognition in self-consistency. In D. J. Bearison and H. Zimiles (Eds.), *Thought and emotion*. Hillsdale, NJ: Erlbaum.

Colby, A., and Kohlberg, L. (1987). *The measurement of moral judgment*. Vol. 1, *Theoretical foundations and research validation*. New York: Cambridge University Press.

Cooley, C. H. (1966). *Social process*. Carbondale: Southern Illinois University Press.

Damon, W. (1977). *The social world of the child*. San Francisco: Jossey-Bass.

Damon, W., and Gerson, R. P. (1978). Moral understanding and children's conduct. In W. Damon (Ed.), *New directions for child development*. San Francisco: Jossey-Bass.

Döbert, R., and Nunner-Winkler, G. (1978). Performanzbestimmende Aspekte des moralischen Bewußtseins. In G. Portele (Ed.), *Sozialisation und Moral.* Weinheim: Beltz.

Edelstein, W., Keller, M., von Essen, C., and Mönnig, M. (1986). Moralische Sensibilität, Handlungsentscheidung und moralische Konsistenz. In F. Oser, W. Althof, and D. Garz (Eds.), *Moralische Zugänge zum Menschen—Zugänge zum moralischen Menschen.* Munich: Peter Kindt Verlag.

Epstein, S. (1973). The self-concept revisited. *American Psychologist,* 18:404–416.

Gibbs, J. C., and Widaman, K. F. (1982). *Social intelligence: Measuring the development of sociomoral reflection.* Englewood Cliffs, NJ: Prentice-Hall.

Hoffman, M. (1984). Empathy, its limitations, and its role in a comprehensive moral theory. In W. Kurtines and J. Gewirtz (Eds.), *Morality, moral behavior, and moral development.* New York: Wiley.

Keller, M. (1984). Rechtfertigungen: Zur Entwicklung praktischer Erklärungen. In W. Edelstein and J. Habermas (Eds.), *Soziale Interaktion und soziales Verstehen.* Frankfurt am Main: Suhrkamp.

Keller, M. (1990). Zur Entwicklung moralischer Reflexion: Eine Kritik und Rekonzeptualisierung der Stufen des präkonventionellen moralischen Urteils in der Theorie von L. Kohlberg. In M. Knopf and W. Schneider (Eds.), *Entwicklung. Allgemeine Verläufe—Individuelle Unterschiede—Pädagogische Konsequenzen. Festschrift für Franz Emanuel Weinert.* Göttingen: Hogrefe.

Keller, M., Eckensberger, L., and von Rosen, K. (1989). A critical note on the conception of preconventional morality: The case of stage 2 in Kohlberg's theory. *International Journal of Behavioral Development,* 12:57–69.

Keller, M., and Edelstein, W. (1990). The emergence of morality in relationships. In T. Wren (Ed.), *The moral domain: Essays in the ongoing discussion between philosophy and the social sciences.* Cambridge: MIT Press.

Keller, M., and Edelstein, W. (1991). The development of sociomoral meaning making: Domains, categories, and perspective-taking. In W. Kurtines and J. Gewirtz (Eds.), *Handbook of moral behavior and development.* Vol. 2. Hillsdale, NJ: Erlbaum.

Keller, M., and Reuss, S. (1984). An action-theoretical reconstruction of the development of social cognitive competence. *Human Development,* 27:211–220.

Kohlberg, L. (1984). *Essays on moral development.* Vol. 2, *The psychology of moral development.* San Francisco: Harper and Row.

Krappmann, L. (1989). Family relationships and peer relationships in middle childhood. In K. Kreppner and R. M. Lerner (Eds.), *Family systems and life-span development.* Hillsdale, NJ: Erlbaum.

Mead, G. H. (1934). *Mind, self, and society.* Chicago: University of Chicago Press.

Melden, A. S. (1977). *Rights and persons.* Berkeley: University of California Press.

Montada, L., and Schneider, A. (1989). Justice and emotional reactions to the disadvantaged. *Social Justice Research,* 3:313–345.

Nunner-Winkler, G., and Sodian, B. (1988). Children's understanding of moral emotions. *Child Development*, 59:1323–1338.

Piaget, J. (1965). *The moral judgment of the child.* New York: Free Press.

Rest, J. R. (1983). Morality. In P. H. Mussen, J. H. Flavell, and E. Markman (Eds.), *Handbook of child psychology.* Vol. 3, *Cognitive development.* New York: Wiley.

Selman, R. L. (1980). *The growth of interpersonal understanding.* New York: Academic Press.

Selman, R. L., and Schultz, L. H. (1990). *Making a friend in youth.* Chicago: University of Chicago Press.

Sullivan, H. S. (1953). *The interpersonal theory of psychiatry.* New York: Norton.

Sykes, G. M., and Matza, D. (1957). Techniques of neutralization: A theory of delinquency. *American Sociological Review*, 22:664–670.

Turiel (1983). *The development of social knowledge: Morality and convention.* Cambridge: Cambridge University Press.

Youniss, J. (1980). *Parents and peers in social development.* Chicago: University of Chicago Press.

Individual and Group Selves: Motivation, Morality, and Evolution

Ervin Staub

Morality is the realm of thoughts, feelings, and behaviors that have direct implications for the welfare of other human beings. In the following pages I will discuss morality as an expression of the relationship between the self and others. This relationship is greatly influenced by the nature of the individual's self, on two dimensions: whether the self is secure or defensive in its orientation to other people, and whether it is connected or disconnected in its relationships with others.

Change—or psychological and social evolution—comes about on both of these dimensions, and on both the individual and group levels. When societal conditions are difficult and basic human needs are met only partly or not at all, individuals and groups can turn toward others in cooperation or even altruism. But more often, they turn against other people or remain passive bystanders to their victimization. As we will see in this chapter, individuals and groups change as a result of their own aggressive and altruistic acts, with the result that selves, orientations toward others, societal standards, and institutions all evolve. I will examine the way in which an individual can evolve toward extreme violence or toward extreme altruism in saving others' lives; I will also examine how a societal evolution can lead to genocide, as it did in the case of the Holocaust. Along the way, I will consider the role played in morality—especially in aggression, altruism, and group violence—by individual and group selves, by basic human needs and their modes of satisfaction, and by the way self-awareness leads individuals and groups to evolve.

The Self as a Source of Motivation

There is motivation inherent in the self, its nature varying with the qualities of the self. The hierarchy of needs that Maslow (1962) described, such as for security, esteem, and (at the highest level) transcendence, arises from the self. The satisfaction or frustration of each of these needs shapes the self.

In Epstein's (1980) self theory, enhancing self-esteem, creating a favorable pleasure-pain balance, comprehending reality, and in a later version (Epstein, 1989) connecting with others are basic functions of one's self-concept or what he calls self-theory. I have proposed as deep human needs the security of one's material self (which includes protecting the self from physical harm and fulfilling its basic physical needs) and of one's psychological self (self-concept, values, and ways of life), a way of interpreting the world and one's place in it or a usable comprehension of reality, and connection with other people (Staub, 1985, 1989).

I regard these as *basic needs*. When basic needs are fulfilled, human lives are likely to center around the fulfillment of wants or desires, or as I have called them, "personal goals" (Staub, 1978, 1980) like personal achievement, affiliation, and helping others. But when basic needs are frustrated, they demand attention, shaping psychological states and directing energy toward attempts to satisfy them. At certain points in life, intrinsic motivation, i.e., the seeking of stimulation and interaction with the environment (Hunt, 1965) and/or achieving competence (White 1959), and going beyond the self, i.e., transcending the self, may also be basic needs of the self.

Defensive and secure selves

While basic needs are universal, they vary in degree in adults and across cultures. Past experiences affect characteristics of the self and its stable needs. When the basic needs of the self are unfulfilled in childhood, an individual is likely to develop a defensive self. People with defensive selves tend to feel vulnerable and insecure. This is partly because they view the world as a dangerous place where they have to be alert and have to defend themselves. They may lack confidence in their ability to protect themselves from threats or attacks by others. They may also lack confidence in their ability to fulfill their important goals.

One is likely to develop a defensive self as a result of the lack of fulfillment of basic needs during childhood. Likely to contribute to the development of defensive selves are criticism, rejection, hostility and abuse in general, threats, danger, attacks or the frequent potential for them, frequent frustration, lack of structure and guidance, and lack of affirmation and support. Many of these conditions incite aggression (Averill, 1982; Baron, 1977), which means that many people with defensive selves will frequently use aggression as a way of relating to the world.

Many violent criminals appear to have defensive selves and to have learned to use force to "defend" themselves. They may react with aggression to mild threats or see threat where it does not exist. Others hold a macho vision of maleness that requires strength and power (Toch, 1969). While this vision may be directly learned from the culture, it can also be a way of compensating for a defensive self. Many delinquents also show poor self-esteem, in a way that reveals a defensive self. For example, they are sensitive to threats, they believe that others' behavior represents attacks, and they "pre-retaliate" (Staub, 1971), or attack before others have actually attacked them believing that their action is a *response* to others' actions (Slavson, 1965).

People with defensive selves tend to have negative views of other people. But the conditions that make them defensive are also likely to make them form negative views of themselves and make aspects of their selves seem unacceptable. While classical psychoanalysts stress anger and sexuality as parts of the self that people often find unacceptable and frequently repress, what these are depends on the values of the parents and other important socializers and their reactions to the child. Disobedience and the desire for independence, or even joy, can become unacceptable. Characteristics not accepted in the self are usually also not accepted in others. People who have them, or onto whom they are projected, are devalued.

The self can also be secure and accepting of its various aspects. Security is often associated with affection and affirmation in childhood and with the ability to predict and control important aspects of one's experience. People with a secure self are likely to perceive the world as benevolent and to see human nature and human beings in a positive light. Valuing the self and others seem connected. Carl Rogers (1961) reported that as clients in the course of therapy begin to express more liking for themselves, they also express more liking for other people. And research on prosocial behavior has shown that positive self-esteem (Yarymovitz, 1977), success on a task, and other positive experiences that presumably temporarily increase self-esteem are associated with helpful or generous acts (Isen, Horn, and Rosenhan, 1973; Rosenhan, Salovey, Karylowski, and Hargis, 1981).

Security and insecurity are opposite poles of a single dimension. Defensiveness is insecurity coupled with a readiness to defend the self, whether by psychological maneuvers or action. Primary motivators of a person with a defensive self are self-defense and self-enhancement. He or she is unlikely to open up to the needs and concerns of others and readily engages in aggressive self-defense. With a secure self, a person is more able to be open to others' needs and concerns. The "economy" of the self, less energy needed for oneself, allows the person to spend energy on behalf of others. Seeing human beings in a positive light, people with secure selves are also less likely to aggress against others.

Security and defensiveness create in people different potentials and possibly inclinations for helpful and aggressive behavior. But people's values also strongly affect their orientation toward others and their moral thoughts and feelings. However, the nature of self makes it more or less likely that a person will possess certain values and emotional propensities. The fear, mistrust, and self-protective stance that are part of the defensive self make genuinely caring about others' welfare through empathy and prosocial values less likely (see below). Still, even people with defensive selves may learn to follow moral rules that prohibit harming others. For example, religious beliefs can lead them to feel obligated to help people, in spite of negative views of human beings. And it is possible for people with secure selves to have learned to strongly devalue certain groups of people and to consider moral values inapplicable to them, or to regard such people as enemies and turn against them.

Defensiveness and security are stable characteristics of the self, but they are also affected by current conditions. Difficult personal circumstances, whether economic, interpersonal, or other kinds, can create or increase defensiveness, while positive circumstances in one's life can support or enhance feelings of security.

Group selves and life conditions

The conditions of life in a society can influence the defensiveness and security of members of a whole group. Difficult conditions of life, like economic problems, political conflict and violence, even great social change, and societal disorganization that results from them, powerfully activate basic needs: defense of the material and psychological selves, comprehension of reality, support and connection, and hope (Staub, 1989). Cultural and societal characteristics strongly affect the intensity of these needs and how they are dealt with. Certain characteristics, some of which are related to defensiveness and other aspects of social and individual selves, predispose groups to deal with difficult life conditions by turning against other groups (Staub, 1989).

One of these cultural characteristics is a group or societal self-concept that evaluates one's group extremely positively and believes in its superiority. A societal self-concept is the dominant view or conception of a society shared by its members. A belief in the group's superiority is not an expression of security, of a feeling of lack of danger and a belief that one can predict and control one's destiny. It has more to do with rights. It can be based on a very positive societal self-concept, one that goes beyond the usual ethnocentrism. But it also confers a belief in the special rights of one's group for power and wealth or for dominance over others. The source of the feeling of superiority may be a history of wealth, power, or influence over other nations, or success in, and admiration from others for the cultural, economic, or other achievements of a nation.

A belief in one's superiority conflicts with the social upheaval and powerlessness created by severe life problems, makes them especially frustrating and threatening, and makes the need to defend the psychological self especially strong. Both Germany before World War I and Argentina after World War II seemed to have been characterized by such feelings of superiority. The intensely difficult life conditions that later developed had especially profound effects in these countries (Staub, 1989).

A deeply vulnerable group self is another predisposing character-istic. This seems directly linked to defensiveness. Frequently a belief in one's superiority and an underlying sense of vulnerability go together. The former can be a way of dealing with the latter. This was true in Germany, which had experienced devastation from wars in previous centuries and had long been fragmented (Craig, 1982; Staub, 1989).

Cultural characteristics that predispose a group to violence also include cultural devaluation of the group of people, a history of devaluation that has become part of the culture; a monolithic rather than pluralistic society with a limited number of predomi-nant values that (often together with the political system) limit the range of views expressed in the public domain; strong respect for and a tendency to obey authority; and a history of the use of aggression (Staub, 1989).[1] These cultural and societal characteris-tics combine with difficult life conditions to activate basic needs and shape the way the group goes about fulfilling them. They make it probable that difficult life conditions give rise to scapegoating. Identifying another group, like a minority group or a historical enemy, as responsible for life problems protects the psychological self: it diminishes the individual's and group's responsibility for the problems, helps make sense of events that may otherwise be incomprehensible, offers the perception of potential control, and creates support among those who scapegoat. These cultural char-acteristics usually also lead the group to an ideology that provides a new comprehension of life and promises a better future. The ideology usually identifies an enemy that must be destroyed be-cause it stands in the way of the ideology's fulfillment.

Personal-Goal Theory, Motivations for Moral Behavior, and the Self

In prior research and theory, I have focused on "personal goals" as an important motivational concept. Personal goals are classes of desired outcomes and networks of cognitions associated with them. They express the purposiveness of human beings. They tend to be future-oriented, and their motivational force is incentive-like, a pull toward something desirable rather than a push arising from deficiency, which characterizes needs (Staub, 1978, 1980, 1989).

While I identified different kinds of motives, I named the theory "personal-goals theory" because they are the most evolved motives. All motives have the potential to become goal-like in nature. The other types of motives are biological needs, the "basic needs" described earlier, rules and customs (norms and standards), and unconscious motivations (Staub, 1989). Personal goals, and all other motives, can be arranged in a hierarchy. Personal goals represent motivational potentials within a person which can become active under certain conditions. Different environments have potentials for activating different goals. Goals and other motives can be environmentally activated or self-activated.

All motives are located in the self, but I think that it is conceptually useful to differentiate between motives inherent in the self, which are the basic needs, and other learned motives. Personal goals may be further differentiated, according to their aims, into *self-related* goals like achievement or wealth, and *other-oriented* goals, which serve morality.

Other-oriented motives are primarily moral values. Their properties are goal-like in that they have classes of desirable outcomes and networks of cognitions associated with them. Three primary motives for altruism, or unselfishly helping others, have been stressed: *a prosocial value orientation, moral-rule orientations,* and *empathy.* A prosocial orientation seems to consist of a positive evaluation of human beings, concern about their welfare, and a feeling of personal responsibility for others' welfare. It is associated with people helping others in physical or psychological distress (Feinberg, 1978; Grodman, 1979; Staub, 1974, 1978) and with self-reports of varied forms of helping (Staub, 1990b). Its focus is people and their welfare.

Moral-rule orientations are a class of motives rather than a single motive, ranging from internalized standards and norms of conduct to commitment to the principle of justice. Their distinguishing characteristic is that their aims or desired outcomes are to fulfill rules or principles. These rules were presumably created to serve human needs and to protect and enhance human welfare. However, the commitment is to the rules, which can become reified, rigid, distorted, or disconnected from the human needs they were meant to serve.

Empathy is a feeling or emotion that arises because another person experiences an emotion. The behavior that arises from empathy varies; it partly depends on the nature of the empathy. People who feel distress because another feels distress may simply escape from the presence of the distressed other. People who feel sympathy and caring are more likely to help (Batson, 1990; Staub and Feinberg, 1980).

The self is deeply involved in these motives. It is the self that is responsible for others' welfare or is obligated to fulfill rules or values. Genuine empathy requires giving the self over to another, so that the self becomes a receptacle for the other's experience. As already noted, the nature of the self, the level of security or defensiveness, strongly affects a person's potential for these motives, but it does not by itself determine whether a person actually has these three types of motives. A reasonably secure self seems to be a precondition for opening up to others but does not by itself create the inclination to do so. A defensive self seems inherently contradictory to a prosocial orientation, a positive evaluation of other people, and concern for their welfare. Although a child in an environment requiring a defensive self may have learned to "read" others feelings, which is a valuable skill to avoid harm, in defensive persons this capacity for role taking is unlikely to lead to empathy.

The self as part of constellations of characteristics

While the nature of a person's self, the way a person's identity is constructed, has direct implications for morality, it is usually a combination of the self with values as well as other characteristics that creates a disposition for moral thoughts, feelings, and action. According to personal-goal theory, an individual may have to have such *supporting* characteristics as role taking or competence to become morally motivated and especially to translate such motivation into action (Staub, 1978, 1980).

I have proposed two constellations of characteristics that predispose people to become perpetrators of great violence, like genocide or mass killing. Such violence is the outcome of a societal process, in which many people are involved as part of an ideological movement, or by serving the institutions of the society, or as passive bystanders whose passivity encourages perpetrators. It is the outcome of the cultural-social characteristics previously enumerated and difficult conditions of life in a society, of motivations that arise from these and ways of fulfilling the motives that turn the majority against a victim group, and of an evolution toward increasing violence. The constellations of characteristics I have proposed (e.g., the *potential antisocial* and the *authority oriented* personalities), lead some people to become perpetrators or to enter roles in which they evolve into perpetrators (Staub, 1989).

The nature of an individual's identity or self is important in both orientations. People with either constellation tend to lack self-awareness. Potentially antisocial persons have a poor, shaky self-image, so they are easily threatened and tend to see the world as hostile. In other words, they have defensive selves, which may cause a fairly constant need for self-defense and elevation of the self. The experiences that gave rise to such selves sometimes lead to an antisocial orientation, characterized by a devaluation of human beings and the desire to harm them. Experiencing hostility and aggression, witnessing aggression and the defensive use of aggression, often lead a child to develop a potentially antisocial personality. As a result, aggressive scripts or schemata (Heusmann and Eron, 1984), representations of reality that make aggression self-perpetuating, are often part of this constellation.

An authority orientation means a preference for hierarchical relationships and social systems, and a predisposition to obey authority. This orientation is often the result of authoritarian child rearing: adults laying down rules based on authority rather than reason and using the punitive power of authority to enforce them. These practices make it difficult for children to develop separate selves and independent beliefs, and to recognize and use their own feelings as guides for action (Miller, 1983). Instead, they use authorities as guides. Facing threats and life problems that make coping difficult, authority-oriented persons tend to seek guidance from authorities and to surrender their powers to make decisions to leaders and the group. However, the leaders or the group may be agents of immoral conduct. Here again, the nature of an individual's self, the lack of a separate and secure identity, can have important moral implications.

Degrees and Types of Relatedness between Self, Others, and the Group

The nature of our selves evolves in the course of our experience in groups: the family, ethnic or religious subcultures, the nation (Mack, 1983; Staub, 1989). Thus, individual identity is inevitably rooted in group membership. One result of this, as Tajfel has noted (Tajfel, 1982; Tajfel and Turner, 1979), is that individuals define themselves in terms of broad, superimposed social categories, which describe their social identity.

In addition to individual selves, we also have group selves; in addition to our individual self-concepts, we also have a conception of our group, a group self-concept. Individual self-concepts are affected by the culture and experiences in it; group self-concepts tend to be shared by the group and are even more strongly shaped by culture. As I suggested earlier, the way a group deals with difficult life conditions is affected by its societal self-concept.

Different cultures and social institutions shape identities that stand in different relations to other people. A number of social scientists have described the current emphasis on individualism in the United States, and the ideal of an autonomous, self-contained identity (Bellah, Madsen, Sullivan, Swindler, and Lipton, 1985; Sampson, 1988). In contrast, a growing feminist psychology has claimed that while men's identities are self-contained, women's identities are connected to others. One expression of this is that women develop a self-in-relation (e.g., Surrey, 1985). Cultural comparisons indicate that connected identities of some form dominate the world (Sampson, 1988); for example, they are characteristic of Japan (Weisz, Rothbaum, and Blackburn, 1984).

For people with self-contained or autonomous identities, the other and connection to the other are external to the self. Presumably, an individual can still develop connections, but since the self has firm rather than fluid boundaries, this is more difficult, and perhaps the connections that develop are less deep. On the other hand, a possible danger for selves deeply connected to other selves is that they are embedded in relationships and connect to their group so deeply that, even when it is morally important, they cannot separate themselves from other people and their group.

As with all psychological states I discuss here, embeddedness in a group can result from characteristics of the self and/or be induced by the environment. Officers of the U.S. military in Vietnam, when they were interviewed after the war, claimed that they disagreed with practices like search and destroy missions and body counts, but they did not express their disagreement during the war (Egendorf, 1986). Military officers are usually self-selected; they choose the military as a career. The combination of initial characteristics and socialization into the military often results in embedded selves and inclines officers to give their selves over to the group. In addition, the structure of the military constantly promotes and reinforces embeddedness. And the conditions of war, with its we-versus-them thinking and the intense ties that can develop facing an enemy, also contribute to embeddedness. Their embedded identities, apart from concerns about careers, were likely to inhibit these officers from speaking out.

Embeddedness can even inhibit a separate perspective. Embeddedness in their group was probably one important reason that Germans did not speak out against the increasing persecution of Jews in Nazi Germany. People have greater capacity for moral thought, feeling, and action when they can psychologically separate themselves from their group, and so can critically evaluate the meaning and consequences of their group's behavior. Such separation may enable them to not only see but also to oppose a destructive or immoral course of action.

I am focusing here on a potential problem in the moral domain for one kind of connected self, an *embedded self*. Such selves are insufficiently differentiated from other members of the family or group. Family therapists regard differentiating the self and developing an autonomous identity as essential for psychological health. Embeddedness in the group poses a danger for the moral well-being of both the individual and the group.

But this is not the only kind of connected self possible. Surrey (1985) and others describe the *self-in-relation* as an outcome of self-development that takes place in relationship to others. Connection is inherent in such a self. And while this aspect is not clear in self-in-relation theory, in my view, such a self can also differentiate itself and develop a capacity to stand on its own. I will call this the *connected self.*

A self that lacks connectedness (in degree and quality) is the *disconnected self.* An autonomous self is self-contained but capable of connection. Autonomous people can develop other-oriented values and the capacity for empathy that connect them to others. People with disconnected selves are emotionally cut off from others. Their difficulty in experiencing connection makes them unlikely to feel empathy and genuine concern for others' welfare. Their moral inclinations, whatever their degree, are likely to be rule-driven. Perhaps one form of attachment that infants form with caretakers, avoidant attachment, can be a starting point in the evolution of a disconnected self (Sroufe, 1979).

What is the relationship between the secure-versus-defensive dimension of the self and this dimension of connectedness? They are separate, although not necessarily independent. For example, defensiveness and disconnection are probably related. But defensive people can be connected to others in negative ways. This connection is one source of others' power to psychologically threaten the person. The defensive self can also be embedded, gaining security from deep connection to a group. It can find security in group identification, which it experiences as protecting it from dangers represented by the rest of the world (and the weakness and negativity of one's own self).

Evolution in Selves, Groups, and Morality

Selves, motivations, and moral orientations develop as a result of experience in interaction with other people. Parental warmth and affection, responsiveness to the child's needs, reasoning with children, effective but not forceful control by adults, and positive example from adults are likely to lead to caring for other people (a prosocial orientation and the capacity for empathy, perhaps integrated with some degree of rule orientation) as well as positive self-esteem in children (Staub, 1979, 1986, 1993).

A great deal of learning also takes place as a result of children's own behavior. Children (and adults) learn by doing. When they are led to help others, they become more helpful (Staub, 1975, 1979); when they are led to harm others, they become more capable of harming others (Goldstein, Davis, and Herman, 1975; Staub,

1989). As they help or harm others, people change their evaluations of the targets of their actions, their concern about the others'
welfare, and their perception of themselves as willing and capable
of helping or harming others (usually for "good" reasons). The
effects of learning by doing also depend on supportive conditions,
for example whether the child is made aware of the benefits caused
by helping or is affirmed rather than punished for helping. In the
case of harmful acts, people often see others' silence as acceptance
and approval.

Once children and adults have developed certain characteristics
and behavioral tendencies, they further shape who they are by *self-
socialization*. That is, they perceive and respond to other people
around them in ways consistent with who they are, and this behavior brings forth reactions consistent with their already formed
expectations about people and social relations. As a result, they
evolve further in already established directions. For example, they
develop more secure or defensive selves and perceive other people
as more malevolent or benevolent.

Adults and whole groups also learn by doing. I have described the
evolution that frequently precedes genocide as "steps along a
continuum of destruction" (Staub, 1989). When a groups turns
against a scapegoat or ideological enemy to deal with needs that
arise from difficult life conditions and cultural characteristics,
this is only a starting point. Mass killing and genocide are the end
points of a progression along a continuum of destruction. As
people begin to discriminate against and harm victims, they become capable of inflicting greater harm. Members of society are
resocialized, and the group develops new standards. They create
institutions that serve discrimination and violence. Part of the
change in people's selves is that they change their orientation
toward victims, whom they further devalue, often to the point
where they exclude victims from the moral realm (Opawa, 1990;
Staub, 1978, 1989, 1990a). Moral exclusion means that people see
moral rules as not applying to members of the excluded group.

Learning by doing and the resulting evolution often bring about
intense, "fanatic" commitment to a group goal, such as fulfilling an
ideology or eliminating a group defined as an enemy that interferes
with the fulfillment of the ideology. This intense commitment can

benefit perpetrators by furthering psychological integration. In this way previously unrelated or even conflicting motives and aspects of the self can be integrated in the service of "higher" ideals and overriding goals. Motives and aspects of the self can be partly subordinated to, partly placed in the service of, these newly created "higher" motives.

There is an unfortunate contradiction here: the greater integrity and wholeness of the self and greater connection to others can result from "ideals" and actions that serve human destruction. The self can feel more whole, more connected to others, and more secure in the perpetrator group and even in the larger society (e.g., Germans in Nazi Germany) as a result of internal integration and external joining with others in a destructive cause.

Resocialization and the evolution of selves, motivations, and values can also occur when people benefit rather than harm others. In my view, many rescuers of Jews in Nazi Europe underwent a similar evolution (Staub, 1989). Oliner and Oliner (1988) describe many rescuers as deeply connected to other people. The theoretical perspective I am presenting suggests that though many probably started out as connected people, they became more connected and caring while helping others. Thus, when helping or harming others, people undergo a resocialization in values or a change in orientation to at least some other people.

While they were connected to other people, rescuers of Jews avoided becoming embedded in their own, dominant group. In fact, some rescuers were marginal to the group, differing in religion from their immediate community, having one foreign parent, or being unusual in some other way (London, 1970; Tec, 1986). This marginality probably enabled some rescuers in anti-Semitic communities to take a perspective different from the rest of the group about the destruction of Jews and to deviate in action from the rest of the group.

Other research findings offer a further perspective on embeddedness in the group. Oliner and Oliner (1988) describe about 50 percent of their rescuers as "normocentric"—guided not by moral principles, "caring" (which is similar to prosocial orientation), or empathy but by connection to a group and its norms. They acted when group leaders, like priests or leaders of resistance groups, or when group norms activated in other ways, guided them to help Jews. Writing about Poland, Tec (1986) noted that while some priests encouraged their communities to help, others encouraged them to join the Germans in anti-Jewish actions. To the extent that individuals are embedded in the group as selves and as moral beings, their actions will depend not on their own moral nature but on that of the group or its leaders.

The Self and Others: From Relatedness to Unity

The usual stance in research and theory is to regard moral action as behavior that requires self-sacrifice. The paradox of altruism, as some have called it, is that people are willing to benefit others even when this brings no material reward and requires self-sacrifice. Exchange theories (Gouldner, 1960; Staub, 1978) suggest that in relationships people try to maximize their own benefits. The self and the other share interests only to the extent that they mutually fulfill each other's needs. According to self-comparison and social-identity theories (Tajfel, 1982; Tajfel and Turner, 1979), positive social comparison, a favorable evaluation of one's self relative to other individuals or of one's group relative to other groups, is essential for satisfaction.

People with embedded selves may perceive the interests of their own selves and of the individuals or groups to whom they are tied as identical. This is an identity of interests that grows out of dependency and need. Is it possible to experience a unity of self and other, or at least of the interests of self and other, without embeddedness or a merging of selves? People in love, occasionally people in families or other tight-knit groups, perhaps connected by love, and at times members of a group facing an enemy or shared threat seem to experience such unity. If I experience others' gains and losses as my own and others experience my gains and losses as their own, we cannot elevate ourselves by diminishing the other.

Presumably, experiencing unity requires a secure and connected self, a deep sense of common humanity with others, and an evolution in consciousness. Conditions in our age—the shared nuclear threat, the shared threat to the environment—can give impetus to it. The moral implications are great: acting in behalf of the other is experienced as acting in behalf of one's self.

In a healthy person, the experience of such unity will not be rigid, which would turn unity into embeddedness, but responsive to circumstances. For example, trusting people are not gullible; they are responsive to others' actions and come to perceive some people as untrustworthy (Rotter, 1971). Similarly, people can come to experience unity with others and still sensitively perceive hostility or exploitative behavior. Having a connected self with well-developed identity and values, they can critically perceive when their group follows a course contrary to their own values. Their commitment to the group's welfare may lead them to practice "critical loyalty" and actively oppose the group's course (see Staub, 1989). A connected self and inclusive other-oriented values can give rise to both unity and the capacity to oppose.

Self-Awareness, Morality, and Freedom of Choice

Self-awareness is an important aspect of morality. It is not a product but an ongoing process. Self-awareness can be of our thoughts and feelings. Or awareness can be of relationships, for example, a person's awareness of his or her embeddedness in a group.

A person can develop the capacity to see the psychological processes or experiences within herself (and the characteristics and processes within her group) that lead to turning against others. These include differentiating "us" from "them," devaluating "them," and "just-world thinking"—the belief that the world is just and that people tend to deserve their good or bad fate (Lerner, 1980). Becoming aware that seeing others in a negative light may be not the result of who they are but a devaluation, can be a significant, even transforming experience. Becoming aware of destructive practices in one's group can lead to critical loyalty, a willingness to oppose group policy for the ultimate benefit of the group.

Frequently people respond to others without going through a process of decision-making. Their response is an expression of who they are but is not based on reflection. Speedy, spontaneous reactions can be helpful (Staub, 1978) or harmful. For example, some police officers resort to aggression in this way (Novaco, 1975). Slowing down these automatic reactions, becoming aware of what happens between stimulus and response, can enable people to change their reactions. In the case of police aggression, it makes self-control possible (Staub, 1991). The "decisions" that people make as they move along the continuum of destruction are often automatic, unreflective. Being self-aware makes reflection and change possible.

But how is change possible if our behavior is determined by who we are? First, our selves and personalities have many different parts and usually some quite contradictory aspects. As we become reflective or aware in our decision making, we can shift from one domain of beliefs and values to another as guides for our motivation and action. For example, we may begin to see moral obligation to all human beings as the basis for action, rather than moral devaluation and the moral exclusion of certain people. We can lessen mistrust by granting others the benefit of doubt.

Does everyone have the same potential to change with increased self-awareness? For one thing, not everyone has the same potential for self-awareness. People with defensive selves and in embedded relations have less potential. Both Eichmann and Himmler got sick when they witnessed the killing of Jews in gas chambers (Hilberg, 1961), but their embeddedness in their group and commitment to its goals made it impossible for them to use their own internal reactions as a force for change (Staub, 1989). The nature of their selves and their moral orientations also made change unlikely. Such an experience of distress might have made some people aware of the shared humanity of all people.

Selves differ in many ways, one of which is the degree of internal differentiation. Self-awareness makes for less rigid selves, for greater differentiation of aspects of one's self, and for responding less automatically and more reflectively to events. This creates greater flexibility and choice. Who we are limits or increases the possibilities inherent in choosing, and thereby limits or enlarges our "freedom of will" (Staub, 1989; see also Rogers, 1961).

A Comparison with Cognitive-Developmental Perspectives

The conception of how moral behavior comes about that I present in this chapter differs from aspects of cognitive-developmental theory. In the conception presented here, moral choice may be avoided, preempted, or its nature changed. Even if a person possesses certain moral values (or has the competence to reason about morality at a certain stage), this value (or reasoning capacity) may never be applied to a particular situation.

Potential and actual victims of immoral or violent action may be excluded from the moral universe, so that moral values (or reasoning) don't apply to them. Or a person or group may resort to "moral equilibration" (Staub, 1989). When there is motivation to harm someone, moral values and inhibitions (or reasoning) that prohibit such harm doing may create conflict. One can reduce the conflict by shifting to a different moral value (or level of reasoning) that allows the harmful action. The new value need not actually be moral but can be used as a moral value. For example, Eisenberg (1986) reported that as prosocial action became more costly, both children and adults shifted to a lower level of reasoning. The Nazis replaced values of the sanctity of human life with values of loyalty and obedience to leaders and the group. Harm doers often create ideologies with "higher values" that provide both the motivation and moral justification for harming certain people. Killing racially "inferior" people was seen by the Nazis as improving and thereby serving all humanity. "Self control" becomes irrelevant. The dominant motive now includes harming the victims, and opposing moral motives have been subverted, replaced, or deactivated. There is no reason to restrain, inhibit, or "control" harmful actions.

This conception also has implications for the responsibility of perpetrators. People must be regarded as responsible (and hence accountable) for their actions. This is as true of perpetrators as of bystanders, who by their words and actions may be able to influence perpetrators (Staub, 1992). Conceptions that help us understand the roots of violence do not diminish the responsibility of perpetrators, who make many small and large decisions along the way (Staub, 1989).

But responsibility can be an expectation and demand, or a psychological reality. People with highly defensive and embedded selves must still be held accountable. But true responsibility follows from the genuine possibility of choice, and a person's potential for choice is greater when she is self-aware and internally flexible, which seems to require a secure self. To make choices that limit harm doing and promote helping also requires a connected self, a prosocial value orientation, and the inclusion of all human beings in the moral realm. These characteristics depend on socialization and lifelong experience. Through positive socialization practices that lead to these characteristics (Staub, 1979, 1986, 1993) and through later experiences (Staub, 1989, 1992), people can become genuinely capable of choice and hence genuinely responsible.

Summary

While I explored many aspects of how selves are related to morality, my focus has been on security versus defensiveness (insecurity and a self-protective orientation inclined toward aggression) and on the degree and nature of the self's relation to others (discon-nected, autonomous, connected, and embedded). Another form of connectedness is unity, where the interests of the self and others are experienced as identical.

I stressed that these aspects of individual (and group) selves are partly stable and partly the result of surrounding conditions and their impact on persons. Individual and group selves also evolve and change in the course of helping and harming. I discussed different moral orientations and explored the relationship be-tween dimensions of selves and moral orientations. I suggested that self-awareness, which some people (and groups) are more capable of than others, is important if people are to decrease the influence of automatic tendencies on their behavior, especially harmful ones, and increase their capacity for choice.

Note

1. All along in this chapter reference is made to the concepts and analyses of genocides and mass killings described in Staub, 1989. However, the brief presentation along the way does not provide a complete picture of the origins of such group violence.

References

Averill, J. R. (1982). *Anger and aggression: An essay on emotion.* New York: Springer.

Baron, R. A. (1977). *Human aggression.* New York: Plenum Press.

Batson, D. (1990). How social an animal? The human capacity for caring. *American Psychologist,* 45:336–347.

Bellah, P. N., Madsen, R., Sullivan, W. M., Swindler, A., and Lipton, S. M. (1985). *Habits of the heart: Individualism and commitment in American life*. New York: Harper and Row.

Craig, G. A. (1982). *The Germans*. New York: New American Library.

Egendorf, A. (1986). *Healing from the war: Trauma and transformation after Vietnam*. Boston: Shambhala.

Eisenberg, N. (1986). *Altruistic emotion, cognition, and behavior*. Hillsdale, NJ: Erlbaum.

Epstein, S. (1980). The self-concept: A review and the proposal of an integrated theory of personality. In E. Staub (Ed.), *Personality: Basic aspects and current research*. Englewood Cliffs, NJ: Prentice-Hall.

Epstein, S. (1989). Values from the perspective of cognitive-experiential self-theory. In N. Eisenberg, J. Rekowski, and E. Staub (Eds.), *Social and moral values: Individual and societal perspectives*. Hillsdale, NJ: Erlbaum.

Feinberg, J. K. (1978). *Anatomy of a helping situation: Some personality and situational determinants of helping in a conflict situation involving another's psychological distress*. Unpublished doctoral dissertation, University of Massachusetts, Amherst.

Goldstein, J. H., Davis, R. W., and Herman, D. (1975). Escalation of aggression: Experimental studies. *Journal of Personality and Social Psychology*, 31:162–170.

Gouldner, A. W. (1960). The norm of reciprocity: A preliminary statement. *American Sociological Review*, 25:161–179.

Grodman, S. M. (1979). *The role of personality and situational variables in responding to and helping an individual in psychological distress*. Unpublished doctoral dissertation, University Massachusetts, Amherst.

Hilberg, R. (1961). *The destruction of the European Jews*. New York: Harper and Row.

Heusmann, L. R., and Eron, L. D. (1984). Cognitive processes and the persistence of aggressive behavior. *Aggressive Behavior*, 10:243–251.

Hunt, J. M. (1965). Intrinsic motivation and its role in psychological development. In D. Levine (Ed.), *Nebraska symposium on motivation*. Lincoln: University of Nebraska Press.

Isen, A. M., Horn, N., and Rosenhan, D. L. (1973). Effects of success and failure on children's generosity. *Journal of Personality and Social Psychology*, 27:239–248.

Lerner, M. (1980). *The belief in a just world: A fundamental delusion*. New York: Plenum Press.

London, P. (1970). The rescuers: Motivational hypotheses about Christians who saved Jews from the Nazis. In J. Macaulay and L. Berkowitz (Eds.), *Altruism and helping behavior*. New York: Academic Press.

Mack, J. (1983). Nationalism and the self. *Psychology Review*, 2:47–69.

Maslow, A. H. (1962). *Toward a psychology of being*. New York: Van Nostrand.

Miller, A. (1983). *For your own good: Hidden cruelty in child-rearing and the roots of violence*. New York: Farrar, Straus, and Giroux.

Novaco, R. (1975). *Anger control: The development and evaluation of an experimental treatment.* Lexington, MA: Heath.

Oliner, S. B., and Oliner, P. (1988). *The altruistic personality: Rescuers of Jews in Nazi Europe.* New York: Free Press.

Opawa, S., Ed. (1990). Moral exclusion and injustice. *Journal of Social Issues,* 46.

Rogers, C. R. (1961). *On becoming a person.* Boston: Houghton Mifflin.

Rosenhan, D. L., Salovey, P., Karylowski, J., and Hargis, K. (1981). Emotion and altruism. In J. P. Rushton and R. M. Sorrentino (Eds.), *Altruism and helping behavior.* Hillsdale, NJ: Erlbaum.

Rotter, J. B. (1971). Generalized expectancies for interpersonal trust. *American Psychologist,* 26:443–452.

Sampson, E. E. (1988). The debate on individualism. *American Psychologist,* 47:15–22.

Slavson, S. R. (1965). *Reclaiming the delinquent.* New York: Free Press.

Sroufe, L. A. (1979). The coherence of individual development: Early care, attachment, and subsequent developmental issues. *American Psychologist,* 34:834–842.

Staub, E. (1971). The learning and unlearning of aggression: The role of anxiety, empathy, efficacy, and prosocial values. In J. Singer (Ed.), *The control of aggression and violence: Cognitive and physiological factors.* New York: Academic Press.

Staub, E. (1974). Helping a distressed person: Social, personality, and stimulus determinants. In L. Berkowitz (Ed.), *Advances in experimental social psychology.* Vol. 7. New York: Academic Press.

Staub, E. (1978). *Positive social behavior and morality: Social and personal influences.* Vol. 1. New York: Academic Press.

Staub, E. (1979). *Positive social behavior and morality: Socialization and development.* Vol. 2. New York: Academic Press.

Staub, E. (1980). Social and prosocial behavior: Personal and situational influences and their interactions. In E. Staub (Ed.), *Personality: Basic aspects and current research.* Englewood Cliffs, NJ: Prentice-Hall.

Staub, E. (1985). The psychology of perpetrators and bystanders. *Political Psychology,* 6:61–86.

Staub, E. (1986). A conception of the determinants and development of altruism and aggression: Motives, the self, the environment. In C. Zahn-Waxler (Ed.), *Altruism and aggression: Social and biological origins.* Cambridge: Cambridge University Press.

Staub, E. (1989). *The roots of evil: The psychological and cultural origins of genocide.* New York: Cambridge University Press.

Staub, E. (1990a). Moral exclusion, personal goal theory, and extreme destructiveness. *Journal of Social Issues,* 46:47–65.

Staub, E. (1990b). The power to help others. Unpublished manuscript. University of Massachusetts, Amherst.

Staub, E. (1991). Understanding and overcoming police violence. Paper based on lecture at the POST (Police Officers Standards and Training). Symposium on Law Enforcement Training Issues. San Diego, California, September 26.

Staub, E. (1992). Transforming the bystander: Altruism, caring and social responsibility. In H. Fein (Ed.), *Genocide Watch*. New Haven: Yale University Press.

Staub, E. (1993). The origins of caring, helping, and nonaggression: Parental socialization, the family system, schools, and cultural influence. In S. Oliner et al. (Eds.), *Embracing the other: Philosophical, psychological, and historical perspectives on altruism*. New York: New York University Press.

Staub, E., and Feinberg, H. (1980). Regularities in peer interaction, empathy, and sensitivity to others. Paper presented at the Development of Prosocial Behavior and Cognitions Symposium held during American Psychological Association Meetings, Montreal.

Surrey, J. (1985). *Self-in-relation: A theory of women's development*. The Stone Center, Wellesley College.

Tajfel, H. (1982). Social psychology of intergroup relations. *Annual Review of Psychology*, 33:1–39.

Tajfel, H., and Turner, J. C. (1979). An integrative theory of intergroup conflict. In W. G. Austin and S. Worchel (Eds.), *The social psychology of intergroup relations*. Monterey, CA: Brooks-Cole.

Tec, N. (1986). *When light pierced the darkness: Christian rescue of Jews in Nazi-occupied Poland*. New York: Oxford University Press.

Toch, H. (1969). *Violent men*. Chicago: Aldine.

Weisz, J. R., Rothbaum, F. M., and Blackburn, T. C. (1984). Standing out and standing in: The psychology of control in America and Japan. *American Psychologist*, 39:955–969.

White, R. W. (1959). Motivation reconsidered: The concept of competence. *Psychological Review*, 66:297–333.

Wilson, J. P. (1976). Motivation, modeling, and altruism: A person × situation analysis. *Journal of Personality and Social Psychology*, 34:1078–1086.

Yarymovitz, M. (1977). Modification of self-worth and increment of prosocial sensitivity. *Polish Psychological Bulletin*, 8:45–53.

Threats to the Self in the Peer World: Observations of Twelve-Year-Old Children in Natural Settings

Lothar Krappmann

General Problem and Aim of the Study

Following the symbolic interactionist view, I define the self as an organized set of ideas that the person possesses about himself or herself in relation to others. This set of ideas serves to orient persons as they participate in social interactions, so that they feel committed to this set of ideas and want relevant others to respect them. Hence people care about presenting themselves to others in a favorable light and tend to defend themselves against misunderstandings and attacks (Goffman, 1959).

Researchers have chosen to investigate the self, either (1) by emphasizing the differentiation of the self as an object of perception and as a subject of action (James, 1961), or (2) by focusing on the unity and continuity of the self when one faces divergent expectations or contexts (e.g., Krappmann, 1988), or (3) by examining the cognitive representations of the self (Harter, 1983; Keller and Edelstein, in this volume; Noam, in this volume) or the conditions that influence the formation of one's self-concepts and self-esteem (Oppenheimer, 1990; Wolf, in this volume). Especially when researchers' attention is not restricted to cognitive representations, the self appears as a structure that unites value orientations, motives, competencies, trust, and commitment in a sociocultural pattern (Taylor, 1989; Krewer and Eckensberger, 1991; Wren, in this volume). Consequently, in critical situations not only does the cognitive representation of one's self break down, but the self as a whole is threatened with the loss of its place in the social world.

Humans are not born supplied with a self. As G. H. Mead (1934) explained, it is only by participating in cooperative action directed at a commonly pursued social objective that the individual can acquire a self and assume the roles by which social interaction is controlled. The evolution of the self is a basic aspect of childhood and adolescent socialization. By integration in socializing interactions with significant others, children construct a conception of themselves based on what they have learned in the exchanges of perspectives with others. Aware of the self constructed so far, the growing child or adolescent enters interactions in which his or her presented self is tested by others.

The formation of the self is an unending process. Though Erikson (1956) emphasized that the development of "identity" has special relevance during the period of adolescence, other students of the self have demonstrated that all stages of development contribute in important ways to the formation of a self and that the self is a major concern already in preadolescence and even in childhood (e.g., Damon and Hart, 1982; Kegan, 1982). Nevertheless, our knowledge about the development of the self in social interaction is still very incomplete. As Damon and Hart (1982) have pointed out, the majority of studies investigating the self in childhood have focused on the evaluative dimension of self-development (self-esteem) and have neglected its cognitive dimensions (self-understanding), on which children draw as they become increasingly aware of themselves. Fortunately, social aspects of the self have not been completely overlooked. The developmental models of self-understanding proposed by Damon and Hart (1982), Kegan (1982), Selman (1980), and Noam (1985) underscore the importance of social experience in the course of self-development, either by including the "social self" as a constituent of the self during the entire process of development or by positing the need to define and redefine the self in relation to others at each developmental stage. None of these models are based sufficiently on analyses of interactions that can demonstrate how the self is constructed in social processes; rather, all infer which aspects of social experience are salient from other sociocognitive research or from retrospective reports on clients' childhoods.

Although symbolic interactionists stress that the self is a fragile structure emerging from the interplay of tentative presentations of the self and various reactions of others, we have to assume that children's and adults' selves are not an ever-new, momentary invention reflecting only the actual negotiations of the interacting partners. The compromises whereby one resolves conflicts between the self claimed by the ego and the self expected by the others are limited by the continuing interaction process, relationship affiliations, and interpersonal regulations that guide behaviors when actors negotiate issues relevant to the selves of the participants.

In view of the continuing interaction process, participants in an interaction must make sure that their contributions are predictable. Only if the self and others can exchange their perspectives across changing interaction situations is participation in interactions unproblematic. In relationships, the contributions of persons must fit the selves on which their relationships are grounded. In interpersonal regulations, participants are expected to keep to values and norms shared in their social group. These moral orientations define what one person owes to another, what care must be given, and what conceptions of justice and fairness must be obeyed by the negotiators when the negotiations result in commitment. These regulations, which are not always abided by, but to which one can always appeal, provide protection to a self based on a shared morality and allow one to push legitimate demands. Thus a self that is integrated in a network of relationships and founded on interpersonal morality is best safeguarded against misinterpretations and attacks (e.g., Kegan, 1982).

The empirical study presented here explores those experiences relevant to the construction of one's self that are contained in children's peer interactions. In it I ask whether children interacting with peers show concern for whether their claimed selves are socially accepted and how they attempt to defend their selves if questioned or attacked by others. My focus is not on "critical life events" (e.g., Filipp, 1981), although many children do indeed experience such crises as failure in school or a move to another neighborhood. Instead, I look at everyday misunderstandings and minor mistakes, mishaps, and deviations from routines, all of which cause embarrassed adults to eliminate the problems or irritations and reestablish their reputable selves (Goffman, 1967; Mummendey, 1990). Do such occurrences, which apparently are even more frequent in childhood than in adulthood, also threaten children's selves?

I presume that children's selves are challenged especially in their interactions with adults, because adults often confront children with standards of competent behaviors and because children cannot or do not overlook these demands, especially if these adults are caring parents or admired models. Thus children take pains to accommodate themselves to what they understand as the adults' expectations. I also assume, however, that the nature of their selves and their self-protective strategies cannot be completely understood by observing these interactions. Children may mechanically copy the demanded behaviors from adults and neglect their own constructive capacities. Though these adults care for their children, they often misinterpret children's problems and influence children in ways that distort the children's frames of orientation. Thus we encounter a complicated mixture of behaviors in which children's own contributions are not easily discovered.

For this reason, I have analyzed the interaction sequences among peers, bearing in mind Piaget's conviction of the developmental relevance of the peer. While the child has difficulties in separating his or her own view from that of the parent, the peer "presents a new problem: that of continually distinguishing the ego from the other person, and the reciprocity of these two views" (Piaget, 1971, p. 278). Interactions with peers not only present crucial tasks stimulating the development of language and thought, as elaborated by Piaget, but also offer key situations for experiencing one's self, since within these interactions, in contrast to interactions with benevolent adults, children cannot hope for care and support from others of the same age (Youniss, 1983). Thus, by looking at children's reactions to threats to the self emerging in peer interactions, we can see which aspects of children's selves are especially vulnerable and forcibly defended, because children do not accommodate themselves to authorities or avoid conflicts with peers about self-relevant behaviors. Children can easily express demands they want to be respected, and they freely use strategies that seem adequate to attack other selves or to protect qualities of their own selves. This study reveals what conceptions of a respectable self and what rules of interpersonal morality guide a child when he or she tries to establish a self among peers.

In this study I also investigate the ways in which threats to the self and the responding defense and protection of the self are influenced by children's friendships. Some research suggests that friendships promote perspective-taking and empathy (e.g., McGuire and Weisz, 1982). Thus friends may respect one's claimed self by not questioning the beliefs and commitments of the claimed self. In contrast, other research indicates that friends compete more than nonfriends (Berndt, 1985) and more critically compare self-relevant behaviors than do other unrelated children (Tesser, Campbell, and Smith, 1984). I side with the second group and also assume that friends provoke self-threatening events and that children must protect themselves against attacks. Perhaps friends even more clearly than nonfriends follow rules of interpersonal morality when they mutually construct, or better, *negotiate*, their selves, because friends must try harder than nonfriends to find acceptable solutions to interpersonal conflict (e.g., Keller and Edelstein, in this volume).

Method of the Study

Since the self, in the outlined approach, is the active base of a person's participation in interaction rather than a mere concept, observation of these interactions is the appropriate method for investigating children's strategies to establish their selves. Children's characteristic procedures should appear most clearly in interactions in which their selves are threatened, because threats reveal vulnerable aspects and show which rules children abide by in their interactions. Additionally, observation of interactions provides data about everyday processes about which persons interviewed are usually not able to report because the occurrences are too trivial to be a focus of awareness.

My analyses of interactions in which a child's self is threatened are based on field notes taken in a sixth-grade classroom in an inner-city neighborhood of mostly upper-lower and lower middle-class families. For the purpose of the planned exploration, twelve-year-olds were chosen as the preferred group of the study because we assumed that children of this age are concerned about challenges to their selves, while younger children may tend to worry less about such challenges. Because of the transition from childhood to adolescence at this age, insecurity about the self as well as defenses against threats should be relatively apparent.

Two observers focused on the interactions of two children sitting next to each other at a table in the classroom. Each observer recorded the interactions between these two children as well as between these children and others with whom they had contact during lessons and breaks spent on the school's playground. During most of the observation in the classroom, the conversations of the focus children were tape-recorded. Both observers elaborated their field notes independently and later compared their descriptions of the observed social processes for congruence. Doubtful recordings were omitted. By this procedure, all 30 children enrolled in this sixth-grade class (20 girls and 10 boys, mean age 12.4) were observed for about three school periods and some recreation time outside the classroom. Although the investigators tried hard to spend an equal time observing each child, this proved impossible for some of the children for various reasons (see Oswald and Krappmann, 1988, for a more detailed description of design and procedures). In spite of these disadvantages, we chose this unstandardized method of collecting data, following Glaser-Strauss (1967), in order to collect ecologically valid data on the natural peer world.

We thoroughly scrutinized the recordings to find episodes in which the self of a participant was threatened.[1] We categorized an episode as containing a threat to a person's self on the basis of a commonsense assessment of whether one participant was threatening the self of another. To these cases we added others in which the reactions of participants indicated that they felt ill-treated or misunderstood with regard to their claimed selves, or in which they sought to establish a desired self in a situation even though their selves had not been ostensibly questioned by others. Thus, we also included in the category or "file" of threats to the self episodes in which the threat emerges from a discrepancy between the claimed and acknowledged self that, although apparent only to the threatened person, was publicly expressed by reactions showing concern about his or her self. Not included were episodes in which the threatened child is not known (a few cases only) or in which the threat emerges in a group situation in which the protagonists cannot be identified, as when several classmates yell at a child's failure (quite a number of cases).

Certainly there are threats to a person's self that can hardly be recognized by others, including researchers, because the self's experience has a subjective dimension that, at least for a while, is inaccessible to others. Only if threats to selves leave visible marks in interactions can an episode be identified as threatening. As the self is dependent on social interaction, children whose selves are discredited often react to these occurrences. If they did not, their selves would be reduced to objects, and active contributions to the coordination of actions would be denied. There are children who try to stand aside and are marginalized by the others because they are "boring." Their social fate indicates that conflicts about one's self should not be avoided and may even contribute to integration into the social world of peers. When, therefore, negotiations about the self are an essential and inevitable part of children's social activities, most of them should be detectable in the recordings of the interactions.[2]

Altogether 129 episodes of threats to the self were compiled.[3] Most of them (99 threats) occurred among children of the same gender (77 percent), 27 in cross-gender interactions (21 percent; in three cases the threatening child is not identified). Since threats in cross-gender interactions have a special character, we did not include these episodes in this analysis. Among the 99 same-gender interactions, 63 threats to selves occurred among girls, and 36 among boys. These proportions reflect boys' and girls' unequal attendance in the classroom; they do not significantly differ in their involvement in interactions containing threats. Almost all children participated in such episodes, in the mean about three times as a target of a threat and about three times as an intentional or casual originator of a threat (the exceptions were one girl who never participated and a boy who was involved 21 times).

To examine the influence of children's social relationships on their behaviors in threat situations, we interviewed the children about their friendships, and we categorized all relationships among the children of the classroom as "best friend," "friend," or "not a friend" (the variable being friendship status). This measure is not a sociometric procedure derived from children's votes but a rating measure that makes use of all relevant information about the quality of existing friendships available from both children (for details of the categorization procedure, see Oswald and Krappmann, 1988). Two other measures give the social position that a child maintains in the network of relationships in the classroom. First, children were distinguished by the number of their mutual best friends and friends (the variable being mutual relationships). Second, children who had three or more mutual best friends or friends were assigned to the category of well-integrated children, the others to the category of poorly or unintegrated children (the variable being social integration).

Though the measures are not independent of each other, they highlight different issues. Friendship status indicates whether two children observed in interaction are friends, whereas the two other measures, mutual relationships and social integration, show whether a child takes part in the social life of the classroom. Two interacting children may be friends and yet be socially marginalized in the classroom; in contrast, two interacting nonfriends may be well integrated in the social network of the classroom. Thus the two variables mutual relationships and social integration reflect a child's general experience with relationships, whereas the variable friendship status refers to the quality of the relationship within the dyad only.

The analyses in the following section are based on the 99 interaction episodes of threats to the self among children of the same gender (the episode file). My examination of the influence of children's relationships additionally uses a data file that reorganizes the information by individuals so that the 30 individual children who attend the classroom can be characterized (the personal-data file).

Threats to the Self

The episodes sometimes comprise short verbal exchanges, sometimes enduring conflicts renewed again and again. This is a typical episode:

Sitting among a group of chatting girls, Elke attacks Bille in a derogatory manner. "Sometimes you're really kinky!" Rebuking Bille, she accuses her of thinking that a certain kind of wool is itchy though it really is smooth. Bille looks irritated and does not know how to answer. First another girl defends her, and only later does she insist on her opinion.

Threats to children's selves in school fall into two categories. They are either related to demands of school and instruction or result from the social world of peers. Examples of threats to the self related to instruction and school are reproaches for "stupid" mistakes or sloppiness. Typical threats among peers are reproaches for bragging, inability to contribute to peer gossip, or liking a member of the other sex. In spite of our observing children in schools, almost two thirds of the issues causing a threat to the self (62 percent) belong to the peer world.[4]

This description seems to suggest that the threatened child is the "victim," and the threatening child the "offender." However, the reality is more complicated. According to the opinion of the raters, about two thirds of the threats were not totally unpredictable but emerged in situations actively produced by all of the children involved, including the "victim." Children apparently enter into risky situations. Most probably they do not intend to endanger their selves on purpose. However, it may be characteristic of children's peer life that they test which behaviors they may inflict on others and how others will respond, in order to learn about selves in interactions.

Furthermore, the finding that in only half of the cases the threats involve verbal or, very rarely, physical aggression indicates that most children do not seriously want to harm the other but are negotiating what is acceptable and what is intolerable. Astonishingly, rude behaviors often are not retaliations, and the debate is not diverted to the rude behavior but continues to be focused on the issue eliciting the threat. Almost all children learn about their selves from both the perspective of the threatening child and that of the threatened child as well.

Our detailed analyses address the following four questions: What are the vulnerable areas of the twelve-year-olds' selves? Which strategies do the children apply to defend their selves? Are the chosen strategies appropriate? Which are the consequences for the children's selves? We shall now discuss these questions.

Vulnerable areas of the self

Threats can endanger children's selves in different respects. In the observed interactions children directed their threats at four different issues (these appear to be relevant from a theoretical perspective as well): (1) The other children view the claimed competence as either substandard or superior, i.e., as not being *equal;* (2) they challenge one's self territory or *sovereignty;* (3) they criticize one's *student performance;* (4) they do not offer *social acceptance.*

Equality
Frequently children are blamed for deviating from standards for all peers with whom the children are prepared to cooperate, e.g., for not knowing or not being able to do what every child knows or is capable of, or, on the other hand, for demonstrating more knowledge or capacity. Children must stick to this norm.

Andrea mentions work she has finished during the "painting lesson." She uses a very old-fashioned German word, which Susi repeats in a mimicking way. Susi continues her mockery until Andrea, who feels bothered, switches to the term used in the schools today.

Children are also blamed for their actual or alleged individual characteristics or performances that distinguish them, even if the child cannot be held responsible for these qualities (e.g., properties such as hair color). Children are also blamed for violating often rigidly interpreted rules of fairness and justice if the others suspect that the child does not contribute sufficiently to common undertakings. Thus a child's self is vulnerable to attack when the child deviates from standards and norms that must be observed by "everybody." Equality is also at issue when a child seems unable to conform (lack of competence) or is not willing to conform (rejection of diversity). Almost one half of the threats to selves observed in same-gender interactions (48 percent) were assigned to the issue of equality.

Sovereignty
Others' attempts to restrict one's own actions are regarded as

serious offenses. Likewise, children feel disrespected when they are kept from contributing to joint decision making.

Klaus has given a sheet of paper to Jan, who often forgets his exercise book. Now he observes that Jan is lazy. Klaus shouts at him, "You still haven't written a single word!" Thereupon Jan paints a big letter on the paper and shows it to Klaus. Klaus is enraged and replies, "That's a letter and not a word! Man, you must write! I didn't give you the paper for that." Jan throws the paper back to Klaus. Klaus furiously returns it to Jan, saying, "I don't need it any more!" The teacher intervenes.

If children feared that their own responsibility was discredited, they tended to deny negotiations also in cases where it was necessary and no longer accepted reasonable suggestions. Often the conflict arises about control over "territories of the self" (Goffman, 1971)—body, possessions, space—that others are not allowed to invade without permission. This issue is called sovereignty rather than autonomy because children at this age tend to defend their selves by establishing control over a fenced-in territory, whereas autonomy consists in standing up for one's own position in domains of common responsibility. We assigned about one fifth of the threats to selves (21 percent) to the issue of sovereignty. Both issues, equality and sovereignty, were observed mostly in the peer world of the classroom.

Student performance
Children challenge each other for inadequate performance of the student's role in school. Here the focus is not the demands that are valid for every child in the same manner but rather the student's differential achievements. Threats result also from failures to observe rules of cooperation or failures in determining which sources of support may be used. Only one fifth of the observed threats fall in the category of student's performance (20 percent), a relatively small portion in view of the fact that we conducted our observations in the classroom. It is also worth noting that quite a number of threats arising from instruction were reinterpreted by the children as challenges to their sovereignty.

Social acceptance
Here threats to the self emerge from challenges to children's

relationships to others when these relationships are not respected by others, when children's contributions to group activities are overlooked, or when children are denied full membership rights or are even excluded from cooperation. As friendships are important for these children, it is surprising that only 11 percent of observed threats involve this issue.

Strategies for defending the self

After a threat children very seldom simply refrained from reactions. By their counterstrategies they addressed the threatening child in different ways:

Communication
In about one fifth of the episodes (22 percent) the threatened child attempts to analyze with the threatener what caused the threat and to settle the problem in a way that satisfied both children's expectations.

Bernd asks Thomas for a special pen. Thomas rejects the request in a rough manner, saying, "Buy yourself your own pen!" (These pens are expensive and quickly used up. Frequent requests for borrowing these pens are regarded as exploitation.) Bernd inquires, "Do you have a new one?" (indicating that he knows about the pen's value). Thomas keeps Bernd waiting, who respects his hesitation, but soon gives him the pen and later even tolerates Bernd's putting it in the middle of the table so that both can easily reach and use it.

Demonstration of sovereignty
While communication integrates both sides of a conflict, children demonstrating their sovereignty pursue their rights or claim their competence without asking for others' views. They rebuke or disparage the threatening child, punish the attacker, or start a counterattack. About one third of the episodes (31 percent) were demonstrations of sovereignty.

When it is Sabine's turn, she jumps and unexpectedly gets some sand on Gabi, who was watching the game. Gabi shouts at Sabine, calling her bad names, and Sabine retaliates loudly. Then Gabi moves toward Sabine, demonstrating anger and decision. (The observer expects that she will hit Sabine.) Sabine, also demonstrating her power, does not step aside. Gabi passes by Sabine very narrowly, addresses Wally, and walks away with her.

Yielding

This kind of strategy also is one-sided, since children yield in the face of an attack on the self. They deny the relevance of the threat or try to change the meaning of what happened, for instance, by joking or clowning. Sometimes they claim incompetence, use empty excuses, comply, or just keep silent even though a reaction is needed and possible. In about one third of the episodes (32 percent) children did not stand up for their demands.

Matthias continues to repeat a funny story, imitating a popular comic actor. Mirko and Gabi remain stone-faced. The embarrassing silence is terminated by Matthias, who starts laughing in a very affected way about his own show.

Confused reactions

We categorized reactions as "confused" when they were clear but children failed to deal with the problem or to address the opponent. Apparently, the reason is not casual misunderstanding but an inability to conceive of the self as an object of conflicts. Children's reactions were confused in 16 percent of the episodes.

Children's strategies show four levels of coordinating perspectives and intentions in considering others' points of view. "Communicative" strategies were the highest, since both sides are integrated in the search for a solution. The "demonstration of sovereignty" and "yielding" strategies consider only one side of the conflict. By demonstrating sovereignty, the self is defended, while the child who yields and leaves gives up essential claims, at least for the moment. We regarded "confused reactions" as the least competent strategy, since the child does not deal with the challenge at all. Children chose strategies with respect to the issue eliciting the threat ($p < .01$). Children chose communicative strategies more frequently than expected when the issue was "equality," less frequently when the issue was "sovereignty." When "student performance" was the issue, children tended to yield and leave. Confused reactions were particularly frequent when threateners raised the issue of "social acceptance."

Appropriateness of the strategies chosen

Communicative strategies of explaining, negotiating, and revising behaviors are sometimes not good responses to threats. "Demonstration of sovereignty" or "yielding" may be a better course. We therefore rated children's chosen strategies with respect to how appropriate they were for achieving a favorable outcome or avoiding more damage to the self. We assessed them as "constructive," "defensive," and "inappropriate." Children proceed in a "constructive" way when they use the situation to gain positive affirmation of their selves, in a "defensive" way when they repel the threat without strengthening their position, in an "inappropriate" way when they do not stand up for themselves. The order reflects the quality of the child's self-affirmation.

These assessments caused extensive discussions among the raters, since subjective experience influences their judgments. I report the findings to draw attention to the fact that a child's strategy may be rated as competent vis-à-vis the threat but is ineffective in protecting the self under the present circumstances.[5] In only 26 percent of the threats did children react in a way judged as "constructive," whereas in more than half of the incidents (52 percent) they behaved in a "defensive" way. In 21 percent of the threatening episodes, we rated their reactions as "inappropriate."

Despite the mentioned differences between competence and effectiveness, appropriateness is highly correlated with the level of coordination of the strategy chosen by the children ($r = .63$; $p < .01$). Raters very often judged communicative strategies as "constructive," while they assessed "demonstration of sovereignty" and "yielding" as "defensive" more often than expected ($p < .01$). With regard to the issues of threat, children reacted to "equality" threats in a "constructive" way more often than expected and in a "defensive" way less often than expected.

Consequences for the self

The threatened child's reaction can lead to a "positive affirmation" or even an "upgrading" of the self, to the "preservation" of the self (no advantage, no loss), or to "diminution" of the claimed self.

Again, we based our assignments to these categories on common-sense judgments. An examination of the episodes shows that after children received threats to their selves, they positively affirmed their selves in 37 percent of the cases, in 33 percent they preserved their selves without advantage or loss, and in 29 percent they lost reputation. "Sovereignty" and "equality" were the issues where children achieved a favorable outcome relatively often, "student performance" and "social acceptance" were the issues where children often failed to positively affirm their threatened selves ($p < .01$). Children often enhanced their selves with "communicative" strategies and "demonstrations of sovereignty," but rarely with "yielding" strategies or "confused" reactions ($p < .01$). We found that appropriateness of the strategy and a positive affirmation of the self were highly correlated ($r = .54$; $p < .01$).

Friendships and Social Integration of Children Involved in Threats to the Self

Children dealing with threats to their selves are mutual "best friends" in 27 percent of the cases observed in same-sex interactions and are mutual best friends or friends in 44 percent of the cases. If one-sided friendships are added, 75 percent of the threats occur between children who are somewhat related from at least one side. Although more than two thirds of possible relationships among the classmates are neither mutual nor one-sided friendships, they account for only 25 percent of the threats.

The friendship status of the interacting children only moderately shaped interactions containing a threat. While differences in the issue of the threat are insignificant, friendship status does correlate with the strategy chosen by the threatened child. Better friends tend to explain ($r = .14$; $p < .08$), better friends tend to react in a more appropriate manner ($r = .28$; $p < .01$), and better friends tend to achieve a more favorable outcome ($r = .26$; $p < .01$).

When we used the variable of "children's social integration" in the peer world instead of "friendship status," correlations with the behaviors adopted by threatening or threatened children became even clearer. Threats to selves were more frequent when both children were well integrated, as well as when both children were marginal members of the class. We found no significant difference between these groups with regard to the issues of threats. However, well-integrated children more often used communicative strategies ($r = .56$; $p < .01$), more often behaved in an appropriate way ($r = .42$; $p < .01$), and more often positively affirmed their selves ($r = .39$; $p < .01$), always in comparison with poorly integrated children. These correlations are higher than those obtained between friendship status and these behavioral variables.

The findings reported so far are based on the episode-data file ($N = 99$). The personal-data file ($N = 30$) shows the extent to which children became involved in threats, which strategies individual children used, whether observers judged their strategies to be appropriate, and whether they achieved a positive affirmation of their threatened selves. Our analyses show that children's participation was not correlated with the number of their friends, that children maintaining a higher number of mutual friendships applied more "communicative" strategies ($r = .34$; $p < .05$), that their strategies were more "constructive" ($r = .37$; $p < .05$), and that they achieved more positive affirmations of their selves than children with fewer mutual friendships ($r = .27$; $p < .10$).

We used various multiple regression models to predict the number of mutual friendships from children's behaviors when their selves were threatened by others, but they all failed. However, we could predict the appropriateness of children's strategies with a multiple regression model that included the number of mutual friendships maintained by a child. Other predictors were the number of times children actively and passively participated in threat episodes and the proportion of equality issues among received threats. This model explained 39 percent of the variance connected with the "appropriateness of the strategy" ($p = .015$). Children behaved "constructively" who maintained more mutual friendships, were involved in fewer threat episodes, and who had to deal with equality issues when their selves were threatened.[6]

Discussion

Our observations of twelve-year-olds in the natural setting of a classroom demonstrate that establishing and protecting the self is a relevant element of preadolescents' interactions. The total number of interactions containing a threat to the self lies within the range of incidents of other important activities of twelve-year-olds that observers identified in their field notes, e.g., helping and negotiating (Krappmann and Oswald, 1987, 1991). Children are thus concerned about their selves in the face of challenges that come not only from adult authorities but also from peers.

The issues that prompted children to defend and affirm threatened selves show that twelve-year-olds want to be respected as equals ("equality"), that they demand control over personal territories ("sovereignty"), that they are willing to be measured against fair standards of achievement in school ("student performance"), and that they wish to be a part of the peer networks ("social acceptance"). These dimensions of interpersonal morality define the conditions of participation in the peer world, at least in Western societies.

Our observations attest that these twelve-year-olds react mainly to two threat issues, "equality" and "sovereignty," which cause conflicts in more than two thirds of all episodes and in even more than three fourths of episodes belonging to the peer world as a whole, including cross-gender interactions. The prevalence of threats involving "equality" suggests that children at this age find it difficult to deal with personal differences; they tend to feel threatened when a peer suspects that they deviate from behaviors and standards to which all preadolescents should keep. Already minor violations of stereotypes lead to serious accusations and strong reactions. Children hid or diminished personal idiosyncracies to avoid reproaches of being a show-off. Likewise, children also cautiously avoid being ridiculed as "babies" because they fall behind standards. The same problem arises in group cooperation: a child who contributes too wholeheartedly may be suspected of selfishly wanting to determine the group's activities; a child who is less engaged may be accused of taking advantage of others.[7]

A closer look at the episodes in which children defend their sovereignty shows that this issue is connected with the problem of equality. Other children questioned a child's sovereignty when the child was not respected as a person who can act in a competent and sensible way. To gain respect, children reacted with rude rejections or ostentatious ignoring to show that they are sovereign individuals. Children reacted in this way not only when others challenged their sovereignty but also when others made an issue of their claim to be equal. With these procedures children seek not to dominate others but to protect the territory of each against intervention. Children force each other to respect the borders within which everybody cares for his or her own concerns. The concept of a peer contains the notion that the peer group is a society of sovereigns and equal individuals free to make agreements. If everybody's sovereignty is mutually recognized, cooperation continues.[8]

This interpretation of children's ideas about the self in relation to others is supported by our observation that these preadolescents seldom explicitly negotiate protection of their selves. Their close connection of the problems of equality and sovereignty leads them to expect that their selves are best safeguarded when others clearly respect "territorial borders" and keep agreements, not when the children permanently and consciously negotiate rights and duties. Thus the children behaved "conventionally," which means that they cautiously observed whether all kept to given norms and standards so that nobody gains an unfair advantage.

I emphasize children's efforts to achieve equality among peers of equal ranking in order to refute the common view that, although equality is an ideal in the peer world, the reality of the peer world consists in hierarchies, domination, and submission. Noisy quarrels and aggressive fights seem to confirm this latter opinion. Closer examination, however, leads to my conclusion that equality is not only a desired ideal but also a regulatory principle of high practical relevance. As children emphatically push for this principle, they sometimes use means that contradict their professed aim of reestablishing equality among partners who mutually respect their self-determination. Yet these acts of doubtful value also result from their eager attempts to enter into relationships based on a moral conception of equality.

I do not mean to deny that children engage in aggression. Dominant children sometimes cannot easily be controlled by other children demanding mutual respect and joint consideration. But domination is not the way to stable integration into the peer world, even though acts of usurpation and unilateral decision are not always clearly condemned. The reason may be caution, a realistic judgment of power, hope for an advantage, disappointment about never ending negotiations among "equals," or the fact that some children are less willing or capable of conforming to these standards.

Interestingly, friendship does not protect children against threats to their selves. Indeed, interacting children often incur threats by creating risky situations. This finding does not reflect the fact that friends in general interact more often. When we compare threats with negotiations, which form another type of interaction examined in the study, we find that friends were more often involved in threat episodes than in negotiations. Remarkably, friends and nonfriends, as well as well-integrated children and poorly integrated children, do not differ with regard to threats, but do differ with regard to the procedures and outcomes. Friends and well-integrated children made more use of communicative strategies, which more often were appropriate, and they achieved more positive affirmation of their selves, than did children with fewer friendships and at the margin of the peer networks.

The correlations I have reported may result from two directions of influence. Either children who know to deal with self threats in an adequate way can establish more friendships and therefore become well integrated, or socially well-integrated children have ample social experiences to draw on to protect their selves in appropriate ways. It is reasonable to assume that influences operate in both directions, but our statistical analyses do not support such a hypothesis. Multiple regression analyses support only one of these mechanisms: intense social experience in friendships enables a child to positively affirm a threatened self. Also pointing in the same direction is the fact that successful protection of the self is more strongly correlated with the social integration of the children than with friendship status.

Why do friends as well as socially experienced children question the selves of their interaction partners? G. H. Mead (1934) maintained that children shape their behaviors in cooperation with significant others. Tesser, Campbell, and Smith (1984) concluded that friendships strongly affect children's self-evaluations because friends often deal with issues regarded as relevant to self-definition and often critically react to each other. People often think that friends mutually further their development because they offer each other friendly assistance. Our data as well as that of other researchers show that this is an inadequate description of the social reality between friends (e.g., Berndt, 1985; Hartup, Laursen, Stewart, and Eastenson, 1988; Krappmann and Oswald, 1987; Selman and Schultz, 1991). In fact, friends often behave toward each other much as nonfriends do, and often even the outcomes of their actions are quite similar. As I reported above, friends and nonfriends alike not only attacked and finally positively maintained each other's selves, but also harmed and hurt one another's selves. So we must examine other aspects of friendship than friendliness to understand why children benefit from their friendship experiences.

Presumably, these are the qualities of friendships that enable children to constructively deal with controversies, reproaches, and accusations: friends owe each other answers reacting to what has occurred. These reactions can become part of a long-term exchange in which, if necessary, a solution can be further elaborated. Friends must be able to look beyond the current problem and consider consequences for their relationship. They must seek solutions that sensible partners can agree on and that permanently settle the dispute. This is accomplished by solutions that are reasonable and grounded in interpersonal morality. Good solutions bring the additional reward of enhancing friendships. These developmental mechanisms also enable friends to develop socially accepted selves. Our observations attest that preadolescent friends use these chances for development.

The majority of our observed twelve-year-old preadolescents can be seen as belonging to Kegan's (1982) sovereignty stage. Although children's attempts at equality, which is an important aspect of children's interpersonal activities, seem to orient them to the needs and expectations of others, they often abstain from dealing with conflicts in a communicative way. As I explained above, children seek equality not yet as a way of building a relationship but as a way of defending the ego's interests and demands against the interests and demands of others, which, by equality, must be recognized as legitimate claims. Thus these twelve-year-olds have not yet entered the stage at which the self *is* one's interpersonal relationship, as Kegan puts it. The behaviors manifested by these children recall Noam's (1985) description of the reciprocal-instrumental self, since children's relationships are primarily based on interests rather than on trust and intimacy.[9] Some of these children give indications that they still fear the loss of impulsive control, which indicates that they have not yet completely mastered the task of the preceding developmental stage. Rigid behavioral patterns that everyone must observe can be seen as a barrier against these "regressions."

The same considerations raise doubts about assigning these children to the category of interpersonal selves as described in Damon and Hart's (1988) model. We can interpret the children's emphasis on equality as an alternative outcome of the process of social comparison characterizing the development of a self concept at Damon and Hart's level 2. Our observations suggest that these early adolescents do not seek to affirm differences with their comparisons but to reveal what qualities peers have in common and what differences do not endanger cooperation.

These considerations show that children's selves, as inferred from observed peer interactions in which these selves were threatened, are basically moral concepts in a double sense. The children's selves reflect their convictions about principles that should regulate interpersonal conduct. Also, protecting their selves stimulates children to shape their interactions in ways that consider these interpersonal rules. However, as is evident from the observations reported here, the restricted morality on which these twelve-year-olds base their selves is but a stage on the path to autonomy and social responsibility.

Notes

1. The interactions analyzed in this chapter are part of the data collected in the study "Everyday life of primary school students," which is a joint project of the Free University of Berlin (with Hans Oswald) and the Max Planck Institute for Human Development and Education. Thanks are due to Martina Krollmann and Marita Schulz for their valuable assistance in the analyses of the interaction episodes.

2. Assignment to the data file is restricted to episodes. Encompassing psychological states, like anxiety or shyness, are not included, although they are elements

of a child's self and may influence a child's behavior during recorded interactions. My focus is on microsocial processes and not on the fundamental psychodynamics of a child.

3. The field notes contain more interactions in which aspects of selves are addressed, though not in connection with threats (statements about selves, positive evaluations of one's own or others' selves).

4. We statistically tested quantitative statements and have reported them only if differences are reliable according to conventional criteria.

5. We do not know how reliable our coding procedure is, since we used the incidents to develop our rules of categorization.

6. We found no significant differences between girls and boys with regard to participation, strategies, appropriateness, and outcomes when we tested using the personal-data file.

7. Threats were very rare in situations of competition with the exception of reproaches that rules of fairness had been broken. Efforts to be first apparently do not contradict the demand for equality if the competitors keep to the common rules.

8. I will not further comment on the two other issues causing threats to the self, "student performance" and "social acceptance," other than to say this: The issue of social acceptance may be underrepresented, since our observations focus on trivial occurrences of everyday interactions and losing a friend or being excluded from a group does not happen several times in the course of a school morning. Authorities and institutions strongly influence threats arising from inadequate student performance. Interestingly, children often shift from the original source of threat to issues of "sovereignty" or "equality."

9. Since children were interviewed about their friendship conception using Selman's (1981) procedure, we know that many children still have problems of arguing at stage 2 as defined by Selman ("fair-weather cooperation"). The majority of children argue at stage 2, the others still below stage 2.

References

Berndt, T. J. (1985). Prosocial behavior between friends in middle childhood and early adolescence. *Journal of Early Adolescence,* 5:307–317.

Damon, W., and Hart, D. (1982). The development of self-understanding from infancy through adolescence. *Child Development,* 53:841–864.

Damon, W., and Hart, D. (1988). The self-understanding interview and scoring procedures. In M. L. Hoffman (Ed.), *Self-understanding in childhood and adolescence.* Cambridge: Cambridge University Press.

Erikson, E. H. (1956). The problem of ego identity. *Journal of the American Psychiatric Association,* 4:56–121.

Filipp, S.-H., Ed. (1981). *Kritische Lebensereignisse*. Munich: Urban and Schwarzenberg.

Glaser, B. G., and Strauss, A. L. (1967). *The discovery of grounded theory*. Chicago: Aldine.

Goffman, E. (1959). *The presentation of self in everyday life*. Garden City, NJ: Doubleday Anchor.

Goffman, E. (1967). *Interaction ritual*. London: Penguin.

Goffman, E. (1971). *Relation in public*. New York: Basic Books.

Harter, S. (1983). Developmental perspectives on the self-system. In P. H. Mussen (Ed.), *Handbook of child psychology*. Vol. 4, *Socialization, personality, and social development*, edited by E. M. Hetherington. New York: Wiley.

Hartup, W. W., Laursen, B. S., Stewart, M. I., and Eastenson, A. (1988). Conflict and the friendship relations of young children. *Child Development*, 59:1590–1600.

James, W. (1961). *Psychology: The briefer course*. New York: Harper. Originally published in 1892.

Kegan, R. (1982). *The evolving self: Problem and process in human development*. Cambridge: Harvard University Press.

Krappmann, L. (1988). *Soziologische Dimensionen der Identität*. Stuttgart: Klett.

Krappmann, L., and Oswald, H. (1987). Negotiation strategies in peer conflicts: A follow-up study in natural settings. Paper presented at the biennial meeting of the Society for Research in Child Development, Baltimore.

Krappmann, L., and Oswald, H. (1991). Problems of helping among ten-year-old children—Results of a qualitative study in natural settings. In L. Montada and H. W. Bierhoff (Eds.), *Altruism in social systems*. Toronto: Hogrefe and Huber.

Krewer, B., and Eckensberger, L. H. (1991). Selbstentwicklung und kulturelle Identität. In K. Hurrelmann and D. Ulich (Eds.), *Neues Handbuch der Sozialisationsforschung*. Weinheim and Basel: Beltz.

McGuire, K. D., and Weisz, J. R. (1982). Social cognition and behavior correlates of preadolescent chumships. *Child Development*, 53:1478–1484.

Mead, G. H. (1934). *Mind, self, and society*. Chicago: University of Chicago Press.

Mummendey, H. D. (1990). *Psychologie der Selbstdarstellung*. Göttingen: Verlag für Psychologie.

Noam, G. (1985). Stage, phase, and style: A developmental dynamics of the self. In M. Berkowitz and F. Oser (Eds.), *Moral education: Theory and application*. Hillsdale, NJ: Erlbaum.

Oppenheimer, L., Ed. (1990). *The self-concept*. Berlin: Springer.

Oswald, H., and Krappmann, L. (1988). Soziale Beziehungen und Interaktionen unter Grundschulkindern—Methoden und ausgewählte Ergebnisse eines qualitativen Forschungsprojektes. Materialien aus der Bildungsforschung No. 33. Berlin: Max-Planck Institut für Bildungsforschung.

Piaget, J. (1971). *The language and the thought of the child.* New York: Harcourt and Brace.

Selman, R. L. (1980). *The growth of interpersonal understanding: Developmental and clinical analyses.* New York: Academic Press.

Selman, R. L. (1981). The child as a friendship philosopher. In S. R. Asher and J. M. Gottman (Eds.), *The development of children's friendships.* Cambridge: Cambridge University Press.

Selman, R. L., and Schultz, L. H. (1991). *Making a friend in youth.* Chicago: University of Chicago Press.

Taylor, C. (1989). *Sources of the self: The making of the modern identity.* Cambridge: Harvard University Press.

Tesser, A., Campbell, J., and Smith, M. (1984). Friendship choice and performance: Self-evaluation maintenance in children. *Journal of Personality and Social Psychology,* 46:561–574.

Youniss, J. (1983). Piaget and the self constituted through relations. In W. F. Overton (Ed.), *The relationship between social and cognitive development.* Hillsdale, NJ: Erlbaum.

Contributors

Augusto Blasi is a professor in the Psychology Department of the University of Massachusetts at Boston. His research interests and principal publications are in the areas of moral cognition, the development of self-identity, and the relationship between responsibility and behavior.

Anne Colby is the director of the Henry A. Murray Research Center of Radcliffe College. Her principal publications are in the areas of moral judgment, the development of extraordinary moral commitment, and adult development.

William Damon is professor of education and director of the Child Study Center at Brown University. His numerous books and articles have focused on social and cognitive development through the course of life.

Wolfgang Edelstein is a professor at the Free University of Berlin and codirector of the Max Planck Institute of Human Development and Education (Berlin). His research deals with the interface of development and socialization in the areas of cognition and sociomoral development.

Harry Frankfurt is professor of philosophy at Princeton University. Most of his books and articles focus on issues concerning moral philosophy and the structure of the self, though he has also written extensively on the history of modern philosophy.

Helen Haste is reader in psychology at the University of Bath. Her work has dealt with the nature and interrelationships of moral, political, and social development, as well as the relationship between career and values, the social-psychological aspects of sex roles (especially the nature and effect of stereotyping), and the social image of science. She is presently engaged in research on the social and cognitive aspects of metaphor.

Monika Keller is a developmental psychologist and research fellow at the Max Planck Institute of Human Development and Education (Berlin). Her research and publications focus primarily on social cognition and moral development.

Lothar Krappmann is a sociologist and senior researcher at the Max Planck Institute for Human Development and Education (Berlin) and adjunct professor in the School of Education of the Free University of Berlin. His research focuses on the question of how children's relationships shape and enrich their social experiences and foster their social, moral, and cognitive development. He has published books and articles on social development, the culture of childhood, and social processes in the classroom.

John Lee is a doctoral student in the College of Education at the University of Illinois at Chicago. His research interests and publications are concerned with the role of subjectivity and personal desires in the definition of personal autonomy and morality.

Leo Montada is professor of psychology at the University of Trier. His current research is on social emotions such as guilt, resentment, envy, and jealousy, as well as on social justice, the experience of injustice and how people cope with it, and prosocial and ecological commitments.

Mordecai Nisan is professor of educational psychology in the School of Education at the Hebrew University of Jerusalem. His main publications and research interests have to do with moral development and behavior, human motivation, and self-control.

Gil G. Noam is associate professor of psychology, psychiatry, and education at Harvard University and director of the Laboratory of Developmental Psychology and Developmental Psychopathology, McLean Hospital. His research interests and publications deal with the relationship between cognitive development and psychoanalytic theory, developmental psychopathology, self-interpretation, and communicative discourse.

Larry Nucci is chair of the Department of Educational Psychology at the University of Illinois at Chicago. He has published books and articles in the areas of moral development and moral education. He is presently engaged in cross-cultural studies of family interactions and the development of concepts of personal freedom and sociomoral regulation in children and adolescents.

Gertrud Nunner-Winkler is a sociologist and research fellow at the Max Planck Institute for Psychological Research (Munich). She has published books and articles on educational sociology and, with R. Döbert, on adolescence, identity formation and moral development, suicide, and the problem of judgment and action. Recently she edited a book on female morality, and she is presently engaged in a research project on the development of moral understanding and moral motivation in early childhood.

Amélie Oksenberg Rorty is Martina Horner Distinguished Visiting Professor at Radcliffe College and professor of philosophy at Mount Holyoke College. She is the author of numerous books and papers in moral psychology, the history of ethics, and other philosophical topics.

Ervin Staub is professor of psychology at the University of Massachusetts at Amherst. He has conducted research and published books and articles on the socialization and developmental origins of prosocial behavior and altruism, and on social influence and personal characteristics as determinants of altruism.

Ernst Tugendhat is professor of philosophy at the Pontifical University of Chile in Santiago, where he teaches philosophy of language and moral philosophy. He has published numerous books and articles in English and German on these and other philosophical topics.

Ernest S. Wolf is a faculty, supervising, and training psychoanalyst at the Chicago Institute for Psychoanalysis and assistant professor of psychiatry at Northwestern University Medical School. His main interests and publications have been in the theoretical, clinical, and developmental aspects of the psychoanalytic psychology of the self.

Thomas E. Wren is professor of philosophy at Loyola University of Chicago, where he teaches moral philosophy and philosophical psychology. He has published books and articles on these topics as well as on moral motivation, the philosophy of human action, and a variety of historical figures, including Spinoza, Hume, Macmurray, and Kohlberg.

Index